The Good News About Depression

The Good News About
Depression

Cures and Treatments in
the New Age of Psychiatry

Mark S. Gold, MD,

with Lois B. Morris

BANTAM BOOKS
TORONTO · NEW YORK · LONDON · SYDNEY · AUCKLAND

Although the case histories in this book are accurate, the names and identifying characteristics of the persons described have been changed to protect their privacy.

This edition contains the complete text of the orginal hardcover edition.
NOT ONE WORD HAS BEEN OMITTED.

THE GOOD NEWS ABOUT DEPRESSION
A Bantam Book / published by arrangement with Villard Books

PRINTING HISTORY
Villard edition published February 1987
    The charts "Endocrine Mimickers" (page 141), "Infectious Disease Mimickers" (page 85), "Central Nervous System Mimickers" (page 89), and "Toxic Mimickers" (page 127) are reprinted by permission from *Advances in Psychopharmacology: Predicting and Improving Treatment Response*, copyright © 1984 by CRC Press, Inc., Boca Raton, Florida.
    The chart "Nosology of Depression" (page 62) is reprinted by permision from *Inpatient Psychiatry: Diagnosis and Treatment* by Lloyd I. Sederer, M.D.
    The chart "Doctor's Earnings" (page 20) is reprinted by permission of Medical Economics Co., Inc.
    The chart "Signs and Symptoms of Hypothyroidism and Depression" (page 148) is reprinted by permission from *Handbook of Psychiatric Diagnostic Procedures*, Vol. 1, edited by R.C.W. Hall, MD, and T. P. Beresford, MD. Copyright © 1984 by Pergamon Press, Inc.
Bantam edition/March 1988

Library of Congress Cataloging-in-Publication Data

Gold, Mark S.
    The good news about depression.

    Bibliography: p. 313
    Includes index.
    1. Depression, Mental—Popular works.   2. Biological psychiatry.   3. Psychological manifestations of general diseases.   I. Morris, Lois B.   II. Title.
RC537.G64   1988   616.85′27   87-33373
ISBN 0-553-34511-7 (pbk.)

Published simultaneously in the United States and Canada

9-89

PRINTED IN THE UNITED STATES OF AMERICA
FG   0 9 8 7 6 5 4 3 2 1

For Samuel and Belle Gold

Acknowledgments

I am deeply grateful to the patients who taught me to appreciate the pain and suffering of having and being treated for depression, and to my collaborators at Yale University School of Medicine and Fair Oaks Hospital, whose research has helped me understand the diseases that cause depression.

For their many contributions to the research for and preparation of this project from its inception, heartfelt thanks go to A. Carter Pottash, MD, Steven Stanzione, MD, Eugene Borkan, MD, Becky Cole, Judy Andraski, and Barbara Capone.

Sincere appreciation to my biopsychiatric colleagues across the country for the clinical experiences that enlighten these pages.

Contents

Introduction:
The Good News

YOU COULDN'T HAVE picked a better time in human history to feel miserable.

At long last there are effective treatments and cures for depression. These have been developed and implemented by a handful of psychiatrists and neuroscientists who have worked tirelessly, and often without recognition, throughout the past two decades to bring a new *science* to the practice of psychiatry and the relief of mental suffering.

We who work in this new field call our science *biopsychiatry,* the new medicine of the mind. If you have ever sought help from a psychiatrist, your doctor, a psychologist, a social worker, a nurse, or a minister because you're depressed and can't seem to shake it, you will see as you read this book just how different, how straightforward, is the biopsychiatric approach to your pain. Biopsychiatry *works,* and because it works, it is sweeping through the top academic and research centers in the United States and abroad, ushering in a new age of optimism in psychiatry and psychotherapy after years of treatments —from talking to taking pills—that don't work, or don't last.

What is biopsychiatry? In two words it is *medical psychiatry.* It returns psychiatry to the medical model, incorporating all the latest advances in scientific research, and, for the first time in history, providing a systematic method of diagnosis, treatment, cure, and even prevention of mental suffering.

Mental suffering comes in many forms; depression is the most common. Throughout the world, *one hundred million* people are estimated to be suffering from severe biological depression requiring, although not necessarily receiving, a doctor's care. In the United States, that number may be as high as sixteen million. Along with the millions who exhibit overt symptoms of depression, hundreds of thousands of others suffer "masked depression," in which they do not realize that their physical aches and pains are actually symptoms of depression.

Overall, depression is the "common cold" of psychiatry *and* medicine, the condition for which more people seek care than any other, including viruses, high blood pressure, headaches, and, indeed, the common cold.

What is depression and why is it so common? The extraordinarily high incidence of this condition of misery made it a first priority for study by biopsychiatrists in research and laboratory settings, in hospitals and clinics. Through intensive efforts we have amassed an impressive amount of theoretical and practical knowledge, so that today we know more about depression than any other psychiatric affliction.

In this book I will use the phenomenon of depression to demonstrate the tenets and advances of biopsychiatry, and to show you how and why it is a truly optimistic new science. Through the "microscope" of depression I'll be showing you how biopsychiatry works and what practitioners like myself can offer those who suffer mental—and physical—agony. By comparison, you'll see how and why traditional psychiatric and psychological approaches do not—indeed, *cannot*—work.

Adventures on the Frontiers of Science

Imagine the questions we as scientists had to ask ourselves. Not only did we have to learn what depression is, we also had to find out what it *isn't*. How does it work in the body? Which parts of the brain are involved in depression? What are the psychological and physiological causes of depression? What is the relationship, if any, between the symptoms of depression and its cause or causes? Do animals get depressed? Why? Is there an evolutionary advantage to depression?

What happens to brain cells during depression? Which body chemicals are involved? Which genes? Which glands? Why do depressed people have bodily symptoms? How many kinds of depression are there, and what are the different criteria of each? Are there types of depression which are not physiological and if so, how can we tell?

What is the relationship between stress and depression? Is depression related to other emotional disorders, such as anorexia and related eating disorders, school phobia, impulsiveness? Are people who commit suicide physiologically and/or psychologically different from other depressed people or the population at large?

Can we develop laboratory tests to diagnose depression and to follow the progress of treatment? What makes some people subject to depression and others not? Is there a relationship between depression and personality?

What's "body"? What's "mind"? Does depression have a lasting effect on the body? On behavior? Are there biochemical or behavioral or genetic traits that can indicate who is or will be subject to depression? How can we treat the symptoms of depression? How can we cure it? How can we prevent it?

Question after question led us into some of the most incredible medical research ever done. Together with the leading minds in all areas of the life sciences, we have probed the frontiers of science and human understanding wherein lie the ultimate comprehension and cure of *all* mental illness. Already we have so many answers, even to our most exotic questions, as you'll see when you read the chapters that follow.

Biopsychiatry is closing the conceptual gap between body and mind. Our understanding has penetrated the very cells of key brain areas, to the submicroscopic spaces between nerve cells and structures on the cells, the chemicals that are synthesized in tiny amounts, the cell walls, the ions that penetrate them.

We now have a working conception of the brain's mood anatomy, including which of the brain's chemical "messengers" are important in good and bad moods. Embracing the most advanced laboratory technology, we've developed tests to diagnose, to monitor, and to predict the course of depression. We now have tests to identify subtypes of depression in order to choose the appropriate treatment or blend of treatments. When medication is required, other tests can identify the correct dosage for each individual and still others can tell when it's working.

Incredibly, we are on the verge of identifying chemical and genetic traits in children and relatives of depressed people to let them know who will be at risk of severe depressive disease during their lifetimes. This means that someday soon, as we develop appropriate precautions for the at-risk population, we will be able to prevent depression from taking its deadly toll. By identifying certain chemicals in the blood, we may even soon be able to predict who is at risk of suicide.

Although some of the "tools" we use to treat depression are

newly developed (including light therapy and tinted glasses for seasonal emotional disorders), we also use such traditional treatments as medication and psychotherapy. The difference between biopsychiatry and traditional psychiatry and psychology, however, is that we use these treatments in a much more systematic and creative way, determining which patient requires which specific medication or medications, which type of psychotherapy, how much and for how long, and who's likely to get better without any major intervention.

The Not So Good News

"No one has real reason to fear that his or her depression is untreatable," asserts an article in a recent publication of the American Psychiatric Association, the preeminent professional organization of psychiatrists.

Unfortunately, there are many reasons why depressed people and other suffering individuals remain in pain and are likely to continue to do so despite the advances of biopsychiatry and the emerging new age of optimism. We have the technology, the tests, the treatments. We have the backing of all the best minds in psychiatry. What we lack is practitioners within the community who are truly qualified and/or willing to practice what we preach. In fact, some of the practitioners out there—from psychiatrists to internists to psychologists to social workers—are the real reason to fear that your depression *will* be untreatable.

Who practices biopsychiatry? Every psychiatrist *should*—but often doesn't. This is one of my reasons for writing this book: to air some uncomfortable truths about my profession today.

Biopsychiatry is likely to be the only viable form of psychiatry now and in the future. To practice it, psychiatrists must return to being doctors and to *thinking like doctors.* As you'll see in the following chapters, that's about the last thing that most psychiatrists want to do. Once they get through their technical training in medical school and receive their MD degrees, most of them set up shop in the practice of *psychology.* When was the last time you saw a psychiatrist carrying a physician's black bag? When was the last time a psychiatrist you consulted, or someone you knew consulted, performed a complete physical exam, or even took a complete medical history? When was the last time your psychiatrist took blood tests or urine tests and worked with a laboratory?

Medicine, as the saying goes, is as much art as science. Psychiatrists have long practiced their art without the science to back it up and make it work. In part, this is because until recently little was known about the interactions of the brain, the body, and behavior. I'm not against psychotherapy (the "talking cure"); on the contrary, when it comes to problems of living and being, the psychotherapist's art is *de rigueur* in helping you get your life on track and achieve a larger measure of gratification and effectiveness. Depression, however, is not necessarily the kind of problem for which talking to someone can help you.

Depression can be a biological illness for which you need a doctor. It can be the first sign of a developing, perhaps deadly physical illness. It can be a "side effect" of virtually any prescription or illegal drug, or of physical illness. In any of these cases, traditional psychotherapy in the absence of appropriate medical diagnosis and care will not help you and may even hurt you. One recent study shows, for example, that the longer the delay in receiving appropriate medical care for major (biological) depression, the more likely it is that the condition will become chronic and possibly untreatable. All these types of depression share the same constellation of symptoms. You cannot know what kind of depression you have unless you consult a specialist in the *differential diagnosis* of depression: a biopsychiatrist.

Of all the mental health professionals who practice in this country, only psychiatrists are MDs. Society has conferred a particular mandate on physicians: to heal the sick. Having been trained to fulfill this mandate, psychiatrists have the moral and ethical responsibility to return to the medical practice of their specialty. At present, psychiatrists routinely fail to recognize medical diseases in their patients. Study after study reveals that *up to 40 percent of all diagnoses of depression are misdiagnoses of common and uncommon physical illnesses.*

You may feel and act like you're miserably depressed, and your psychiatrist or other therapist may well agree with you, when actually your emotional symptoms may be an early indication of thyroid disease, heart disease, alcoholism, Alzheimer's disease, diabetes, mononucleosis, nutritional deficiencies, even (and not unusually) cancer. There are at least seventy-five diseases that first appear with emotional symptoms. People with these diseases often get locked up in psychiatric hospitals. Biopsychiatrists, with their medical approach, make their first order of business to look for and rule out these diseases *before* beginning to treat you for depression.

Once the diagnostic process has ruled out physical diseases and causes and ruled in primary depression, the next step for the biopsychiatric physician is to identify which type of depression you are suffering from. You will see shortly just how many types and subtypes of "actual" depression our research has identified: from "normal" depression, which affects every human being in the course of life—for example, after a death or job loss—and which always goes away; to types of recurring depression that depend on the oversupply or undersupply of certain minute amounts of a number of chemicals deep inside key areas of your brain.

Effective, lasting treatment of depression depends entirely on matching the treatment to the kind of depression you have. Again, a psychologist or a traditional psychiatrist, including one who dispenses drugs (and most psychiatrists who do prescribe drugs don't know how to use them correctly), cannot or does not make these essential distinctions, which is one of many reasons why the treatment you or a family member has received for depression may not have worked.

Everybody's Doing Something Wrong

Psychiatrists aren't the only ones to misdiagnose depression and treat it incorrectly or ineffectively.

- Primary-care physicians prescribe most of the antidepressant medications that are sold in this country. Unfortunately, as studies show, they have a poor record in diagnosing depression correctly or in treating it properly.
- There are more psychologists (PhDs) and social workers (MSWs) in mental health practice today than there are psychiatrists. Most of them are not educated as to the medical diseases that masquerade as depression and to the importance of differential diagnosis. Rather than cooperating with psychiatrists on behalf of the total health of their patients, nonmedical therapists and their professional organizations frequently act competitively and defensively, promoting certain myths, such as: chemical theories of depression are "hype"; antidepressant medication is a crutch—it is addicting, and it interferes with therapy; biopsychiatrists give all their patients pills, no matter what's wrong with them.
- Have you been reading in the newspapers about the "epidemic" of teenage suicides? Every time the aggrieved parents are interviewed, they insist that Johnny gave no sign of his unhappiness. Well, Johnny in all likelihood did offer plenty of evidence, if only his parents had known how to read him. Kids do get depressed, and

parents (and teachers) must begin to learn how to recognize and deal with this before it's too late.

- Two to one, women bear the greater burden of depression, yet they are commonly told by the doctors and therapists they consult for premenstrual, postpartum, and postmenopausal depression that the problem is "all in their heads." Even those doctors who recognize the legitimacy of these conditions commit some fundamental errors in diagnosis and treatment.

- The elderly are true victims of depression—victims because their families as well as their doctors routinely make matters worse. They're diagnosed as senile or demented and stuck prematurely in nursing homes, when, even in the elderly, depression is reversible. And the elderly are especially prone to the diseases that masquerade as depression; too many doctors are likely to treat them as grouchy time-wasters, instead of seeking the source of their symptoms.

- And what about you? Yes, *you.* Depression is among the worst experiences in life, granted. If you're depressed and doing things to get rid of the pain, well, that makes sense. But what you are doing! Daily jogging or aerobic exercise is one thing, but taking tranquilizers, painkillers, drinking, doing drugs . . . ! Do you know that drugs and alcohol *cause* depression? Though they may have a temporarily lifting effect, they will make any preexisting depression you have worse, much worse.

And you don't go for help. Only 10 percent of the millions of people estimated to be biologically depressed in this country ever seek help. Maybe you believe what you think when you're depressed —that you're no good, so what's the use of going for help when there's no hope for somebody like you anyway. Maybe you'd like to see someone about it but you think that being depressed is something to be ashamed of, that it's all your fault.

Maybe you've had some bad luck with depression treatment in the past. Maybe you lay on the couch for ten years while your shrink assured you that in time you would "get to the bottom" of your depression, only you never did. Maybe you've taken pills that just made you miserable and didn't work.

Maybe you don't know that what you're feeling is depression.

Back to the Good News

Although most psychiatrists do not yet practice the science of biopsychiatry, there *is* plenty of help out there for depression. More and more biopsychiatrists can now be found all over the country, at the finest hospitals and academic centers. You just have to know where to look (the first place is the Appendix at the end of this book) and what to ask for—to insist on—in terms of good care for yourself and those you care about.

The time it takes a new form of practice to filter from the profession's leadership to its everyday practitioners can be long; in psychiatry, where many practitioners follow their own set of rules (there are as many as 140 different "schools" of psychotherapy), that lag time can go on seemingly forever. Did you know that lithium, the wonder drug used in treatment of manic-depressive (bipolar) illness, was available *twenty years* before U.S. psychiatrists started using it?!

You, the reader, can help reduce that lag time—and this, overall, is the main reason I'm writing this book. In hundreds of professional publications, in symposia and lectures, I have patiently and steadfastly educated my colleagues. Now I turn to you.

You'll be learning a lot of inside information in these pages: how psychotherapists think, how doctors think, how they arrive at their conclusions regarding you, how and why they treat you the way they do. By rights, this information, along with information about all the recent advances in medical science, belongs to you now—not twenty years from now. Well informed, you can begin to demand better treatment when mental illness strikes you or your family. You can ask questions of your therapist to see how educated he or she is in the psychobiological aspects of depression. You can seek help among those practitioners who are up-to-date in diagnosis and treatment. You can evaluate the treatment you're getting before it's too late. And —this is no small point—you can know what is expected of you in order to achieve fully successful treatment. You can, in a word, be happy.

The Key to Happiness

The ultimate aims of biopsychiatry are identical to those of all the mental health professions: to remove or lessen the obstacles that stand in the way of living a healthy and productive life. Once depression is cured, you can pursue and experience happiness.

The great thing about biopsychiatry is that it covers so much territory on your behalf. Although critics accuse us of disregarding psychology in favor of biology because we insist on additional medical training (especially in neurology and endocrinology) and a medical approach, biopsychiatry is the first science of the mind to include *all* of you. Science will no longer allow us to separate the mind from the body. Ongoing research reveals more and more the complex, exquisite interrelationships between physical illness and behavior, between the state of your mind and the state of your body.

Psychiatry has had to wait a long time, longer than other medical specialties, for knowledge and technology to advance sufficiently to penetrate the inner workings of the brain. Now we have done so, and at long last we are beginning to comprehend the biology, the etiology, the physiology of mental illness, and to develop treatments corresponding to our new knowledge. We must not be afraid of this knowledge.

For biopsychiatry—for those who suffer mental agonies—the age of optimism has only just begun.

The Good News
About Depression

Part I

What Is a Psychiatrist?

1

The Case of the Famous Actor Who Couldn't Go On

HE WAS A HOLLYWOOD legend, one of the most well-known and be-loved stars of all time. He had come to Fair Oaks Hospital in Summit, New Jersey. We had to tell him he had cancer. *It was the best news he had heard in years.*

Fortunately, we don't often have to deliver a diagnosis of cancer. Still, this case was not unusual for us. Psychiatrists in private practice or at other psychiatric hospitals often refer their "nonresponders"—their hopeless cases—to us for our evaluation. Or people call us up saying they've been treated for depression for umpteen years and they're not getting any better. Their friends and families and even their doctors urge them to *learn to live with it;* this misery is part of who they are. Is there anything we can do for them? They're at the end of their ropes, a lot of them.

So often what we find is that their misery results from a *disease* that they have. Sometimes that disease is the brain lesion we call major depression. Sometimes that disease is drug toxicity. Or it is hyper-parathyroidism or hypothyroidism or ovarian cysts or pancreatitis or folic acid deficiency or diabetes or heart disease or Parkinson's disease . . . or cancer.

Prologue: The Actor's Entrance

This very famous actor—let's call him FA—had been treated for de-pression without success for three and a half tormented years. Famous and wealthy as he was, he was able to consult some of the best-reputed and most expensive psychiatrists in New York, and to afford any treatment they recommended. Still, in this day of "miracle cures" for depression, instead of getting better, FA grew worse. His personality seemed to change and, beloved though he had been to friends and fans alike, he had become distinctly unlikable. His doctors washed their hands of him and turned him over to us.

Well-known people are not unusual among our inpatients and outpatients at Fair Oaks; our staff doesn't often blink an eye at celebrities. But anticipating the arrival of this man—this star of some of the finest classic movies, this heartthrob and role model, still so virile in his early sixties, silver hair matched by a softly curving silver mustache, with steel-gray eyes and rugged features—well, we were all rather weak in the knees!

When he checked in, however, he barely resembled that familiar face and sinewy body. His skin was pale, his eyebrows were knitted, and his whole face drooped. He looked as if he hadn't been eating or sleeping. His gait was ponderous; he walked like an old man.

And was he in a rotten mood! It was his first day on our evaluation unit, and he lashed out when anyone approached him. At a psychiatric hospital, the staff doesn't take a patient's angry outbursts personally. Patients are referred to us or approach us directly because of their behavioral difficulties; if they acted normally, we'd wonder what they were doing here. But with FA, who had been known so long for his gentle manner, the hostile, angry behavior was disconcerting. As far as he was concerned, we couldn't do anything right—and he was sure to let us know about it.

It all started when the nurse asked him to take off all his clothes and put on a hospital gown. She handed him the white gown, and he let her have it: "What the hell kind of place am I in—who the hell do you think you are? Look, miss, or is it *ms.*," he said with a sneer, "I'm in this nuthouse with a bunch of lunatics because I've been stinking depressed for five years. Get it? I say that to that doctor out there and it's like he hasn't heard me. He just smiles and says, 'Pee in this jug, please.' Now I've got to strip. I've already had a physical—I've had *two* physicals. I've come here for my head, get it?" He drew his finger across his neck in an off-with-his-head gesture that conveyed all too well how desperate he was feeling.

FA was behaving badly, but who wouldn't, after all he had been through? For the past three and a half years he'd suffered progressively worsening symptoms despite the ministrations of well-meaning doctors. Each of them had diagnosed his condition as depression. His symptoms ran the gamut from hopelessness and lack of self-esteem to loss of energy, appetite, and sleeplessness, an inability to concentrate, and the disappearance of all interest in sex. From this list of rather typical symptoms, there was no reason to think that he didn't have major depression. However—and here's the "secret" to the approach my colleagues and I use at Fair Oaks—*neither was there any reason to suspect that he did.*

The Actor's Downfall

The beginning of FA's suffering had coincided with his return to Broadway after nearly forty years. The dramatic role he was playing was demanding. He had worked harder at it than he had in a long time, for which he was rewarded with good reviews. He remembers beginning to feel exhausted and low after the third or fourth week of performances. "I'd be onstage, involved completely in my role, then all of a sudden I'd feel like calling it quits. I'd looked forward to my return to Broadway as coming full circle in my life. But now that I was here I felt that my life had no meaning—that it never had had meaning."

It wasn't the first time that FA had suffered a down mood. "I was a stage actor originally," he says, "and every young actor who comes to New York fully prepared to triumph gets hit with a painful dose of reality. I was no different from anyone else—although I thought, of course, that because I had been in summer stock for three seasons I was extraordinarily superior to all the other actors and actresses in New York who were waiting tables while waiting for their big break." He smiles that soft familiar smile known so well to generations of moviegoers.

"I couldn't even get an audition," he remembers woefully, "and when I did, it seemed an exercise in humiliation. They would cut me off after two sentences and sometimes call out the next name without even acknowledging I'd been there. I'd go back to my rented room and feel like hell." FA groaned in reminiscence. "But I *had* to be an actor, I *had* to make it, because there wasn't anything else I could do. I couldn't even wait tables without dropping something."

As frequently happens, FA's down mood strengthened his resolve and dedication. It took him two and a half years to land a decent role on Broadway. Critics and audiences loved him. From that point on, he seemed blessed. He went straight to Hollywood for forty years of uninterrupted stardom.

But this depressed mood, four decades later, had taken everything out of him. His guardian angel had deserted him. He didn't enjoy his work. He didn't enjoy anything. He couldn't sleep, but he was so tired he couldn't get up. And for the first time in his adult life he wasn't at all interested—it took him a while to admit this, even to himself—in sex. He'd been married only a few months, to a woman who was twenty-five years younger. After several nights of excuses, which he blamed on exhaustion from eight performances a week, he would push her away angrily when she approached him. His wife began to think it must be her fault. She tried to talk to FA about it but he didn't want to discuss it. His angry outbursts became more frequent. Afterward he felt guilty and disgusted with himself. But he couldn't tell her—this young, beautiful, sexual woman with whom he had hoped to spend the rest of his life—that he believed in the depths of his heart that age had caught up with him. From now on, he "knew" it was all over for him. He allowed her to leave him rather than tell her what he was so sure was the truth.

His wife was the first to seek psychiatric help. Her psychiatrist suggested that it was FA who needed the help.

Mr. Famous Actor remained in touch with his estranged wife, but he was reluctant to consult a psychiatrist. He wasn't the type to seek help; he would tough it out as best he could. Then the night came when he faced the audience and knew, despite a contract obligating him to four more months of performances, that he could no longer go on. He broke his contract, and his life seemed to collapse around him. He lay in bed for days, hating himself, regretting his lost youth, knowing he had no more future.

Then one day, weeks later, he got up and went outside. It was a clear, sharp late-winter day that promised the arrival of spring to those who could hold out just a bit longer. FA went for a walk in Central Park. He sat down on a bench and watched the joggers and bike riders and the nannies with their tiny charges. It became clear that it was time to take action. He went back to his hotel and made an appointment with a psychoanalyst.

The Actor Becomes a Treatment Failure

Dr. Pierce, we'll call him, had been recommended to FA by his director as being "brilliant" with creative people. He was a psychiatrist who had taken analytic training and worked with his patients using that Freudian technique. He worked with FA for two years, four days a week. At first they discussed FA's immediate symptoms—the onset of his depression at that particular time in his life, and its consequences, such as the shattered relationship with his new, young wife and his abandoned Broadway role.

Mr. Famous Actor learned a great deal about himself in his two years with Dr. Pierce; his depression did not improve. Sometimes the symptoms would lift, only to return. Slowly but surely, things got worse. During bad times FA found it difficult to concentrate; he lost his ability to have an erection, he became angry and withdrawn, and he hated himself. He couldn't get himself to look at scripts or to talk about working again. Gossip columns were full of items about his "changed personality." Though never directly stated, it was implied that FA was an alcoholic.

A concerned friend who knew the truth of FA's erratic behavior, and who had suffered a bout of depression himself a few years before, told FA how much he had been helped by antidepressant medication. He was surprised to find out that Dr. Pierce, who was, after all, a physician, had never recommended a trial of medication. FA mentioned this conversation to the doctor, who wondered why, after two years of therapy, FA would now be bringing this up. His implication was that FA's question was a wish to escape the work of the analysis, and this in itself should be explored. Dr. Pierce was a psychoanalyst of the "old school," and would not under any circumstances prescribe medication.

FA could bear his symptoms—and the vicious gossip—no longer. Now that he knew that there were other approaches to his depression, he felt he owed it to himself to try them. He parted from his analyst and made an appointment with his friend's psychiatrist.

The first session was a great relief for FA. The doctor listened to his symptoms and agreed that FA was certainly depressed. He reassured him that medication was available and that from his symptoms it sounded as if FA would be a good candidate for drug treatment. Before he would prescribe anything, however, he wanted FA first to undergo a physical exam. He wanted to make sure, he said, that FA would be able to tolerate the potential side effects of the medication. Mr. Famous Actor went to the internist that the psychiatrist had recommended. The exam lasted twenty minutes, followed by an electrocardiogram. The internist told him his heart was sound and in his opinion there was no reason why FA should not take antidepressants.

FA returned to the psychiatrist, who reached for his prescription pad. "What about the reasons why I'm depressed?" asked FA. "We've plenty of time to talk about that, if we need to," replied the doctor, and he wrote a prescription for Elavil. He explained that they would be slowly building up to the proper dosage, and that the pills would take anywhere from days to weeks before they achieved their desired effect. He told him, too, that he might experience some possibly disconcerting side effects, such as exhaustion, dry mouth, palpitations, constipation, and confusion. These, he said reassuringly, would probably disappear in time. He also explained that if this initial choice of antidepressant medication proved ineffective—which they wouldn't know until at least six weeks after they had built up to the proper dosage—that they would try another type of medication. There was no lack of pills to try, he said, urging FA to have patience.

Mr. Famous Actor took the pills as prescribed, and he had a rough go with them. He had heart palpitations, he was anxious and restless and couldn't concentrate, he was dizzy, he sucked hard candies constantly because his mouth was painfully dry, he was constipated and occasionally nauseated. He stuck it out for two months because he believed this was finally going to work for him. The side effects lessened. The depression didn't. Still, the psychiatrist reassured him that given time they would find a medication that would work for him.

They didn't. Two changes of prescription and almost five months later, FA was even worse off than he had been before, and he felt that he was getting to the end of his rope. The doctor admitted him to the psychiatric unit of a famous teaching hospital. There the resident gave him another brief physical exam, in which he found nothing unusual. He prescribed various drugs and then more innovative combinations of medications for close to five months, during which time FA's behavior deteriorated—he was angry, impatient, belligerent, and often downright rude to the staff, who expected him to be his Famous Actor self, no matter what he was suffering from.

When FA refused shock treatments, the staff gave up and called me. "Treatment failure," said the psychiatrist in charge of his case. "The guy's an old crock," he added.

Enter the Biopsychiatrists

Nobody likes to fail. So when you do fail, why not blame the patient? I can't tell you how often I hear the words "nonresponder" or "treatment failure" coupled with a negative view of the patient. Here all these doctors had spent so much time and energy on Mr. Famous Actor. Because he was who he was, they might even have worked harder than with a more "ordinary" patient. Yet he had the temerity not to get better! To add insult to injury, he did not seem grateful to them for their failed efforts.

To be sure, he was difficult. The disease he was suffering from, which everybody took to be depression because it looked and sounded like it, had changed him. So had the frustration of trying to find help. I doubt there's a psychiatrist in this country who wouldn't claim that he or she could offer a depressed patient significant help. Mr. Famous Actor had believed his doctors' claims. And still . . .

To him, my colleagues and I were yet another stop on the train to nowhere. So if he took extreme offense at us for making him undress in order for us to examine every nook and cranny of his body, well, so what?

It was the urological exam that made him angriest. "I want a goddamn psychiatrist," he growled. Calmly the doctor, now examining his testicles, looked up and said, "I am a psychiatrist."

There was a moment of silence. FA sighed. "I give up," he said. "Five years of headshrinkers and I haven't the vaguest idea what a psychiatrist does—what a psychiatrist *is.*" He was quiet for the remainder of the physical examination portion of the evaluation.

A complete medical history and evaluation always come first in our evaluation of each new psychiatric patient, including outpatients, at Fair Oaks. For many of our patients, it is the most thorough physical they have ever had. If nothing abnormal shows up that could explain the patient's psychiatric symptoms, we then proceed to an equally thorough diagnosis of the psychiatric condition. If patients are surprised at the physicals, they're doubly so when we start taking blood and urine specimens for laboratory analysis, to confirm, first, the existence of depression, then the type of depression, then blood levels of medication, and then physiological responses to it. Usually, they're pleased. Here we are, psychiatrists, getting up from our consulting chairs and aggressively and energetically taking their problems as seriously as if they'd told us they had chest pain.

As it happened, we did not have to go on to test FA specifically for depression. Examining physicians, lab work, and a biopsy all confirmed that Mr. Famous Actor was suffering from a disease that would account for all his symptoms: a low-grade seminoma, which is a form of testicular cancer. Despite his symptoms, depression was a *misdiagnosis.* Thus, all the treatments he had undergone were incorrect. His symptoms arose out of his medical condition and would disappear only when the cancer was treated.

We referred FA to the appropriate specialists for treatment of his illness. He was hardly cheered when he heard that he had cancer. This time he got depressed for real—a normal reaction to what he was at first convinced was the worst news he'd ever heard. But when we told him that we had caught the disease in time and that the likelihood of a complete cure was 95 percent, he began to cheer up.

He asked the logical question: "Why didn't any of the other doctors pick it up?"

There are several answers to his question. One is that no one was looking for this illness—or any illness at all. He was a psychiatric patient, and to most internists and psychiatrists, that means the problem is located somewhere above the neck and between the ears. The last thing they consider—despite indisputable evidence to the contrary—is that emotional symptoms can often be the first and long the only signs of serious physical illness. By the time the distressing physical symptoms suddenly appear and the diagnosis is made, it is often too late for a cure.

The Happy Ending

Our diagnosis, even though it was cancer, truly was the best news he had had in three and a half years. We identified what FA really was suffering from, so that at long last he could receive the proper treatment. That's what it took for Mr. Famous Actor's "depression" to go away—along with his cancer.

Biopsychiatrists save lives. Any more treatment for "depression" and our famous patient might have died.

Surgeons removed the malignancy; afterward he undertook a course of radiation therapy. Chemotherapy was not considered necessary. FA has had no recurrence of cancer, or depression, in almost five years.

Mr. Famous Actor is back in front of the cameras. He is thinking of returning to Broadway in a revival of his original success forty-plus years ago. He and his wife have reunited, their sex life is great, and he is his former self again, almost. Unfortunately but not surprisingly, his years-long experience of trying to get help has left a deep scar, a suggestion of bitterness toward psychiatrists.

What Everybody Did Wrong

This subject is going to come up again and again in this book: what everybody's doing wrong. So far what we have is one psychoanalyst, who, although trained as a psychiatric physician, abjures his medical training. He makes no effort to diagnose his patient's depression. He assumes the symptoms arise from FA's psyche and that they can be explained by FA's life experiences. He could be right. Any biopsychiatrist can tell you there are a number of reasons why a person will exhibit symptoms of depression; some, indeed, may be imbedded in an individual's personality.

But Dr. Pierce makes no attempt to verify his assumptions by ruling out any of the many other diseases or conditions that could just as well explain his patient's suffering. And since he never prescribes medication for his patients, he apparently does not believe that depression can in itself be a biological illness, much less a symptom of a medical illness. Doctor though he may be, he has not remained in touch with current medical knowledge.

The psychiatrist who prescribed medication for FA made the same initial error: diagnosis by description of symptoms. Unlike his predecessor, however, he did request a medical consultation, but only to make certain his patient could tolerate the side effects of the pills, and probably to protect himself in the event of a malpractice suit. If he was willing to prescribe medication, he obviously accepted the notion of depressive illness, but despite the increasing number of laboratory tests available to psychiatrists, he did nothing to prove or disprove that FA was an appropriate candidate for medication. Neither did he use any of the available laboratory techniques to identify the medication most likely to be effective; to estimate the dosage, which varies from individual to individual; or to follow the course of treatment. His treatment of his patient was nothing more than trial and error, which prolonged the suffering of his patient and—since he was working from an incorrect diagnosis—was doomed to fail.

Let's not forget the internist whom FA visited. Because his patient had been referred by a psychiatrist, he apparently assumed that all FA's problems were in his head and thus performed only a perfunctory examination. He probably was uncomfortable dealing with psychiatric patients. Yet he must have known that psychiatric symptoms are frequently caused by an extraordinary number of physical illnesses.

In terms of both physical examination of the patient and differential diagnosis of his condition, the doctors at the hospital were no better. Even in a hospital setting, they made no use of psychiatric laboratory technology (which at their hospital was used routinely only for patients participating in research projects). Their contribution was to try the patient on newer, more innovative combinations of medications. Throwing pills at people can be very effective for the treatment-resistant or treatment-refractory patient—but only if depression is the problem. Which it wasn't.

Our famous actor friend made his own mistakes, not that he could be held accountable. He too operated by assumption: that a psychiatrist is a psychiatrist is a psychiatrist. That they all have the same training, the same point of view. That they are all equally capable of recognizing what lurks behind psychiatric symptoms and will provide similar treatment for it. Not until he looked down and found a psychiatrist squeezing his testicles did FA ask himself an essential question: What is a psychiatrist?

What *Is* a Psychiatrist?

If Mr. Famous Actor thought he was confused about the definition of a psychiatrist, he should only have known how confused psychiatry is itself.

Is a psychiatrist a psychotherapist who uses verbal therapeutic techniques to treat all patients, regardless of their complaints?

Is a psychiatrist a drug therapist who believes that medication can help most patients who complain of psychiatric symptoms?

Is a psychiatrist a professional spokesperson for social causes?

Is a psychiatrist a consultant to defense and prosecuting attorneys?

Is a psychiatrist a specialist who believes that normal behavior is a matter of relearning more appropriate actions or thoughts?

Is a psychiatrist an "allergist"?

Is a psychiatrist a kind of counselor who assists essentially normal people to achieve more fulfilled existences?

The answer is yes to *any* of these definitions of psychiatry. Each psychiatrist has his or her own "thing." Each will claim a therapy for —and an interpretation of—depression. Analytic-style psychiatrists, for example, will investigate early loss, rage, and self-esteem issues. Cognitive doctors will say you learned your depression and you can unlearn it. Feminist therapists may find sufficient explanation for a woman's depression in the dependent position into which women are forced, and by way of "cure" help the woman to assert her rightful place in society. A family therapist will find the roots of a family member's depression within the functioning of the family as a whole. Psychopharmacologists are likely to explain that your depression is the result of a chemical deficiency, and recommend medication . . . and on and on and on.

Basic Requirements

PSYCHIATRISTS

- To become a psychiatrist, one must complete four years of medical school and receive an MD degree. At present, one internship year of general clinical medicine in a hospital is required prior to specialization. Specialists in adult psychiatry must complete a three-year hospital residency training program; child psychiatrists must complete two additional training years.
- All psychiatrists must be licensed to practice medicine in their state.
- To become a Diplomate of the American Board of Psychiatry and Neurology, a psychiatrist must practice for two years following completion of the residency and pass oral and written exams. A psychiatrist who becomes a Diplomate is, in effect, certified as fully trained and competent. Diplomate standing is not required to practice psychiatry, and, in fact, many well-qualified psychiatrists choose not to join the specialty organization.
- A psychiatrist who practices psychotherapy is not required to undergo psychotherapy personally.

PSYCHOANALYSTS

- Psychoanalysis is a specific type of psychotherapy.
- An MD, a PhD, or an MSW (Master of Social Work) degree usually is required for admission to a psychoanalytic training institute. Some institutes accept MDs only. While an MD need not have trained as a psychiatrist to be eligible, most MD psychoanalysts are in fact psychiatrists who have completed the requirements discussed above.
- Psychoanalytic candidates must complete at least three years of course work, closely supervised work with patients, and a formal case study which is prepared in writing and defended orally. In addition, to be certified as psychoanalysts, all candidates must successfully complete their own personal analysis.

None of these approaches is necessarily "wrong"—but who says which one is right for you? The burden falls on the patient, as it did on Mr. Famous Actor, to know what the problem really is in order to get help for it. What if you were having a heart attack and the cardiologists in your city each had a different "cure"? Whom would you consult? How would you know which one had the right treatment for you? Trial and error would kill you. Fortunately, cardiology and most of the other medical specialties have come a long way since those days, not so long ago, when diagnosis and treatment might depend on the beliefs or idiosyncrasies of a particular practitioner.

Cardiology consists of a body of knowledge and procedures that are universally applied. The only variable in treatment is the competence of the particular physician using these procedures, which is why most people rely on referrals from doctors they trust.

As a subspecialty of medicine, psychiatry espouses no such consistency. While controversy exists throughout all of medicine (is bypass surgery any more effective in prolonging life than medical treatment?), it leads to research that advances medical care. In psychiatry, disagreements are often based on theory and are not resolved through research. Psychiatrists are notoriously contentious and frequently view other approaches with contempt rather than with an interest in learning from one another and in unifying the field within itself and within medicine.

The identity confusion in psychiatry reaches to the deepest roots of the profession. Biopsychiatry has appeared on its white charger, in effect, to rescue the profession and its patients. What is a biopsychiatrist? Simply put, he or she is a specialist in all problems affecting human behavior, who is trained to perform a differential diagnosis assisted by all available technology, and who can then choose and/or institute the most effective treatment for the patient based on the diagnosis.

Biopsychiatrist and *psychiatrist* ought to be synonymous terms. And if biopsychiatric theory and practice—beginning with *standardized, medically based diagnostic procedures for all patients*—are not immediately adopted by every psychiatric practitioner, the profession will collapse.

2

Where Have All the
Psychiatrists Gone?

YOU MAY THINK THAT the world is crawling with shrinks, especially if you live in California or New York. Clinical psychologists are hanging out their shingles in increasing numbers. Then there are the psychiatric social workers, the nurse therapists, the pastoral counselors, the lay therapists—all doing psychotherapy. But where are the psychiatrists?

The year is 1970. Psychiatry is alive and well. Seven to 10 percent of all graduating medical students have chosen it as their area of specialization. Competition for the best hospital residency positions is ferocious.

Now it is 1980. Psychiatry is sick and dying. Only 2 percent of graduating medical students have decided to become psychiatrists. Hospital administrators are faced with a real problem: Less than half of all hospital psychiatric positions can be filled by graduates of U.S. medical schools.

Advance to 1984. The situation has barely improved: 57 percent of first-year psychiatric residencies are filled by U.S. graduates. Administrators have to take what they get, for competition is nonexistent: 88 percent of applicants are accepted by their first-choice hospital. Eighteen percent of the remaining first-year positions are filled by graduates of foreign medical schools (outside the United States and Canada). Practicing in the area of medicine most dependent on comprehending the words and culturally based nuances of language and behavior of their patients, foreign psychiatric trainees often speak English as a second language and are unfamiliar with our culture. Worse, their training is often way below par. In a recent year, a third of all applicants for the specialty exams given by the American Board of Psychiatry and Neurology were foreign medical grads; their failure rate was eight times higher than that of their American colleagues.

Psychiatry today is staffed with more foreign graduates than any other medical subspecialty except one (physical and rehabilitative medicine). Even so, in 1984, 25 percent of all the first-year residencies remained empty. The shortage of psychiatrists is critical. If the trend continues, by 1990, even though an estimated 12 percent of the U.S. population will require psychiatric care, we'll be short 8,000 general psychiatrists and 5,000 child psychiatrists.

For the profession, the situation is *depressing*. Not only is the body count down, the talent has sunk to a new low. Attend a meeting of academic psychiatrists and watch the training directors sigh and roll their eyes when they discuss the latest crop of trainees. Used to be, they say, you could get the students who had graduated at the very top of their classes. Now . . .

"I'd Rather Be a Real Doctor Than a Psychiatrist"

The wholesale abandonment of psychiatry began suddenly in the mid-1970s. It was unexpected, and psychiatric educators have been busy ever since trying to figure it out. They've conducted opinion polls in medical schools. Here's what some of the future doctors of America have to say:

- Psychiatry is unscientific and imprecise.
- Nonmedical specialists are equally qualified to treat patients.
- Psychiatrists do not make use of their medical training.
- Patients do not get better fast enough.
- Psychiatry is low in status relative to other specialties.
- Psychiatrists earn too little compared to other specialties.
- Psychiatry is confused about its role and skills.
- In the 1950s and 1960s, psychiatry promised more than it could accomplish.
- Psychiatry has a poor public image.

These young people see that psychiatry is out of sync with the rest of medicine, that it has no credibility, and therefore, the rewards of choosing to work in psychiatry are few. Medicine has moved into a new era of applied science, and that's the kind of medicine they went to med school to practice. They may read and hear the psychiatric leadership and researchers/practitioners like me propounding the scientific principles of biopsychiatry. But then they look around and see the average psychiatrist practicing nonmedicine and squabbling over the neuropsychiatric discoveries and technological applications that have been made.

Delayed Progress: The Lithium Story

In the mid-1960s, a greatly loved and admired psychiatrist who taught at Johns Hopkins Hospital hanged himself. For years he had suffered severe mood swings, and despite all the resources available to him from the hospital and his caring colleagues, nothing and no one had been able to help him. Yet a medicine that had proved remarkably successful in controlling the very condition that he had—manic-depression, now known as bipolar disorder—had been discovered nearly two decades before.

The drug was lithium carbonate, a naturally occurring mineral salt, whose usefulness in the control of mania had been discovered in Australia by psychiatrist John F. Cade in 1949. In Australia and Europe—but not the United States—researchers began immediately to experiment with it. A major study by Mogens Schou in Denmark was published in 1954 and led to the development and successful use of lithium throughout Europe.

Nevertheless, the psychiatric establishment in the United States expressed little interest in lithium. It was just a mineral salt, whose use as a salt substitute in the 1940s had proved problematic. The drug companies were even less enthusiastic, since they couldn't patent a natural element. Finally, in 1958 and 1960, a few U.S. physicians and institutions began to test lithium's effectiveness. For many subsequent years, lithium was dispensed only by these specialists or by the National Institutes of Health, while most psychiatrists remained unaware of it.

Just one year after his teacher's suicide at Johns Hopkins, psychiatrist Bernard Levy, who is now a professor at Harvard Medical School and founder of a Boston psychiatric hospital, went to work at the National Institute of Mental Health. One of the psychiatrists there "had somehow learned of the use of lithium in manic-depressive illness and introduced it into our clinical work," writes Levy. "My teacher's dying of an illness untreated by a medicine that was available, but unfamiliar, has been a central stimulus to my interest in sharing knowledge. . . ."

Although all who worked with lithium found it remarkably effective, the FDA did not approve lithium as a prescription drug for mania until 1970; the following year it was okayed as a maintenance therapy for manic-depression.

Many more years remained before psychiatric practitioners included its use in standard practice, although lithium was psychiatry's first "wonder drug" and remains to this day perhaps the greatest of all psychiatric medications that have been developed in drug company laboratories.

The Lab Lag

Many psychiatrists point thumbs down on all that is promising and hopeful and *helpful* in the new psychiatry: the drawing of blood, the lab tests, the understanding of and testing for neuroanatomical, neuroendocrine, neuropathological, and genetic abnormalities. Anti-technology psychiatrists include those who find it incompatible with their own theoretical systems as well as those who argue vehemently that the tests are unusable because they're not perfect. Yet any graduating medical student knows that *no test in all of medicine is or ever will be perfect.* The public—and some psychiatrists—may believe, for example, that the glucose tolerance test, in use for the last half-century, is all a physician needs for the diagnosis of diabetes. Actually, researchers are discovering that some types of diabetes exist in the presence of an apparently normal test and, conversely, that abnormal tests may give false readings. Physicians do not react by tossing the test out the window. Instead, the more they know about the diabetes disease process, the better they become at interpreting test findings.

Where could psychiatrists have come by their misunderstanding of the role of the laboratory in medicine? Did they sleep through medical school? Apparently.

Many of the old-style psychiatrists, who practice psychotherapy and often do not prescribe medication (if they do, they dispense it like aspirin), survived med school by the skin of their teeth. One 50-year-old MD psychoanalyst confided that, having been accepted by a number of medical schools, he chose the one that gave no exams; to graduate, students were required only to pass the national boards, which were given after the second and fourth years. He crammed and he passed. He had never intended to practice medicine, he said; his sole interest was in becoming a psychoanalyst.

During his psychiatric residency he began his studies at a psychoanalytic institute, of which he is now a leading light. He reads psychoanalytic journals and is better informed than many of his colleagues in that area. He almost never looks at the psychiatric literature concerning biopsychiatry, which he disdains, claiming that all that is necessary to know about depression and other forms of mental suffering has already been written, by Freud and later psychoanalysts. He speaks of the new psychiatry in rather the same snide tone he uses when remembering medical school. He may be the best psychoanalyst in his city, rendering an important service to some patients. But a doctor he's not.

"I'd Rather Be a Psychiatrist Than a Psychologist"

Why would people put themselves through the torture of four years of medical school if they didn't want to become doctors? Why not simply become a psychologist and not bother with all that dreadful stuff like biochemistry and patients leaking blood and oozing pus, not to mention the internship and residency years, in which you work yourself to death with little sleep and less financial reward?

The answer is *prestige*. Psychiatrists may be the butt of jokes, but an MD is an MD. A few decades ago medicine had a hammerlock on psychoanalysis, and medical school was thus the best route to a psychoanalytic institute. Psychologists and other professionals established their own institutes, and only during the psychiatrist shortage have some of the MD-only institutes opened their doors to psychologists. Nonetheless, doctors are esteemed in our society far more than are PhDs. This esteem is bankable. A young woman in New York wanted to be analyzed. She obtained the names of two well-known psychoanalysts, one an MD and one a PhD. Both had roughly the same number of years of experience and a similar reputation in professional circles. The MD charged $125 an hour, the PhD $90.

Psychiatrists could probably charge even more, if psychologists and other nonmedical therapists weren't competing for the dwindling psychotherapeutic dollar. In 1980, the worst year so far in the psychiatrist shortage, U.S. universities awarded 22 percent more PhDs in clinical psychology and counseling than they had the year before.

The Reduction of Insurance Benefits— and a Possible Solution

In relation to other doctors, however, a psychiatrist's fee is low for forty-five to fifty minutes of uninterrupted time. Psychiatrists have sunk bottomward on the earnings totem pole in medicine. They can expect to make some 30 percent less than the average physician: $79,850 net for psychiatrists to $115,600 for all physicians.

DOCTORS' EARNINGS* ACCORDING TO SPECIALTY

Specialty	Net Income	Specialty	Net Income
NEUROSURGEONS	$179,690	GENERAL SURGEONS	$117,940
ORTHOPEDIC SURGEONS	$173,030	OB-GYN SPECIALISTS	$112,110
RADIOLOGISTS	$159,820	NEUROLOGISTS	$108,830
OPHTHALMOLOGISTS	$150,000	DERMATOLOGISTS	$107,750
THORACIC SURGEONS	$149,250	INTERNISTS	$86,660
PLASTIC SURGEONS	$144,250	PSYCHIATRISTS	$79,850
GASTROENTEROLOGISTS	$139,500	FAMILY PRACTITIONERS	$76,810
CARDIOLOGISTS	$131,940	PEDIATRICIANS	$76,470
UROLOGISTS	$126,820	GENERAL PRACTITIONERS	$68,600

*Amounts represent average net practice income. When ranked by gross income, psychiatrists place last among the specialties listed. Adapted from *Medical Economics*, September 9, 1985.

If you are or have been a psychiatric patient, your heart probably isn't bleeding for your "poor" shrink. In your experience, no doubt, consulting a psychiatrist for your depression is far more costly than going to a gastroenterologist for your ulcer. Your insurance company pays for your tummy. You pay for your head.

Over the last decade, insurers have consistently reduced their coverage of outpatient psychiatric expenses. These days, a major medical policy that covers 80 percent of all outpatient doctors' fees and a maximum of $500 a year for outpatient psychiatric care is considered "generous." How many people can afford a long-term course in psychotherapy anymore? Ten years of analysis could easily run $100,000—minus $5,000 reimbursable (that is, if the insurance carrier doesn't impose a lower limit). Patients—from those who just want to figure themselves out to those who are ill and in pain but not sick enough to be hospitalized—will have to hand over their life savings to get help.

In 1984, at the order of the federal Office of Personnel Management, Blue Cross/Blue Shield substantially reduced mental health benefits for federal workers. Psychiatrists in the Washington, D.C., area experienced an immediate 10 to 15 percent reduction in billable hours.

Some medical students, as well as psychiatrists, inaccurately blame the insurance pullback on psychologists and, in some states, social workers, who have successfully fought for the right to equal reimbursement for their services. It isn't their fault, however, that they provide the same *nonmedical* services—psychotherapy—for their patients as do psychiatrists.

A Blue Cross spokesperson explained, "With psychotherapy, the problem is that the psychiatrists can't specify the problem or the likely outcome, and can't give a good description of the method in between either."

Health insurance pays for the treatment of medical illness. Are psychiatric patients medically ill?

Much of the remainder of this book will be devoted to this question, to which the answer is very often yes. Some patients with symptoms of depression may not know that they are suffering from serious bodily illnesses (expenses currently reimbursable). Some are suffering the effects of drug and alcohol abuse, although they may not appreciate the relationship of the abuse to their symptoms (treatment reimbursable). Many are suffering the brain disease of depression, often genetic in origin, for which a number of treatments are available, including medication and special types of psychotherapy (partially reimbursable). Others are suffering from life problems that lead to depression and for which psychotherapy is often helpful (rarely reimbursable, at a very low rate).

If tomorrow morning psychiatrists suddenly decided to act like doctors, they'd probably save their patients a lot of money, not to mention torment. They would uncover the predicted high rate of medical illness among their patients with depressive symptoms, and these individuals would find their psychiatric expenses reimbursable at the *medical* rate. This in itself would cheer them up!

Similarly, there is no reason why a psychiatrist cannot provide an accurate diagnosis and prognosis of biological depression, which is, after all, a brain disease. In other words, by approaching psychiatry as a medical specialty, we could easily provide the insurance companies with the information they require (and the patients with the treatment they need) in order to cover psychiatric expenses.

To reverse the trend of reduced benefits—and the shortage of psychiatrists—all psychiatric practitioners, old-time and new, will have to change their ways.

"I'd Rather Be a Psychiatrist Than a Real Doctor"

While a psychiatrist in middle age or older is practicing what was the state of the art in an earlier era, when there was no brain science to speak of, the young psychiatrist fresh out of medical school who perpetuates this time-locked tradition has his or her head in the sand.

It is the strong impression of training directors that the majority of those few students who are gung-ho on psychiatry can't wait to leave doctoring behind them. When they finish their residencies, they will quickly find offices and equip the consulting room with low lights and sedate furniture. They will not have stethoscopes or blood-drawing equipment or examining tables or any traditional medical equipment, except, of course, their prescription pads.

Although during their residencies psychiatric trainees are required to give physical exams to incoming hospital patients, they approach this procedure as a red-tape formality and hurry to get it over with and get on to "real" psychiatry. After the completion of their training, most will never again perform a physical exam. This is despite the fact that the physical may be the most important procedure a psychiatrist can perform for many patients.

Unused, whatever skills they may have as physicians will atrophy. Not only do fewer than 35 percent of psychiatrists ever give their patients any kind of physical; a third of all psychiatrists admit to feeling *incompetent* to do it, and fewer than half even have a fully equipped physician's black bag. Far fewer than that, of course, use any of the new technology for the diagnosis and treatment of depression. They went into psychiatry in the first place because it was free of all that gobbledegook, and that's the way they intend to keep it. These psychiatrists are often those who argue loudest about the fallibility of the emerging psychiatric laboratory science.

These psychiatrists will persist in diagnosing depression by its apparent symptoms and in providing inappropriate treatment for those patients who are thus misdiagnosed. Some of these patients may ultimately die when their medical illnesses manifest themselves in time. The psychiatrist will not realize that he or she had any responsibility in this.

Misdiagnosis and Malpractice

A few years ago several psychiatric researchers reexamined one hundred consecutive patients at a psychiatric center who had already been examined and diagnosed. They found that 46 percent had an undiagnosed medical illness which either exacerbated their psychiatric symptoms or fully accounted for them. Of these, 61 percent showed a dramatic clearing of their psychiatric symptoms once they were properly treated medically, and the remaining 39 percent were substantially improved. *Without this intervention, all of these individuals would have been committed to a state mental institution.* An additional 34 percent of the patients had an undiagnosed physical illness that was unrelated to their psychiatric problems but which required treatment. In all, psychiatrists missed the presence of physical illness in 80 percent of the cases.

The same team had earlier investigated over six hundred outpatients—those with less serious symptoms who were referred for routine psychiatric care. Close to 10 percent of them turned out to have medical disorders that produced their symptoms.

Another investigator compared studies of outpatients whose symptoms were caused by undiagnosed physical illness and found that one-third of them end up being tagged as having "functional psychoses."

In our own outpatient department at Fair Oaks, of one hundred supposedly depressed patients we evaluated, 35 percent of those who were referred by psychiatrists turned out to have an underlying physical reason for their psychiatric symptoms. Once their medical problems were controlled, they had no reason to take the antidepressants the original doctors had prescribed.

"Well," you say, "what can you really expect of psychiatrists when it comes to physical illness? If these patients had been seen first by internists, the story would be different." Unfortunately, according to my experience and to a recent article in the *Journal of the American Medical Association,* not only psychiatrists but other physicians misdiagnose behavioral disorders 40 percent of the time.

How and why "body doctors" miss these diagnoses will be discussed in a later chapter. Psychiatrists cannot pass the buck for these errors, however; clearly it's their job to determine the origin of their patients' symptoms.

Easy Money: Malpractice Claims Against Psychiatrists

Malpractice claims against a psychiatrist based on misdiagnosis are the easiest to win and commonly earn the largest awards. They are the most frequent source of loss to psychiatrists, because the courts assume that since a psychiatrist is a medical doctor, he or she has fully evaluated the patient and ruled out other conditions that can cause the same symptoms. That is the informal contract between patient and doctor. The most common misdiagnosis is "depression neurosis," according to a five-year overview of malpractice claims against psychiatrists.

The Undereducated Psychiatrist

I am embarrassed that psychiatrists are so bad at doctoring. Psychiatry has lost so much esteem within the medical inner sanctum that those qualified medical students who had strongly wanted to be psychiatrists do not have the courage to buck the system; they choose other specialties.

These young men and women, who could contribute so much to the field of psychiatry, are being repelled by the profession's tendency to ignore scientific advances and allow its practitioners to dwell in ignorance. Unlike other, more "respectable" medical fields, psychiatry has no tradition requiring practitioners to accumulate continuing medical education credits to maintain their specialty standing.

What would happen if an orthopedic surgeon didn't bother to learn the procedure that has lately revolutionized that field: arthroscopy? (No longer do orthopedic surgeons have to cut open an athlete's knee, for example, to diagnose as well as correct an injury. They can insert the scope, look around, and often snip away the offending tissue. A few hours later, the patient limps out and hails a cab for home.) Here's what would happen: The patients would say, "This guy's behind the times," and head for another orthopedist. Why suffer through a major operation and long convalescence when there may be a more up-to-date alternative? So many people, especially athletes, are aware of arthroscopy that specialists in orthopedic medicine simply can't get away with ignorance. The doctors who don't keep up will eventually feel it most in the pocketbook.

There's Good News in This Chapter Too

And this is what will happen in psychiatry—why I'm sure that psychiatric medicine in the United States has a great future. The more that those of you who are depressed (or severely anxious, or subject to panic attacks, or a host of other anguished conditions) become aware of the treatment advances that are available, and the more you see other people finally *feeling better,* the more you'll insist on benefiting from the new psychiatry yourself. And the more you seek help from biopsychiatrists, the more tempting psychiatry will once again become to the talented young scientist-doctors of America.

I have a hunch the current shortage of qualified young psychiatrists is good news too. It represents significant, even revolutionary change, which will probably be accelerated by psychiatry's failure to compete with the other medical specialties for new recruits. An old way of thinking that has outlived its usefulness is dying and making way for the new.

My research and teaching and patient treatment are the basis of my good-news view. My work with patients has achieved what they call "amazing" results, yet I have no secret cure, no special magic. All I do is diagnose my patients before I treat them. And I know how to use the new tools. I'm a doctor.

The best news is from a potential patient's point of view. My concern as a psychiatrist is for *you*, now and in the future. I don't want you to suffer, and one way I can reduce your pain is to reach those practitioners who resist progress and instead insist that their long-suffering depressed patients are refusing to be cured. I must demonstrate to them with hard, cold facts that frequently this just isn't true. In this way I can promise you better care in the future.

You need not wait. The biopsychiatric approach has become *the* way at many of the best psychiatric centers in the country. For the person who is hurting, or who has a loved one suffering mental pain, biopsychiatrists are available right now to help you. Someday they'll be everywhere.

3

I Am a Psychiatrist

IT WAS MY SENIOR year in medical school. My professors thought I was going off the deep end. They tried desperately to stop me.

"Psychiatry?!" exclaimed my neurology chairman. "How could you throw away your career?"

My neurosurgery professor talked about my love for pure science. He recalled the years I had spent in labs working on special research projects, my dedication to medicine. It sounded like a eulogy. He called it my "death wish."

These two men were my mentors, and it was difficult not to have their support. I understood their objections, of course. At that very moment in the mid-1970s, while the rest of medicine was reveling in a new era of scientific discovery and advances, psychiatrists were expending their energy in backbiting and attacking each other's competing approaches. The psychodynamic psychiatrists fought the biological psychiatrists who fought the social psychiatrists who attacked the behavioral psychiatrists—pity the poor patients who were trapped in between. Psychiatry had lost its focus.

Fortunately, the dean and dean of students of the medical school recognized my mission. As they put it, what psychiatry needed above all was individuals to make it important again and relevant to the rest of medicine without sacrifice to the "mind" advances that had been made. It would take scientists, pioneers, individuals with a steadfast and single-minded vision to attach the body to the mind, the mind to the body, once and for all.

That thought struck me. No doubt that the discoveries of the extraordinary complexities of the mind and the corresponding development of psychology have been giant steps forward. But the insistence on separating the head from its own corporeal existence is an even larger step backward, toward some of the least enlightened times in our history.

From the Pharaohs to Freud

Some four thousand years ago, the ancient Egyptians did not differentiate between mental and physical illnesses; they believed that despite their manifestations, all diseases had physical causes. They thought the heart was responsible for mental symptoms. Hippocrates and the early Greeks believed as well that all illness resulted from a biological malfunction; in the case of depression, from an excess of "black bile."

The ancients may have been off the mark as to specific causes, but their nonpejorative view of mental suffering and their search for medical causes were right on track. As history progressed, however, the "mind" view of mental illness came to predominate, and with it the conviction that the victim was to blame. Possession by evil spirits, moral weakness, and other such "explanations" made a stigma of mental illness and placed the responsibility for a cure on the resulting outcasts themselves. The most apparently ill were chained to walls in institutions such as the infamous Bedlam, where the rest of society could forget they existed.

ANCIENT VIEWS OF DEPRESSION

	Causation	Treatment
Early Egypt	Loss of status or money	Talking it out Religion Suicide is accepted
Job/Old Testament	Despair Cognition	Faith
Homer Aeschylus	Gods take mind away Demons	Exorcism
Socrates	Heaven-sent *Not* shameful	None A blessing
Aristotle	Melancholia	Music
Hippocrates	Melancholia Natural Medical causes	Abstinence from all excesses Vegetable diet Exercise
Celsus	A form of madness	Entertaining stories Diversion Persuasion therapy
Galen	Psychic functions of brain affected	Confrontation Humor Exercise

In our supposedly more humane era, we have freed the mentally ill from institutions and, instead of providing continuing care, have left them to fend for themselves. Forced to be aware of them, we disdain the "crazies" out there and wish they would get it together and behave themselves; down deep, we really believe that if they had the strength of character, they would straighten out.

The stigma of illness of the mind is all-pervasive. If we or members of our families experience mental illness, the shame may prevent us from seeking available help or even from following the doctor's advice. Psychiatrists often fail at effecting a cure because patients resist taking the prescribed medication. I had a patient not long ago —a woman named Julie—who at age 38 had earned a top executive position at a major manufacturing company. She had been referred to Fair Oaks by her family physician because she suffered severe, recurrent depressions. Lately she had found herself contemplating suicide, and her fear of what she might do forced her for the first time to reveal a history of desperate anguish on and off for almost twenty years. It was her "secret shame."

Julie appeared extraordinarily well put together in her dark suit, off-white high-neck blouse, and colorful little bow tie. Her medium-length auburn hair was conservatively cut and carefully combed. Her makeup was perfect. It took much of her strength to maintain this façade, behind which she hid her true feelings. No wonder she seemed so aloof and chilly.

We were able to determine that Julie was biologically depressed, and our lab quickly identified the type of antidepressant that she would respond to. We worked to get the concentration of medication in her blood up to the optimum level. Results were dramatic. For the first time in years her mood range was normal. Her facial expression had lost its disdainful severity, and she smiled warmly and often.

Yet we weren't able to maintain Julie at an effective medication level, because every time she had to go out of town on business, which was about twice a month for a week each time, she'd manage to "forget" her pills. After protesting that she really had forgotten them, she finally confessed that she was terrified one of her customers or colleagues would find out what she was taking and why, and that would be the end of their respect for her and, what she most feared, the end of her rapid progress in her corporate career.

She could imagine them buzzing behind her back that her depression was so bad she had to take *pills* for it. I pointed out that she regularly took pain medication for a jogging injury. "That's not the same thing," she insisted. "In fact, that's something to be proud of

—it makes me 'one of the guys.' But depression," she said, her voice rising in self-disgust, "that makes it seem like I can't control my own emotions, like the stereotypical, weak, afflicted, helpless *woman.*"

I told her that she didn't seem to understand what depressive illness was; her tests clearly showed her to be suffering from a biological disease that afflicted even male presidents of corporations. She waved away my explanation with a hint of tears in her eyes. The "weakness" view of mental symptoms has too strong a footing in our culture to be able to let go of it in just one straightforward sentence.

I told her she might want to talk about this with a psychotherapist, explaining that people who have suffered a lot of depression end up distorting their lives in order to survive what they believe to be shameful pain. If she would take her medication she would be free of the pain and in a good state to work with a therapist to help her straighten out what she'd done to her life. She seemed skeptical, until I added that therapy was likely to help her understand and achieve her career goals. She brightened and asked me for the names of some therapists.

Once you determine that a "head problem" is, in fact, a body problem, the stigma evaporates. Until only a few years ago, an alcoholic in the family was the skeleton in the closet. Now we're calling alcoholism a disease, and it has become much easier to admit to needing help for it.

Emil Who?

Within the last century, Western psychiatry has followed separate "head" and "body" routes.

The founders of these two traditions were Sigmund Freud and Emil Kraepelin, both of whom were German-speaking men born in 1856. Although most Americans consider Freud the father of modern psychiatry, medical people, especially those in Europe, are likely to name Emil Kraepelin as the actual founder of the medical science of psychiatry. Sigmund Freud originated *psychoanalysis,* from which today's psychotherapies based on psychodynamic theories and techniques derive.

Both men were physicians, Kraepelin practicing in Munich and Freud in Vienna. Freud's theories attempted to demonstrate an order within the chaos of the human mind. Kraepelin's work created order of the chaotic thinking about mental disease among doctors of the late nineteenth and early twentieth centuries.

Kraepelin's method was empirical: He observed mentally ill patients, described their symptoms, followed their courses for some years. By doing so, he was able to discover similarities among patients and to identify distinct syndromes (a syndrome in medicine is a collection of symptoms that frequently occur together) and predict their outcome. He identified what he termed *manic-depressive psychosis* (now termed bipolar disorder) and *dementia praecox* (schizophrenia). He showed that manic-depressives tended to get better spontaneously and that schizophrenics tended to deteriorate over time.

Before Kraepelin, psychiatrists were dealing with each patient as an idiosyncratic set of confusing symptoms whose causes, future course, and treatments were unknown and unpredictable. So-called diagnoses were descriptive and often had little relationship to anyone else's use of the same terms. Once Kraepelin showed that psychiatrists were dealing with the same illnesses among their patients, they could at last begin to make diagnoses.

A diagnosis in medicine implies *prognosis* (prediction of the probable course of an illness) and treatment. In those days, once a physician knew, for example, that manic-depressives get better in time, he could prepare the patient and the patient's family for a short-term hospitalization. These serious mental diseases had no effective treatment, but at least psychiatrists could begin to research systematic treatment approaches.

Its house in order, late-nineteenth- and early-twentieth-century psychiatry was now in a position to take advantage of the medical advances of those days. It was the era of the *microbe,* the disease-causing agent. Using the available technology of the times, such as the microscope, and applying the advances of the new science of bacteriology, psychiatrists immediately made some startling discoveries. A number of their "schizophrenic" patients had bacterial illnesses. These were syphilitics suffering from general paresis, the late stage of that disease, which causes schizophrenia-like symptoms. These patients required medical treatment, not psychiatric incarceration. Penicillin eventually proved to be the treatment of choice, and lo and behold, the mental hospitals emptied out by some 10 percent.

Even more dramatically, in the South, nearly half the patients in some mental hospitals walked out suddenly sane when niacin was added to their diet. They were discovered to be suffering from pellagra, which results from a chronic deficiency of that B vitamin.

It seemed that the future of psychiatry was set on this firm medical footing. The first part of the twentieth century, however, was to provide psychiatrists with few advances with which to find the pathogens or biochemical and structural defects in the brain which they were hoping to discover as the causes of mental illnesses. And the questionable use or overenthusiastic application of such physical treatments as shock therapy, psychosurgery, and even teeth-pulling, combined with gross insensitivity to the experiences of their patients, led medically oriented psychiatrists quickly down the path of ignominy.

The Talking Cure

Biological research into the brain and its functions and the origins of mental illness continued, but it fell increasingly to neuroscientists in fields other than psychiatry. In psychiatry, for some forty years following World War I, the dominant intellectual influence was psychoanalysis.

Sigmund Freud was a physician and began his career as a neurologist. He was a brilliant physiologist, and many of his speculations about the structure of the brain and its biochemistry have turned out to be accurate now that we have the technology to investigate this.

Like Kraepelin, Freud believed that biological correlates would be found to explain mental malfunctioning. "In view of the intimate connection between things physical and mental," he once said, "we may look forward to a day when paths of knowledge will be opened up leading from organic biology and chemistry to the field of neurotic phenomena."

In the absence of the technical laboratory skills necessary to prove this point, Freud set up the best construct that he could: that *neurosis* (disorder of personality rather than a disease syndrome) derived from key experiences of the child as it passed from one predictable developmental stage to another. The remedy was to explore the unconscious mind through uncensored talking and through the patient's reactions to the analyst, thereby identifying and reconstructing these early life experiences and working through their influence on adult life.

In theory and practice, Freud's ideas were revolutionary. Psychotherapy in the many forms it has taken since Freud has become an essential tool—sometimes the only tool—for mental health professionals. But it was never meant for serious illnesses. "Psychoses, states of confusion and deeply rooted (I might say toxic) depressions . . . are not suitable for psychoanalysis," Freud stated. All too many therapists have ignored Freud's advice and kept their patients with active brain disease on the couch for, literally, decades. These therapists don't "believe" in brain disease, despite all the recent evidence for it.

There are several other drawbacks to using "the talking cure" as the one and only method of treatment. For one thing, patients have to be sufficiently intelligent and motivated to apply the results of this *learning experience* to their lives. And, of course, they have to be good talkers. Not long ago the best candidates for psychotherapy were described as "young, physically attractive, well-educated members of the upper middle class, intelligent, verbal, willing to talk about and have responsibility for their problems, and showing no signs of gross pathology."

Of course, they have to be able to afford it as well. Got a spare hundred grand?

Still, Freud and his followers offered a rich and innovative approach to understanding human experience. The early decades of psychoanalytic influence were rife with intellectual fervor. Analysts saw themselves as medical subspecialists, researchers into the human psyche. They kept notes, went to meetings, presented cases, published them in journals. Unfortunately, they and the therapists to come were never able to provide acceptable documentation that psychoanalysis works. Limited to each practitioner's private experience in the consulting room, without the presence of another therapist or film or videotape to document the progress of the analysis, "the self-congratulatory clinical histories in the analytic literature cannot be accepted as evidence of anything beyond the writers' self-regard," wrote one commentator recently.

Under the psychoanalytic influence, the 1930s and 1940s were the heyday of psychiatry and psychosomatic medicine. Many psychiatrists took additional training in internal medicine and walked around hospitals in white coats like the other doctors, and tried to figure out why people get ulcers, or ulcerative colitis, or high blood pressure. Without today's technology they didn't get very far. But their concern with the relationship of mind and body was appropriate for a physician, as witness our developing understanding today regarding, for example, the link between "Type A personality" and heart disease, and between cancer and loss (research, I might add, that was accomplished largely by nonpsychiatric investigators). These early psychoanalytic physicians recognized that their patients also had bodies!

Overall it was a time of enormous prestige for psychiatry, and the profession attracted the cream of the crop of medical school graduates.

As the years passed, however, practitioners of psychoanalytic psychotherapy were to abandon medical science altogether and all categories of mental diseases within it. In 1963, Karl Menninger, founder of the Menninger Clinic in Topeka, Kansas, published *The Vital Balance,* an influential book in which he insisted that all mental afflictions were degrees of a single disease and therefore responsive to the same technique: psychotherapy. This view doomed depressed people to another decade of noncures on the couch. Psychiatrist Thomas Szasz, in *The Myth of Mental Illness,* published in 1961, insisted there wasn't even one disease.

Psychiatrists had become doctors who treated no diseases. How Kraepelin's ghost must have shuddered. Moreover, this theoretical stance blurred all distinctions between psychiatrists and psychologists, who had multiplied greatly since World War II. Psychotherapy requires no medical background. It's rather like getting eyeglasses fitted: Why go to an expensive ophthalmologist, a doctor who specializes in the eye, just to have your glasses checked, when you can consult an optometrist, who has gone to optometry school to learn this one technical skill? Ophthalmologists do, of course, fit eyeglasses, but as physicians they primarily diagnose and treat eye *disease.* If there were no more diseases for psychiatrists to treat, who needed them?

Psychologists and other nonmedical mental health workers (many of whom were trained by psychiatrists during the community mental health movement of the 1970s) further "nonmedicalized" prevailing views of the etiology of mental suffering and the corresponding treatment. Psychotherapy is good for "whatever ails ya," from severe depression or mania to problems with your spouse. And if it has taken psychiatrists forever to begin to recognize the possibility that psychological symptoms may actually be symptoms of physical disease that must be treated, nonmedical therapists have yet to take this reality seriously.

The Psychiatrist as Clown

Ironically, psychotherapy prospered in an illness-free environment: You didn't have to be "sick" to get your head on straight or to learn to open up or to sweeten your relationships or to handle money better or to overcome your sexual inhibitions. Whatever you wanted to accomplish, by the late 1960s there was sure to be a therapy somewhere to serve you. Psychotherapy was a growth industry. Shrinks with MDs or PhDs or no degrees at all created liberating therapies founded on little legitimate theory and much popular hype. These might have been fun, even enlightening for the participant who was basically okay, but the seriously depressed or otherwise ill person was likely to be lost in the melee.

Still, psychotherapists could see into your mind, predict your future, and cure you of anything that held you back. Such was the message of psychology and psychiatry, and the public wanted to hear it. Psychiatrists were elevated to high priests of the courtroom and seers of the future. Supposedly the psychiatrists had the knowledge to determine whether a criminal or mentally ill individual would be dangerous to self or others and therefore to determine his or her future. The courts listened; they continue to listen as evidence piles up against psychiatric fortune-telling. A study published in 1984 suggests that nobody even knows what "dangerous" means. Psychiatrists and nonpsychiatrists were asked to rate sixteen criminals for dangerousness. Hardly any of the 193 raters agreed with each other; only on four of the cases was there as much as 60 percent agreement. Psychiatrists reached no higher level of agreement than anyone else.

Psychiatric performance in the courtroom has led to such absurdities as the "Twinkie defense" of Dan White, who killed San Francisco Supervisor Harvey Milk. Psychiatrists testified that White had become deranged by eating too much junk food. No research evidence was submitted.

The trial of John Hinckley for his attempted assassination of President Ronald Reagan in 1981 was the last straw. So many psychiatrists were called to testify that Hinckley was insane or wasn't insane that the public became convinced, once and for all, that psychiatrists could be paid by lawyers to say anything. In all, they were a bunch of silly people who didn't know much of anything. Why, Hinckley's own psychiatrist had thought he was essentially a normal kid who needed more discipline!

Psychiatrists came tumbling off the pedestal that society had helped put them on. Ironically, despite its poor performance as an expert witness, the courts won't let psychiatry step down. The American Psychiatric Association in 1984 declared that psychiatry did not belong in the courtroom. Despite attacks on the legitimacy of psychiatric testimony in several recent court decisions, the Supreme Court has determined that psychiatrists can and should testify, even if their opinions are hypothetical and they never meet the person they are testifying about.

Pill Time

The development of an arsenal of psychiatric medication by the 1970s both helped and hurt the profession's public image.

The age of the wonder drug in psychiatry had begun in the 1950s, when a French surgeon who was experimenting with a medication to reduce surgical shock discovered what would become the first antipsychotic drug: chlorpromazine (Thorazine). Many others soon were synthesized, for purposes of profit to drug companies as well as benefit to patients.

Prior to that time, most psychiatrists had dumped their psychotic patients in mental institutions and more or less forgotten about them, since there was no treatment to help them and few believed that psychotherapy made any sense for someone not grounded in reality. Medication liberated many of them both from lifetime sentences of bizarre behavior and thinking, and from the disregard of their psychiatrists.

The first of a class of drugs called *tricyclic antidepressants,* imipramine entered the world as a possible new antipsychotic. It turned out not to work, but it did have a lifting effect on the spirits of depressed patients. Development of tricyclics and other classes of antidepressants immediately followed. Tranquilizers first appeared on the market in the late 1950s; lithium, finally, in 1970 (see Chapter 2).

Pharmaceutical companies have poured billions of dollars into the development and marketing of psychiatric drugs. Despite this phenomenal amount of money and the proliferation of medications, few essentially new drugs have appeared. Almost all are variations of earlier formulas or concepts. Each variation does, however, entitle the drug companies to a new patent, and it gives psychiatrists or other physicians with little knowledge of psychopharmacology but much trust in the drug-company detail men hope that this new drug might work.

Under attack for their inability to prove the effectiveness of psychotherapy, frustrated by their lack of progress with severely depressed and/or anxious patients, and feeling the economic strain of competition from all the nonmedical therapists, psychiatrists were relieved to have chemical agents at their disposal. At last they had differentiated themselves from psychologists. And the prescriptions often worked.

Many psychiatrists and physicians in other specialties began to prescribe psychiatric medication with an excess of enthusiasm—a common phenomenon in medicine when a "new cure" makes its appearance. The huge doses of antipsychotics which they were dispensing turned out to have a ghastly and often irreversible side effect called tardive dyskinesia, which causes involuntary movements of the face and tongue. Tranquilizers were prescribed for every little twinge of anxiety, and they turned out to be addicting. Antidepressants caused such unpleasant, and occasionally dangerous, side effects that many patients quit taking them.

These excesses received wide public attention and further eroded the image of psychiatry. Psychiatrists came to be seen as pill pushers, no better than the "druggies" who had emerged from the 1960s. Many psychiatrists panicked. As a result, a serious problem in medicine today is the *underprescription* of medication for pain and for some psychiatric conditions, especially depression. Patients dying of cancer receive too little pain medication for fear that they'll become addicted to it. And patients suffering the pain of depression are often given tiny little doses of medication—so tiny that the brain doesn't even notice. We get so many cases of hopeless or "intractable" depression at Fair Oaks that we can "cure" in a blink simply by adjusting the medication level.

Still, despite their initial inexperience with the new psychiatric drugs, psychiatrists became convinced that at last they could actually *do* something for their more seriously ill patients. For patients who had to be hospitalized, medication was usually the treatment of choice. Beyond a doubt, most depressed patients who were given a course of medication improved and went home. Books were written about the wondrous new cures. Psychiatry as a whole began to feel a lot better.

Crash!

If all those books had been correct, you wouldn't be reading this one now. After nearly thirty years of the use of "miracle drugs," the verdict has just come in: They don't work miracles.

Study after study reveals that patients who are vigorously treated with drugs or even shock therapy by the most well-intentioned practitioners have a response rate that is about the same as those who receive cognitive psychotherapy (see Chapter 22). Even when initial response is dramatic and the patient is soon discharged from the hospital, the risk of relapse is extraordinary. The ongoing NIMH Collaborative Study of the Psychobiology of Depression, conducted at America's premier academic hospitals, reports that only 60 percent of depressed patients have recovered six months after treatment, and only 34 percent are completely free of symptoms. Of those who fully "recover" during treatment, 19 percent relapse within six months and 24 percent develop new symptoms.

The fact is, depressed patients wonder whether they would be better off if psychiatrists left them alone. That same 60 percent will get better no matter what we do—the rate of spontaneous recovery is that high.

Findings such as these pulled the rug out from under traditional psychiatry. Down it went in a final crisis of confidence and credibility.

Biopsychiatry to the Rescue

The apparent ineffectiveness of the most modern treatments for depression hardly surprised me. Having hung my hat with the new psychiatry, until then forced to remain behind the scenes, I knew why traditional methods had failed. It wasn't the fault of the treatments available; it was failure of the practitioner to apply these treatments in rigorously scientific ways.

Antidepressant medication can work extraordinarily well—*if* the patient needs it. Much of the work of biopsychiatry has gone into defining what biological depression is, developing a technology to aid in accurately diagnosing who has it, and determining through laboratory methods what is the most appropriate treatment.

Of course, success rates will turn out low if you're prescribing antidepressant medication for everybody who seems depressed, including the patients whose depressive symptoms have to do with other undiagnosed diseases.

But let's say you are a psychiatrist and your patient really is biologically depressed. Which of all the medications available are you going to prescribe? For how long? How do you really know it's working? You'll have to use the laboratory to be sure. Many a patient starts to seem okay, but tests reveal that the biological condition remains active. Removing medication at the patient's first sunny smile and apparent remission of symptoms ensures relapse.

Biopsychiatry is rigorous medical science. That's the major difference between "us" and "them." And it's the reason why—here comes the good news—using many of the same treatments at which others fail, we can make them work.

Where Biopsychiatry Came From

The discovery of the psychiatric wonder drugs back in the 1950s led to some essential questions about the nature of psychiatric illness, which only biological research scientists were equipped to resolve. Why did these drugs work? How? Which brain structures and processes were affected? If chemicals could alter the behavior of someone termed psychotic, but leave a depressed person essentially unchanged, was there some *organic* difference between these two individuals? Which conditions would be most responsive to which drugs, and why? If drugs altered brain chemistry, was brain chemistry the cause of mental illness? Suddenly a group of psychiatrists began to reconsider the discarded notion of separate psychiatric illnesses. Antidepressants worked on some people with symptoms of depression and not others. Were the differences in their brains or in their minds?

At the same time, neuroscientists in fields such as neurochemistry, neuroendocrinology (study of the brain's hormonal system), and neurobehavior were asking a number of related questions about normal and abnormal brain function and its relation to feelings and behavior. The new organic psychiatrists remained alone and unloved in psychiatry, but they had lots of friends in these other sciences. All began to learn from one another. Suddenly there was an explosion in technological development, and the tools they all needed to answer their questions began to become available. They were peering into the very cells of the brain and beginning to discover how it, and psychiatric drugs, worked. The next step was to begin to investigate the physiology of mental illness and perhaps even discover its causes. Then they could correct them.

The Good News:
I Am a Psychiatrist

I entered psychiatry at the very beginning of its recruitment crisis— no better time to get involved in the new psychiatry. The technology was in place, the greatest minds in the field were allying themselves with the new work, and the unraveling of the mysteries of the mind was imminent. Any serious psychiatrist who joined in could make a practical contribution to basic science and to patient care. Results were formidable. Traditional psychiatrists were in the doldrums, but we were—we are—a bunch of cheerful optimists.

We continue to provide evidence that patients with brain disease are different from those with problems of living. This couldn't be more important for depressed people, whose conditions can be anything from a perfectly appropriate reaction to a life situation to a serious biological illness. We are in the process of delineating subtypes of depression that respond to different treatments. We are discovering the relationship of genetics to the development of psychiatric illness and learning about the environmental, psychological, and biological factors that trigger it. We have amassed a gold mine of data on the relationship of illnesses like depression to the endocrine system. We're discovering the biochemistry behind the relationship of depression to the immune system.

Overall, we've learned how to piece together the biochemistry, neuropharmacology, and neuroendocrinology of mental illness. Lab reports from high-performance liquid chromatographs, receptor-binding assays, and immunochemistry augment and rival the notepad, and the straitjacket.

We've begun to influence the way psychiatrists are trained. The American Psychiatric Association has published a manual of therapeutics which for the first time in its history includes a chapter on the psychiatric laboratory. Educators agree finally that a psychiatrist must be a skilled physician who can diagnose illness using an interview, patient history, laboratory tests, and a complete physical exam—even if he or she goes on to practice psychotherapy. They insist that trainees have a broad knowledge of other specialties.

What does all this mean to the depressed person? It means that we are finally beginning to learn what depression is: a disease that is treatable. Psychiatrists who treat depression traditionally with medication use the trial-and-error method. They say that you have a 50 to 60 percent chance of getting better on the first antidepressant tried. If that doesn't work, you'll be switched to another one, which increases the chances to 65 to 80 percent. This will cost you twelve to thirty weeks in treatment.

We say that we'll test you to make sure you really are a candidate for medication. If you are, we'll test you again to make sure we "hit" on the first try. Biopsychiatry will get you better faster, more efficiently, and with less suffering. At Fair Oaks, our treatment-resistant rate for depression is less than ten out of one hundred. If you are not getting better in your current psychotherapeutic treatment, chances are close to 100 percent that biopsychiatric evaluation will yield either medical illness or active brain disease.

It means that you can begin to trust psychiatrists again. "That'll be the day," muttered a down-in-the-dumps woman patient who'd gone the shrink route and gave us a try only because she couldn't live with her condition and didn't know what else to do. She went home with a prescription for thyroid medication. No one had performed the right kind of thyroid test on her, so her thyroid disease—at the root of her mental symptoms—had never been treated. "Maybe you guys aren't so bad after all," she laughed in parting.

Yeah, maybe.

Over 90 percent of those who are suffering depression are not being treated for it. You stay home and watch Phil Donahue because you are embarrassed to be depressed and you don't think it's a disease, or because you think this head doctor is going to make you talk for fifteen years. You don't want to talk. You want to die.

"Medicine is pragmatic," writes Canadian psychiatrist Myre Sim, MD. "One must constantly seek better remedies and discard the old. Authority must have its credentials repeatedly examined and tested."

This process is ongoing in medicine. Biopsychiatrists have managed to reestablish psychiatry as a branch of medicine. This has been our greatest accomplishment, and in itself is and will be responsible for the onrush of advances in our field.

Addressing the American Psychiatric Association upon his election as president, John Talbott, MD, a few years ago spoke of psychiatry's new agenda:

> While most physicians and, indeed, most laymen still perceive of psychiatry only as a couch-bound psychotherapeutic discipline, this is no longer the case, and we have to struggle not only with our sense of integrity in the face of such rapid changes but attempt to inform the rest of medicine and society about our changing world. This is not to say that psychotherapy no longer is valued or has value, but rather with our increasing ability to diagnose accurately and thereby treat effectively . . . we become more broad based and better therapeutically armed.

So maybe it's time to have that depression of yours (or your spouse's or your child's or your grandfather's) looked at. By a biopsychiatrist.

Part II
Diagnosis and Misdiagnosis

4

All That Wheezes Isn't Asthma

THERE'S A JOKE MAKING the rounds of psychiatrists' cocktail parties about a woman who wakes up one morning with a sore throat. She's new in town and doesn't have a doctor, so she looks in the Yellow Pages under "Physicians." She finds a doctor in her neighborhood and calls for an appointment. When the woman is shown into the doctor's office, she describes her symptoms. He takes a history, then directs her to the examining room. It just so happens that this doctor is a gynecologist. He performs a pelvic examination and discovers that she has a low-grade vaginal infection. He prescribes antibiotics, and her sore throat clears up.

In medicine, treatment follows from diagnosis. If lab results show you have a strep throat, you'll get a prescription for an antibiotic that will go to war with the streptococcus bacterium. Should your sore throat prove to be caused by a virus, against which antibiotics are ineffective, your doctor still may recommend antibiotics, feeling (improperly, of course) that he or she has to prescribe something to appear doctorlike and knowing that this kind of sore throat will go away anyway. As long as the doctor can figure out what's wrong with you, he or she can choose the treatment that is most likely to work. But should you really have a strep infection and your doctor jumps to the conclusion "it's just a virus; stay in bed, keep warm, it'll go away," you're in trouble. Wrong diagnosis leads to wrong treatment. Unless, of course, your doctor, like the gynecologist, gets lucky and prescribes the right treatment from the wrong diagnosis.

Few doctors, psychiatrists included, can keep blind luck going for long. More likely, a high rate of misdiagnosis will yield a low rate of treatment response. This is what has happened in psychiatry.

The problem stems from: (1) the medically outmoded diagnostic system psychiatry uses, combined with (2) the nonmedical propensities of the practitioners, (3) often hostile competition among the many psychiatric approaches, as well as (4) reluctance, or downright refusal, to incorporate in the diagnosis the new knowledge about mind-brain function gained in the laboratory using the new technology.

"Psychiatry . . . tends to run about two hundred years behind the rest of medicine," comments Donald W. Goodwin, MD, one of the new psychiatry's leading lights. The system of diagnosis, which classifies psychiatric illness largely through description of symptoms, was appropriate when doctors knew nothing about underlying causes or treatment. Today, psychiatric knowledge about both causes and treatments is exploding. Nonetheless, when it comes to step one, diagnosis, psychiatry relies on a system that can at best yield incomplete information. At worst it encourages misdiagnosis. Adding insult to injury, when treatment fails, instead of questioning the diagnosis that encouraged them to choose an ineffective approach, psychiatrists accuse the patient of being a "nonresponder."

The Case of Ms. A

Ms. A, the 25-year-old patient of a Providence, Rhode Island, psychiatrist, had been misdiagnosed as schizophrenic by at least three different psychiatrists for the seven years before she consulted him. He correctly identified her illness as bipolar (manic-depressive) disorder. During a manic phase, bipolar and schizophrenic patients may behave in a similarly bizarre fashion. The bipolar patient, however, will exhibit powerful mood fluctuations, and if the psychiatrist is diagnosing only by the appearance of the patient, this is the giveaway. Confusing the two illnesses is common, although they are in fact very different, from diagnosis to treatment to prognosis. Bipolar illness responds almost immediately to lithium, which not only restores normalcy but controls the disease's seesaw course. Schizophrenics can be helped back into this world with neuroleptic (antipsychotic) medication, but their illness remains chronic, and medication only manages it.

The Providence doctor's patient did not believe that she was schizophrenic and refused to take her medication. Even so, her condition returned to normal between episodes—another bipolar diagnostic giveaway.

"The lack of early correct diagnosis led to a series of mutually reinforcing complications for Ms. A that were all potentially avoidable," her psychiatrist wrote in a letter to the editor of the *American Journal of Psychiatry*. "Maintenance treatment was attempted with neuroleptics (with significant side effects) rather than with lithium, which might have minimized the chances of recurrences. Her dislike of the neuroleptics and her disagreement with her diagnosis led to confrontations with and distrust of her physicians. Her conflict with authority widened to her family, particularly her father, who blamed her for the episodes because she did not comply with the recommended treatment. She increasingly came to feel misunderstood and isolated. She did not know where to turn for guidance and support. This sense of isolation and confusion occurred during adolescence, a critical developmental stage, and was aggravated by the continued cycling of her illness. Once the initial diagnosis of schizophrenia was made, there seemed to be a strong reluctance to reexamine it, even with growing evidence against it."

Get it right from the beginning and you're more than halfway there, say the biopsychiatrists. Our treatment results are demonstrably better than those of psychiatry as a whole, because we begin by applying the more rigorous, medically current diagnostic system that is used in all other areas of medicine today.

Making a Diagnosis, Medical Style

Arriving at a diagnosis can be the longest, most challenging, and most difficult step for a doctor. No two patients are identical in health or illness. Virtually no one will exhibit the "classic" symptom and test result patterns described in textbooks. Often, too, a physician will be searching for a disease that is in a stage of development in which it does not exhibit its characteristic appearance.

The time it may take a physician to diagnose your problem may be long and frustrating, but it's worth the wait. The doctor who can pinpoint your problem is best equipped to target the treatment precisely.

The medical diagnostic process begins with a clinical interview in which the doctor takes a history of the specific complaint and of your overall health as well as your family's health patterns. The doctor next performs an examination in which he or she hopes to see, feel, or demonstrate the presence of a particular illness or condition. Usually the physician will order lab tests. The laboratory is central to modern medicine because to the well-trained physician it can provide highly specific, objective information of a kind that in previous years might have been available only at autopsy. (If you want the most accurate diagnosis, wait!) Together with the physician's clinical impression, the laboratory will help to confirm a diagnosis as well as to verify the progress of treatment.

Diagnoses made on the basis solely of a patient's symptoms are the least accurate or useful to a physician. Symptoms are usually vague and often difficult to describe and to remember. Emotional symptoms tend to be the most unreliable because the patient's description of them is colored by the emotion itself. For example, if you are depressed and a doctor asks you how long you have felt that way, unintentionally you will probably exaggerate because depression distorts your sense of time. In addition, when you're depressed, it's difficult to remember events or experiences that occurred when you were not depressed. Similarly, if you're not depressed now, you won't remember many of the details of your last depression.

The single greatest reason why symptoms are only part of the picture in medical diagnoses, however, is that symptoms are not specific. In other words, any one symptom can indicate a host of conditions. If you have a pain in your big toe, maybe you broke it. Or maybe you have gout. Or an ingrown toenail.

If you are depressed, maybe you have infectious mononucleosis. Or maybe you have a bad marriage. Or a genetic deficiency of enzymes that synthesize the brain chemical norepinephrine.

Before the development of objective measures to verify or clarify particular diagnoses, medicine had little choice but to depend on symptoms or clusters of symptoms (syndromes) to try to identify a disease. In medicine this era has ended.

Making a Diagnosis, Psychiatric Style

Despite their long years of medical training, and despite the increasing sophistication of the psychiatric laboratory, psychiatrists continue to diagnose their patients solely on the basis of their symptoms.

Frequently a psychiatric diagnosis goes like this:

"Oh, Doctor, I'm so depressed."

"Tell me about it."

You talk about your feelings of worthlessness and hopelessness, your difficulties concentrating and making decisions, your insomnia, your loss of interest in just about everything, including food and sex. The psychiatrist asks how long this has been going on, whether you have experienced these feelings before, whether anything might have happened to bring on this episode.

At the end of the interview, the psychiatrist agrees that you are indeed depressed because the symptoms you describe fit the descriptive diagnostic criteria (see box on page 50).

It's as if you went to your internist with a sore throat only to discover that you had . . . a sore throat.

The "diagnosis" thus quickly established, the psychiatrist will begin treatment equally peremptorily—no tests, no verification of the diagnosis, no uncertainty about what these symptoms may mean.

This in a nutshell is where most psychiatrists (and nonmedical therapists) go astray: They *rule in* their diagnoses. In other words, they take the subjective details of symptoms and history described by their patients and fit them to the condition that appears the most obvious explanation for them.

It's Obvious

In medicine there's a saying: All that wheezes isn't asthma. This serves to remind physicians to look beyond the obvious before they jump to conclusions about their patients' conditions. And in fact, in the differential diagnosis of asthma, the treating physician must rule out thirty-four other possible causes for wheezing before he or she can safely rule in a diagnosis of asthma.

A friend of mine suddenly experienced a terrible pain and tightening in his chest. The pain radiated down his left arm. Dizzy and faint, nearly overwhelmed with nausea and barely able to breathe, he somehow managed to get himself to the nearest emergency room. "I'm having a heart attack!" he gasped, clutching his chest, and collapsed. In a split second he was on a hospital gurney surrounded by the ER staff. A doctor was listening to his heart while one nurse was hooking up the electrocardiogram, another taking his blood pressure, and another drawing blood to rush it to the lab for serum enzyme analysis. My friend lay there in terror of dying.

Thank goodness, he pulled through. His tests all turned out negative. He hadn't had a heart attack after all. He had had an anxiety attack.

Any doctor would have suspected a coronary, for my friend's symptoms so closely fit those we all learned in medical school. But a decent medical workup always consists of a ruling out/ruling in—what we call a differential diagnostic procedure. This is absolutely essential to good medical practice, because what if it isn't the obvious condition? Jumping to conclusions can have tragic, irreversible consequences.

The Case of Donald Snow

A recent, well-publicized malpractice case in New York involved a man named Donald Snow, now 23, who had been diagnosed as retarded and committed to the Willowbrook State School before he was 3 years old. As an infant he had not developed properly; he learned extremely slowly and he could not speak. His pediatrician advised his parents to take him to Willowbrook for testing. As a result of these tests he was allotted an IQ of 24, which put him in the Imbecile category; he was considered uneducable and untrainable. Under the circumstances, his parents felt they had no choice but to commit him.

To make a painfully long story short, the child wasn't retarded. He was deaf. Willowbrook did not test his hearing, and the test they gave him was for babies who could hear the examiner. He hadn't heard anything in his life. Everyone was so focused on his "retardation" that they missed the disability that Donald was truly suffering from.

His deafness was discovered when Donald was 10, and the boy finally went home. The ending, however, is not a happy one. Because of Donald's early deprivation, he may never develop into a truly normal, if deaf, person.

At the schools for the deaf Donald attended until he was 21, he was never able to catch up to his appropriate level. "In a report to the court, Jerome D. Schein, director of the New York University School for Deafness Rehabilitation, said that because of his experience at Willowbrook, Donald will never learn to speak, that he will have trouble establishing personal relationships, finding a job or even going shopping, and that his true personality will always be masked by the 'passivity, overdependence, and immaturity' that he learned at Willowbrook," reports newsman Robin Topping.

Unfortunately, the deaf are frequent victims of other incorrect diagnoses, including autism and childhood psychosis.

The Psychological Explanation

It is human nature to try to make sense of experience. Psychologically, there is almost always an explanation for why we feel the way we do. Sometimes that explanation is irresistible. Let's say you meet a middle-aged man who is in terrible pain from depression. After talking to him for a while, you find out he recently lost his wife in an automobile accident. Of course he's depressed! Need you explore further?

The answer is an unqualified yes, because it is precisely when the allure of the obvious is that powerful, serious mistakes are most likely to be made. Just because this explanation for the man's distress makes sense, who's to say it is the only one to make sense? Where is it written that the explanation for his distress must have a single facet? Indeed, with evidence mounting for a causal relationship between severe stress and physical, often fatal, illness, a physician is compelled to go further.

This man became a patient at Fair Oaks, and just in time. He had seen three doctors before he was referred to us for psychiatric evaluation. By the time he arrived he was only hours from death. He was deeply depressed and fit the necessary criteria for a major depressive episode. Within moments of his admission, our alert evaluations team noticed that his lips were vaguely blue. We took his blood pressure and discovered it was very low. Immediately, we ran emergency tests and found that his potassium level was high enough for his heart to stop beating. An electrocardiogram revealed a heart rhythm so disturbed he could indeed die at any moment. Quickly we provided intravenous fluids to bring down his potassium level and bring up his sodium level. This is standard procedure, but it didn't work. Within twenty-four hours we had discovered why: his cortisol test confirmed that he had Addison's disease (see page 153), in which the adrenal glands shut down. Without treatment Addison's is fatal. Twenty minutes after we gave him intravenous cortisone, an adrenal hormone, he started feeling better.

Every physician knows that Addison's, an extremely rare disease, causes severe depression. Psychiatrists say: "Sure, Addison's causes depression, but I've never seen a case in all the years I've practiced." To this I respond, "When was the last time you looked for it, or any other not-so-obvious diagnosis? How can you find it when you hang your diagnostic hat on your patients' outward symptoms?"

Our files are filled with all too many of these avoidable horror stories. As we pointed out in Chapter 2, misdiagnosis brings the most suffering to patients and the highest awards in psychiatric malpractice cases. Still, instead of returning to the medical model of diagnosis, psychiatrists continue to string descriptive symptoms together until they neatly fit the diagnosis. Why? In part the answer is to be found in a manual possessed by all psychiatrists and published by the American Psychiatric Association.

The DSM-III

Published in 1980 and revised in 1986–87, *The Diagnostic and Statistical Manual of Mental Disorders* (Third Edition), popularly termed the *DSM-III,* is the bible of psychiatric diagnosis. Its influence is enormous even outside psychiatry, for its diagnostic codes are used by all mental health providers whose services are reimbursable by insurance companies. Although the APA lately supports biopsychiatric concepts, this important manual paradoxically promotes a descriptive, symptom-based system that is at best reductionistic. At worst, it discourages practitioners from looking beyond the obvious.

The box on this page quotes the DSM-III criteria for a "major depressive episode" (sometimes called a "clinical" depression—see Part III of this book for the sundry names depression can go by). All psychiatric conditions in the DSM-III are diagnosed in this peculiar "Chinese menu" style: one symptom from column A, two from column B. . . .

Diagnostic Criteria for Major Depressive Episode

A. Dysphoric [unpleasant] mood or loss of interest or pleasure in all or almost all usual activities and pastimes. The dysphoric mood is characterized by symptoms such as the following: depressed, sad, blue, hopeless, low, down in the dumps, irritable. The mood disturbance must be prominent and relatively persistent, but not necessarily the most dominant symptom, and does not include momentary shifts from one dysphoric mood to another dysphoric mood, e.g., anxiety to depression to anger, such as are seen in states of acute psychotic turmoil. (For children under six, dysphoric mood may have to be inferred from a persistently sad facial expression.)
B. At least four of the following symptoms have each been present nearly every day for a period of at least two weeks (in children under six, at least three of the first four):
   1. poor appetite or significant weight loss (when not dieting) or increased appetite or significant weight gain (in children under six, consider failure to make expected weight gains)
   2. insomnia or hypersomnia [excessive sleeping]
   3. psychomotor agitation or retardation (but not merely subjective feelings of restlessness or being slowed down) (in children under six, hypoactivity)
   4. loss of interest or pleasure in usual activities, or decrease in

sexual drive not limited to a period when delusional or hallucinating (in children under six, signs of apathy)

5. loss of energy; fatigue

6. feelings of worthlessness, self-reproach, or excessive or inappropriate guilt (either may be delusional)

7. complaints or evidence of diminished ability to think or concentrate, such as slowed thinking, or indecisiveness, not associated with loosening of associations or incoherence

8. recurrent thoughts of death, suicidal ideation, wishes to be dead, or suicide attempt

C. Neither of the following dominate the clinical picture when an affective syndrome (i.e., criteria A and B above) is not present, that is, before it developed or after it has remitted:

1. preoccupation with a mood-incongruent [content unrelated to depressed-type thinking] delusion or hallucination (see definition below)

2. bizarre behavior

D. not superimposed on either Schizophrenia, Schizophreniform Disorder, or a Paranoid Disorder.

E. Not due to any Organic Mental Disorder or Uncomplicated Bereavement.

**. . . CRITERIA FOR SUBCLASSIFICATION
OF MAJOR DEPRESSIVE EPISODE**
(When psychotic features and Melancholia are present the coding systems require that the clinician record the single most clinically significant characteristic.)

. . . In Remission. This . . . category should be used when in the past the individual met the full criteria for a major depressive episode but now is essentially free of depressive symptoms or has some signs of the disorder but does not meet the full criteria.

. . . With Psychotic Features. This . . . category should be used when there apparently is gross impairment in reality testing, as when there are delusions or hallucinations, or depressive stupor (the individual is mute and unresponsive). . . .

Mood-congruent Psychotic Features. Delusions or hallucinations whose content is entirely consistent with the themes of either personal inadequacy, guilt, disease, death, nihilism, or deserved punishment; depressive stupor. . . .

Mood-incongruent Psychotic Features. Delusions or hallucinations whose content does not involve themes of either personal inadequacy, guilt, disease, death, nihilism, or deserved punishment. Included here are such symptoms as persecutory delusions, thought insertion, thought broadcasting, and delusions of control, whose content has no apparent relationship to any of the themes noted above.

With Melancholia

A. Loss of pleasure in all or almost all activities.

B. Lack of reactivity to usually pleasurable stimuli (doesn't feel much better, even temporarily, when something good happens).

C. At least three of the following:

    (a) distinct quality of depressed mood, i.e., the depressed mood is perceived as distinctly different from the kind of feeling experienced following the death of a loved one

    (b) the depression is regularly worse in the morning

    (c) early morning awakening (at least two hours before usual time of awakening)

    (d) marked psychomotor retardation or agitation

    (e) significant anorexia or weight loss

    (f) excessive or inappropriate guilt

The Trouble with Symptoms, Continued

We have already discussed some of the drawbacks of symptom-based, ruling-in diagnosis. The DSM-III glaringly demonstrates others.

1. Without objective verification, how can you be sure you have the correct diagnosis if the symptoms of two different disorders are similar?

A patient shows up talking a mile a minute about how God instructed him to take a supersonic airplane to Paris and back. This grandiose delusion could fit someone in the midst of a manic episode *or* a schizophrenic. Get the diagnosis wrong and, as in the case of Ms. A, you can effectively destroy a patient's life. You can also possibly give a patient a bright new future—but to do that, as we said, you must first get the diagnosis right.

2. Patients tend to evaluate symptoms differently. "How's your appetite?" "Fine," answers the patient, who is grateful that for once she has no appetite.

"Are you in pain?" "Not particularly," answers the person who has lived with pain so long that it no longer seems unusual. "Oh, terrible!" responds another person, who makes much of a transitory experience.

3. Patients of differing ages and backgrounds display differing symptoms, for in sickness and in health behavior is shaped by generation and culture, even by sex. Women tend to display more of the emotional symptoms of depression, while many men mask them with physical complaints or activities. A colleague had a patient whose career had collapsed and whose wife had thrown him out of the house who would build a new piece of audio equipment each time he got depressed. When he ran out of room in his one-room apartment he experienced the depression he'd been fending off, and finally went for help.

DSM-III makes no mention of the manifestations of depression in different cultures, even though late in the last century Kraepelin noted their existence and contemporary crosscultural studies reveal a wide variation. For example, guilt as a symptom of depression appears to be a Western phenomenon. Kraepelin observed that his Japanese patients were neither guilt-ridden nor suicidal. According to a more recent study, developing cultures tend to emphasize physical symptoms. Asian cultures generally do not reveal their feelings. A study of Hawaii's ethnic groups showed that depressed Japanese showed more suspiciousness, Caucasians more helplessness. So symptoms alone do not a diagnosis make: A disease is a disease is a disease, whether the patient is in New York City or Tokyo.

Virtually every culture and subculture influences the expression and content of symptoms—but not the expression and content of the DSM-III. Blacks and Hispanics with bipolar illness are more likely than whites to be diagnosed as schizophrenic because they tend to have what admitting psychiatrists call delusions and hallucinations that may actually be culturally based religious beliefs.

4. Relying on symptoms often leads to inappropriate evaluation of the patient's progress. Biopsychiatrists have shown that patients may continue to show biological evidence of depressive illness even though many of their symptoms have disappeared. To stop treatment measures when symptoms abate puts these patients at high risk of relapse.

Shrewd patients can manipulate symptoms to get their shrinks off their backs. Nobody likes to be hospitalized, and depressed patients need only appear to have all the "right" symptoms in order to get out. "How are you feeling today, Joanne?" "Just fine, Doctor. I'm sleeping and eating just fine and I'm full of energy. Why, I've been really excited about the great future I really have." So the psychiatrist releases Joanne prematurely. She goes home and kills herself.

5. The absence of expected symptoms does not necessarily rule out the disease. Certain psychiatric patients diagnosed as suffering from "schizophreniform disorder," for example, show none of the DSM-III symptoms of mood disorders. Nonetheless, researchers have recently demonstrated that when these patients are diagnosed using all the tools of biopsychiatry, including the laboratory, they can be shown to be suffering from mood disorders. Most important, they respond favorably to treatment for depression or bipolar disorder.

Would you call a serial murderer normal? If you go by symptoms, you'd have to, for studies of these people who kill person after person show that using descriptive criteria they appear utterly normal.

Poor Little "E"

Ultimately, the DSM-III is a trap for psychiatrists. It encourages them to believe that behavioral symptoms necessarily mean something psychiatric. This comes from a notion, long discarded in the history of medicine, that the body consists of discrete systems that have nothing to do with one another; emotional symptoms come from the head and physical symptoms come from the body, and never the twain shall meet. If you're acting funny, you need a psychiatrist to straighten out your mind.

You do need a psychiatrist, but not necessarily for that reason. You need a psychiatrist to perform a sophisticated medical diagnosis so that you know exactly what you are suffering from that is affecting your behavior and emotions.

When a person tells me he or she is depressed, I say to myself, "So what? That doesn't tell me anything." If I know that someone is not sleeping, I'm no better off than I was before the patient walked in. For I know—and so do all newly trained biopsychiatrists—that meeting the DSM-III criteria does not tell me what caused the problem or what to do about it.

There is no "mental" symptom that is specific to psychiatric illness alone. You could be standing on a street corner having bizarre Technicolor hallucinations and still not be "crazy"; your visions may indicate you're in the midst of the aura that precedes a small percentage of migraine headaches. Visual hallucinations could also be symptomatic of a brain tumor, of cocaine or MDMA intoxication, or of alcohol or sleeping pill withdrawal. Or they could be a side effect of a commonly prescribed medication. Catatonia—a condition in which the patient stays as still as a statue, utterly unmoving, despite an often bizarre and uncomfortable posture—is the quintessential psychotic symptom, right? Wrong. Catatonia is now known to be more indicative of neurological conditions. The differential diagnosis of catatonia includes at least thirty-nine disorders, varying from lesions, tumors, and malformations of the brain to epilepsy, syphilis, encephalitis, and diabetic ketoacidosis, to chronic amphetamine intoxication and aspirin overdose.

Among the many flaws in the DSM-III, the following is the most shocking. The DSM-III does not consider causes or even tell psychiatrists about the organic conditions that can mimic psychiatric illnesses. Look again at the criteria for major depressive disorder on page 50. Buried deep in the list is poor little letter "E": "Not due to any Organic Mental Disorder or Uncomplicated Bereavement."

This means that no one—psychiatrist, internist, or psychologist—can conclude that a patient is in the midst of a major depressive episode without first ruling out possible organic causes. The DSM-III explains this diagnostic criterion as follows: "An *Organic Affective Syndrome with depression* may be due to substances such as reserpine, to infectious diseases such as influenza, or to hypothyroidism. Only by excluding organic etiology can one make the diagnosis of a major depressive episode."

Only three organic causes of depression are mentioned in the official book of psychiatric diagnosis. Now we can begin to understand why the rate of misdiagnosis in psychiatry is so high: The psychiatric profession's official manual of diagnostics does not provide an inclusive differential diagnostic list of the seventy-five-plus organic conditions that can mimic depression, many of which are not widely known or considered by psychiatrists or internists. Even for the three organic causes the DSM-III *does* mention, no guidance is forthcoming on how to rule them out. In Chapters 6 through 10 of this book we discuss each of these mimickers; read them and you will be much better informed than most doctors and virtually all nonmedical therapists.

To avoid misdiagnosis, poor little "E" should become the first criterion in the differential diagnosis of depression. At present, it appears an afterthought or even a disclaimer. The combined category of organic causes and uncomplicated bereavement misleads further, as if the two were of equal diagnostic weight. (It is important, of course, for the clinician to determine whether the patient's symptoms represent a normal grief reaction; this becomes one more possibility to be ruled out.)

The individual psychiatrist who out of ignorance misdiagnoses depression in the presence, say, of zinc or folic acid or vitamin B12 deficiency, may be in for a costly malpractice judgment. The defending psychiatrist may genuinely believe that he or she was following approved diagnostic procedures. This, of course, is no defense in law, and no defense in medicine. Psychiatrists who love doctoring will hang onto medicine's fundamental principles despite the DSM-III and have faith, as I do, that someday the DSM will catch up with us.

It has far to go. Its mishandling of organic mimickers is not its only major flaw. Once the diagnosis of depression is made, the DSM-III provides the clinician no further guidance. It ignores the many diagnostic steps that now must be taken in order to identify the appropriate treatment.

I require far more than a knowledge of symptoms to treat unhappy people who come to me in good faith, expecting me to help them. Fortunately, I know what to do. My physician's black bag is close at hand, and my lab is just down the hall.

5

The Baby and
the Bathwater

"WHAT'S WRONG, KATHARINE?"

She sits across from me hugging herself. She doesn't answer, and I'm worried.

"Katharine?" I repeat.

Finally in a voice that is barely audible, she says, "I'm back just where I started, Dr. Gold. I thought there was a way out of this. That's why I came here. I don't know what I'm going to do now. . . ."

I've just told this bright, attractive, talented woman that all her tests are normal; she has no organic illness causing her symptoms. She treats the news as if I have just proclaimed her death sentence. Katharine, who is 34, has been depressed for approximately seven years. She has had all the usual treatments and she has not improved. She came to me after seeing an article in a local newspaper about our success at diagnosing mimickers. As she sees it, unless she has a curable organic illness causing her depression, she has no hope.

Many psychiatrists would regard Katharine's reaction to my good news as typical of a depressed person's negative attitude. I find her despair understandable, considering what she has been through.

Ruling out "E" leaves Katharine stuck, she thinks, with a DSM-III diagnosis of major depression—the same diagnosis given her by every psychiatrist she has consulted.

A Woman Robbed of Tears

Neither Katharine nor her husband, Steve, can remember exactly when she became depressed. She was fine—just the usual ups and downs—when they married, and for the first few years after their kids were born. "The uglies," as they called it, seemed to creep up on her, robbing her first of the bright smile that Steve remembers most about her from "the old days." Ultimately, it took everything away: her energy, her desire to paint, her pleasure in her family, her desire to live.

Ironically, Katharine is one of those people who seem to have everything. She has a solid, twelve-year marriage, a husband who loves her and understands the demands of her art, and two healthy, smart, well-behaved preteen kids. Her paintings have been well received by local critics, and she even has financial security now that Steve has been made a partner in his firm.

Katharine makes a striking first impression. She's five foot seven, with long blond hair carefully combed in a quiet, conservative style. Her makeup is subtle, her clothes sophisticated and well chosen. She walks slowly and with apparent determination—determination not to reveal the struggle with depression that she says is always going on underneath that careful exterior. She is ashamed of her suffering.

Katharine's depression has robbed her of the experience of what otherwise would be a good, accomplished life. She hasn't painted in almost three years, since her first hospitalization. Her kids don't understand what's happening to her, and her youngest has suddenly begun to fail in school. Steve may seem devoted now, but it's hard on him, he'll admit when pressed. Once he nearly left her, so convinced was he that her changed attitude toward the family and him meant that she had found someone else.

Steve is a stoic, unused to sharing his feelings. He just couldn't talk to Katharine about his suspicions.

Finally, at an elegant French restaurant, as he watched his wife pick at a meal he couldn't really afford, under the influence of one too many glasses of expensive wine, he burst out, "I can't stand this anymore, Katharine. The kids bore you, I bore you. Last night in bed you just lay there as if I was doing something detestable to you. I won't ask you who the guy is. I don't want to know. I just want you to go."

Steve gulped down the rest of his expensive French wine and asked for the check. Katharine hadn't said a word. She looked down at her hands, twisting the pink napkin.

Steve's outburst turned out to be what they both needed. Steve had to let go of some of his smoldering anger. Katharine had to talk about what was happening to her, and she had to understand that her depression was affecting the rest of the family. Both Katharine and Steve had to face that they were in trouble. For the first time since Katharine had become depressed, they talked honestly. She knew she'd been, as she put it, a "miserable blob." She hadn't had any energy, any motivation—hardly a state in which she could have an affair, she reassured Steve. "I'm dead inside, Steve," she said without emotion or expression.

With Steve's encouragement, Katharine made an appointment with their longtime family doctor. He did not examine her. Instead they talked, and he recommended a psychotherapist.

Katharine quit after four sessions. She told me, "He'd say things like, 'I can't understand why you are so unhappy, when you're so pretty, Kathy.' I said, 'Oh, you mean that if I would realize I'm attractive I wouldn't be depressed?'

" 'Well . . . ?' he responded with a big, wide smile.

"My heart just sank," Katherine said. "I felt I'd been trapped in another century, where no one could help me. Before that moment I'd never felt like killing myself. Fortunately I had enough self-esteem left to get up and leave."

She liked her second therapist very much. She treated Katharine and her problem seriously. Katharine went to her twice a week but, except for the first few sessions when she was alive with hope that this would help her, her misery was ever-present. Without results, she couldn't see continuing beyond a year.

Several months later Katharine was recommended to a psychiatrist and for the first time tried various medications. She had trouble with the side effects, though. With one she had cramps, with another her eyes were so blurry she couldn't even watch TV (her one remaining "activity"), and with a third type she frequently became dizzy and faint. The doctor urged her to hang in there, but she began to lose all hope. She began to think seriously of suicide but worried about the effect on her kids. Then again, she pondered, what kind of mother was she when all she could do on her worse days was stay in her room and watch television?

Her dismal mood suddenly plummeted to acute despair. She agreed to be hospitalized. She stayed there for a month while her doctor and the staff psychiatrists dosed her with medications that made her feel even more miserable and confused.

A year and half later she was rehospitalized by a different psychiatrist for a similar sudden "crash." The hospital he chose for her had a more active therapeutic program. Katharine had individual therapy, group therapy, and even family therapy. Although her pain lessened, it did not go away. A few months after she came home, when she seemed to be stabilizing, she left treatment.

Now Katharine confides to me in a flat voice that many nights lately as she begins to drift into sleep she will perceive her life as a short pencil line with a tiny dot on it that inches farther and farther toward the end of the line. She feels that she is that dot on that bleak line. Backwards or forwards, it all looks the same.

I wonder whether Katharine is thinking about taking an eraser and shortening the pencil line. I ask her. She shrugs.

I think, if only she could cry. Katharine had not cried in over three years.

Frankly, I am surprised that we have not turned up a physical condition that would explain Katharine's symptoms. A person like Katharine, who has a history of nonresponse to treatment, is in the highest risk group for a mimicker. I make a note to retest her periodically.

"Katharine," I say, "I understand you were hoping for a physical explanation of your depression. I understand too that you've had a lot of treatment for depression that didn't work. But we haven't even diagnosed your depression yet, so let's hang in there."

"Pardon me, Dr. Gold, but after all these years I don't need you to tell me what kind of depression I have." I have let her down and she is angry. "Good old incurable major depression," she says. Her cynicism is scary.

Quietly I say, "I don't consider 'major depression' a diagnosis."

Katharine stops hugging herself and for the first time today looks me in the eyes.

Katharine, it turns out, has not read the second installment of the newspaper story that brought her to my office. "That explains it," I say. "Then you don't know about the steps we take to diagnose and treat depression."

She shakes her head no.

"Chin up, kid," I say. "You ain't seen nothin' yet."

DSM-III Does It Again

I am a doctor. My charge is the relief of suffering. But suffering cannot be relieved unless treatment can be directed *at* something.

The DSM-III is an exercise in *nosology*, meaning classification of diseases. In medicine we must classify diseases in order to differentiate one from another for treatment, management, and research purposes. In the last chapter we saw that a symptom-based nosology does not differentiate psychiatric depressive conditions from organic illnesses; it leads instead to misdiagnosis and mistreatment. However, misdiagnosis and mistreatment can result even when, as with Katharine, the psychiatrist dutifully rules out organic symptom mimickers.

Katharine is depressed. Clinicians who have worked with depressed patients have long known that all depressions are not alike, and all stages of depression are not alike. Is it simply a matter of psychology versus physiology?

Do not look to the DSM-III for answers. The DSM-III criteria are so broad and overinclusive that they end up saying nothing much about anybody. To say that ten depressed people meet the DSM-III criteria for major depression is not to say that they look, act, or talk alike; nor does it mean that they will respond to the same treatment or even respond at all. Furthermore, it does not indicate who is in spontaneous remission or who is at risk of suicide without hospitalization.

While the point of creating categories is to identify homogeneous groups of patients, two people can have complaints that are polar opposites and still meet the criteria: no appetite, overwhelming appetite; no sleep, too much sleep. Psychiatrists dread going into court to defend how a diagnosis can be made in people who are so different.

Of the DSM-III subtypes of depression, only Melancholia presents more objective and specific criteria: regularly worse in the morning upon awakening, loss of appetite and weight loss, early morning awakening, and so forth. But even then, it doesn't tell the doctor what's wrong or what to do about it.

Neither do the DSM-III categories parallel the biological subtypes that are being revealed in laboratory research. We are learning that there are important biological differences among depressed people. From this perspective, two people with a diagnosis of major depression can be as different as night and day; their treatment will be similarly different. Yet a person with *Dysthymic Disorder* (which used to be called Depressive Neurosis) and another diagnosed as *Atypical* (a wastebasket category for anybody who doesn't fit existing categories) can reveal significant biological similarities and respond well to the same treatments. Only bipolar disorder (manic-depression) generally holds up as a useful category biologically and in terms of treatment, with lithium.

Thus, despite the rigor with which the DSM-III team has differentiated symptomatic categories of depression, none except the bipolar category is clinically useful. Conclusion: The DSM-III nosology of affective (mood) disorders is invalid.

But I have to begin somewhere. In order to relieve Katharine's suffering, first I have to understand her illness in terms of categories that mean something useful.

NOSOLOGY OF DEPRESSION
Affective Disorders (Depression and Mania)

Primary affective disorder		Secondary affective disorder	
Unipolar affective disorder	Bipolar affective disorder	Other psychiatric disorder	Systemic medical diseases
Single or recurrent episode	Mania or manic-depressive disorder	Schizophrenia, alcoholism, dementia	CNS disorders, endocrine disorder, drug-induced disorder, infections

A Diagnosis for Katharine: Step One

Many of my biopsychiatric colleagues and I are guided by a nosology of affective disorders which, as you can see above, is far more pragmatic than the DSM-III. Following this scheme step-by-step, any knowledgeable practitioner will find the category of disease he or she is dealing with and from there can take steps to identify the specific disorder. Treatment decisions easily follow. Faithful adherence to this scheme will steer the practitioner clear of misdiagnosis.

Let us say Katharine just walked in my door. I will show you how I organize my approach to her:

First I need to establish whether her symptoms represent a *primary* or a *secondary* affective disorder. Prominent in the secondary category are the organic mimickers that could cause or worsen her symptoms. Here, too, are other psychiatric conditions that have been known to produce depressive symptoms. If I determine one or the other is true, I proceed to identify precisely the causal condition from the list of major categories of mimickers that this scheme provides.

In Katharine's case, through an extensive history (including a family history and a discussion with Steve), physical and psychological exam, and laboratory work, I have ruled out this secondary category. I must now work my way through the primary category. First I must establish whether Katharine's depression is unipolar or bipolar—in other words, does her mood also soar, or does it always plummet? Both Katharine and Steve have told me that hers is the plummet-only variety. Now all I need to know to establish the category into which

Katharine's illness falls is whether this is her first episode or one among many; further conversations with Katharine reveal it is her fourteenth.

The result: Katharine's depression is of the *primary unipolar recurrent* type. In arriving at this category of illness I have been able to separate Katharine's depression from other disorders. I am now on the path which, once I identify the subtype of her depression, will lead me to *specific* treatment of her condition.

If my nosological chart were part of a diagnostic manual such as the DSM-III, it would of course instruct the psychiatrist at great length each step of the way. It would list the mimickers in detail, providing necessary diagnostic information on each. And of course it would provide extensive coverage of causes and treatments for the primary affective disorders, not to mention appropriate symptomatic treatment of patients in the secondary category.

The steps I must take now are to identify the subtype of Katharine's depression. When I determine it I will have a diagnosis. This diagnosis will suggest a specific treatment.

How Psychiatrists Make Treatment Decisions

Psychiatry offers three major approaches for the treatment of depression: psychotherapy, medication, and electroconvulsive therapy (ECT, popularly known as shock therapy). All of them work on some patients. But which patients? The point of diagnosis is to answer this all-important question. For all its pages, the DSM-III breathes not one word about treatment. One must play match-the-symptoms without reward. What is the best way to treat Katharine's major depression? In the tradition of psychiatry, the answer is: whatever works.

Prevailing textbook wisdom—not the DSM-III or systematic research—tells the psychiatrist that patients who are having psychotic delusions, who cannot tolerate the pills, or who require emergency treatment to survive (such as those who are starving to death) get ECT; those with numerous physical symptoms get pills; all who have ups along with downs (bipolars) get lithium; and patients with few physical symptoms and a chronic history get psychotherapy—or some combination of these four.

Usually, if one approach or one type of medication doesn't work, the psychiatrist tries another, or combines them, until something works, if only temporarily.

In other words, psychiatric treatment is trial and error, broadly aimed.

As Katharine's experience exemplifies, psychiatry's poor treatment-response record results as much from this nonspecific approach as it does from misdiagnosis of organic conditions. It is rife with clinical pitfalls. Without a systematic attack on a particular target, for one, you as treating psychiatrist can never know why a treatment works or why it doesn't. Thus, you will rarely be able to replicate your success; you will have to start from scratch with each patient. With luck your patient will be able to continue treatment and not quit out of frustration or become uncooperative or even give up and commit suicide before you happen upon the right formula.

Not that you will recognize a good treatment when you find it. There are just too many patient and treatment variables. Instead of having moved on to a new treatment, maybe you should have given the last approach more time, or, with medication, maybe you should simply have adjusted the dosage or switched to another type in the same category which produces side effects that may prove more tolerable.

A few months before Katharine came to me, I had a case that illustrates this last point. I treated an obese woman who was referred to me as a nonresponder. To no avail she had been medicated with many types of antidepressants, the last of which was in a class called monoaminoxidase inhibitors (MAOIs). It turned out that the woman had not been taking the MAOIs as prescribed, because she seemed to feel they made her gain weight. Her psychiatrist reassured her that they had no such effect, implying she was being neurotic. The last thing she needed was to gain more weight. So she stopped taking the pills, but she didn't tell her psychiatrist.

She was right about the weight gain; the MAOIs she was taking do occasionally have that side effect. Her psychiatrist was not familiar with all the literature. The results of our laboratory work confirmed that MAOIs were a good choice of drug class for this patient. I switched her to a slightly different formulation which did not contribute to her weight problem; she took them as directed and within a month experienced her first real relief in many years.

Although the overall approach is trial and error, each psychiatrist of course has a rationale for choosing a particular treatment for a particular patient and criteria for evaluating the results. When subjected to scientific scrutiny, however, treatment and results may not hold up. Question: How would you as treating psychiatrist know whether your depressed patient was better? When his or her symptoms went away—in other words when the patient felt better? That seems to make sense and is, indeed, how most psychiatrists evaluate the progress of their patients. However, upon close biopsychiatric investigation, it turns out that relief of symptoms is an unreliable measure of progress in treatment. We have discovered that patients who have biological depressions will relapse if they are not treated until their biological abnormalities disappear, regardless of how much better they feel and look and function.

How Patients Make Treatment Decisions

Few psychiatrists are generalists who use all treatment modalities. Most psychiatrists specialize in one or perhaps two approaches. Some psychiatrists provide medication, while others offer talk-only cures, and some will even shock all comers (hospitalized patients mostly). Each of these treatments is appropriate for different types of depression, or the same type of depression at different times. For instance, while a psychotherapeutic and a biological approach may prove equally effective over time, medicating the patient may stabilize a severely suffering patient far more quickly. After the acute phase, psychotherapy may be the treatment of choice. Possibly a patient will require no somatic (bodily) treatment and would be more likely to get better in therapy. But the types of therapy differ. Should this patient undergo a long course of psychoanalysis or a short course of cognitive therapy?

Who decides? Without knowing it, you do. You feel rotten, you ask a friend or a doctor for the name of a good shrink, you make an appointment, you go, and you take the cure that is offered. You don't know whether the therapist is an analyst, a medication specialist, a behaviorist, a cognitive specialist, or an orthomolecular practitioner. You may not even know whether he or she is a doctor or a psychologist or a social worker. You take the cure that is offered, but if you went to the therapist down the hall, or the one down the street, you could get entirely different treatment.

Ultimately, the burden of trial and error falls squarely on the depressed patient. Katharine, as have many of my patients, has gone from therapist to therapist and cure to cure. It has only made her depression worse.

Depressed Physician Sues Hospital and Wins

Although the DSM-III results in part from the call for a new, more precise psychiatry, it does not provide procedural guidance whereby the diagnosing psychiatrist can choose the most appropriate treatment(s) independent of his or her own theoretical bias.

If all the recent disappointing response-to-treatment statistics do not convince professional psychiatry of the need for objective diagnostic and treatment criteria, perhaps a recent landmark malpractice decision will.

A former patient, himself a physician, sued a private psychiatric hospital for negligence because the staff treated him with psychotherapy, with which he did not improve, rather than with medication. When he transferred to another hospital and was treated with antidepressants, he recovered quickly. Obviously, a key issue in his suit was the propriety of the diagnosis, which precedes treatment choice. Was it a narcissistic personality disorder, also a DSM-III diagnosis, or a type of biological depression? Depending on their theoretical orientation, experts argued for each. The fact is, the *treatment* for the diagnosis of depression worked. Early in 1984 a Maryland malpractice board awarded the ex-patient $250,000. But the real issue of the case —whether the right diagnosis was made—remained unresolved.

That the antidepressants worked does not in itself confirm the diagnosis. There are many reasons why patients improve; sometimes a change of scene or a new psychiatrist is sufficient to effect a "miraculous" recovery. I would have to review his history and to see the results of laboratory tests before and after his treatment to form an opinion. While this case represents many complex medico-legal issues for psychiatry, our concern with it here is as follows:

Is there not a way to insure that any suffering person can receive an *accurate* diagnosis, predictive of treatment? In psychiatry as in other branches of medicine, are there not objective scientific criteria with which any two psychiatrists, whether psychoanalyst or biological psychiatrist, can arrive at a diagnosis that will pinpoint a proper treatment plan regardless of their personal modes of practice?

Another Missing Link

We have seen that: (1) The DSM-III employs broad, descriptive criteria that can apply to more than one disorder; and (2) resulting diagnoses are not treatment-specific. There is another, related missing link: (3) The DSM-III does not address causation or pathology (an understanding of the disease process in the body).

If a doctor does not know what is causing your symptoms and/or how the underlying condition is affecting body tissues, there's not much he or she can do besides provide symptomatic relief. Probably the symptoms will come back. In medicine, established diagnostic procedures are designed to lead all physicians to a uniform understanding of the cause and the pathology behind the patient's complaints. This information in turn yields uniform treatment options. For example, a man reports a persistent urethral discharge to his physician, who takes a gonorrheal culture; the test is positive, and the physician prescribes penicillin. A mother tells a pediatrician that her daughter's teachers say she's been daydreaming and seems to have a concentration problem; the pediatrician orders an EEG, diagnoses petit mal epileptic seizures, and prescribes anticonvulsants.

Psychiatry has no history of uniform procedures. A practitioner's understanding of causation and pathology may follow the body of thought of one of the numerous psychiatric theoretical schools, or it may be derived idiosyncratically.

One of Katharine's therapists decided her depression had to do with her early relationship with her mother, which led her to become depressed in adulthood; accordingly, he designed a psychotherapeutic approach to lead her into the past and back again. Another therapist saw it as more a here-and-now problem and discouraged any talk of past relationships; he prescribed medication because he believed it would alleviate Katharine's symptoms and make her more amenable to treatment. The first time Katharine was hospitalized, without any testing to find out what was causing her condition, the resident doctors decided that her depression was caused by biological factors. They gave her medication to correct her supposedly faulty biochemistry. The doctors were most familiar with three of the many antidepressant formulations; they gave Katharine the one they used most commonly.

Why would the DSM-III authors promote such confusion? Apparently, they chose not to play favorites among the many competing, often mutually hostile "camps," each of which offers a different understanding of the causes of and treatment for mental suffering. They decided instead to stick to the so-called facts.

Katharine, the Baby, and the Bathwater

Politically, the decision to eliminate any suggestion of causation/ treatment may be wise. Medically, it is disastrous. Existing in a conceptual vacuum, the DSM-III "facts" are useless. It's tantamount to throwing away everything we know in an attempt to clean house: Down the drain goes the baby, and my patient, with the bathwater.

"We need conceptual frameworks within which to place our data of observation. It matters not if there are many; it matters much if there are none," Dr. Donald Langsley, a past president of the APA, has said. "With concepts, new data will distinguish those which are useful from those that are not. This has been the history of all medicine."

Indeed, it has been the history of all *applied* science.

American psychiatry has a peculiar fondness for the one answer, the one concept with which all will be explained. The DSM-III's de facto denial of all concepts is an example of this all-or-nothing point of view. This single-mindedness has contributed to the failure of psychiatrists to consider the presence of organic illness in their patients. And it accounts for the slow integration of medical advances, or change of any kind, into the diagnosis and treatment of so many suffering human beings.

A Diagnosis for Katharine, Step Two

Biopsychiatry is an integrative science of the mind. We are equally a product of psychiatry and of the neurosciences, which are brand-new to psychiatry. Conceptually we understand mental illness as a dysfunction of brain/body/mind/environment. One aspect may predominate, and we may choose to intervene on that level using medical or psychological techniques. Our responsibility is to the entire patient—as a biological, psychological, and social being—from diagnosis through recovery.

Above all we are doctors; we owe our theoretic allegiance only to medical science in the service of the patient.

To Katharine I owe a diagnosis worthy of a medical doctor. It must reflect causation and pathology and point toward a specific treatment. I have thus far decided that Katharine's illness falls within the primary unipolar recurrent category. Good medical practice dictates that I verify this largely subjective finding using objective measures. The fact is, any psychiatrist's clinical impression is likely to be inaccurate 25 percent of the time. Therefore I turn to biopsychiatry's essential resource, called "the right hand of modern medicine": the laboratory.

Immediately I will give Katharine a battery of neuroendocrine tests. These tests reveal abnormalities in brain-body systems which control both mood and endocrine gland function and which are thought to be *biological markers* of primary depression. Together the dexamethasone suppression test (DST) and the TRH (thyroid releasing hormone) stimulation test verify the presence of a neuroendocrine type of depression.

The DST and the TRH test will provide the initial findings to confirm Katharine's diagnosis. If one or both turn out positive, I can be sure we are on a biological track. If so, I will proceed to look for markers of her particular subtype.

Biopsychiatric research is almost daily revealing extraordinary information about brain dysfunction in depression at the level of the individual nerve cell and the chemicals which are synthesized in tiny amounts to carry messages across the synapses (spaces) between cells. The chemicals are called neurotransmitters, and depression is one powerful message. The task with every patient is to identify *which* neurotransmitter system seems to be at fault. The resulting diagnosis yields a subtype of depression that we can match specifically to medications that act on these specific systems. We can't, however, get a measurement of these neurotransmitters without poking around Katharine's brain—rather an extreme way to arrive at a diagnosis. So we've developed clever ways to figure out what's going on in there from measuring breakdown products (metabolites) of "used" neurotransmitters in blood or urine or other fluids. As many as three depressive subtypes can be identified from the results of one urine test.

Katharine may suffer from a serotonin type of depression, a possible marker of suicide, toward which Katharine is well on her way if I don't help her out fast. Importantly, she has a positive family history of suicide. Her maternal grandfather—the skeleton in the family closet—shot himself to death "accidentally," according to the official family version. The unofficial version is that his death was self-inflicted. Katharine's mother later died in a car accident which may have been intentional, as many fatal crashes are. She supposedly fell asleep at the wheel early in the evening and drove off the road into a steep ravine. While Katharine denied that her mother was depressed, Steve thought that in some ways her persistent aloofness and coldness reminded him of Katharine during "the uglies."

The possibility of being able to predict true suicidal risk before anything happens, and being able to correct it readily is almost too exciting for words—a psychiatrist's dream come true. One out of twenty patients ends up killing himself or herself because psychiatry has never been much good at predicting suicide.

The present and future biopsychiatric possibilities on behalf of patients like Katharine are extraordinary. The laboratory is the key to our work, testing our major tool.

The Final Missing Link

By now it will not surprise you to learn that no tests are mentioned in the DSM-III. Even in areas in which the DSM overlaps other areas of medicine, such as drug abuse detection, it omits the tests that are standard operating procedures in all other branches of medicine.

Most medical diagnoses derive from the physician's clinical suspicion combined with external, objective, authenticated laboratory tests. When clinical impression and test results differ, the physician will often give an abnormal test the greater weight. Certainly no doctor would ignore abnormal electrocardiogram results just because the patient feels fine and the stethoscope doesn't detect any problems.

Psychiatrists would never accept treatment for their own or family members' medical problems without first being convinced that laboratory findings back up the diagnosis. Yet in their own practices, they are willing to dispense powerful and possibly dangerous medications on the basis of a patient's history and nonspecific behavior. Just as in medicine, the defining criteria for psychiatric disease must ultimately be pathology, which can be demonstrated only in the laboratory.

The psychiatric laboratory has applications to virtually all areas of clinical practice, from differential diagnosis to choice of medication and appropriate dosage to measurement of recovery and prediction of relapse. Yet the majority of practicing psychiatrists are reluctant to test patients. Their stated reasons are these:

1. The tests do not reliably confirm DSM-III diagnostic categories.

2. The tests do not provide a diagnosis.

3. The causes of depression have not been proved, so testing is pointless.

Each of these objections is *true*. Nonetheless, to discard the use of tests for these reasons reveals psychiatry's fundamental ignorance of the principles of laboratory medicine.

In the first place, the tests cannot confirm DSM-III diagnoses because, as we have seen, they are not true medical illnesses or categories. There is no one-to-one correspondence between a symptom and specific pathology. To come up with a test for feeling rotten and eating too much or too little and sleeping too much or too little would be impossible. The insistence that the only acceptable test would be one that proves the existence of major depression is like saying the only valid test for a sore throat is one that proves all sufferers have a strep throat.

The dexamethasone suppression test is continually being criticized because it does not seem specific to depression. Some patients with other DSM-III diagnoses, such as borderline personality disorder, keep turning up positive on this test. "See!" critics say. "The test doesn't work." Biopsychiatry's response is that we ought to rethink diagnostic criteria and reorganize them on the basis of neurophysiological measures, because persons with the same laboratory findings tend to respond to the same treatment, regardless of descriptive diagnosis. Starting from these findings, we could then work backwards to determine whether common behavioral criteria also exist.

Next, tests rarely in themselves provide a diagnosis. Laboratory data are evaluated along with other clinical information to create a total picture. (See Chapter 20.) No test is the perfect final version; it is the best available at any point in time. The more clinicians use tests, the more the tests are improved and refined. But first, psychiatrists must reeducate themselves in laboratory medicine, which means they must overcome their reluctance to act and think like doctors.

Finally, psychiatry is not the only medical field in which causes elude us: The causes of *most* medical illnesses remain to be proved. These range from heart and circulatory disease to diabetes and kidney disease to allergy and migraine headache to gastrointestinal disease to the common cold. Nonetheless, the laboratory gives us important clues that meanwhile we can use to refine our understanding and treatment. The lack of ultimate proof must never prevent us from applying what we have thus far learned to relieve our patients' suffering. Knowledge develops incrementally. What we learn today may show that we were wrong yesterday; more likely it will show that there's more to it than we thought yesterday.

The Gift of Hope

So I will continue the differential diagnostic procedure with Katharine. I tell her about each step I will take. Should her neuroendocrine tests prove positive and further testing reveal a targeted treatment, I will not stop there. I'll test to see that the medication has reached the proper level in her blood to be effective. And I'll continue my diagnostic tests throughout her treatment to determine her progress, relief of symptoms being as unreliable as I've previously described. I will also refer her for a short-term psychotherapy designed particularly for people with depression.

This type of psychotherapy will be my sole treatment choice for the time being if her neuroendocrine tests are negative. I'll watch her progress carefully. If she still does not improve I will retest her both for biological depression and for organic illness. Katharine might have a still-undetected illness that is developing and displaying as yet only emotional and behavioral symptoms.

"As soon as I have a final diagnosis for you, Katharine, I expect you to improve rapidly," I tell her, "because unlike any treatment you have received before, mine will be targeted to exactly what's wrong with you. Our research at this hospital shows that nine out of every ten women and men with your problem get better."

Katharine smiles shyly. I get a glimmer of the life that was once in her, and the hope that remains despite her pain.

Four months have passed. Katharine has just been in to have her medication blood levels checked. She is all smiles. She told me she hopes to start painting again soon.

Katharine did not have a serotonin type of depression. However, we discovered abnormalities on two other biological tests that helped explain the chronic, relapsing course of her illness. I began to treat her with a type of antidepressant targeted to her diagnosed pathology. Katharine was far from pleased when she heard which drug I had chosen; one of her previous doctors had prescribed the same type of medication. Not only had it not worked, but Katharine had also suffered badly from its side effects. I told her that I believed the dosage she had been given was far too low to be effective, and that we had strategies to help prevent side effects.

We discovered that Katharine's body metabolized most of the drug before it reached her brain. As a result, she needed more than twice the amount of medication than she had been given before. The doctor who had prescribed it for her had not performed the laboratory work necessary to determine the required dosage. Frequently checking the amount of medication in her blood, I slowly built Katharine up to the effective dosage. She did not have as much difficulty with side effects as she expected. The greatest problem was drowsiness, so I changed the timing instructions. Instead of taking the pills twice a day, she began to take them all at bedtime; by the time she awoke, this side effect had worn off.

A month passed before we were able to get enough antidepressant medication into Katharine's system. Results were dramatic. She became able to laugh, able to cry.

Katharine feels a million times better but is not cured yet. Her tests reveal that the fundamental biological abnormalities remain. I will continue her on the medication until they at least normalize. Only then can I be sure she will not suffer a relapse.

Six weeks ago Katharine entered short-term psychotherapy. I felt she needed to work on some of her depression-related attitudes. Katharine's depression had been central to her existence for so many years that she did not know how to live without it. For example, she had a great deal of time on her hands and did not know how to fill it. Before her illness she would have been grateful to have that time for her artwork. Now she felt that her depression had destroyed her talent.

When she tells me today she's off to buy art supplies, I know her faith in herself is returning. Four months after we established a diagnosis based on specific pathology, Katharine is on her way to a complete recovery.

6

When Depression Isn't

As MANY AS 20 percent of the average psychiatrist's patients are being treated for mental disorders that they do not have. Their psychiatric symptoms are directly caused by a physical illness of which the psychiatrist is unaware. For hospitalized patients, the situation is even worse. Almost a third have undiagnosed physical diseases rather than the psychiatric illnesses for which they have been confined. Half have illnesses which substantially worsen their psychiatric symptoms.

I find previously undetected physical illness in approximately one out of four of my Fair Oaks patients. This higher-than-average rate results from the nature of my practice, which includes a number of men and women who have been considered psychiatric treatment failures; risk of a physical disease masquerading as an emotional problem is highest among this group.

At least seventy-five illnesses or conditions can cause symptoms of apparent mental disorder; some estimates range as high as ninety-one. I call these diseases the Great Mimickers of Psychiatry, for they imitate the disorders that psychiatrists are trained to treat. Without diagnostic examination and testing, rarely can any physician, or any patient, tell the difference between a true psychiatric illness and a mimicker.

Routine physical examination and testing are often insufficient. To uncover many mimickers, the examining physician must first stop to consider that an organic condition may be causing a patient's emotional symptoms. Then he or she must know which diseases to look for, and how.

Physical and Psychiatric Illness: How They Interact

As you read the following chapters, keep in mind that the coexistence of physical illness and mental symptoms does not necessarily mean they are related. If you are depressed and have physical symptoms, it is no simple matter to determine what is causing what. For example, you can be depressed and have an unrelated physical problem. You can also be depressed and have physical symptoms as a direct result of the depression.

Physical and psychiatric illness interact in five different ways. In most cases, the specialized diagnostic skills of a biopsychiatrist will be required to untangle these complex possibilities.

1. *Physical illness can intensify emotional disorders.* The more serious or chronic the illness, the greater the emotional stress. Treating the illness will lighten the emotional load but it will not remove pre-existing difficulties. A major reason why many people suffer a relapse or do not respond completely to psychiatric treatment is that these exacerbating illnesses are undiagnosed or untreated.

2. *Psychiatric symptoms can develop in reaction to a previously existing illness.* Following major heart surgery, for example, recovering patients almost always get depressed. This type of depression will generally lift as patients recover and readjust.

3. *Physical and psychiatric illness may coexist without relationship to one another.* Hospitalized psychiatric patients have a high rate of physical illness, in part because in a psychiatric setting they receive generally poor medical care. Dr. Milton Erman reports that "in one emergency setting, 66 percent of staff psychiatrists did not perform physical examinations, nor did 59 percent of psychiatric residents." Treatment of the physical illness, however, may have little or no bearing on the psychiatric symptoms.

4. *Physical illness may be the direct result of emotional problems.* Sometimes a person who turns out to be depressed will have few of the classic symptoms of depression but many physical symptoms. This is called *masked depression* and is discussed in Chapter 13. Also, depression may weaken the immune system, which then cannot fend off life-threatening illness such as cancer. This is an important area of mind-body investigation and is covered in Chapter 19.

In either case, treating the physical illness will not remove the underlying depression.

5. *Certain physical illnesses may cause emotional disorders.* The psychiatric symptoms will clear only if the underlying physical condition is

> medically treated. These diseases are the Great Mimickers of Psychiatry, the subject of the chapters remaining in this section.

The Most Unforgiving Organ

Confusion between physical and mental disorders occurs frequently because *psychiatric symptoms are often the first and only signs of a developing illness.* Mental symptoms may precede the appearance of overt physical symptoms by weeks, months, years, even decades. The Famous Actor's depression (Chapter 1) was his only symptom of testicular cancer for three and a half years. A 66-year-old man was depressed for ten years before he developed jaundice and itching, his first bodily symptom of a pancreatic tumor. His depression finally abated after the removal of most of his pancreas. But the "cure" was too late in coming. He died two months after the surgery.

Few if any diseases just "happen." You don't come down with an infectious illness the moment the offending virus or bacteria invade your system. Your immune system will have begun its struggle with the attackers, which continue to reproduce until finally you have that miserable feeling that you're coming down with something. Neither do you become diabetic the day your doctor announces you have diabetes; even if you "passed" your glucose tolerance test last year, the disease was there but undetectable by that particular measure. You may have felt depressed, but you would hardly have associated such a feeling with diabetes.

In all illness, the body undergoes subtle changes that will develop into the gross pathological states, the destruction of body tissue, that doctors associate with disease. One of the greatest challenges in medicine today is to detect these early stages before damage is done. This is a high priority in diseases like heart disease and cancer, which often cannot be diagnosed until they are in their final stages. Early detection may be able to prevent the disease from developing further.

Early detection requires early suspicion. Standard screening exams reveal relatively little of what could possibly go wrong with your body. Generally the doctor starts a determined search only when you come in for treatment of specific complaints.

Ironically, considering psychiatry's longtime medical backwardness, our recognition that mental symptoms are frequently the earliest clues has moved biopsychiatry to the forefront of medical diagnostics. Psychiatric symptoms occur first, we have learned, because as many diseases develop, they slowly, imperceptibly begin to alter the chemistry of the body. The brain will not forgive this; even the most subtle changes will affect it long before they appear to influence the normal functioning of other organ systems.

For example, as the thyroid gland stops functioning, the smallest reduction in the output of thyroid hormone can change the sensitivity of nerve cell receptors in the brain and produce a chemical state conducive to depression long before classic physical symptoms of hypothyroidism occur (see Chapter 10). Standard tests will show a normal amount of thyroid hormone in the blood. Only one test, rarely administered by doctors other than biopsychiatrists, can reveal this physical state. The difference between the two tests is often striking.

Psychiatrist as Medical Superspecialist

In an important study of misdiagnosed psychiatric patients, Dr. Richard Hall found that most of these individuals had no idea they were physically ill before they developed mental symptoms. Says Hall, a professor of psychiatry and internal medicine who is a seminal researcher in the mimickers, ". . . when a psychiatrist evaluates an adult who has recently developed a major psychiatric symptom or a severe personality change, a thorough, detailed physical examination should be conducted. . . ."

While all physicians would do well to take emotional symptoms as indications of early illness, differential diagnosis of the Great Mimickers is one area of medicine in which all psychiatrists must become *better* clinicians than internists, pediatricians, neurologists, and other medical and surgical subspecialists. The reason is practical: Because of the nature of the presenting symptoms, psychiatrists (indeed, all mental health practitioners) encounter more patients suffering from mimickers than do any other physicians. Some of these diseases, as you will see in upcoming chapters, have a fatal outcome if not detected very early in their course. Psychiatrists can—they *must*—save lives.

Referral to a psychiatrist is appropriate in any case, since a psychiatrist is, or is supposed to be, a medical specialist in all illnesses that affect a person's mental and emotional existence.

Admittedly, this is a lot to ask of most of today's psychiatrists, who were relieved to abandon disease detection at the medical school door. But there is no excuse for lack of awareness: All mental health practitioners must become aware of the mimickers, their prevalence within their practices, and the need for professional medical diagnosis of all patients before deciding on a treatment plan.

At present only a biopsychiatrist is likely to consider the presence of a mimicker in a patient complaining of depression, anxiety, confusion, and the myriad other symptoms these diseases may cause. The diagnostic acumen should not become the rarefied province of only a few psychiatric subspecialists, however. Psychiatrists are *physicians*, not psychologists or social workers. All are obligated morally, ethically, and legally to provide state-of-the-art medical care to every patient.

How to Detect a Mimicker

An active evaluation program can totally eliminate misdiagnosis. My biopsychiatric colleagues and I do not prejudge our patients' symptoms. We take a detailed personal and family history, then conduct a mental status exam, and perform a complete physical, including neurological and endocrinological examinations. Now, working with clinical findings and the frequency with which each mimicker tends to occur in each of our settings, we develop an "index of suspicion."

The index of suspicion will determine which of the possible tests to run to rule out a diagnosis for which suspicion is high. The laboratory is *always* part of the process. Neither psychiatrist nor internist has sufficient clinical skills to pick up the majority of the mimickers without diagnostic testing. As we said in the previous chapter, clinical impression alone is wrong one out of four times.

FAIR OAKS PROTOCOL TO RULE OUT PHYSICAL ILLNESS WITH A PSYCHIATRIC PRESENTATION

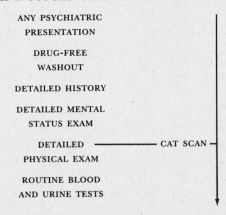

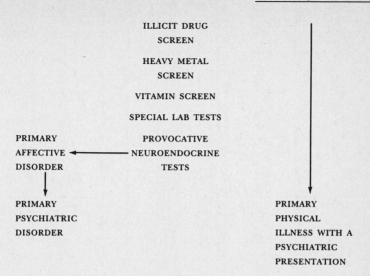

The expense of such an examination, which can take up to two weeks, is substantially higher, of course, than the one psychiatric session in which a person with depressive symptoms can earn a diagnosis of major depression. Detection of a mimicker, however, will substantially shorten the hospital stay of many a previously considered "hopeless case"—saving untold amounts of money for whoever foots the bill. Similarly, it can lop years off of a costly long-term psychotherapy.

One cannot, of course, put a price on the relief of suffering. At Fair Oaks, at least eight out of every one hundred severely "depressed" patients we evaluate are found to be suffering from hypothyroidism, our most common mimicker and one which is easily treatable. These eight lives are utterly changed by the evaluation procedure. Their treatment is changed. Their diagnosis is changed. Their depression finally lifts. Life goes on.

Categories of Mimickers

The Great Mimickers of psychiatry fall into a few broad categories. The most common are (1) drug (illicit, prescribed, and over-the-counter) and alcohol reactions and (2) endocrine disorders (e.g., hypothyroidism, diabetes). Other categories include diseases of the central nervous system (including Alzheimer's disease and multiple sclerosis), infectious diseases, cancers, metabolic conditions, nutritional and toxic disorders, plus a large miscellaneous category.

In the remainder of this chapter and in the four that follow, we'll explore these categories, describing a number of the individual illnesses or conditions within them. We will cover psychiatric symptoms and later physical manifestations, and include some case vignettes. No doubt, like most medical students, you will be certain that you or someone you know who is depressed has this or that mimicker, most certainly one that is fatal and/or most difficult to treat. Be aware, however, that when it comes to diagnosing medical problems, most patients are as bad as most psychiatrists.

Cancer

Many types of tumors throughout the body can exhibit mental symptoms, which may be the only symptoms to appear for weeks, months, or years.

How many times have you heard the following story? "My mother has bone cancer. They found it in her hip. For years she's been depressed and feeling vaguely ill. Until the diagnosis was made, doctors told my mother it was all in her head. Now she has six months to a year to live."

Or this: "Aunt Lu was 55 when Uncle John told her he wanted a divorce so that he could marry another woman. Aunt Lu had been very dependent on Uncle John. Now here she was on her own. As you can imagine, she had a rough time starting a new life. Oddly, she didn't get really depressed for about a year after the divorce. Then she began to get backaches. They became more and more intense, until she could barely walk. My mother, Lu's sister, finally convinced her to go to a doctor. He talked about the back being a common focus for psychological stress and he prescribed pills for the pain. They didn't seem to work. And Aunt Lu started acting crazy—talking a mile a minute, often to herself, then suddenly bursting into tears. She ended up in a mental hospital. Everybody, including the doctors, blamed it on the divorce. My mother arranged to have Aunt Lu transferred to a private psychiatric hospital in our city. The doctor who admitted her there said he thought her symptoms were medical. Everybody was shocked. Sure enough, she had a lymphoma. She was dead within a month."

Cancers are not the most common mimickers. Only 2 percent of all mimickers prove to be cancers. (Among patients who have not responded to psychiatric medications and who have lost at least thirty pounds, however, the diagnosis is very common.) Since they often run a fatal course, *recognition of early psychiatric clues is urgent.*

In particular, tumors of the central nervous system (brain and spine) and those that secrete hormones will present earliest with mental symptoms. Hormones are chemicals that are secreted by the brain and endocrine system, which help to regulate many body functions, including metabolism, growth, development, and numerous others. Overall, they help to keep the body in balance. Hormones are related—sometimes identical—to neurotransmitters, the brain's chemical messengers. Hormones, as we shall see, are highly involved in the genesis of depression, whether mimicker-induced or biological.

LUNG CANCER

Karen B. remembers that her 66-year-old father became inexplicably depressed for three months before his lung cancer was detected. Claiming fatigue, he lost interest in playing golf, meeting friends, watching TV. "It just wasn't like him," says Karen. Her dad began to lose weight, but since loss of appetite is common with depression, no one recognized it as a bad sign. The family searched for a psychological explanation. Says Karen, "It didn't occur to us that there might be any other reason for a really awful mood like that." It was about time for her father to have a checkup, so he made an appointment and during the examination mentioned the mood change. The doctor answered that depression was common in older age, and if he wanted, he would prescribe some pills. Karen's father said he'd think about it.

They never pursued the conversation, for his chest X rays revealed an ominous spot on his right lung. It turned out to be cancer of the oat-cell type. Oat cells secrete ACTH, a pituitary hormone that stimulates the cortex of the adrenal glands and which is thought to cause or encourage depression. Surgery and chemotherapy did not halt the course of the disease, which had already spread to his liver. Karen's father died almost a year after his cancer was diagnosed. Had the diagnosis come three months earlier, at the onset of the depressive symptoms, it might have made a difference. He might have had a chance.

PANCREATIC CANCER

Pituitary, thyroid, parathyroid, renal, ovarian, stomach, and particularly pancreatic cancers also secrete hormones. Pancreatic cancer, a swift and painful killer, is notorious among biopsychiatrists for presenting first with depression in half to three-quarters of all patients. The pancreas lies behind the stomach and normally secretes juices which are essential to digestion. The severe depression of pancreatic cancer is often accompanied by crying spells, insomnia unresponsive to medication, and anxiety associated with the fear of having a serious illness.

While a small percentage of patients with pancreatic cancer are candidates for surgery, which extends life for only 10 percent of them, half of all patients die within three months of the diagnosis, most within a year. The mortality may be so rapid because of the physical silence of the disease. When physical pain (constant and radiating toward the back), weight loss, and jaundice occur, the disease is quite advanced. Here is a real opportunity for a psychiatrist to save or prolong a life, for, as we saw earlier in this chapter, the depression of pancreatic cancer can precede the physical symptoms by as much as ten years.

Pancreatic cancer is somewhat more common among men than women and rarely occurs before age 40. Other symptoms include indigestion and constipation. The psychiatrist should be on the lookout for it when presented with a patient over 50 with severe depression and weight loss, or with diabetes, who may also be a heavy drinker. (Alcohol is a common cause of pancreatic disease.)

CARCINOID SYNDROME

Carcinoid tumors are sometimes called functioning endocrine tumors. Although they can occur throughout the body, usually they grow from endocrine cells in the small intestine, appendix, or stomach. Patients can live ten to fifteen years following diagnosis, even though the tumors usually spread to other organs. They are accompanied by a bizarre set of symptoms called the carcinoid syndrome. Food, excitement, exertion, or alcohol may bring on an attack of flushing of the head and neck, color changes from bloodless to blue, and diarrhea and abdominal cramps. Forty percent of patients exhibit mental symptoms. Depression is most common.

Carcinoid tumors secrete substances, including most commonly serotonin, which are implicated in depression.

CENTRAL NERVOUS SYSTEM TUMORS

Tumors of the left temporal (near the temple) and frontal (above the forehead) lobes of the brain and of the limbic system (deep inside the brain) are those most likely to produce early symptoms of depression and irritability. The most common psychiatric symptom of brain tumor, however, is personality change. Psychiatrists Linda Gay Peterson and Mark Perl report a case of a 38-year-old woman with multiple sclerosis, itself a frequent mimicker, who was hospitalized because of physical symptoms. Psychiatrists were called in because her husband mentioned that she had been acting strangely. A year earlier, he said, after ten years of marriage, she began having unexplained emotional outbursts. She started having an affair, which she flaunted, and moved back and forth several times between her mother's house and their own.

The consulting psychiatrists ordered a CAT scan and found brain tumors in the frontal, temporal, and parietal lobes (behind the frontal lobe at the back of the head). "Would earlier diagnosis have improved the woman's survival?" ask the psychiatrists. "This is not clear, but early recognition of the tumor could have reduced the marital strife and family disruption that occurred because of her symptoms."

Suspecting Cancer

Anyone who has an abrupt personality change, depression without a history of mood disorders, or weight loss of greater than twenty pounds—or who is unresponsive to standard psychiatric treatment—should be evaluated for cancer or other mimickers.

Heart Disease

Depression may be an early clue to impending heart attack. A five-year study conducted by British researchers showed recently that the men they studied, 40 to 65 years old, often had depressed moods, lost their sex drive, were exhausted, and worried excessively in the months before they suffered heart attacks. Examination prior to their attacks detected no physical symptoms of heart damage.

Infectious Diseases

Many infectious diseases can exhibit psychiatric symptoms. Viral pneumonia is accompanied by depression. In early stages of tuberculosis, many people become irritable and apathetic; excitement and hypomania (mild mania) characterize later stages. More commonly misdiagnosed infectious mimickers include mononucleosis and infectious hepatitis.

DISEASES MOST LIKELY TO PRODUCE PSYCHIATRIC SYMPTOMS

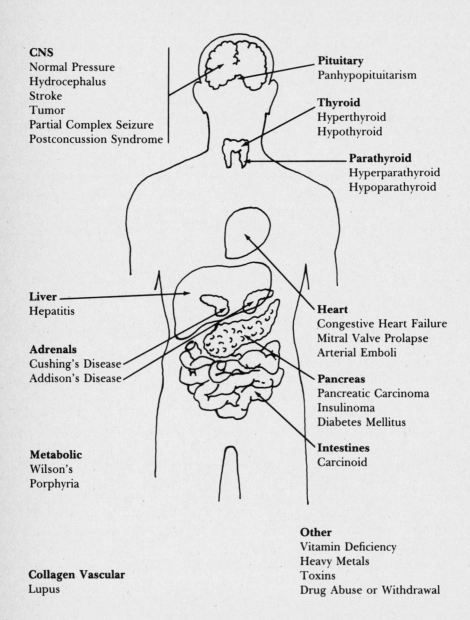

CNS
Normal Pressure
Hydrocephalus
Stroke
Tumor
Partial Complex Seizure
Postconcussion Syndrome

Pituitary
Panhypopituitarism

Thyroid
Hyperthyroid
Hypothyroid

Parathyroid
Hyperparathyroid
Hypoparathyroid

Liver
Hepatitis

Adrenals
Cushing's Disease
Addison's Disease

Heart
Congestive Heart Failure
Mitral Valve Prolapse
Arterial Emboli

Pancreas
Pancreatic Carcinoma
Insulinoma
Diabetes Mellitus

Intestines
Carcinoid

Metabolic
Wilson's
Porphyria

Collagen Vascular
Lupus

Other
Vitamin Deficiency
Heavy Metals
Toxins
Drug Abuse or Withdrawal

INFECTIOUS DISEASE MIMICKERS

Disease	Major Depression	Manic-depression
Syphilis	+	+
Infectious mononucleosis	+	
Pneumonia (bacterial)		
Pneumonia (viral)	+	
Brucella	+	
Tuberculosis	+	

INFECTIOUS MONONUCLEOSIS

Doctors in student health services ought to know that "mono" commonly shows up as depression—especially around exam time, when college students are generally run-down and susceptible. It occurs most commonly among adolescents and young adults, and has been called "the kissing disease," because it is spread by close oral contact. It is not very contagious, however.

Mono is caused by the Epstein-Barr virus (named for its discoverers), one of the many herpes viruses. The virus attacks and transforms the lymphocytes in the lymph glands, the white blood cells which fight disease. For four to seven weeks no physical symptoms will be apparent.

When symptoms of illness do occur, they may be so mild, like a barely noticeable cold, that some people don't know they have it. Others become extremely ill. Symptoms may include a persistent sore throat and fever, swollen glands in the neck, throat, armpit, and groin, plus headache, weakness, swollen eyelids, and a rash.

The virus can infect many organs, making it difficult to diagnose and increasing the risk of complications. The liver is involved in almost all patients, and in about 50 percent the spleen is enlarged and may easily rupture.

Diagnosis is by blood tests, which are frequently negative. It may take two or three tests over several weeks to make an accurate diagnosis. Thus, when a student is so depressed he or she thinks she's going insane and tests out negative the first time around, the doctor should resist delivering his standard speech about the stresses of exam time, etcetera.

When depression and tiredness are the only symptoms, many

young people will not seek medical help. A young man I know was so run-down and depressed that he actually left his Ivy League medical school. This was proof, he discussed with his therapist, that he didn't really want to be a doctor. When he told his father, a physician, about his decision to quit, the older man convinced him to take a leave of absence and think it over. So he did his dad a favor and applied for and received a leave. He was certain that his symptoms would disappear with this decision. They didn't, so he gave it another week—after all, leaving medical school is itself a major stress. Another week went by and his eyes puffed up, his liver became swollen—and his test for mono was positive.

Mono lasts from a couple of weeks to a few months to a few years. Treatment includes bedrest and relief of symptoms as necessary. A depressive syndrome may follow the disease and it may be the last symptom to depart.

INFECTIOUS HEPATITIS
This liver infection can be caused by three and possibly four different viruses as well as by drugs and alcohol. Type A and Type B are most common. Type A is transmitted by contaminated food (such as raw shellfish) or water, or contact with infected feces (sewage contamination, etcetera). Hepatitis B is called serum hepatitis; it usually enters the bloodstream directly, through transfusion or infected needles, although it can be passed among sexual partners. One may be a carrier of the virus and continue to pass it on to others without becoming ill oneself.

Following infection, the symptom phase of hepatitis may take from two to twenty-five weeks to appear. The resulting illness may be unnoticeably mild, fatal, or anything in between. While symptoms vary, commonly they begin with loss of appetite and distaste for cigarettes, malaise, nausea, vomiting, and fever. Itching and joint aches may occur. Next comes a darkening of the urine and jaundice, a yellowing of the skin and whites of the eyes. Following the jaundice, the disease usually begins to disappear, although Type B may become chronic.

Strict bedrest is the treatment of choice for hepatitis, which the body will fight off eventually. Extremely ill patients may require hospitalization and transfusions.

Before, during, or after hepatitis of any type, mental symptoms ranging from mild lethargy to outright psychosis are possible. Anxiety and/or depression are very common. Suicides and acute delusional mania following hepatitis have been reported. Despite the regular occurrence of these symptoms, their existence is rarely mentioned in texts, or even in publications for the layperson. This is unfortunate, since hepatitis is a common disease throughout the world.

Immune and Autoimmune Disorders

The body's immune system is supposed to protect it from outside invaders. Sometimes, however, these invaders attack the cells of the immune system itself, weakening its effectiveness. Or our inner defense system may malfunction, mistaking some of our own cells for invaders, attacking them, and causing autoimmune disorders.

A relatively new area of interest and inquiry in medicine, autoimmune factors appear to be at work in many diseases, including diabetes and endocrine gland failure (which are covered in Chapter 10), rheumatoid arthritis, and possibly some psychiatric afflictions.

SYSTEMIC LUPUS ERYTHEMATOSIS

Usually called lupus or SLE, this grave, uncommon illness affects women nine out of ten times. Most victims are young, although the disease can strike at any age. It is a chronic and relapsing inflammatory disease of the connective tissue that can involve many organ systems in an unpredictable course. The disease may develop over years with frequent, unexplained fevers; in early stages it is very difficult to diagnose. Painful joints, which may become misshapen, are common. Many sufferers have an itchy, scaly skin rash in the shape of a butterfly on body surfaces exposed to light. Lungs, spleen, kidneys, and heart often become diseased. Baldness, seizures, and anemia may occur. Lupus patients are weak and prone to infection.

Lupus has no cure. Treatment usually includes antiinflammatory medication but otherwise depends on disease manifestations. Certain drugs may exacerbate lupus and these are eliminated. Patients are urged to avoid emotional stress, physical fatigue, and overexposure to the sun.

Lupus can mimic any kind of psychiatric disorder, ranging from mild anxiety to severe psychosis. These occur early in the course of the illness and may be the only symptoms for quite some time. Among 140 lupus patients studied, 3 percent presented with solely psychiatric phenomena, and close to 24 percent had mental symptoms along with others prior to or just after diagnosis. Even though the psychiatric manifestations of lupus are well known, the diagnosis is routinely ignored or overlooked in young women with psychiatric symptoms plus joint pain, which ought to be a giveaway.

ACQUIRED IMMUNE DEFICIENCY SYNDROME (AIDS)

Thus far, no one has recovered from AIDS, a viral disease of the immune system cells that was identified as recently as 1981. The disease is transmitted sexually as well as by transfusion of blood from an infected person or by a contaminated hypodermic needle. In the United States, AIDS occurs mostly among homosexual and bisexual men and intravenous drug users; in Africa, where the disease may have originated among monkeys, men and women are equally afflicted. Once the immune system has been invaded by the virus, the body's natural defenses become crippled. The victim is now susceptible to "opportunistic" infections, killers like Kaposi's sarcoma, a once-rare skin cancer that appears with bruise-like lesions. Approximately one in ten persons exposed to the disease actually develops it; all ten may be carriers capable of spreading it.

Many exposed persons have *AIDS-related complex,* considered to be an early sign of the disease. Symptoms include swollen glands, fever, fatigue, diarrhea, weight loss, and night sweats. An estimated 30 percent of AIDS patients reveal brain involvement, marked by depression, dementia, paralysis, seizures, and loss of control of body functions; scientists now fear that the virus may infect the brain directly, independent of the immune system.

A monumental research effort is underway worldwide to understand, control, treat, and prevent the illness from spreading further.

7

It's in Your Head

DISEASES OR INJURIES to the central nervous system can be some of the trickiest mimickers for psychiatrists. The same organ system—the brain—produces both psychiatric and neurological symptoms. Symptoms of some CNS diseases or injuries may mimic psychiatric syndromes so closely that the psychiatrist who does not always consider organic alternatives will easily be fooled. Delaying treatment for many central nervous system diseases can lead to permanent brain damage.

CENTRAL NERVOUS SYSTEM MIMICKERS

Disease	Major Depression	Manic-depression
Narcolepsy	+	
Epilepsy	+	
Partial complex seizures	+	+
Normal pressure hydrocephalus	+	
Huntington's chorea	+	
Multiple sclerosis	+	+
Post-concussion syndrome	+	+
Pick's disease	+	
Tumors	+	+

The Dementias

Dementia is a condition in which the brain, and therefore brain function, deteriorates, often irreversibly. It occurs most frequently in older age and is often mistaken for "senility." While some degree of brain function deterioration is natural with aging, because of shrinkage of the outer layer of the brain (the cortex), site of most of our intellectual and social functioning, even mild dementia is *un*natural. In dementia, pathological processes that cause intellectual functioning and personality to disintegrate are at work on the brain. Eventually, as behavior and self-care deteriorate, a person with a dementing disease will require total nursing care.

Dementia in younger persons is usually caused by alcoholism, chronic stimulant-drug abuse, infection, brain trauma, diabetes, and kidney failure.

Dementia may also occur in several central nervous system disorders (such as Huntington's chorea and Parkinson's disease, discussed below), as well as in AIDS. Differential diagnosis is critical, for the dementia may be reversible if the disease is properly identified. The dementias we are discussing here, however, are primary, that is to say they are diseases in themselves. They are pitilessly progressive and irreversible.

PSEUDODEMENTIA VS. DEMENTIA:
THE CASE OF MR. R

As dementia progresses, emotional response usually flattens. At first, however, it can be highly exaggerated and produce quite peculiar behavior. Other early symptoms include changes in appetite and sleep habits, and wild mood fluctuations. For example, Jack K. had always been quiet and polite. With the onset of as-yet undiagnosed dementia, however, he demanded to be the center of attention at every opportunity. As soon as all eyes were on him, he'd start to tell jokes that only he could appreciate. His moods went from pussycat to tiger to cowardly lion. At this stage, all roads lead to the psychiatrist's office. Since depression in older age is very common (see Chapter 23), major affective disorder is a tempting misdiagnosis for these patients, as it was for Jack, who, in fact, suffered from an irreversible dementia.

Psychiatrists who recognize a dementing process are more apt to fall into the related *pseudodementia* misdiagnosis trap; many depressed older persons develop a psychological dementia, reversible when their depression is treated. The irony in this misdiagnosis is that depressed older persons have too often been tossed into nursing homes with an incorrect diagnosis of dementia.

"I am much gladdened by this recognition of the fact that many elderly people appear demented when they really have a treatable depression," comments Canadian psychiatrist Robert O. Jones. "I now have some feelings, however, that perhaps this concept of pseudodementia has gone too far and leads to diagnostic errors in the opposite direction, i.e., we call people with an organic dementia depressed, and miss the true diagnosis of the underlying dementia. As a result . . . we sometimes . . . make the dementia worse by our treatment."

Dr. Jones relates the case of Mr. R, who at age 62 was referred to him because of nonresponse to treatment. "His history and mental status examination persuaded me that he had a unipolar depression." A decade earlier the local government had taken over land on which Mr. R had run a store. Three months later, Mr. R showed the classic symptoms of depression: He couldn't sleep, lost interest in his usual activities and declared that life wasn't worth living, seemed slowed down, and so on. Says Dr. Jones, "I had no doubt about my diagnosis." He hospitalized Mr. R "with the objective of pushing one or another of the antidepressant drugs to a dosage higher than one would prescribe for an outpatient. . . . He had the usual admission investigations, including an EEG [electroencephalogram]," which did reveal some abnormalities, as did a mental status examination. "However, I and my colleagues on staff rounds were quite willing to put this down as an example of pseudodementia."

The staff psychologist disagreed with this diagnosis. She noted many areas in which Mr. R seemed impaired. In her report she wrote, "While depression tends to interfere with one's efficiency in this area, the discrepancy revealed is marked and points to the likelihood of organic impairment."

Admits Jones, "With the weight of my medical authority (not to mention my medical arrogance), it was not hard to beat her into submission and have her agree to a diagnosis of pseudodementia."

The punch line is that the psychologist was right, and Mr. R's illness had to progress for eighteen more months before his doctor saw the light. "I was in the process of writing a prescription for more [antidepressant medication] at a higher dosage," relates Dr. Jones, "when he casually said, 'You know there have been two or three times recently that I wet myself.' My pen stopped in midair. . . ." Detailed questioning of Mr. R and his wife revealed that Mr. R's physical and intellectual functioning was deteriorating. Mrs. R "told me of an incident in which he looked a number up in the phone book quite correctly but then seemed completely unable to utilize the information by successfully dialing the phone."

Immediately Dr. Jones hospitalized his patient. His EEG showed the same mild impairments as it had a year and a half before. But this time Dr. Jones investigated further. He ordered a CAT scan. In the meantime he called in a consulting neurologist. Says Jones, "The neurologist noted the same sensorial difficulties that we had found and reported that his neurological examination had uncovered nothing and that Mr. R had a depression and was a good example of the pseudodementia of the depression." The neurologist hadn't yet seen the results of the CAT scan. When he did, "he immediately recognized that it was grossly abnormal. . . ."

Mr. R was ultimately diagnosed as having *Binswanger's disease,* associated with a chronic low-grade high blood pressure. "Unfortunately," concludes Dr. Jones, "these findings increase our medical satisfaction but not our ability to intervene in a useful way for Mr. R." There is no cure for the progressive dementia of Binswanger's.

ALZHEIMER'S DISEASE

Approximately two million Americans, most over 65, suffer from dementia of the Alzheimer's type, or Alzheimer's disease, described by the National Institute on Aging as "the most common cause of severe intellectual impairment in older individuals." The most serious form of the disease will strike in middle age, however.

Alzheimer's usually becomes apparent with the onset of mild confusion and forgetfulness, especially for recent events, although other symptoms may predominate. Family members have a tough time dealing with Alzheimer's victims, who will deny anything is out of the ordinary. ("The loss of a mind is too terrible a thing for conscious contemplation," comments geriatric expert Dr. Barry Reisberg.) Yet they will drive others crazy repeating questions that have already been answered, and they'll show appallingly bad judgment that could get them into serious trouble. One undiagnosed Alzheimer's sufferer, for example, nearly lost his job as a road maintenance worker when he tickled a fellow crew member who was operating a chainsaw. Alzheimer's patients can be alternately loud and embarrassing, then sad and depressed. Frustrated families often force the person to see a psychiatrist. During the evaluation the patient will typically joke around and chatter, then possibly break into tears. The family's irritation and anxiety, combined with the patient's behavior and symptoms, may tempt the practitioner into a misdiagnosis of depression.

The disease progresses horribly. Memory gaps begin to include names, even identities of friends and family members. Comprehension of numbers and words starts to go. Victims lose their ability to organize their days or to complete tasks. They become painfully frustrated and irritable. Judgment, orientation, and concentration disappear. Victims often suffer from an extreme restlessness and need to move around constantly, frequently wandering off. Eventually, they lose control over bowels and bladder. In time, the Alzheimer's patient will require total care.

When Alzheimer's strikes in middle age, the course of the disease can be as long as twenty years. The patient will lose awareness of the agony, but the family will suffer the burden of this consciousness.

Alzheimer's disease has no cure. The disease is being studied extensively, however, in hopes of finding the causes of characteristic brain-cell changes. Scientists are studying the neurotransmitter acetylcholine, which is implicated in the disease, and an enzyme necessary to the synthesis of acetylcholine. A possible accumulation of aluminum in the brain may contribute to it, as may a slow-acting virus or a tangling of temporal lobe somatostatin cells or a newly identified infectious particle called a prion. Alzheimer's may be genetic, since it seems to cluster in families.

If Alzheimer's is correctly diagnosed in the early stages, experts can intervene to make life a little easier for the victim and for the family. Memory aids can help, and medication to reduce agitation, improve sleep, and treat disease-produced depression can be effective.

Infectious Brain Diseases

Virtually any brain infection can bring on a confusing array of psychiatric symptoms in lieu of physical symptoms. We will survey a few of them.

SYPHILIS (GENERAL PARESIS)

One of the most devastating sexually transmitted diseases, syphilis can immediately invade the central nervous system. In addition, 10 to 15 percent of all untreated individuals will eventually develop brain infection, called general paresis or paretic neurosyphilis.

Early in the century, before antibiotics were discovered, general paresis was the greatest of all mimickers, accounting for 10 to 20 percent of all admissions to state hospitals for the insane. Today most psychiatrists have never seen it, and probably would not recognize it. In the study (mentioned in Chapter 2) of one hundred state hospital patients in whom physical disorders had supposedly been eliminated, researchers found two cases of syphilis, one diagnosed as schizophrenia, the other as manic-depressive illness. General paresis can mimic virtually any psychiatric disorder.

Syphilis is caused by a spirochete bacterium, which is transmitted by sexual contact. Typically the chronic disease has active phases interspersed with long symptom-free periods. General paretic symptoms, which progress to dementia, seizures, and paralysis, may be completely reversed if diagnosed when they appear. Penicillin is the usual treatment at all stages.

VIRAL ENCEPHALITIS

This inflammation of the brain often occurs following other infections, such as measles or mumps. Also, in warm weather, it may be caused by bites from infected mosquitoes. The herpes simplex virus causes most cases of nonepidemic encephalitis, which usually will follow a skin infection by the same virus. It affects mostly children and young people, 50 to 70 percent of whom die of the disease. With immediate treatment, the mortality rate can be reduced to less than 30 percent. The physician who does not suspect a mimicker is not likely to diagnose encephalitis at this stage; behavioral changes, including psychoses and manic-depressive illness, may be the only initial signs.

Add those symptoms to a previous history of mental illness, and misdiagnosis is assured. We stated in the previous chapter that psychiatric patients get poor medical care. Dr. Milton Erman relates a case of misdiagnosed encephalitis in a former psychiatric inpatient in which doctors assumed that her past illness explained all future symptoms. Would the emergency room doctors have ignored the neurological signs in a person who had not had the misfortune to suffer a painful emotional disease?

At 21, Miss V had already been the victim of apparent psychiatric misdiagnosis. Of the previous two years, she had spent all but six months as a psychiatric inpatient diagnosed schizophrenic, even though she did not respond to antipsychotic medication. Her recovery was quick and impressive, however, once she was given lithium. Six months after she went home, she came to the emergency room with some physical symptoms, including headache, nausea, and blurred vision, and plenty of mental ones, including visual hallucinations and impaired thinking. The doctors tested the level of lithium in her blood to rule out lithium poisoning. A neurologist took a look at her and concluded—without performing a lumbar puncture, which would have revealed infection—that she had a "hysterical psychosis." Back to the psychiatric floor she went. Her behavioral symptoms worsened in the following week, and when organic involvement became painfully obvious—she was becoming less and less alert and beginning to wet herself—finally an organic condition was suspected and the appropriate diagnostic tests performed. Miss V had viral encephalitis. She survived, but it took five weeks before she was well enough to leave the hospital. A year later she felt she had not recovered her previous alertness.

Normal Pressure Hydrocephalus

When normal absorption of cerebrospinal fluid becomes blocked, it builds up in brain cavities, principally the ventricles. The accumulation produces a swelling which compresses brain tissue. In medical school students learn that dementia, loss of gait coordination, and incontinence mark this syndrome. Psychiatric symptoms may be the most apparent, however, ranging from behavior problems to persecutory delusions and psychotic depression. Since this condition is most common in older individuals, it should always be considered when an apparent psychiatric illness strikes seemingly out of nowhere. Timely diagnosis is critical: The only treatment is the insertion of a shunt (tube) in the brain to drain the fluid; the earlier in the illness the shunt is inserted, the more likely it will help.

Causes of this syndrome are unclear. Prior brain infection or inflammation may predispose an individual to it.

Post-Concussion Syndrome

It doesn't happen only in the movies: A blow on the head *can* cause a personality change. We treated a man who had been a bystander at a barroom brawl and accidentally got hit with a nightstick when the police came to break it up. He had been a nice, placid guy, a cook at the restaurant across the street from the bar. The injury was bad, damaging the frontal lobe of his brain. He went from being a sweetheart to a living terror, prone to attacks of rage and severe depression. He also lost his sense of smell, so he was fired from his job as cook. The psychiatrist who was treating him figured that his moods were related to the job loss. It was an obvious conclusion—except that when he was referred to us and we gave him an EEG, we discovered his attacks were actually seizures. The medication he takes now has restored his more pleasant nature, although he still cannot smell things.

Post-concussion syndrome occurs as the aftereffect of brain damage from severe head injury. Depending on which part of the brain is affected, it can mimic anxiety, depression, excess anger, loss of emotional and/or social control, mood swings from euphoria to depression, and psychotic symptoms. Even mild injury may bring on fatigue, nervousness, anxiety, depression, restlessness, irritability, and prolonged elation for as long as several months after head trauma.

No tests exist for post-concussion syndrome. A history of severe head injury, particularly one that resulted in a coma lasting more than two days, is highly suggestive of this diagnosis. Treatment is symptomatic where possible, but damage and resulting symptoms may be permanent.

Narcolepsy

Narcoleptics suffer from a sleep disorder that makes their lives literally a nightmare. They continually fall asleep, often experiencing terribly vivid illusions or even hallucinations as they drift off. The desire to sleep, which may occur from a few to many times a day, is impossible to resist. Attacks may last from minutes to hours. Rousing a narcoleptic is no more difficult than waking a normal person. Nighttime sleep is poor and filled with bad dreams.

Sleep has two cycles, NREM and REM. REM stands for "rapid eye movements," which are characteristic of dream states. NREM means non-REM. Normally in the first hour or so of sleep, a person sinks deeper and deeper into NREM before going into REM and starting to dream. In narcoleptics, REM usually occurs immediately, and their dreams are usually vivid because they are barely asleep.

Other symptoms considered typical of narcolepsy include: cataplexy, which is a brief paralysis usually brought on by strong emotion; and sleep paralysis, an occasional inability to move when falling asleep or waking up. (This is present also in some normal people.)

Firm diagnosis is often made by taking an EEG during sleep and finding the REM sleep brain patterns at the beginning of sleep. Repeated testing may be necessary, however, because narcoleptics do not necessarily show the abnormal pattern every time they fall asleep. Few narcoleptics, in fact, evidence all the symptoms of this rare syndrome. In the absence of the complete symptom picture, or when a single test does not reveal the only measurable finding, narcoleptics are often condemned to misdiagnoses of major depression, schizophrenia, thyroid disease, or just plain malingering.

No one knows what causes narcolepsy, which is far more common among men than among women. The syndrome usually begins in adolescence or early adulthood and persists for a lifetime. Stimulant drugs are usually prescribed. Although narcolepsy is not a depressive disorder, recent evidence suggests certain antidepressants may be effective in treating it.

Epilepsy

"The number of patients with schizophrenia diagnosed and treated as epilepsy by neurologists is equaled only by the number of patients with psychomotor epilepsy diagnosed and treated as schizophrenia by psychiatrists," noted Dr. D. A. Treffert in the *American Journal of Psychiatry* two decades ago. Not much has changed since then.

Epilepsy refers to any recurrent pattern of seizures. Along with syphilis, epilepsy is one of history's all-time great mimickers. Since earliest times epileptics have been considered "mental." Although at long last these seizure disorders are treatable, persons with the illness still must struggle against its stigma. Thus it is particularly tragic when psychiatric symptoms associated with certain types of epilepsy lead to a psychiatric rather than neurological diagnosis.

The brain is a usually smoothly functioning electrochemical "machine." In epilepsy, sudden surges of electricity will disorganize brain activity and bring on a seizure. Just before the seizure, most people have premonitory experiences, ranging from déjà vu to mystical experiences to headaches to visual hallucinations to an overall undefinable feeling of oddness.

Stress, especially the everyday kind, is a potent seizure trigger. Not all persons suffering from epilepsy experience the classic convulsions and fall to the floor in a complete loss of control, however, although this type of seizure is most common. Some will either stop all movement or begin to repeat actions inappropriately. Still others will briefly "tune out," staring off into space, as if daydreaming. Even if they remain conscious during the seizure, sufferers will have no memory of it. When seizures are the subtle variety, an undiagnosed epileptic often does not even know he or she is subject to them.

Persons with partial complex seizures (temporal lobe epilepsy and psychomotor epilepsy) are most likely to suffer the symptoms that tempt psychiatrists into misdiagnoses. Between seizures, some become super-good—excessively religious and ethical, with a corresponding reduction of sexual interest and activity. In others this super-goodness may alternate with a super-badness, à la Jekyll and Hyde. These behaviors and hallucinations of any type may be associated with depression, anxiety, hysteria, hypochondriasis, apparent schizophrenia, confusion, and antisocial personality. Whether this form of epilepsy is related to violence and aggression is currently a hot topic among neurologists and psychiatrists.

Epilepsy can occur as a result of:

1. An unidentified inborn metabolic error or possible birth injury or developmental defect.

2. Brain injury, tumor, brain infections, drug overdose or withdrawal, poisoning, endocrine diseases such as hypoglycemia, drug allergy—virtually anything, in other words, that affects the brain. (Indeed, "seizure" or "epilepsy," like "depression," is more a statement of symptoms than a diagnosis.) Usually the seizures will disappear as the disease moderates or the drug or poison clears the system. But when misdiagnosis leads to incorrect or delayed treatment, permanent brain damage may occur, seizures may continue, and the diagnosis of epilepsy will be made.

Diagnosis of epilepsy consists of a careful history and examination to discover causative illnesses or conditions. The EEG can detect abnormal brain electrical activity, but it is not foolproof. A normal EEG does not rule out the disease, and, in the absence of clinical symptoms, an abnormal test does not always guarantee its presence.

Anticonvulsant medications, singly or in combination, are highly effective in helping to prevent and/or control epileptic seizures. In severe cases, brain surgery is usually effective. Once the disease is controlled, epileptics can lead virtually normal lives.

Seizures, by the way, aren't all bad. ECT, or shock therapy, relieves symptoms of depression by *inducing* convulsions (in an anesthetized patient).

Multiple Sclerosis

Is it multiple sclerosis (MS) or is it a "conversion disorder" or is it depression? Conversion disorder is a psychiatric condition in which repressed emotional conflicts are unconsciously converted into bodily symptoms usually involving the nervous system. (In psychosomatic illness, psychological stresses cause actual damage to the body; in conversion disorder, sometimes called hysteria, no pathology is present.) If it's a conversion disorder, psychotherapy is the treatment. If it's MS, prompt medical attention is essential.

MS is a chronic degenerative disease of the central nervous system. Nerves lose the myelin sheaths that protect and insulate them, and virtually all body systems slowly begin to deteriorate. It usually strikes between ages twenty and forty. Women are affected somewhat more often than men. Oddly, MS is uncommon in tropical climates.

A puzzling array of psychiatric and neurologic symptoms often appears years ahead of the diagnosis. Early neurologic symptoms can include fleeting visual problems, transient weakness and tingling of an arm or leg, and vague bladder problems. Usually the psychiatric symptoms, including emotional upsets that can't be explained, depression, and euphoria, are more "convincing." All the symptoms will come and go, in this way too mimicking a primary emotional problem.

When MS ultimately reveals itself, limbs begin to go weak, an eye may lose its sight or its movement or double vision may occur, dizziness is frequent, loss of sensation is common, urinating becomes difficult, gait is unsteady, impotency and vaginal numbness strike, speech becomes slurred, seizures may occur, euphoria and/or depression continue, bladder and rectal control are lost—among many other possibilities, depending on how the disease progresses and which nerves are affected.

Usually the disease does not continue on a steady downhill course. It is marked by unexplained remissions, which may last for years. Recurrence usually brings a worsening of symptoms. Most people with MS end up in wheelchairs.

Like many diseases of the central nervous system, the causes of MS are unproved. Possibilities include: (1) a virus to which the victim was once exposed and which eventually is activated either by reexposure or because of stress; and (2) a defect in the immune system, making certain individuals more vulnerable, perhaps for genetic reasons.

No cure for MS has been found. Steroid medication may help shorten attacks. Care and treatment of symptoms is about all that can be done, and it is essential to provide this assistance as soon as possible, in order to strengthen muscles and to improve morale. A fighting spirit is the best friend an MS sufferer can have to postpone or even avoid total invalidism. Needless to say, no progress can be made when a psychiatrist sets out to convince the unfortunate patient that the problem is in his or her head. At this writing, we have just diagnosed MS in three psychiatric patients at Fair Oaks, each of them referred to us for *depression*. None was overjoyed to learn the diagnosis, but what relief to have a doctor confirm what they've been trying to get across all this time: There *is* something wrong.

Huntington's Chorea

"The tendency to insanity and sometimes that form of insanity which leads to suicide is marked," noted George Sumner Huntington in 1872, when he described the hereditary degenerative disease that bears his name. Nonetheless, psychiatrists and other physicians continue to be deluded by obstinacy, moodiness, apathy, violence, paranoia, euphoria, psychosis, and a host of other psychiatric symptoms that mark Huntington's in its earliest presentation. While the giveaway should be the typical spasmodic, uncontrolled "choreiform" movements ("involuntary twisting and movements of the whole body, including the face and tongue," as Dr. Stephanie J. Bird describes it) and dementia, some psychiatrists will conclude that the movement problems are caused by the antipsychotic medication they have been prescribing. A family history of Huntington's should lock in the correct diagnosis of this horrible disease.

Huntington's leads invariably to total mental deterioration. While medication can help control the movements, nothing can help the mind. Still, sufferers can live ten to twenty years.

Huntington's develops between ages 30 and 50. Genetically, half of all offspring will be affected. A genetic marker for the disease has very recently been identified, and development of a presymptomatic test is in the works. But there is no cure. The only preventive measure is for offspring carrying the defective gene not to be born.

The most commonly inherited neurological disease, Huntington's afflicts 10,000 to 25,000 persons in the United States; an additional 20,000 to 50,000 are at risk of passing it on.

Parkinson's Disease

Parkinson's has been called "shaking palsy," which describes the most familiar aspect of this motor (movement) disorder of the post-60 set. Except in sleep, the involuntary tremor in the hands is persistent. In resting as well as anxious states the shaking gets even worse, and yet under stress, when purposeful action must be taken, the tremor may briefly disappear.

Parkinson's is chronic and progressive. It goes from tremor to a slowing of movement and muscular rigidity. The facial expression becomes fixed, with unblinking and staring eyes, and slightly open, drooling mouth. Posture is stooped, gait shuffling; worst of all, voluntary movement, such as walking, is difficult to get started, and once begun, is hard to stop. The speech of a Parkinson's patient becomes so soft and slow that it is unintelligible. Mild dementia is common among half of Parkinson's patients. The mind is intact in the other half.

Easy to diagnose? If all patients exhibited the textbook symptoms of every disease, and if nothing was happening during the presymptomatic phase, all doctors could go home early. A 62-year-old woman we'll call Mrs. X was referred to biopsychiatrist Harvey Sternbach, because a few months earlier she had begun an increasingly depressed downward course. She cried, she couldn't sleep, she had no hope, she was agitated, and she just couldn't complete a day's work. She had good reason to be depressed: Her alcoholic husband, who had recently had a heart attack, had just been demoted at work. Her internist gave her a clean bill of health so she went to a psychiatrist, who prescribed antidepressant medication. But her depression and agitation worsened, and now Mrs. X was becoming confused. A CAT scan revealed nothing significant, but neurological examination did show muscular changes in her legs.

What seemed more serious were results of Mrs. X's electrocardiogram, which indicated that her heart could not tolerate the antidepressants. Dr. Sternbach took her off the medication and instead ordered a course of ECT (shock therapy). It worked, to everyone's relief. Unfortunately, the results did not last. Within four months, however, Mrs. X's depression was of less immediate interest than her increasingly apparent dementia. Neurological examination revealed some Parkinson's findings, and the CAT scan now revealed subtle changes in the basal ganglia, the area of the brain that controls starting and stopping movement. Dr. Sternbach prescribed an anti-Parkinson's drug, and Mrs. X's depression and movement difficulties began to subside. Her dementia improved also, but less dramatically. Mrs. X does require help in the tasks of daily living, but at least her downward spiral has been halted.

The treatment of Parkinson's is one of the success stories of modern neuroscience—a good place to end this otherwise gloomy chapter.

The whys of Parkinson's are unknown—no hints of genetic factors, viruses, or autoimmune factors. The whats and hows, however, began to fall into place in 1955, when a German scientist discovered that Parkinson's sufferers have lost many brain cells in an area of the basal ganglia called the substantia nigra. Cell pathways extend from this area to the caudate nucleus, which was already known to play a role in movement. (The caudate nucleus is affected in Huntington's chorea.) Later, when the Swedes discovered how to see what was going on inside nerve cells, they found that substantia nigra cells contain significant amounts of the neurotransmitter dopamine. Neurotransmitters are a part of the brain's electrochemical communication system among cells. It seemed a reasonable conclusion that because of the death of dopamine-containing cells in the substantia nigra, certain movement messages were not being effectively transmitted.

The logical treatment would be to replace the dopamine, but that proved easier said than done. Dopamine does not cross the blood-brain barrier (that is, the brain will not absorb it from the blood). The brain does absorb levodopa, however, which is a chemical from which the brain makes its own supply of dopamine. Soon L-dopa, as it came to be called, was the Parkinson's treatment of choice, for, prodded by this precursor chemical, the remaining cells in the substantia nigra proved amenable to the manufacture of a "replacement" dopamine supply.

Years of experience with L-dopa have revealed it to be, like all drugs, less than perfect. It can have side effects varying from the annoying to the serious, depending on dosage and length of treatment. Unfortunately, large amounts must be taken because much of the chemical is metabolized by other organs before it reaches the brain. Over the years, however, other drugs have been developed that modulate, enhance, or mimic L-dopa's actions.

Speaking of mimicking: Mrs. X's first symptom of Parkinson's was a physiological depression brought on by the developing illness. The medication lifted her mood. Anti-Parkinson's drugs are not antidepressants, so why would they work? We do not know precisely, but the interrelationship of physical illness and psychiatric symptomatology puts us in that most important, most exciting area where mind and body link. Mrs. X consulted a psychiatrist because she was depressed. Later she developed a confusion similar to that suffered by many schizophrenic patients. But her problem was a disease of the central nervous system. Mr. Y might go to a doctor with difficulties in initiating movement, even shaking, to discover that the diagnosis is biological depression. Add profound confusion and the diagnosis might be schizophrenia.

We call Parkinson's *organic* and depression or schizophrenia *psy-*

chiatric—in other words, not of the body. Nonetheless, neuroscientific study of diseases such as Parkinson's yields important similarities between physical and mental processes.

Parkinson's, schizophrenia, and depression, for example, may all be related biochemically. Dopamine cell circuitry is found in two brain areas besides the basal ganglia. One pathway reaches from the midbrain to an area of the cortex (our highest brain regions, site of consciousness and intellectual function) that is believed to be involved in schizophrenia. In schizophrenia, one may be oversensitive to a normal amount of dopamine; already it is well established that the drugs that help control schizophrenia block the body's use of that neurotransmitter. Contrary to the action of L-dopa, antipsychotics reduce the body's supply of dopamine, as does Parkinson's; indeed, taken over a long period, antipsychotic drugs cause an irreversible movement disorder similar to Parkinson's (tardive dyskinesia).

The third dopamine pathway extends from the hypothalamus to the pituitary in the limbic system. Between them these two brain structures regulate stress response, sleeping and waking, appetite, body temperature, hormones, sex, and emotion, all or many of which are involved in biological depression. Persons with this illness often exhibit a slowness and difficulty in moving as in Parkinson's; many also suffer delusions while ill, as in schizophrenia.

Of course Parkinson's is different from schizophrenia, which is different from depression. The point of this chapter, after all, is that psychiatrists and physicians must learn to recognize and/or search for the differences among them, so that their patients receive prompt, correct, and effective care. The differences are not to be found, as we have seen, by separating diseases into mental or physical *symptom* categories.

Overall, the study of diseases such as Parkinson's, schizophrenia, and depression is blurring the traditional conceptual distinctions between mental and physical diseases. Mental disease, too, is "of the body." Elucidation of its physical mechanisms has already led to laboratory diagnostic tests for depression and much more scientifically based treatment.

8

Drugs: Rx and Otherwise

COURTESY OF THEIR doctors, their bartenders, their pharmacists, and/ or their dealers, virtually everybody in America takes drugs. All drugs are chemicals that enter the body and influence its physiology, causing their desired effects as well as other, unwanted reactions.

From prescriptions to over-the-counter preparations to alcohol and illicit drugs, no drug is free of side or adverse effects. Some unwanted effects are dose- and time-related; others vary with a person's age and state of health, while still others play against the individual's genetic makeup and predispositions. When a drug directly or indirectly influences brain chemistry even slightly, psychiatric symptoms result. Because of ignorance of the psychiatric effects of many drugs, or a quickness to jump to conclusions about "mental" symptoms, doctors often do not consider the adverse influence of drugs in the differential diagnoses of their patients. For all these reasons, drug effects are Mimicker Number One, causing more diagnostic confusion

DRUG MIMICKERS

Drug	Major Depression	Manic-depression
PCP	+	+
Toluene	+	
Marijuana	+	+
Amphetamines	+	+
Cocaine	+	+
Sedative-Hypnotic	+	
Heroin	+	
Methadone	+	

than any other substance, disease, or condition. *Drugs must be considered in all psychiatric diagnoses, no matter how classically "psychiatric" the person may appear.* Because, as we said, everybody takes them.

"Recreational" Drugs and Alcohol

THE CASE OF ALISON R.

It was easy to see why Alison's therapist believed that Alison's problem was her relationship with her parents. Alison, the daughter of prominent physicians, was a junior at Harvard, and she was about to drop out of school. For a year Alison had been tangling with an intractable depression, complete with lethargy and an inability to concentrate. Her parents had sent her money to go into therapy, but when the therapist suggested, a year later, that Alison take a leave of absence, get a menial job, and enter four-day-a-week psychoanalysis, her parents had had it.

Alison's father called me in for a second opinion. This physician couple was trouble from the very beginning. "You seem too smart to be a psychiatrist," her father said snidely. Her mother objected to my fee. I began, "If you have a financial hardship—" but the mother interrupted me with, "We make more money in a month than you make in a year."

Finally I met with Alison. I was tempted to make the diagnosis on the basis of her downcast expression alone. She described a depressive-melancholic episode that had lasted for at least a year—decreased sex drive, loss of energy, memory problems, loss of interest in her favorite friends and her number one love, skiing. When I asked how her physical health had been during the year, she said she had had a number of upper respiratory infections and had an occasional cough. Also twice she had thought she was pregnant, but she had just skipped a period. She said she didn't use drugs, except for an occasional drink at a party, and a couple of times she had taken some speed to stay up and study. "It really gave me energy, a real boost," she said, adding, "I was afraid to take it again."

I did a complete physical, including neurological and endocrinological examinations. I called her gynecologist about her last exam, which was normal. I interviewed her less than cooperative family. My examinations and interviews revealed nothing of interest. So far everything appeared to be within the depression spectrum. Depressed women frequently skip a period or even stop menstruating, and depressed people in general appear to be at greater risk for infections. Still, I told her, I wanted to take some tests.

"That's fine," answered Alison, "do anything you want, but I don't think anything is wrong with me except *me.*" Score ten for depressed self-image.

But Alison's mother didn't want to spend the money on the tests. I'd had enough time with her—did she or did she not seem depressed? If she did, did I think she needed to drop out or "just take a few antidepressants"?

I explained in no uncertain terms that this is how I work. The mother backed off and I went ahead and ordered a complete blood count (CBC) and a folate level. Folate, or folic acid, acts like a vitamin; a folic acid deficiency can eventually lead to anemia. A woman can have no obvious anemia on a CBC and still test out deficient in folate. Birth control pills can reduce the available supply of folate, and Alison had been taking them until recently. I ordered a complete review of medical systems (liver, kidney, cholesterol, etcetera), a comprehensive drug screen, and a pregnancy test. I would test for mononucleosis if all else was negative.

In addition I scheduled a TRH stimulation test of thyroid function for the coming week. An early grade of thyroid failure was possible, especially since one of Alison's maternal aunts had thyroid problems. I also scheduled a dexamethasone suppression test (DST) to confirm the diagnosis of biological, treatment-reversible depression. I ordered a blood alcohol test for the first blood draw of the DST.

All the tests were normal, but her urine showed THC, the active ingredient in marijuana. I called up the lab and asked them to run a THC/marijuana at the same time they did the blood alcohol. The alcohol was negative, but the THC showed recent smoking.

When Alison and I met again I had a thick file of interviews and examinations and tests. I said, "My guess is that something is going on with you at school and you want to leave, Alison." This she vigorously denied. I said that I'd try to help her stay in school, but she would have to stop smoking marijuana, see a psychiatrist who specialized in substance-induced syndromes, and be reevaluated in six weeks.

Alison blushed. She had not mentioned a word about marijuana. Now it all came out. She had been smoking three to four joints per day since she'd arrived at college. She got involved with a boy who now wanted her to move in with him. Alison was feeling overwhelmed.

She agreed to sign a contract to refrain from using any mood-altering drugs or alcohol, go to ninety Alcoholics Anonymous meetings in the next ninety days (helpful for anyone who has a substance-abuse problem), go to the psychiatrist as often as she suggested, and to have comprehensive urine testing for drugs at random.

It took six weeks for Alison's urine to stop showing evidence of THC. Her depression disappeared, and she asked her psychiatrist if she could return to her former therapist to continue to work out her feelings toward her parents. She became a pre-law student and eventually was accepted at an Ivy League law school. The last time I saw Alison she seemed very happy.

I'M NOT A COP . . .

. . . I'm a doctor. People like Alison come to me for help, and I can't provide it if I don't know the facts. You bet I test all my patients for drugs, because drug use is commonplace—and drugs cause more depressive symptoms than all diseases or substances. Most patients do not tell their doctors about their drug or alcohol use, or admit to its full extent, even if they come for help with a drug problem. They can't tell us, but they are relieved when we find out. I don't blame the patient—that's the reality of the behavior. I *do* blame the psychiatrist who rules out drug or alcohol reactions just because the patient has denied any significant use.

Like Alison, individuals often will confess to occasional use of a particular drug but not mention the drug that they use regularly. A priest came to me with depression, told me about his drinking problem, but did not confess to using cocaine. An airline pilot told me he occasionally smoked a little marijuana. What he didn't say was that he had a huge cocaine habit and snorted constantly, including before and during flights. And I treated a senior flight attendant who complained of a classical medical depression and who said that she smoked a few joints of marijuana a week. Tests confirmed her use of marijuana— and cocaine and opium. She told me, "I was sure you'd throw me out of the office if you knew I smoke opium as often as I can get it, and use coke to stay awake enough to go to work."

RECREATIONAL DRUGS AND DEPRESSION

We used to think that people used drugs and drank because they were depressed to begin with. While certain people say they get high to escape a rotten mood, evidence now suggests that most often it's the drugs themselves that create the depression. One study found, for example, that 95 percent of opiate addicts (heroin, methadone) with a diagnosis of major depression experienced their first depression only after they started using the drugs.

We studied seventy consecutive patients admitted to our alcohol rehabilitation program. While a large number were seriously depressed on admission, only 7 percent remained in the dumps two to three weeks following detoxification.

Another study showed quite dramatically that alcohol increases depression. Alcoholics in a hospital detox center were briefly allowed to drink as much as they wanted. Twelve percent were depressed before, 41 percent after. Once they were abstinent, their rate of depression was no greater than that of the general population.

Cocaine abusers have a terrible time with depression. Callers to our 800-COCAINE help line at Fair Oaks repeatedly tell us how down they are—83 percent in all. Chronic fatigue and sleep problems are the rule. The depression will remit spontaneously in the majority of those who quit in a supportive, structured setting, or after prolonged abstinence.

Another common drug syndrome commonly confused with depression is "burnout." Chronic apathy, low energy, inability to function in a meaningful way in society, plus some intellectual deterioration are the consequences of long-term, chronic drug use.

LOW-LEVEL DRUG USE

"But I only smoke maybe half a joint every couple of days. Don't tell me I have a drug problem."

"I don't really *drink*—a couple of cocktails after work."

"Listen, Dr. Gold. You're not going to convince me I'm hooked on coke because I do a few lines on weekends."

I hear these kinds of comments frequently from persons who use drugs regularly but in small quantities. Their lives continue as productively as always; they are not experiencing the well-publicized horrors of drug use. Many of them, however, are feeling kind of anxious or down, tired, perhaps less able to sustain their concentration—nothing "serious." They don't mention their symptoms to me, because they don't associate them with their drug use. Instead, they see their mood as something about their emotional makeup, or a reaction to life events. Worse, so do their psychiatrists, who commonly do not realize that low-level drug use may prove the genesis of a depressive syndrome. *No drug use is without consequence.*

DRUGS AND THE BRAIN

Drugs and alcohol are powerful mood-altering substances—that's why most people take them. They achieve their effects by interacting with the brain's own mood-regulating systems. The high from drugs may be short-lived, but the effect on the brain's chemical physiology is long-lasting. With regular use, drugs end up substituting for natural brain's chemicals, which probably cease to function in the presence of the drug. When drug use stops, the systems do not necessarily return to immediate working order; during this phase withdrawal occurs.

The big question is, Will the mood-regulating systems resume functioning at all? Sometimes the answer is no, and just as if you'd contracted an irreversible neurological illness, this means brain damage.

Sleep, appetite, sexual function, and energy are often profoundly affected by the psychological and physiological effects of drugs and withdrawal from them. Related nutritional deficiencies and infections, such as viral hepatitis, common in intravenous users, or hepatitis or cirrhosis in alcoholics, can all contribute to a very convincing "major depression."

Depression is but one of the psychiatric symptoms of drug use, overuse, and abuse. As you can see in the charts on page 104, adverse reactions to any abusable drug can resemble any known psychiatric symptom—from psychosis to mild anxiety states.

PSYCHIATRIC DIAGNOSIS OF DRUG EFFECTS
Except for practitioners who specialize in substance abuse, most psychiatrists remain inexcusably naive about diagnosing drug problems. With the encouragement of the DSM-III they first ask the patient, "Do you take any drugs?" If the patient says, "No," they proceed to observe the person only for supposedly typical signs of drug abuse. The DSM-III criteria for cocaine intoxication (see below) are a prime example of the bankruptcy of psychiatry's diagnostic practices in this all-important area.

DSM-III Criteria for Cocaine Intoxication

A. Recent use of cocaine. ["Oh, I've done a little coke at parties, but nothing regular, Doctor." "When was the last time?" "Gee, let me think. Yeah, must have been three weeks ago. . . ."]
B. At least two of the following psychological symptoms within one hour of using cocaine:
   1. psychomotor agitation
   2. elation
   3. grandiosity

4. loquacity

5. hypervigilance

[These symptoms are indeed true of many cocaine users, also of people who have had too much coffee. They are equally true of most people who are happy or had something wonderful happen to them.]

C. At least two of the following symptoms within one hour of using cocaine:

1. tachycardia

2. pupillary dilation

3. elevated blood pressure

4. perspiration or chills

5. nausea and vomiting

All these are dose- and duration-related effects that can also be caused by fever, caffeine, atropine, and hundreds of other possibilities.

D. Maladaptive behavioral effects, e.g., fighting, impaired judgment, interference with social or occupational functioning. [These "effects" are hardly specific to cocaine.]

5. Not due to any other physical or mental disorder.

[Which disorders? How do you rule them out or rule cocaine intoxication in?]

THE MEDICAL VERSION

The American Medical Association (AMA) is wiser. You want to know if your patient's "maladaptive behavioral effects" result from cocaine intoxication. The AMA manual on drug abuse will tell you to find cocaine levels in blood and/or urine that spell intoxication. These are simple laboratory procedures and provide important data fast. Treatment for the patient's actual problem can begin almost immediately.

Always the point of diagnosis is to help the patient. Many people would rather spend ten years in therapy than face the fact that a drug is causing them to feel like jumping off the nearest bridge. They don't want to give it up; this is the nature of a drug problem. It is far from proper for a psychiatrist to encourage this escape from reality, which will contribute to the patient's continuing mental and physical deterioration.

Not using the lab to rule out drugs also can affect *future* psychiatric patients profoundly. Many persons with drug-related mimickers make their way into studies of depressed subjects, polluting the results. In our own research at Fair Oaks, of course, we test for drug-related problems before we embark on a research project. And as I said, we test all patients who come for diagnosis and treatment of an apparent psychiatric condition.

WASHING OUT DEPRESSION

But the testing is only the first step in determining the contribution of drugs to the patient's misery. Next comes a two-week supervised drug-free "washout." All drugs, prescribed medication included whenever possible, are removed to assess their influence. All patients are of course supervised and supported during this period.

It is gratifying to observe a severe depression lift during this drug-free period. Drug-induced depressions will clear most often in users of alcohol and other sedatives, marijuana, and cocaine. (Detoxification from heroin and especially methadone often causes a long-term depression.) Unfortunately, too many psychiatrists immediately reach for their prescription pads and dose the depressed, recovering drug user with antidepressants and/or tranquilizers. At best, medication at this time muddles the determination of what the patient's depression comes from; at worst, it creates yet another drug problem, especially when addicting drugs like tranquilizers are prescribed.

Prescribed Drugs

The drug washout can be equally dramatic for persons who are doing no more than following doctor's orders. Laurie K. suffered ferocious depressions two weeks out of every month, during which she would berate her husband and then herself. She was convinced she was both evil and crazy. Her psychiatrist suggested she stop taking birth control pills. She pooh-poohed his advice, convinced her moods were far too complicated for something as simple as that. When she heard about our diagnostic work, she was certain we would correctly diagnose her severe mental illness. We took her off birth control pills, and to her husband's relief, and her own, there went her "severe mental illness."

In 1971, investigators found that approximately 3 percent of all persons taking *any* prescribed drug experienced psychiatric symptoms. Hallucinations, delusions, psychosis, agitation, anxiety, weird feelings, depression, fatigue, nervousness, and nightmares were all reported.

Today the incidence is probably much higher, because, for one, so many medications have been introduced since 1971. Secondly, advances in disease control have led to concurrent use of numerous drugs, which separately might be safe but in some persons interact dangerously. Older persons, who do not metabolize drugs efficiently or clear them from their systems normally, are at risk for this category of mimicker. Yet when psychiatric symptoms develop, they often are whisked into nursing homes without being properly evaluated.

KNOW WHAT YOU'RE TAKING

The list of prescribed drugs that have provoked mimickers is encyclopedic. The drug or drug types we'll be discussing are those which have caused the *greatest* number of psychiatric reactions. You may wish to look up the types of drugs you or family members are taking, if you know. Be aware as you read these pages that most drugs have more than one use, often unrelated to their primary application. Dilantin, for example, is classified as an anticonvulsive drug; it is also sometimes given for ventricular arrhythmias. Tranquilizers, listed as psychiatric medication, are commonly prescribed for high blood pressure and muscle relaxation. Even antipsychotics such as Thorazine have medical applications.

If you are medically ill, getting on in age, or have a predisposition or history of depression or other psychiatric illness, you are especially vulnerable to the psychiatric side effects of the following drugs. When a doctor prescribes a medication, be sure to find out what it is and what is in it. Your pharmacist may also be a good source of information. To look up the pills you are presently taking, consult reference books for the layperson, such as those in *The Pill Book* series, which contain inclusive drug guides as well as separate reference guides for particular kinds of drugs or conditions. Whether or not you are among the more vulnerable population, it is always a good idea to know what you're taking and to volunteer the information to the doctors that you consult.

PSYCHIATRIC MEDICATIONS

Antidepressants can make you more depressed, tranquilizers more anxious, antipsychotics more psychotic. These reactions are most likely to occur when the medications are removed suddenly. The tricyclic type of antidepressants may cause a flaming mania or even a psychotic episode in a person who is in a depressed phase of bipolar illness. Tricyclics can also make a schizophrenic person more psychotic. Monoamine oxidase inhibitor antidepressants can cause anxiety, nervousness, agitation, insomnia, depression and/or euphoria, or full-blown mania.

Antipsychotics can create a host of mimickers, including mutism and catatonia, parkinsonism (symptoms similar to those seen in Parkinson's disease, page 100), tardive dyskinesia (page 36), extreme restlessness, and delirium. Woe to the patient whose psychiatrist thinks that the medication isn't working and prescribes more of the same.

When blood levels of lithium (prescribed for bipolar disorder and often for depression) get too high, inability to concentrate, depression, and sometimes delirium will result. At greatest risk are patients of doctors who do not carefully monitor blood levels. It is an uncommon reaction and therefore not easily recognized for what it is.

Benzodiazepine tranquilizers and sleeping pills, which include Valium, Librium, Xanax, Restoril, and just about all types that are prescribed these days, have been known to cause severe depression with suicidal thoughts, even psychosis. These medications will produce dependency over the long term; sudden withdrawal can bring on a host of psychiatric symptoms and invite misdiagnosis and inappropriate treatment.

Antabuse is prescribed for alcoholics to make them sick to their stomachs if they take a drink. Additional reactions have included anxiety, severe depression, successful suicide, manic psychoses, schizophrenia, and delirium. The doctor who is unaware either that the patient has taken this medication or that it can have these side effects risks exacerbating the symptoms by prescribing antipsychotics.

For more drugs prescribed by psychiatrists, see the sections that follow on anticonvulsants and barbiturates.

ANTIHYPERTENSIVE AGENTS

Many of the ingredients in medications prescribed for high blood pressure, particularly reserpine, are notorious for precipitating depression. Persons with a past history of depression are most vulnerable to a reserpine-induced depressive mimicker. Hank, 62, had the misfortune to fall into a deep depression a few months after his internist switched him to a blood pressure medication that contained reserpine. Hank, a wholesale shoe salesman, wasn't the kind of person to share these kinds of feelings, so he didn't tell his internist how rotten he was feeling. His wife finally convinced him to return to the psychiatrist he had seen when he'd become depressed several years before. He felt ashamed to return—he felt as if he'd failed. "How's your health, Hank?" inquired the doctor. "Fine," Hank replied. Hank didn't think to mention the blood pressure pills, and the psychiatrist did not inquire specifically about medications he was taking. He wrote a prescription for the same antidepressant which had worked for Hank the last time. It didn't work this time. Now Hank was positive he'd failed. The psychiatrist wanted to try a different medication, but Hank quit. He couldn't see the point of going to a psychiatrist if it didn't work. His depression continued. It was Hank's wife who came to see us. She said her husband was depressed but she couldn't get him to go to another psychiatrist. We asked if his depression had been medically evaluated, and she said no. It took her months to get Hank to make an appointment with us, but when he called he said he wanted a *physical* doctor.

You know the rest: the reserpine in his blood pressure pills. We called his internist and discussed changing to a different medication. For us this was a simple case. Not so for Hank, because of a series of errors and omissions by doctors and because of his own reticence to share his feelings. The internist did not ask about Hank's history of depression or inquire specifically about side effects while Hank was on the medication. The psychiatrist committed a serious, potentially life-threatening error in prescribing a drug without asking which other medications Hank was taking. He also made a false assumption that Hank's present depression was a recurrence of his last depression.

Alpha methyldopa, another antihypertensive agent, causes depression at high dosages. Other psychiatric side effects include sleep problems complete with bad dreams and nightmares and, rarely, psychosis. Clonidine occasionally will induce depression, nervousness, irritability, paranoia, and hypomania (a low-level mania). And propranolol (Inderal), besides occasional depression and sleep problems, has been known to cause sleep-related hallucinations.

CARDIOVASCULAR DRUGS

Mental symptoms may be the first and only signs of digitalis overdose. Digitalis toxicity is often confused with "intensive care unit psychosis," a syndrome resulting from the sensory deprivation of the intensive care unit environment, and usually treated psychiatrically. Death from heart failure, heart block, or cardiovascular collapse can be the result of this misdiagnosis and mistreatment. Monitoring of digitalis blood levels prevents overdose.

Psychosis is also a possibility with antiarrhythmics, such as lidocaine and procainamide, generally administered in an emergency setting.

DRUGS FOR ARTHRITIS
AND JOINT/MUSCLE PAIN

Nonsteroidal antiinflammatory analgesics constitute a relatively new class of drugs prescribed for joint diseases such as arthritis and bursitis and for sports injuries. The pills act much like aspirin to relieve pain, reduce swelling, and lower fever. Two related drugs in this category, Indocin and Clinoril, have been reported to cause psychiatric symptoms with only one dose. Indocin has caused anxiety, agitation, hostility, paranoia, depersonalization (feelings of unreality about oneself or the environment), hallucinations, and psychosis. For Clinoril the list includes bizarre behavior, obsessive talking, delusions, paranoia, combative behavior, irritability, depression, and homicidal threats.

GASTROINTESTINAL MEDICATION
Cimetidine (Tagamet) is widely prescribed for ulcers and other conditions marked by excessive gastrointestinal secretions. A wide spectrum of mental changes has been reported from cimetidine therapy, especially among alcoholics with liver damage, the elderly, and persons who are seriously ill. Symptoms range from mild to severe confusion, depression, agitation, hallucinations, peculiar speech, fluctuating levels of consciousness, and extreme paranoia.

ANTICONVULSANTS
Traditionally these medications are used to treat seizure disorders. Lately, however, some of the drugs in this category are proving helpful for persons with bipolar disorder who do not respond to lithium.

Phenytoin (Dilantin) has long been the drug of choice for seizure control. High blood levels will bring on symptoms that are easily confused with psychosis: delirium, hallucinations of all kinds, delusions. Carbamazepine (Tegretol), lately a psychiatric as well as a neurologic drug, has fewer mimicking effects but is not free of them.

BARBITURATES
Barbiturates have a wide range of uses. They are sedative-hypnotic drugs, inducing sedation or sleep. They are often ingredients in pain medication, such as Fiornal, prescribed for headaches. Some types of barbiturates, notably phenobarbital, are also used as anticonvulsants. Still others are included in antispasmodic medication. All types of barbiturates are addictive drugs of abuse.

Barbiturates are among the more challenging mimickers, since they tend to cause opposite psychiatric effects in adults and children. Adults suffer confusion, drowsiness, oversedation, and depression. Kids are more prone to excitement, irritability, tearfulness, aggression, and hyperactivity. Many of these effects will besiege those who are in withdrawal from a barbiturate, which can be addictive whether it is used to get high or to get better. Toxic or withdrawal reactions frequently are not recognized for what they are.

ANTIPARKINSON'S DRUGS
Parkinson's disease (page 100) is a top mimicker among the older set; so, too, are the drugs used to treat it. L-dopa has a 20 percent rate of psychiatric side effects, including confusion, delirium, depression, agitation or activation, psychosis, delusion or paranoia, hypomania, and hypersexuality. Bromocriptine, related to LSD, tends to encourage hallucinations, vivid dreams, mania, and paranoid delusions, symptoms which can be quite prolonged. (I might mention that I have recently begun to use bromocriptine very successfully in the treatment of cocaine addiction. Side effects are rare because the drug is taken at low dosage over a short period of time.)

CANCER CHEMOTHERAPY
If your Aunt Sylvia is depressed and she has cancer, everybody around her whispers, "Well, *of course* Aunt Sylvia's depressed. She's got *cancer.*" Her doctors also think her frame of mind is natural and understandable. They may be right, but they may not realize that the drugs they are giving her are making matters much worse. Even if Aunt Sylvia starts acting "crazy," the family may believe it is her way of dealing with it. Or they begin to pull away from her, believing her hopeless and near death.

Side effects of cancer chemotherapy are not limited to nausea and vomiting and hair loss. Psychiatric side effects are numerous. Chemical treatments for cancer can cause Aunt Sylvia to suffer depression and/or confusion, hallucinations, anxiety, agitation, delirium, and so on. Vinblastine, for example, produces depression and anxiety in 80 percent of patients within two to three days after treatment. Twenty percent of patients treated with hexamethylamine have had severe psychiatric side effects, including attempts at suicide.

State of mind is all-important in the struggle against cancer (indeed, against all disease). Aunt Sylvia can put up a fight if she realizes the depression and confusion, the bizarre behavior, aren't "her" or the deadly effects of the disease. The family too will be helped, relieved, able to remain close to her.

CORTICOSTEROIDS
Resembling hormones produced by the adrenal glands, corticosteroids can replace the natural hormones when the glands no longer

function adequately on their own. Because they are very powerful antiinflammatory drugs, corticosteroids are also useful in a wide variety of diseases and conditions. Lupus (page 87), asthma, hay fever, drug and transfusion reactions, skin rashes, psoriasis, eye inflammations, cancer . . . the list is endless. Patients are usually warned about the many physical side effects of these drugs. That they also have "head" manifestations comes as a terrible surprise—everything from depression to mania to schizophreniform psychoses (like schizophrenia but shorter in duration). These reactions occur in approximately 5 percent of persons taking the drugs.

A major corporation referred an employee to Dr. Irl Extein for hospitalization. The man was 50 and had already been in three general hospital psychiatric units for depression.

No contributing medical problems, concluded his internist.

Dependent personality, concluded his psychiatrist.

Hypoadrenal state, concluded Dr. Extein.

The man gave every appearance of DSM-III major depression: He felt worthless and hopeless, he had no interest in anything anymore, he cried a lot. Dr. Extein, a biopsychiatrist, did a depression workup, which included a standard measurement of the adrenal hormone cortisol at various times throughout the day. "The levels were extremely low," says Dr. Extein. "On careful review of this man's medical history, it was revealed for the first time that he had been treated with corticosteroid hormones for a gastrointestinal condition. This medication had been stopped just prior to the onset of his depression. In retrospect, the diagnosis was clear—his own adrenal glands had 'turned off' when he was prescribed corticosteroids and, as is sometimes the case, had not 'turned on' again. His depression was a result of his hypoadrenal state.

"The treatment was then clear also. He was prescribed corticosteroid replacement medication and within a few weeks his depression and apathy vanished. He did not require antidepressant medications. He returned happily to his family and to his job. Once more he was a productive employee."

OTHER Rx'S
Half of all women taking oral contraceptives experience varying degrees of depression, irritability, tiredness, reduced sex drive, and even reduced capacity for orgasm. . . . Certain general anesthesias can produce a month's worth of depression and other symptoms that are indistinguishable from the real thing. . . . Many of the drugs for

tuberculosis have a long list of psychiatric side effects. . . . Temporary psychosis could be the result of therapy with Chloroquine for malaria and skin problems, or quinacrine for intestinal parasites.

Over-the-Counter Medication

"The availability of approximately 100,000 over-the-counter drugs complicates the picture," writes Dr. Richard Hall and colleagues. "Adverse drug reactions to over-the-counter preparations occur more frequently than most people imagine. The elderly, children, patients with medical and psychiatric illness, and those using other prescribed or over-the-counter medications are the populations most at risk. Psychiatric complications may include nervousness, anxiety, depression, psychosis, or delirium."

The medical community now frowns upon doctors prescribing diet pills (amphetamines, also known as "speed"), which produce too many physical and mental side effects—including dependency and addiction, depression, and psychosis—to be worth the pounds. Reducing pills are easily obtained at the drugstore, however, complete with their share of problems. These pills contain stimulants that mimic both the effects and side effects of amphetamines.

In a personal communication Dr. Hall tells us about a 20-year-old college student who came to him because she was so anxious and depressed that she couldn't concentrate and would suddenly break into tears without any reason. She couldn't sleep, either, which always makes everything worse. She'd been in this state for about a month and a half. A couple of weeks before her symptoms had started, she had decided she needed to do something about those extra fifteen pounds, so she had bought some diet pills at her local drugstore. "Sometimes she took more than the manufacturer recommended on the label," Dr. Hall says. "The symptoms abated when the diet pills were discontinued."

Cold and cough preparations contain similar stimulant ingredients, plus antihistamines and nonnarcotic anti-cough chemicals. From these last two ingredients some people suffer tiredness, slowed or impaired judgment, central nervous system depression, possibly convulsions. According to Hall and colleagues, cough and cold remedies "are the most frequently used over-the-counter drugs."

And watch out for laxatives. Overuse of types that contain mercurous chloride (usually foreign brands) can lead to the tremor and dementia of mercury poisoning (see page 134). Anorexics and the elderly most frequently overdo laxatives.

Over-the-counter medications must list all ingredients on the label. Phenylpropanolamine, ephedrine, pseudoephedrine, and aminophylline are among the greatest offenders.

9

You Are What You Eat.
And Breathe.

YOUR BODY REQUIRES a basic environmental survival kit of food, water, air. It's fussy about this threesome, though. To thrive, it insists on a particular balance of ingredients in each category. All bodies will react to a gross deficiency of an essential ingredient or an overabundance of a potentially toxic material. The fine tuning, however, is individual. The amounts of nutrients required to be at your best are particular to you and no other. Similarly individual is the point at which a toxic substance in air, food, or water will affect you.

The brain is greedy and supersensitive. Over all other organs, its cells have first call on oxygen and energy-producing sugars. Deprive the brain of even small amounts of these and other nutrients, and it will often turn "psychiatric" on you. Introduce a toxin and it will often be the first organ to react.

Nutritional and toxic disorders are making a "comeback" in biopsychiatric circles. Diet, air, and water are changing, yielding new deficiencies, new pollutants. Of course these changes will affect us. Sometimes it seems as if the only thing that is not changing is our way of thinking about mental disturbance and nutrition.

Nutritional and toxic disorders will not be discovered without laboratory testing. Even so, deficiencies or excesses that are marginal or "subclinical" may not be considered significant, and your doctor may tell you your vague complaints are all in your mind. "Among doctors, the idea of a marginal nutrient deficiency has been about as prevalent as belief in a marginal broken leg," quipped one pundit. Thus, unless the index of suspicion is extremely high, as it might be if you work in an indoor garage, breathing carbon monoxide exhaust, nutritional and toxic mimickers will not be detected.

Certain populations are more vulnerable to mild nutritional and toxic mimickers. The elderly are the most susceptible and, as always, end up the victims of antiquated thinking. "I think it likely that in older people subclinical deficiencies can indeed lead to less-than-optimal mental performance," says Dr. James S. Goodwin.

Vitamins

"I asked my shrink whether he thought my depression might have something to do with a vitamin deficiency and he was dead silent," reports 36-year-old Linda F. " 'Well, I guess you don't think so,' " I sighed, feeling more depressed than when I'd walked in for my session. Then I couldn't think of anything else to say. Finally my shrink suggested that my inquiry about vitamins and my subsequent silence meant I was trying to avoid the 'real' work of the therapy."

Linda, in fact, turned out to have a deficiency of vitamin B6. With treatment, her longtime depression lifted substantially.

Some psychiatrists think that a patient's interest in a vitamin "cure" is yet another neurotic symptom. Others go the opposite route and believe that all mental problems result from nutritional deficiencies.

"The psychiatrist should . . . realize that there is tremendous lay interest in the role that vitamins play in mental disorders," says Dr. Frederick C. Goggans, addressing his psychiatric colleagues. "While there is no evidence that the use of vitamins in the therapy of patients without true deficiences is of value, absolute or relative deficiencies will never be discovered if patients are not tested."

Some vitamin deficiencies, particularly of the B vitamins, do indeed present psychiatrically. This should come as no surprise to a physician, since the B vitamins play an important role in brain metabolism. The deficiency is extremely common. Over half of 127 consecutive admissions to a British general hospital psychiatric unit, for example, were deficient in at least one B vitamin, a 1982 study found.

Treatment of vitamin deficiencies should result in reversal of psychiatric and neurologic symptoms. Failure to detect and treat them, however, may result in permanent damage and/or permanent psychiatric or neurologic disability.

VITAMIN B3 (NIACIN)
Pellagra, which earlier this century affected as many as 200,000 people, a third of whom died of the disease, is one of the great historical mimickers. In the South, as many as half the state mental hospital beds were occupied by demented pellagra victims. Pellagra is caused by a dietary deficiency of niacin, which was especially common in the South where many people existed on a diet of corn, fatback, and

molasses. After 1937, when the niacin factor was discovered, the vitamin was added to most commercial cereal products and pellagra disappeared. Besides dermatitis and gastrointestinal problems, pellagra victims suffered depression, intellectual impairment, psychosis, or dementia sufficient to send them to mental institutions. Niacin deficiencies and their attendant mental symptoms are now found principally among drug addicts, alcoholics, elderly persons, and some persons with liver disease. Anti-parkinsonian drugs also can reduce necessary niacin levels.

Agitation and anxiety as well as mental and physical slowing, depression included, are among the symptoms of developing deficiency. Niacin usually cures the condition rapidly, except in cases of longtime niacin dementia.

VITAMIN B12

Ms. A was 47 when she began to see UFOs. Then Jesus commanded her to board one of them. Her family thought she would be better off in a car heading for a hospital. The doctors who admitted her thought she looked older than she was. She was tired, sad, and reclusive. "Jesus has hold of my soul," she declared. "He'll come down in a cloud to take me to be his bride." She would burst out in laughter and just as suddenly be in tears.

Out of her mind or out of B12 (to paraphrase a popular magazine)? Ms. A, who had had no previous psychiatric history, was definitely out of B12. Monthly B12 injections sent the spaceship back to its home planet and returned Ms. A from organic psychosis to mental health.

B12 shortage ultimately leads to pernicious anemia. Anemia refers to a deficiency of red blood cells or of hemoglobin, which transports oxygen to body tissues. B12 is necessary for production of red blood cells in bone marrow. Intrinsic factor, an enzyme secreted in the stomach, allows the vitamin to be absorbed in the intestine. Pernicious anemia occurs most often because of an autoimmune deficiency of intrinsic factor. Stomach illnesses, thyroid disease, and certain drugs are among other causes. B12 is found most commonly in meat and animal protein foods; thus, "vegans" (vegetarians who eat neither eggs nor dairy products) are at risk for a dietary deficiency. So, too, are older persons.

The body stores B12 in the liver, generally building up a three- to five-year reserve. Symptoms develop as the stores are slowly used up, psychiatric and neurologic manifestations often long preceding the appearance of diagnosable anemia. Early diagnosis is crucial, however, for mental changes can become permanent. These include dementia, mood changes, paranoia, irritability, hallucinations, confusion, mania, etcetera. Physical symptoms of pernicious anemia include weakness, shortness of breath, heart palpitations, appetite loss, diarrhea, dizziness, burning of the tongue, and tingling sensations in the limbs. In addition, gait is often disturbed.

FOLIC ACID

Folic acid, or folate, is essential to hemoglobin production; deficiency also leads to anemia. But here, too, psychiatric symptoms commonly preexist a diagnosable anemia. A number of recent studies have shown that psychiatric patients have lower folic acid levels than normal subjects and that at least 20 percent of depressed inpatients with no anemia have abnormally low levels. Deficiency of the B vitamin was present in 67 percent of those in one psychiatric unit for geriatric patients. Still another study showed that folic acid treatment shortened hospital stays of patients with depression, schizophrenia, and organic psychosis.

Green leafy vegetables are the main source of folic acid, but cooking destroys more than half the available vitamin, making deficiency of this vitamin the most common overall. "In general, folate levels reflect the overall nutritional status of an individual," says Dr. Goggans.

A nutritionally inadequate diet, as in alcoholism (alcohol also interferes with metabolism of the vitamin), illness, poverty, poor eating habits, and many reducing diets, contributes to folic acid deficiency. In addition, barbiturates, aspirin, anticonvulsants, oral contraceptives, and other drugs interfere with its absorption into the body.

Fatigue and lassitude are early signs of folic acid deficiency. As the condition worsens, depression, burning feet, restless leg syndrome, and dementia are common. Deficiency during pregnancy increases the likelihood of premature delivery and of birth defects.

VITAMIN B6 (PYRIDOXINE)

Research strongly correlates B6 deficiency with depression in hospitalized patients or those taking part in depression treatment studies. As many as 20 percent of study subjects revealed a B6 deficiency without any physical symptoms, or with neurological symptoms such as tingling sensations in the limbs, numbness, and sensations reminiscent of electric shocks. B6 is important for blood, nervous system, and skin. Deficiency is yet another path to anemia. In children convulsions are a major consequence.

Vitamin B6 is present in most foods. Deficiency results from malabsorption diseases, certain drugs (including antihypertensive medication containing hydralazine, oral contraceptives containing estrogen, L-dopa, and MAO inhibitor antidepressant medications), and increased metabolism.

Caution: Vitamin B6 is damaging to sensory nerves at high doses.

VITAMIN B2 (RIBOFLAVIN)

Like vitamin B6, B2 is associated with depression in the absence of signs of malnutrition or other evidence of disease. A British study of 127 consecutive admissions to a psychiatric unit in a general hospital found B2 deficiency in 29 percent of patients, most of whom exhibited depressed symptoms.

Vitamin B2 is essential for growth and tissue function. In deficiency states, lips and mouth can become cracked and scaly, vulnerable to fungus infection. Skin around nose, ears, eyelids, and genitals becomes red, scaly, and greasy, producing a condition called "shark skin." The eyes, too, can become ulcerated and vision impaired.

Deficiency is common in the second trimester of pregnancy. Oral contraceptives reduce available vitamin levels.

VITAMIN B1 (THIAMINE)

Fatigue, irritation, memory problems, difficulty sleeping, chest pain, loss of appetite, abdominal miseries, and constipation—all symptoms of depression—mark the onset of vitamin B1 deficiency. Severe deficiency leads to beriberi, a now-uncommon nutritional illness. Cerebral beriberi, or Wernike-Korsakoff syndrome, characterized psychiatrically by anything from personality change to apathy to confusion, can be mistaken for severe depression. It is most common among chronic alcoholics. Korsakoff's psychosis resembles alcoholic DTs. Also at risk are pregnant and nursing mothers, who have an increased need for the vitamin, and persons who suffer frequent bouts of diarrhea.

Milder forms of B1 deficiency are more common, especially among alcoholics, drug addicts, schizophrenics, the elderly, the chronically ill, and persons existing on polished rice. Junk food consumers are also at risk. In one study, adolescents who ate a lot of junk food, carbonated sugary drinks, and candy showed symptoms of early beriberi.

Vitamin B1 is necessary for brain carbohydrate metabolism. Untreated, deficiency can lead to death. Treatment must begin early to reverse the condition completely.

VITAMIN C (ASCORBIC ACID)

Marginal deficiencies of vitamin C have been reported to influence mood and behavior. Severe deficiency leads to scurvy, in which depression, hypochondria, and hysteria are quite common.

Vitamin C is a busy vitamin. It participates in formation of connective tissue, collagen, and teeth, and it is necessary for wound healing and recovery from burns. In addition, it facilitates iron absorption and is involved in the actions of folic acid and amino acids phenylalanine and tyrosine (see below).

Oral contraceptives, tetracycline, aspirin, stress, pregnancy, lactation, aging, inflammatory diseases, surgery, and burns all increase the body's needs for vitamin C. If the increased requirement is not met, deficiency will occur, as it will in a nutritionally poor diet.

In true mimicker fashion, tiredness, weakness, apathy, weight loss, vague pains, and depression appear three to twelve months before scurvy shows up. Finally, sores will begin to appear, often containing coiled hairs, on the buttocks, thighs, and calves especially. Gums swell and bleed, teeth loosen, and wounds fail to heal.

Amino Acids

All body substances, neurotransmitters included, consist of proteins, which are made of complex molecules called amino acids. The body can produce some of its own amino acid building blocks, but others must come from food. Technically, then, each of these dietary amino acids is a vitamin, which is defined as "a general term for a number of unrelated organic substances that occur in many foods in small amounts and that are necessary in trace amounts for the normal metabolic functioning of the body" in *Dorland's Illustrated Medical Dictionary.*

Does a deficiency of dietary amino acids mimic depression? As Dr. Goggans puts it: "Although it is inherently obvious that availability of the substances in the diet and their presence in blood and brain would be important in the evaluation of mood states, appreciation of their roles and the clinical investigation of such issues as prevalence of amino acid deficiencies in major affective disorder patients and their role as therapeutic agents have only just begun."

Neurotransmitters are manufactured (synthesized) in the brain from substances called "precursors" in the presence of enzymes. The amino acid tryptophan is a precursor of the neurotransmitter serotonin; serotonin levels are low in some depressed people (see Chapter

18). Tyrosine, another amino acid, is a precursor of both norepinephrine and dopamine, both of which are known to be involved in mood; dopamine may play a major role in schizophrenia. Phenylalanine is yet another critical amino acid. All three must be obtained through diet.

Amino-acid replacement therapy for apparent deficiency states is not as easy as it may sound. Ingesting a high-protein meal or the pure amino acid itself does not insure that it will arrive in the brain in the required amount. Some researchers believe that the ratio of desired precursor to other amino acids is all-important. Following a high-protein meal, amino acids will compete with each other to penetrate the blood-brain barrier. A high-carbohydrate, low-protein meal apparently increases brain tryptophan levels by causing insulin secretion, which in turn lowers levels of serotonin's amino acid competitors. But ingesting large amounts of tryptophan is likely to inhibit tyrosine uptake. Phenylalanine may not be metabolized without the addition of vitamin B6. But B6 can be toxic at high levels, and phenylalanine can trigger hypomania.

While this is a promising research area, obviously we know all too little about amino-acid replacement therapy. The good news, however, is that psychiatry is beginning to take seriously the complex interrelationships of food, mood, and behavior. In the past a therapist might have attributed a patient's craving for sweets to a "symbolic feeding of the self by a defeated and depleted psyche," explains John W. Crayton, MD. Today the practitioner might also consider "the effects of carbohydrate loading on brain neurotransmitter metabolism," says psychiatrist Crayton. "Increasing the proportion of carbohydrate in the diet tends to increase the amount of tryptophan entering the brain and consequently raises the amount of serotonin available for neurotransmission." Since some depressed persons reveal a low level of serotonin, "the carbohydrate craver could be attempting to raise serotonin levels via this mechanism. Evidence that central serotonin levels can influence the proportions of carbohydrate and protein selected in the diet support this notion," he reports.

Amino acids hold the most promise as supplements to standard depression treatments, about which more in Chapter 21.

Metals

Although your mother never said, "Eat your metals, dear," she probably did have a few words about all that spinach on your plate. Spinach is a source of iron, one of many metals essential to health. Essential metals, usually called minerals, include: sodium, magnesium, potassium, calcium, vanadium, chromium, manganese, iron, cobalt, copper, zinc, molybdenum, nickel, strontium, and selenium. Most of the essential metals are necessary to the functioning of enzymes, which in turn are essential to metabolic processes throughout the body. When you don't get enough of the essential metals, either because of diet or inability to metabolize them properly, deficiency diseases result. But you can also get too much of a good thing and that spells toxicity —in a word, poisoning.

TOXIC MIMICKERS

Toxin	Major Depression	Manic-depression
Magnesium	+	
Hypocalcemia	+	
Hypercalcemia	+	
Zinc	+	
Manganese	+	
Lead	+	
Mercury	+	+
Thalium	+	
Bismuth	+	
Aluminum		
Lithium		
Arsenic	+	
Bromides	+	
Organophosphates	+	

"Metals are ubiquitous in our environment," notes Neil Edwards, MD. "Of the naturally occurring elements, 69 are metals." While we may require fifteen of them, we come in contact with many more. Since 5,000 B.C. we have learned to use them with increasing sophistication: in tools, shelter, medicines, fuels, jewelry, structural materials, makeup, hair spray, herbicides, kitchen cleansers, insecticides. . . . Overdoing our contact with many nonessential metals turns out not to be so good for us, especially when we eat or breathe them. Lead, mercury, and radioactive metals, not to mention the favorite poison of a good old whodunit, arsenic, can wreak havoc.

Psychiatric complications of essential or nonessential metal deficiency or toxicity, even at low levels, are many. The brain is quicker to react than the rest of the body; thus mental and behavioral symptoms may outweigh organic signs. The result is the usual mimicker story: inappropriate psychiatric treatment or incarceration. We'll look at the most common of these metal mimickers.

Essential Metals

SODIUM

Hyponatremia is the term used to indicate a decrease in sodium (salt) concentration in body water. Usually it represents an increase in body water rather than a decrease in sodium. "Hyponatremia has been associated with numerous psychiatric conditions," says Dr. Goggans. "To some extent symptoms depend on the speed with which hyponatremia develops." When it comes on suddenly, agitated delirium or psychosis often result. In chronic, slowly developing states, however, depression and/or dementia are more likely.

Overdoing diuretic medication, which causes the kidneys to excrete water by removing too much salt from the system, can induce hyponatremia. If you are taking "water pills," be sure to follow your doctor's directions. Call your doctor if you start to feel weird or moody in relation to the medication. Other causes of hyponatremia include: vomiting, diarrhea, porphyria, kidney, adrenal, pituitary, thyroid, brain, lung, heart, or liver diseases. For more information on hyponatremia, see Chapter 10.

POTASSIUM

Diuretics are also a common cause of potassium deficiency, or hypokalemia. Depression is the primary mental manifestation. Reduced potassium slows the whole body, to the point of paralysis and respiratory failure. When the potassium level falls far enough, the heart will lose its rhythm and stop. Hypokalemia "is well known to be the most frequent cause of sudden death" in anorexics and bulimics, "usually because of a hypokalemia-induced cardiac dysrhythmia," reports Dr. Goggans. Persons with these eating disorders deplete themselves of potassium through vomiting and abusing laxatives and diuretics.

IRON

Iron deficiency is on the increase worldwide, possibly because of the increase of refined foods and the decrease in iron cookware. One study indicates that perhaps half of all premenopausal women and a third of all children do not receive enough iron. Athletes—runners in particular—apparently are prone to low-level iron deficiency.

American Health magazine published the "case" of world-class marathoner Alberto Salazar, who suddenly began to run poorly under even the best of conditions. After one race "he poured out his frustrations about his physical state on national television," reported article author Paul Perry. "He hadn't slept well in more than a year," he said. He was listless, irritable, and depressed. Canadian sports medicine specialist Doug Clement, MD, suggested a special diagnostic test to Salazar's coach, and sure enough, he was deficient in iron. He began to take a supplement, and "within two months he ran his second best time ever. . . ."

Doctors often wait for anemia to appear before they will diagnose iron deficiency. In iron-deficiency anemia, the body forms too few red blood cells and tissues end up deprived of oxygen. It may progress from weakness, tiredness, loss of stamina, dizziness, ringing in the ears, irritability, and strange behavior to cessation of menstrual periods, loss of sex drive, congestive heart failure, and shock. Some persons with iron-deficiency anemia crave dirt, paint, or ice. Blood loss is a major cause.

Symptoms of marginal deficiency include depression, fatigue, irritability, reduced attention span, poor work performance, and possibly sleep disturbance. It can be caused by iron-poor diet, heavy exercise (World War II troops became deficient in iron after long marches), insufficient vitamin C, increased nutritional demands (as in pregnancy and adolescence), malabsorption diseases, and menstruation, in addition to the causes mentioned above.

Too much iron, however, can lead to toxicity. Iron poisoning occurs in conjunction with a genetic condition (hemachromatosis) in which iron is overabsorbed, or with various diseases such as alcoholic cirrhosis or diabetes. Taking iron supplements can quickly lead to vomiting, upper abdominal pain, diarrhea, drowsiness, and shock. Hemachromatosis generally develops slowly, however. Skin color turns bronze, cardiac symptoms develop, sex drive is lost, and behavior changes occur. Hemachromatosis usually develops after the age of 50.

Iron poisoning can happen to anyone, however, from overdoing dietary supplements. In children, particularly, iron poisoning from multivitamins usually results in death.

CALCIUM

Depression is the rule in calcium toxicity—which does not mean that a doctor will automatically check a depressed patient's calcium level. Jerry G. was a cranky guy in his mid-seventies who had been depressed on and off for years. He had refused psychiatric help, saying it was nobody's business what went on in his mind. After his wife Frances died from cancer shortly after they moved to a retirement community in the Southwest, Jerry's condition worsened, mentally and physically. He was sure everybody was against him. His blood pressure zoomed, he had digestive problems, and finally he even had triple bypass surgery. Although his recovery was complete, he was frightened of an imminent heart attack or stroke. He would go from doctor to doctor, all of whom quickly tired of his anxieties.

When Jerry's depression worsened suddenly and severely, nobody thought too much about it. Even his children, who tended to be kind and sensitive to him, shrugged it off with: "What do you expect at his age, with Mom gone?" Jerry couldn't sleep, yet he barely had the energy to get up. When he went out of the house he became panicky. He worried continually. He was afraid of dying, but he talked of suicide. He began to lose weight because he couldn't eat; he couldn't keep food down. His regular doctor assured him he was okay; he should "get out more and make some friends." The doctor shooed him off to the nurse, who took his blood pressure and told him to come back in two months.

Finally he went to a doctor with whom he had no history. This time the doctor hospitalized Jerry for testing. Jerry's calcium level was "almost off the charts," as the gastroenterologist put it. Jerry was suffering from two diseases: parathyroid tumors and acute, severe pancreatitis. The parathyroid hormone helps control the body's calcium (see Chapter 10). In Jerry's case the tumors caused oversecretion of the hormone, which in turn increased the concentration of calcium in his blood. The doctors believed that the long-undiagnosed hyperparathyroid condition had led to an accumulation of calcium in Jerry's pancreas, poisoning the digestive organ. Two months after a doctor finally paid attention to Jerry's symptoms, he was dead from complications of the pancreatic illness.

The body is acutely sensitive to changes in calcium. The brain cells will not function normally in the presence of too much of the essential metal. Psychiatric symptoms—typical depressive symptoms plus possible personality change, disorientation, delusions, hallucinations—parallel calcium levels. It is possible that Jerry's "usual" depression was related to calcium, since the parathyroid condition develops slowly over decades.

Depression also occurs in calcium deficiency. Other psychiatric symptoms run the gamut from anxiety, tiredness, weakness, and irritability to psychosis. Deficiency sometimes results from vitamin D deficiency, more often from disease, including kidney failure, hypoparathyroidism, intestinal malabsorption, magnesium deficiency, leukemia, and fluoride intoxication. Here, too, the psychiatric symptoms may long predate the appearance of the organic condition.

Many women have begun to take calcium supplements to prevent osteoporosis, the much-publicized bone-weakening to which they are subject with advancing age. The best way to increase calcium is to eat more milk products and vegetables. Supplements can provoke kidney stones in vulnerable individuals.

MAGNESIUM

Deficiency of magnesium can result from numerous causes, among them inadequate diet, kidney disease, chronic alcoholism, parathyroid disease, and impairment of the intestines, through which magnesium is absorbed into the body. Lactating mothers have an increased need for magnesium and can become deficient by not adding more to their diet. Premature infants tend to suffer from it as do normal-term babies of mothers with diabetes mellitus.

Psychiatric symptoms of magnesium deficiency not only may be the first to appear, but may continue after the others disappear. These include depression, agitation, disorientation, confusion, anxiety, and hallucinations. Patients suffering from the deficiency are irritable and uncooperative, behavior which can lead internists to make a too-hasty referral to a psychiatrist.

Persons with poor kidney function are most prone to magnesium toxicity because healthy kidneys usually clear it from the body fairly rapidly. Generally the poisoning is associated with medical use of magnesium sulfate, which may be given intravenously for high blood pressure or convulsions, or by mouth as a cathartic or antacid. The toxicity results in lassitude, depression, and changes in perception, attention, intellectual function, and personality.

ZINC

More than fifty enzymes need zinc in order to function properly. Thus, zinc deficiency can lead to a number of disorders and difficulties, including loss of appetite, taste, and smell, compromised immune-system functioning, mental slowing, irritability, emotional disorders, impaired healing, and rough skin. Zinc-deficiency depression is seen particularly among the elderly; their complaints about appetite and taste often confirm an erroneous psychiatric diagnosis. Consequences for children include retarded growth, possibly even mental retardation and learning disabilities. Experiments with pregnant monkeys suggest the possibility that even slight zinc deficiencies can seriously affect the health of pregnant women.

Diets high in whole grains (which bind zinc), intestinal malabsorption disorders, many infectious conditions, anemias, diabetes, cirrhosis, dialysis, anorexia, and many other conditions—including, of course, a diet poor in zinc—can all result in zinc deficiency.

MANGANESE

Manic excitement, incoherent speech, depression, irritability, insomnia, refusal of food, spontaneous laughing and crying—these are the symptoms of "manganese madness," and they occur in people who work in manganese mines, steel foundries, and ore-crushing plants, and in anyone who inhales manganese dust regularly. Prolonged exposure leads eventually to symptoms similar to Wilson's (page 138) or Parkinson's (page 100) disease, although once again mental manifestations come first.

To Supplement or Not to Supplement?

All the vitamins, amino acids, and metals we have discussed are available from drugstores, health food stores, or from vitamin suppliers. Self-treating a depression with one or more of them makes little sense, however. Unless a biopsychiatrist diagnoses your depression as a nutritional mimicker, you cannot know whether your problem is lurking in your diet. Neither can you know which substance to take or how much, which only laboratory testing can reveal. The body depends on a balance of nutrients, which can be dangerously altered by adjusting intake of one. The megadoses often recommended by the "expert" behind the counter can be toxic. Taking large doses of amino acids, for example, can lead to "marked food intake suppression, massive tissue damage, and death," warns a recent article in the *Annual Review of Nutrition.* Furthermore, dosing yourself with vitamins, minerals, and amino acids will only confound your diagnosis when you are finally ready to go get one.

You're better off joining a health club. As you will see in Chapter

22, there are a number of ways for you to treat your own depression, but do-it-yourself treatment is not one of them. The best way to be sure you're getting the nutrition you need for your head is to eat a balanced diet.

Nonessential Metals

Since these metals are not essential, you cannot be deficient in them. You can get too much, though—sometimes all too easily. Toxic states result from excessive exposure to all of the following metals.

LEAD

Lead poisoning causes a biochemical malfunction similar to porphyria (see page 137), complete with its wide range of psychiatric manifestations. In children, lead poisoning leads to mental retardation in 25 percent of all cases. Most common are hyperactivity and lower intellectual functioning. Cautions Dr. Neil Edwards, "It would behoove the careful clinician dealing with children who are hyperactive, learning disabled, retarded, or even autistic to obtain a careful history for possible lead exposure" and to take the appropriate tests.

Adults exposed to lead often exhibit depression and cognitive and behavioral changes, even at low levels of toxicity. Indications of high-dose lead poisoning can be abdominal cramps, "dropping" of wrists and ankles and other peripheral nerve disorders, personality changes, metallic taste, headache, vomiting, constipation.

The symptoms of lead poisoning in adults and children can develop slowly or suddenly, often recurring long after the toxicity has been treated, since lead is stored in bone tissue.

Lead is so much a part of our environment that sources of poisoning are numerous. A partial list includes: paint peelings from lead-based paints in old homes (common source among young children, who put the peels in their mouths and swallow them), water that has been standing in lead pipes, solder and lead-emitting smelter fumes, automobile exhaust from old cars using leaded gas, "moonshine" whiskey made in lead stills, burning lead-painted wood or battery casings, and ceramic-ware (usually homemade) that has been improperly lead-glazed.

If you work in the manufacture of ammunition, pipes, brass, bronze, solder cables, lead shielding, pigments, chemicals, or processed metals, you are at risk for low-level lead poisoning.

MERCURY

Do you know anyone who is mad as a hatter? Then your friend must be suffering from mercury poisoning. The expression probably comes from the behavior of English felt-hat makers in the last century, who were exposed to mercury vapor in their work. They suffered severe depression with retarded (slowed) movement, severe irritability, a profound fear of strangers (xenophobia), and such embarrassment and self-consciousness that they could no longer function under direct supervision. Then as now, mercury poisoning progresses to a permanent dementia if the source of exposure is not discovered and avoided. Children with mercury poisoning may appear to have learning disabilities.

Besides mercury vapor, poisoning can occur from mercury dental fillings, douches, skin creams, diuretics, and laxatives containing mercury, and food and water contamination resulting from industrial wastes.

ARSENIC

Arsenic is an ingredient in insecticides, herbicides, rat poisons, antibiotic preparations for amebic infections, and detective novels. Arsenic is a convenient way to kill off characters in a murder mystery, for the poison causes death within hours if ingested in large quantities, or illness and a rather dramatic madness followed by death when exposure occurs over a longer term. Arsenic poisoning generally begins with a feeling of burning in the throat followed by gastrointestinal symptoms. Psychiatric symptoms of arsenic poisoning can include depression, anorexia, lassitude, confusion, disorientation, crying, agitation, paranoia, visual hallucinations.

If you are inexplicably losing your hair, if your skin is thickening and becoming darker, if you find a white line running across your fingernails, and if you are suffering from any or all of the above symptoms, surely it's a case for Agatha Christie.

BISMUTH

Most cases of bismuth poisoning go unrecognized in this country. Worldwide, bismuth is most often used in oral gastrointestinal preparations, including some laxatives, chronic ingestion of which can lead to toxicity. In the United States, skin-lightening creams, unbeknown to most doctors, are the major culprit; bismuth, which can be absorbed into the body through the skin, is a major ingredient in these preparations.

Psychiatric symptoms predominate in the first phase of toxicity. Depression, anxiety, loss of interest, slowed thinking, antisocial behavior, delusions, and hallucinations mark this phase. Often they come and go, just like a psychiatric condition. Complete mental confusion, tremor, and involuntary behavior (walking, standing, speaking) typify later stages. Death can follow.

Correct diagnosis is simple—measure bismuth levels in blood and urine. That is, if it occurs to the treating psychiatrist to take some tests.

ALUMINUM

The principal population for aluminum poisoning are persons undergoing kidney dialysis. In one study, 86 percent of all dialysis patients eventually developed psychiatric symptoms which were misdiagnosed as major depression and mistreated with antidepressants. Dialysis dementia is characterized by progressive mental deterioration. Behavioral changes range from severe depression to memory problems to hallucinations. Reducing aluminum levels in dialysis fluids will prevent the disorder. Continued exposure will lead to coma and death.

BROMIDES—A LITERARY CASE HISTORY

Bromides used to be popular as sedative-hypnotics and anticonvulsants. They were a major mimicker of their day, accounting for 21 percent of all psychiatric admissions in 1927. Since supplanted by our modern drug armamentarium, bromide toxicity accounts for a tiny percentage of mimickers today.

The late British author Evelyn Waugh had used bromides for sleep for ten years prior to his breakdown in 1954. His psychotic collapse was actually a case of bromide poisoning. In his 1957 novel *The Ordeal of Gilbert Pinfold,* Waugh details this experience through the fictional Pinfold.

Pinfold, like Waugh at this period, is an ill-humored, cranky writer who becomes depressed and can no longer write or sleep. Convinced he requires a stronger dose of his medication, he talks his pharmacist into not diluting his bromides, "diluting" them himself with alcohol. Soon Pinfold begins to suffer from bromide poisoning. Waugh describes Pinfold's bromide toxicity as skin blotches, memory lapses, inability to spell, aches and pains, clumsiness, and irritability with his wife. A doctor misdiagnoses his condition as an allergy to an unidentified substance. Advice is to escape the allergen. Pinfold books passage for Ceylon. On board ship he becomes at first delirious, then quickly psychotic, convinced he is involved in an international conspiracy. He hears voices, one of which falls in love with him. Pinfold prepares for an affair. When nothing happens, voices accuse him of impotence.

In his confusion Pinfold has not packed enough bromide, and his supply runs out on the second day. Instead, he takes pills and alcohol. The psychosis continues, interspersed with periods of lucidity as he now goes into withdrawal from his long habit. He returns to London within a month and gradually recovers. The family doctor, who now knows of the bromide use, says, "It sounds like a perfectly simple case of poisoning to me." But the way Pinfold looks at it, ". . . he had endured a great ordeal and unaided, had emerged the victor." When Waugh himself returned from his own journey, a psychiatrist correctly diagnosed his breakdown for what it was.

Environmental Poisons

These are the poisons that "progress" has created. Does a day go by without a report of toxic waste pollution or disaster from chemical fumes? Environmental poisoning need not come from an exotic source, however. The exhaust from any car will do.

CARBON MONOXIDE
Virtually all of us are exposed daily to this colorless, odorless gas. It is a component of automobile exhaust, tobacco smoke, and burning wood, coal, and charcoal, to name a few. Poisoning will occur after prolonged exposure. A faulty automobile exhaust system or fireplace chimney, or a job in a parking garage will do it. Running a car engine in an enclosed space and breathing the fumes will do it unto death.

Carbon monoxide "steals" oxygen from the body. The brain is the organ most immediately sensitive to this oxygen starvation; psychiatric and neurological symptoms are the rule. The symptoms are so unpredictable, however, that carbon monoxide poisoning has been misdiagnosed as hysterical psychosis, borderline personality, schizophrenia, psychotic depression, catatonia, and hysteria. Poisoning must be treated to avoid permanent brain and heart damage.

ORGANOPHOSPHATE INSECTICIDES
Organophosphate insecticides act the same as nerve gases used in chemical warfare; they inhibit acetylcholinesterase, an essential brain enzyme. Chronic exposure results in irritability, tension, anxiety, jitteriness, restlessness, giddiness, emotional withdrawal, depression,

drowsiness, decreased concentration, confusion, and bizarre dreams. Atropine, administered intravenously, usually reverses the condition.

VOLATILE SUBSTANCES
Painters, refinery workers, and persons who work with fuel for many years are at risk of personality change, depression, fatigue, lowered intellectual capacity, irritability, panic disorder symptoms—the works.

Children and adolescents who sniff glue, toluene (a solvent), gasoline, cleaning fluid, and nitrous oxide ("laughing gas") are also in for it, and not just from their parents. After the euphoria come hallucinations and what we psychiatrists call "conduct-disordered behavior." These resulting behavior patterns are usually considered part of the "badness" that led to the drug abuse rather than the brain's organic response to poison. Most of the toxic effects disappear with removal of the substance.

Metabolic Diseases

All the chemical reactions that release energy from food and that convert food into more complex chemical compounds equal the process of metabolism, which takes place in every cell. Some individuals are born with chemical defects that affect this highly complex, essential functioning.

ACUTE INTERMITTENT PORPHYRIA
This is one of a rare group of diseases caused by an inherited defect in the enzymes that produce a constituent of blood. A speaker at the 1985 annual meeting of the American Association for the Advancement of Science suggested that early victims of these diseases could have inspired the myths of werewolves and vampires, because sufferers used to ingest blood to right this defect. Acute intermittent porphyria affects the nervous system and is more common among women. It can exist in a latent form with no physical symptoms. Attacks, however, can be precipitated by various drugs, alcohol, crash diets, or simply reduced intake of carbohydrates; pregnancy, menstruation, or oral contraceptives; and infection.

Since the disease can affect any part of the nervous system, symptoms can include nausea and vomiting or constipation, muscular weakness, loss of vision, paralysis, and/or psychiatric problems. These last run the gamut of virtually everything a psychiatrist has ever seen or studied, including neuroses, hysteria, organic brain syndrome, psychosis, conversion disorder, and depression, which is most common between attacks.

A screening of 2,500 psychiatric patients discovered the presence of the disease in thirty-five patients, a 1.5 percent incidence.

Acute intermittent porphyria can often be controlled by a high-sugar diet or by injections of a blood product. Although it is not a psychiatric disease, phenothiazine medication, ordinarily prescribed for psychosis, may be helpful in controlling pain and psychiatric symptoms.

Avoidance of stressors that provoke attacks is the best approach. Obviously, among women this is not always possible. Neither is it possible when a psychiatrist misdiagnoses a patient with the disease and prescribes medication that will promptly precipitate an attack.

WILSON'S DISEASE

Another rare, inherited disorder, Wilson's disease is caused by an error in copper metabolism that results in copper accumulation in body tissues. Symptoms begin to occur early in life, between the ages of 6 and 20, when binding sites in the liver become saturated with copper. Some Wilson's patients suffer liver disease at this point, which can lead to liver failure. About half of patients develop a golden-brown or gray-green ring around the corneas of their eyes. Eventually in many patients copper will begin to destroy nerve cells, causing tremor, peculiar movements and rigidity, personality changes, and dementia. None but psychiatric symptoms may be present, however, and more Wilson's sufferers are initially sent to psychiatrists than to pediatricians or other physicians. Wilson's symptoms can mimic mania, depression, schizophrenia, schizoaffective disorder, hysteria, conversion disorders, anxiety, confusional state, neurosis, hyperactivity, and school phobia.

Wilson's disease is reversible if it is properly diagnosed when symptoms first begin. Certain death follows on the heels of misdiagnosis.

AN APPLE A DAY

Biopsychiatrist A. James Giannini, not one to fall for a mimicker, recently "solved" a one-of-a-kind metabolic deficiency case.

His patient, a supermarket owner in his early thirties, had emigrated from Greece four years earlier. Every September since his arrival he would suffer disabling depression with anxiety. Every December it would lift. "During this time he had the changes in mood, appetite, sex drive, energy levels, and confidence characteristic of a biological depression," Dr. Giannini tells us. Psychiatrists had dosed him with antidepressants to no effect. Dr. Giannini gave him a battery of biopsychiatric and psychological tests. Negative. "Finally," says Dr. Giannini, "in the manner of a fishing expedition we gave him virtually every test available. His only abnormality was a deficiency of the enzyme G-6-P-D.

"Levels of the enzyme G-6-P-D are frequently lower in Southern Europeans," he explains. "Usually this causes no problem, unless the reduced level of enzyme is overloaded with salicylates. Salicylates are found in aspirin, wintergreen, and most importantly in this case . . . apples."

"This patient rarely ate apples on his Greek isle of birth. Here in Ohio, however, apples are abundant. During the autumn season the excess apple crop is pressed into cider. This patient, who acquired a passion for apple cider, drank several quarts daily throughout the entire cider season—which lasts from September until mid-December.

"When the apples and apple cider were discontinued, the depression lifted." Dr. Giannini is happy to report that his patient has been without cider, and without symptoms, for two years.

Case closed.

10

Hormones

WE DECIDED A FEW years ago to expand our Fair Oaks outpatient evaluations team. We knew it would not be easy to find a psychiatrist with the qualifications we require: excellence in psychiatry combined with a strong medical background. The man we ultimately decided on had terrific medical and psychiatric training. But he was young and brash, convinced that already he had seen everything.

"All this testing is bogus," he declared. "None of the patients are going to be sick."

I smiled—how many times had I heard *that* before? "Do me a favor," I said. "Just work up fifty patients in a row my way. Then write a paper on your results, whatever they are. If the patients turn out to be physically healthy, fine. Then you can go ahead and 'expose' me."

It was his turn to smile. "A deal!" he said.

His paper appeared in the *Journal of the American Medical Association.* It was about the misdiagnosis of thyroid disease.

"If you don't take a temperature, you won't find the fever," the saying goes. Had this young doctor not performed the necessary workup, he never would have discovered that *early thyroid failure is the most common medical condition to mimic depression.* Furthermore, the endocrine system as a whole, of which the thyroid is one small part, is the organ system most commonly associated with psychiatric symptoms. As many as one third of misdiagnosed patients will have one or another endocrine mimicker (including diabetes), with underactive thyroid being the most frequent.

ENDOCRINE MIMICKERS

Disease	Major Depression	Manic-depression
Hypothyroid	+	+
Hyperthyroid	+	+
Hypoglycemia	+	
Cushing's disease	+	+
Addison's disease	+	
Hyperparathyroidism	+	
Hypoparathyroidism	+	
Pheochromocytoma	+	
Carcinoid	+	+
Ovarian failure	+	
Testicular failure	+	
Panhypopituitarism	+	+

A Crash Course in Neuroendocrinology

Endocrine glands are found throughout the body. The thyroid is located in the neck, where it is surrounded by the parathyroid glands. The thymus gland is below the neck. The islets of Langerhans are situated on the pancreas, which is the digestive organ found behind the stomach. The adrenals sit atop the kidneys. Our sex organs, the ovaries and testes, are also endocrine glands. The brain, too, has its endocrine glands—the pituitary, the hypothalamus, and the pineal. These are the "traditional" endocrine glands. We are discovering, however, pockets of cells which act like endocrine glands throughout the body.

HORMONES

All endocrine glands secrete hormones into the blood. Hormones are the body's chemical regulators. Growth and development, reproduction, response to stress, sexual activity, energy, heart rate, blood pressure, body temperature, appetite—all are mediated by hormones. Hormones work to keep the body in a state of balance, or *homeostasis.* If your electrolyte balance is off, for example, the adrenal cortex will secrete aldosterone to increase sodium and decrease potassium and make sure that the body's electrical transmission system can continue uninterrupted.

The endocrine system as a whole functions remarkably like an extension of the nervous system, to communicate with organs and tissues throughout the body and to control their functioning. The differences between the two are that the endocrine system is slower to respond than are nerves, and its effects are longer lasting. Also, it relies on the nerves in the sense organs to tell it what is happening outside the body. The electrochemical nerve impulses triggered by the sight of a bull charging at you are immediate but brief. Nerves communicate the news to the endocrine system, which takes over to direct the response. The pituitary gland will begin to secrete one of its hormones (ACTH) into the blood. When the circulating blood reaches the adrenals, the ACTH "tells" the cortex to secrete cortisol, which helps to stimulate the adrenal medulla to secrete epinephrine (adrenaline) and norepinephrine, its stress hormones. Only now will the "fight or flight" reaction begin; your heart will start pounding, your legs will take you to the nearest tree, and your arms will help pull you up, even though you may never have climbed a tree in your life.

GLANDS IN THE BRAIN

Like the nervous system, too, the endocrine system has a control center, or centers, in the brain which direct their activity. The pituitary gland has long been called the "master gland," because its hormones initiate the secretions of other glands. However, it is the hypothalamus that directs the pituitary.

The pea-sized hypothalamus has been called "the 'brain' of the brain." It has connections to nearly all parts of the brain. Its responsibilities are awesome indeed: to regulate sleep, waking, heart rate, body temperature, hormones, hunger, thirst, sex, and emotions. Keeping them all in balance—particularly that last item—is some chore. No wonder the hypothalamus, and the limbic system of the brain of which it and the pituitary are a part, are of major interest to psychiatry today. Limbic system structures are also involved in learning and long-term memory, creative thinking, decision making, behavioral control. Some psychiatrists believe that mental illness originates right here.

Depression, whether primary or secondary, appears to be a hypothalamic/limbic phenomenon. Look back at the DSM-III symptoms of depression (page 50) and you will see that they refer to functions regulated in this part of the brain.

MIND-BRAIN-BODY BOND

The more we can see into the brain, the more we are discovering just how interconnected are the nervous system and the endocrine system. Here are just a few of the many extraordinary ways in which they interlock and interact:

- The brain's all-important neurotransmitters, those chemicals that carry nerve messages across the gaps (synapses) between neurons (nerve cells), are identical to some hormones. For instance, epinephrine and norepinephrine are adrenal hormones. They are also brain neurotransmitters, playing an important role in the genesis of depression.
- The neurotransmitters, that regulate the hypothalamus, which in turn regulates the endocrine glands, are the same as those that regulate moods.
- Thyroid hormone as well as neurotransmitters norepinephrine and dopamine are all made from the same amino acid, tyrosine.
- The brain is itself a target organ for endocrine hormones. Thyroid hormones, for example, set the tone of receptors for mood-message neurotransmitters. After a drop in thyroid hormone, receptors become "deaf" to messages of good cheer.
- In earlier chapters we referred to the new diagnostic tests for the existence of biological depression. All of them test particular functions of what we have come to call the *neuroendocrine* system, for the great majority of persons with biological depressions demonstrate a variety of brain-endocrine abnormalities.

The endocrine system, then, is as powerfully involved in what depression *isn't* as in what depression *is*. We will investigate more of this intriguing organ system in depth as we move, in the next chapter, from the mimickers to true depression.

The Diagnosis Dilemma

"Since the endocrine system and the nervous system are intimately linked, it is often difficult to distinguish cause from effect," says Dr. Arthur J. Prange, Jr. "In depression, for example, one usually assumes that mental changes cause endocrine changes; in certain endocrinopathies [disorders of endocrine glands], depressive changes or other mental aberrations are usually seen as results."

Little wonder that the psychiatrist or internist who does not test depressed patients confuses these relationships utterly.

But testing itself is not enough. The physician must know which tests to perform, and how to interpret their results.

When an endocrine gland malfunctions, it secretes too little or too much hormone, or it stops secreting altogether and/or responding to "command" hormones. Because of the interrelationship of the brain and the endocrine system with its hormones, mental symptoms will occur far earlier than bodily symptoms of gland disease. Even the smallest alterations in hormonal secretions can upset the chemical balance the brain requires. Traditional endocrinology, however, still relies on a concept of disease that waits for physical pathology to appear. Also, many of the diagnostic tests which endocrinologists use, particularly thyroid function measures, cannot detect developing gland failure. Following these tests, the patient will be told he or she is "normal," despite mood and behavioral changes.

The psychiatrist who bases his or her own judgment on the standard indices will have to conclude that the patient's mood misery is primary. Out comes the prescription pad. But the antidepressants don't work, and the psychiatrist either blames the patient and/or pins on the "nonresponder" label. The patient feels guilty and probably quits treatment. If she or he is "lucky," in ten or fifteen years the dysfunction will have developed into full-blown disease which a doctor at last will diagnose and treat.

Biopsychiatrists are subspecialists in endocrinology, neurology, and particularly in their relationship to each other, which is called neuroendocrinology. In the many hours my colleagues and I have spent in the laboratory seeking to understand the various neuroendocrine disorders, we have learned that we must look at the failing systems on a *continuum* that is unique to each person. Each stage of organ failure, from beginning to traditional disease state, is marked by deviations from the optimum hormone level at which the individual functions best. The changed hormone level may still fall within the normal range. Nonetheless, it is not normal for *you,* which is why you are experiencing emotional difficulties.

The Thyroid

Sometimes at conferences I'll be talking about all the tests to run on patients with mood problems, when somebody will ask: "After a drug screen, if you could do only one test, which one would it be?"

I always answer, "The TRH stimulation test, because it yields ten to fifteen percent. You will find that ten to fifteen percent of the patients you think are depressed have one form or another of thyroid disease, and you wouldn't have found it otherwise. Thyroid dysfunction is the single most important area of misdiagnosis."

The thyroid lies in the neck, just below the larynx and straddling the windpipe. Every cell in the body, brain cells included, depends on thyroid hormones T3 and T4 to function effectively, for the hormones control their rate of metabolism. Thus, this one gland determines the speed of all chemical reactions involved in consuming oxygen and burning energy in each and every cell. Normal growth and development are impossible when the gland is malfunctioning. Mental and physical retardation are the tragic results of thyroid illness in a fetus or young child.

The thyroid is part of a neuroendocrine minisystem called the hypothalamic-pituitary-thyroid (HPT) axis. The hypothalamus secretes a hormone called thyrotropin-releasing hormone (TRH), which travels to the pituitary and stimulates that gland to release thyroid-stimulating hormone (TSH). TSH in turn acts on the thyroid to promote release of thyroid hormones into general circulation. Levels of thyroid hormone in the blood modulate the pituitary's continued release of TSH. This feedback mechanism ultimately switches off the pituitary.

Things start going wrong when the thyroid goes off-system, secreting its hormones against pituitary orders. Thyroid dysfunction will result, too, if disease strikes elsewhere in the HPT axis.

Inherited defects in the immune system are probably responsible for most thyroid malfunction. Other known causes include iodine deficiency or excess, lithium (a common cause of hypothyroidism), and diseases of other endocrine glands.

Thyroid disease is extremely common, especially among women. Perhaps as many as one woman in fifteen is prone to thyroid problems. Overall, an estimated ten million people in the United States have some form of thyroid dysfunction whether they know it or not. The only signs may be depression and/or fatigue.

Thyroid diseases fall into two categories: (1) *hypothyroidism,* in which the gland slows down and secretes less and less thyroid hormone; and (2) *hyperthyroidism,* the reverse condition, in which the gland secretes more hormone than is normal for the person. In either case, and at any level of illness, psychiatric symptoms are the rule.

Hypothyroidism

A TALE OF THREE PATIENTS

It was Ms. A's second overdose in six months. She'd swallowed a bottleful of the antidepressants that were supposed to make her feel better. "I tried to commit suicide twice. I guess that means I'm depressed," she told the emergency room staff sardonically. She was angry that they had pumped her out and ruined her attempt. She said to the admitting psychiatrist at the psychiatric hospital to which she was subsequently referred, "I'll probably try again."

No sense trying to convince Ms. A that she had a good life ahead of her. She was only 27 and held down an extremely responsible executive position with a major local corporation. For a year she had been trying to work out her depression in therapy with a psychologist. For the previous nine months she had also been seeing a psychiatrist for medication.

Ms. A's depression had appeared out of nowhere. She'd never been this depressed before, and there was no history of mood problems in her family. She had zero energy, she said, needed far more sleep than she ever had, and not a thing gave her pleasure anymore. Although she had always liked to go out and have fun, she had withdrawn from her friends and preferred to stay home nights and weekends. She couldn't pay attention, her memory was awful—what was the use of going on?

Meanwhile, in another city, Mrs. T was talking suicide, if not yet acting on it. She was in the midst of an awful crisis: Her husband had just announced he was leaving her the very next week. When she started talking suicide, her psychiatrist had her admitted to the hospital. Hers seemed as sure a case of depression as anyone ever did see: no energy, daily variation in her mood, problems with concentration and paying attention, no appetite, insomnia, bouts of tearfulness. For six months her depression had regularly been getting worse. And for the last two months her marriage had been on the rocks. Now her husband was leaving her. At only 26 years old, Mrs. T was in bad shape. As she saw it, she was utterly without a future.

At the same time in still another city, a police cruiser received instructions to go to the local Catholic church and take away the "crazy." There they found Ms. U, a well-dressed 44-year-old woman, declaring in no uncertain terms that she had the same rights to the church as the priests who ran it. No indeed, she would not leave. The police had to arrest her, but they let her go as soon as she seemed calm. Right back to the church she went and up the winding stone steps to the bell tower. There she rang the church bells, singing out her right to run this church as she wished, denouncing the priests and religious hierarchy for all to hear.

A trip to the local hospital was next in store for Ms. U. The emergency room personnel noticed Ms. U's lethargy and puffy face, but they did not have time to finish their physical examination before an orderly from the psychiatric service came to get her. They kept her in the psychiatric ward for twenty-four hours for observation but released her without a formal diagnosis. Ms. U returned to her own city. Some days later she turned up at the local hospital emergency room, saying she was so tired, so depressed. When she told the staff what she had done when she was away, they quickly transferred her to the psychiatric service with a diagnosis of psychotic depression.

The admitting psychiatrist walked into her room. Ms. U was sitting on the bed in a very warm room wrapped in a blanket and wearing a scarf and cap. She was cold, she said, and no wonder: Her body temperature was only 96.4. Her pulse was so slow that the psychiatrist could hardly believe it: 46! Her expression was dull; she was puffy and swollen, her eyelids drooping. She spoke with a raspy, hoarse voice. The psychiatrist could make a diagnosis virtually by looking at her.

Fortunately, all three women, in separate hospitals across the country, had ended up in the care of biopsychiatrists. The correct diagnosis of their "depression" could now be made. Ms. A, Ms. U, and Mrs. T were all suffering from differing grades of hypothyroidism—symptomatically indistinguishable from DSM-III major depression. Once the correct tests were administered and the diagnoses made, each woman's condition was treatable with hormone replacement medication.

MS. U'S MYXEDEMA MADNESS
Biopsychiatry has identified three stages of thyroid illness.

Ms. U had stage 1, full-blown thyroid illness, called myxedema; her thyroid had virtually ceased functioning. This phase of illness any fourth-year medical student ought to be able to diagnose, because the symptoms are so obvious: puffiness, drooping eyelids, flat expression, sensitivity to cold, raspy voice. Typically, Ms. U was constipated. Her skin was thick and dry, her hair sparse and coarse. Yet, despite all evidence of disease, because she was acting so "crazy," almost everyone jumped to the wrong conclusion. As Dr. Milton Erman said of Ms. U, had she been "transferred to a psychiatric hospital for long-term treatment, the diagnosis might have been missed completely or further delayed."

Ms. U. was suffering from "myxedema madness," which can occur with end-stage hypothyroidism. Her thyroid was swollen (called a goiter), her heart was enlarged, her reflexes slow, her menstrual flow heavy. The longer her condition continued, the more she was at risk of heart attack, coma, and death. At this level of illness, all the standard tests—once someone thinks to take them—reveal frank illness. Indeed, Ms. U's T4 level was 0.5 mcg/dl; normal ranges are from 4.5 to 12.5 mcg/dl.

SIGNS AND SYMPTOMS OF
HYPOTHYROIDISM AND DEPRESSION

Hypothyroidism

Depression

Goiter
Cold intolerance
Brittle hair, loss of
  eyebrow hair
Thickened, dry skin
Bradycardia, cardiac
  failure
Delayed reflexes

Dysphoric mood
  (depressed)
Loss of interest
  or pleasure
Weight gain
Appetite decrease
Sleep increase
Constipation
Decreased libido
Anergia, fatigue
Decreased
  concentration
Suicidal ideation
Delusions

Weight loss
Appetite increase
Sleep decrease

MS. A'S SUBCLINICAL HYPOTHYROIDISM

Ms. A, although she was actively suicidal, was suffering from stage 3 hypothyroidism, the mildest level of dysfunction. Her thyroid was just beginning to go, and her ferocious depression was the only symptom. We call stage 3 illness chemical, or subclinical, hypothyroidism. Stage 2 is termed mild hypothyroidism and reveals a few other symptoms, such as fatigue, dry skin, constipation, weight gain. Data suggest that both forms of illness will develop into myxedema if untreated.

Over 90 percent of the patients with hypothyroid depression have stages 3 and 2 illness—neither of which is detectable on standard tests. Thus, psychiatrists end up seeing most of these patients. If they go by the symptoms, as most do, they will institute treatments for primary depression rather than for hypothyroidism, for symptomatically the two are indistinguishable (see chart on page 148). We find that most of the patients we correctly diagnose have had multiple psychopharmacological treatments.

THE TRH STIMULATION TEST

There is a surefire diagnostic test for subclinical hypothyroidism: the TRH stimulation test. It's a pet peeve of mine that it is not administered more frequently.

As mentioned earlier, the thyroid is not autonomous; it responds to hormones secreted by the pituitary, which in turn responds to hormones from the hypothalamus. The TRH stimulation test provokes the HPT axis into revealing the abnormality in the *system*.

First we take a blood sample to measure the patient's regular (baseline) pituitary TSH level. Then we administer the hypothalamic TRH and at intervals of fifteen, thirty, and ninety minutes, we take more blood to see how the pituitary TSH levels are responding. In persons with no thyroid disease, within an hour the TSH levels will respond to the hypothalamic "command" by secreting modest amounts of TSH over the first measurement. We take the highest level reached, subtract the baseline level, and come up with the "delta TSH" value. We consider any score from 5 to 20 as normal.

In subclinical hypothyroid patients, the delta TSH is markedly increased, even though the thyroid hormone is utterly normal. Apparently, in early thyroid failure, the pituitary has become supersensitive to TRH and secretes lots more hormone, to stimulate the sluggish thyroid to "put out." For the time being it works, and the extra work the system has to do is not detectable until it's turned on. Although the thyroid hormone level remains normal via this mechanism, all is not right in the brain.

MS. A'S SYMPTOMLESS AUTOIMMUNE THYROIDITIS

Ms. A's delta TSH score was 27.1. Mrs. T's delta score was similar, at 27.3. But that wasn't the end of Mrs. T's story. She became a patient of Dr. Ronald Bloodworth, who found antithyroid antibodies in her blood. Diagnosis: subclinical hypothyroidism secondary to "symptomless autoimmune thyroiditis" (SAT). Her thyroid had begun to fail because her immune system was attacking her own gland. The more research we do on this condition, the more common SAT turns out to be. As many as 60 percent of the patients we test have these antibodies.

The whys of SAT are not known. It affects 5 to 15 percent of the general population and is four to eight times more common among women than men. SAT runs in families. It appears most commonly between the ages of 30 and 50, and may be associated with other diseases, such as anemia, diabetes, allergies, and arthritis.

The treatment for SAT is the same as for other thyroid conditions: thyroid hormone replacement.

When Mrs. T began to take this medication, "she showed gradual and sustained improvement in spite of the marriage failing during her hospitalization," reports Dr. Bloodworth. She continued in psychotherapy and at last was able to become actively involved in it. An endocrinologist took over her treatment for SAT.

Hyperthyroidism

In hypothyroidism the metabolic rate gets slower and slower as the gland fails. In hyperthyroidism, as the gland secretes excess hormone, the metabolic rate is correspondingly speeded up.

Consequently, hyperthyroid individuals are often restless and have to keep moving around, and they can't pay attention for long. Neither can they sleep. They are hungrier than usual, but they may lose weight. Physically, too much thyroid hormone can cause abundant sweating, heat sensitivity, tremor, fatigue, soft moist skin, heart palpitations, frequent bowel movements, muscular weakness, and protruding eyeballs. Women have scant periods. In men, swelling of tissue of one or both breasts (gynecomastia) may occur.

A hyperthyroid person will feel anxious, jittery, and irritable, and may have frequent mood swings and emotional explosions. At its emotional worst, the condition is often misdiagnosed as mania or psychosis.

Depression occurs in hyperthyroidism, too, and can substantially worsen a "life events" depression.

Dr. John J. Schwab had a patient consult him for depression who turned out to have Graves disease, a form of hyperthyroidism. The man was 36, a successful and well-to-do accountant. During the first visit he told Dr. Schwab that he no longer felt pleasure or gratification in any area of his life. He was afraid, Dr. Schwab tells us, "that his gloom and despondency might increase to the point that he harmed himself." He worried about his marriage and his work. He had been married ten years and had three young children. Although he cared for his family, he had become increasingly irritable with them and they just weren't getting along. At work he had begun to pass on the more challenging work to his partner.

"During the last six months he had had difficulties with sleeping, especially with frequent awakening, a loss of energy, diminished interest in sexual activity, and some increase in appetite. Prominent mental symptoms were difficulty with concentration, distractibility, and pessimism," reports Dr. Schwab.

During the second visit, he continued to talk about how depressed he was and when it all had started. The alert psychiatrist noticed that his patient had "a fine tremor of the hands and fingers. He denied any history of alcoholism and of tremor in the family. Also, he admitted to perspiring excessively for six to nine months, to some heat intolerance, and to a feeling of muscular weakness."

Subsequent physical examination and testing revealed the existence of hyperthyroidism. The most common treatment, radiation with radioactive iodine, worked. "Many of the symptoms of depression have lessened considerably," reports Dr. Schwab, "and he has begun to enter actively into therapy in order to resolve the conflicts that have imperiled his marriage. He has not needed antidepressant medication."

Because hyperthyroidism is far less common a mimicker than hypothyroidism, we have not yet studied it as deeply. We have reason to believe, however, that it too can be understood on a continuum of malfunction, from subclinical to mild to overt illness. Recently a form of disease called "silent thyroiditis" has been identified. It consists of a mild hyperthyroid condition lasting weeks to months, often followed by a brief flirtation with hypothyroidism. Then the thyroid function returns to normal.

Untreated, severe hyperthyroidism can lead to "thyroid storm," which can be fatal. It comes on abruptly, often preceded by a physical stress such as surgery, diabetic shock, or toxemia of pregnancy. However, severe fright can bring it on as well, as can sudden discontinuance of hyperthyroid medication. Thyroid storm is marked by fever, severe weakness and muscle-wasting, extreme emotionality and restlessness, confusion, psychosis, swollen liver, cardiovascular collapse, and shock. Even with treatment, one fourth of patients die.

Like hypothyroidism, hyperthyroidism appears to be a genetic autoimmune disorder. It too is most common among women, especially those between the ages of 20 and 40.

A Paradox

Administer the TRH stimulation test to a hyperthyroid individual, and the resulting delta scores will be below average. In other words, stimulate the pituitary to produce thyroid-stimulating hormone, and it will secrete very little, because the thyroid is independently putting out so much on its own.

Now give the same test to a biologically depressed person who has no thyroid disease and what will you find? Twenty-five percent of depressed people will show a *low* delta TSH score, as if the person were *hyper*thyroid! This result occurs so consistently that it has become a biological marker for the existence of depression as well as a predictor of response to treatment.

This finding seems to make no sense. It's the *hypo*thyroid people who characteristically are depressed. Why does it happen? You'll find the answer (or at least the *theory*) in upcoming chapters.

CELL SELF-HATRED?

We've been talking about thyroid illness as *autoimmune*—the body mobilizing to fight off its own tissue, as if it were a foreign invader. This is an important area of medicine today—why does the system fail? Attacking one's own cells is the ultimate in self-hatred. Could depression have anything to do with it? Research is providing some surprising answers. Stay tuned.

The Adrenal Glands

With the adrenals we introduce a second neuroendocrine axis that is central to mood regulation in biological depression and mimicked depression: the hypothalamic-pituitary-adrenal (HPA) axis. While diseases of the adrenals are less common mimickers than thyroid malfunction, they too develop along a continuum. Emotional and behavioral symptoms occur earliest, and only the psychiatrist with a nose for medical causation is likely to differentiate adrenal dysfunction from primary psychiatric states.

Diseases of the adrenals can be extremely serious, and waiting to diagnose them until they develop fully can be dangerous—as witness the near-death of the man with Addison's disease we discussed back in Chapter 4; until he came to Fair Oaks, all the doctors whom he consulted were convinced his depression was caused by the recent accidental death of his wife.

WHAT THEY DO AND HOW THEY DO IT

The two adrenal glands, perched atop the kidneys, are each two separate glands in one: the adrenal cortex and the adrenal medulla. Each secretes its own hormones. The hormones of the cortex are called corticoids or corticosteroids. Among them are: aldosterone, which increases sodium and decreases potassium in the blood; androgens, male sex hormones which are also present in women, although at lesser levels; and a number of hormones called glucocorticoids. Glucocorticoids help maintain blood sugar at appropriate levels; they play a role in blood pressure, reduce inflammation, and help fight infection, allergy, and stress. Cortisol, or hydrocortisone, is a major hormone in this category—and one in which psychiatry is extremely interested (see below). Some steroid medications (Chapter 8), such as prednisone and cortisone, are chemically related to adrenal hormones. That steroids are themselves potent mimickers is no accident.

Hormones of the adrenal medulla are epinephrine and norepinephrine, referred to as catecholamines. When secreted by the adrenal glands, the catecholamines are the "fight or flight" hormones released under stress. These hormones also exist in the brain, where they are among the most significant neurotransmitters in depression. They also instruct the hypothalamus to secrete the releasing factors that control pituitary function, and which end up controlling the cortex of the adrenal glands. (Specifically, hypothalamic corticoreleasing factor, or CRF, stimulates the pituitary to release ACTH, which triggers the hormones of the cortex.) The adrenal medulla is triggered directly by the nervous system as well as by some of the cortical hormones.

ADDISON'S DISEASE

President John F. Kennedy suffered from this rare disease, in which the adrenal cortex progressively fails. It may not be detected or diagnosed until severe stress causes an Addisonian crisis, as in our patient described in Chapter 4. However, symptoms of depression and emotional instability may have existed for a long time. Dr. Richard Hall mentions that "mental changes are common, occurring in 64 percent to 84 percent of the cases, and may vary from mild neurotic traits to gross psychosis. The most frequent mental changes are mild disturbances in the level of consciousness, manifested as apathy, somnolence, insomnia, and dulling of intellect. These disturbances are fluctuating and episodic. Most observers report apathetic or depressive moods, poverty of thought, and lack of initiative."

Weakness, fatigue, shortness of breath, and low blood pressure are other early signs. Skin usually becomes darker and black freckles may appear. Loss of appetite, nausea, vomiting, dizziness, sensitivity to cold, and hypoglycemia (low blood sugar) are possibilities. In later stages, resistance to infection and stress is lowered. Addison crisis is marked by severe pain in the legs, belly, or lower back, plus collapse of blood vessels and kidneys. Without treatment, death will follow.

Treatment with steroid medications brings a return to normal functioning.

Tuberculosis used to be the major cause of Addison's. Now, however, in the large majority of cases the gland atrophies for no known reason.

CUSHING'S SYNDROME/DISEASE

The reverse of Addison's disease, Cushing's syndrome refers to overactivity of the adrenal cortex, usually as a result of benign or malignant adrenal tumors or ACTH-secreting tumors elsewhere in the body (as in some lung cancers). Cushing's disease implies a corresponding overproduction of pituitary ACTH to which the adrenals are overresponding. The disease represents two thirds of all Cushing's cases; most victims are women of child-bearing age. In both types, behavior is affected in as high as 90 percent of cases. Depression is the most commonly mentioned symptom; euphoria, anxiety, and psychosis complete the list.

Physical signs of Cushing's include a moon-faced appearance, weight gain, purple stripes on the belly, and accumulations of fat pads (buffalo hump). Wounds heal poorly, and bruising is common. High blood pressure, kidney stones, muscle-wasting, bone weakness (osteoporosis), acne, and diabetes occur frequently, as do menstrual irregularities and excessive hairiness in women.

Frequently, however, none of these symptoms occur, and the only indications of malfunction are periodic behavioral symptoms plus increased cortisol secretions—which earn Cushing's sufferers beds in psychiatric wards, these symptoms being "typical" of major depression. Clearly there are subclinical forms of this adrenal malfunction.

Treatment is surgery, radiation, or drugs, depending on the cause.

CUSHING'S TEST FOR DEPRESSION?

The dexamethasone suppression test (DST), highly touted as *the* diagnostic test for biologic depression, was first developed to discover the excess secretion of cortisol in Cushing's. Then one day not so long ago we discovered that many biologically depressed people also secrete excess cortisol. As a matter of fact, "nearly all of the HPA abnormalities described in Cushing's syndrome can occur in patients with 'primary' psychiatric disorder," Drs. Victor I. Reus and Jeffrey R. Berlant inform psychiatric practitioners.

PHEOCHROMOCYTOMA

Pheochromocytoma are tiny tumors of the adrenal medulla (although occasionally they occur in other areas of the body), generally benign, that secrete catecholamines. They can occur at any age but are most common between 5 and 25. High blood pressure is the most significant physical sign; it may be constant or occur during attacks.

Emotional stress, abdominal massage, standing up or sitting down, anesthesia, laughing, sleeping, sexual intercourse, shaving, gargling, straining during a bowel movement, sneezing, hyperventilating, urinating, pregnancy in young women—all these have been known to provoke acute attacks in vulnerable individuals. Headache, perspiration, and palpitations often characterize attacks. Nausea, weakness, nervousness, chest pain, difficulty breathing, tingling, and other strange feelings in arms and legs, tightness in the throat, dizziness, and faintness have also been mentioned. From headache to faintness, the list of symptoms is consistent with panic attack; during pheochromocytoma attacks, the anxiety may be so intense that it produces acute temporary psychosis. Add to this the fact that symptoms other than the possibly chronic hypertension show up only during attacks, and pheochromocytoma's place among the mimickers is assured. The tumors have also been noted to produce severe chronic depression and depressive psychoses.

The disease is frequently associated with a familial tendency to multiple benign endocrine tumors. Surgical removal cures pheochromocytoma 90 percent of the time.

The Pituitary

Deep inside the brain is this tiny blockbuster of a gland. It influences a number of metabolic processes essential to growth and development and maintains the functioning of other endocrine glands.

Attached by a kind of stalk to the hypothalamus, the pituitary, too, is two glands in one. The anterior pituitary alone secretes six major hormones and some minor ones, each triggered by hypothalamic hormones. Four of the most important anterior pituitary hormones stimulate other endocrine glands to perform their various functions. Besides thyroid-secreting hormone (TSH), these include: adrenocorticotropic hormone (ACTH), which stimulates the adrenal cortex; follicle-stimulating hormone (FSH) and luteinizing hormone (LH), both involved in ovulation. In men, LH is called interstitial cell-stimulating hormone (ICSH), and it stimulates the testicles to secrete testosterone. The other two hormones of the anterior pituitary include growth hormone (GH), a metabolic hormone that is indeed involved in growth in children, and possibly in healing and tissue repair in adults; and prolactin (PRL), which stimulates the growth of breasts during pregnancy and lactation afterward.

The posterior pituitary releases two hormones that are not actually pituitary hormones at all. They are manufactured in the hypothalamus and simply released by the pituitary. They include oxytocin, which causes labor contractions; and vasopressin (also called antidiuretic hormone or ADH), which stimulates the kidneys to reabsorb water.

What with all the hormones flowing to and through this gland, and its direct involvement with the hypothalamus and limbic system, anything that goes wrong with the pituitary is bound to effect mental life. Accordingly, since most of the body's hormones seem to be controlled by the same neurotransmitters that we believe are involved in mood disorders, the functioning of the pituitary and its "client" glands may well provide a window into the brains of depressed people. Many of our neuroendocrine tests for depression do indeed measure fluctuations in pituitary hormone output.

PANHYPOPITUITARISM
This condition refers to a generalized slowing of the anterior pituitary, often because of tumor or other space-occupying mass in the brain or damage to the gland from a disease or burst vessel. Symptoms encompass those of the endocrine glands which are affected. Mental symptoms are present at least 70 percent of the time, usually beginning with depression and lack of sex drive. When the disease comes on suddenly, it is likely to be diagnosed properly. But when it develops slowly, the mimickers will predominate. Besides depression, panhypopituitarism commonly mimics anorexia nervosa.

As the illness progresses, infertility, decreased secondary sex characteristics, hypoglycemia, hypothyroidism, hypotension, and low stress tolerance, susceptibility to infection . . . all may eventuate if the disease is not caught in time.

Panhypopituitarism is treated by replacing the hormones of the target glands, which can no longer function in the absence of pituitary control. Often the gland must also be surgically removed.

ACROMEGALY

Acromegaly refers to pituitary oversecretion of growth hormone in adults. In children the excess hormone leads to pituitary gigantism and growth to more than seven or eight feet.

In acromegaly the bones begin to enlarge. Face, hands, and feet particularly are affected, changing the person's previous appearance completely and unpleasantly. "Little attention has been paid to the psychiatric aspects of acromegaly," says Dr. Hall. "Although it generally does not produce a psychosis, it is regularly accompanied by alterations of personality such as decreased initiative and spontaneity, and mood change."

Pituitary adenomas (benign tumors) are likely to produce this condition; excessive secretion of hypothalamic hormones may also be a factor. Such growth obviously does not happen overnight. Once again, mental symptoms may be important clues. Surgery or radiation are the usual treatments.

HYPONATREMIA

When the posterior pituitary releases too much vasopressin, or ADH, too much water is reabsorbed by the kidneys and delivered into the blood. The blood becomes too dilute, which decreases the necessary salt concentration. Hyponatremia may not reveal itself clinically, but, according to two recent reports, it may well trigger delusional depression. Two psychiatric researchers discovered two such individuals, one a 75-year-old man and the other a 69-year-old woman, who had frequently been hospitalized with delusional depression. The researchers discovered that both suffered from hyponatremia. Fluid restriction and a high-sodium diet substantially cleared their symptoms. (See also Chapter 9.)

Islets of Langerhans

You'll need a microscope to spot these groups of cells ("islets") on the pancreas, discovered by Paul Langerhans. They secrete the hormones glucagon and insulin. Glucagon helps liver cells convert a substance called glycogen into glucose. Insulin helps transport the glucose out of the blood and into cells where it is used as fuel, or back to the liver where it is stored as glycogen.

DIABETES MELLITUS

When the islets of Langerhans underproduce insulin, or when the body cannot use it, glucose continues to accumulate in the blood and the tissues cannot get at it. *Diabetes mellitus* is the result. There are at least five forms of the disease.

Type I diabetes, usually called insulin-dependent diabetes, most often occurs in persons under 30. Their islet cells do not produce adequate insulin and they must depend on replacement hormone for life. This is the most severe form of the disease, affecting about half a million persons in the United States. Their life-span can be reduced by half because of complications developing later in life that can lead to kidney failure or stroke. Often blindness occurs and limbs must be amputated.

Evidence is beginning to accumulate that type I diabetes is an autoimmune disease in which the body attacks its own insulin-secreting cells. Research in this area also reveals that the antibodies are present often long before the disease becomes manifest. Treatment with drugs that inhibit the immune system has met with varying success. The key seems to be to catch the disease before it becomes symptomatic. The best way to do that, researchers at the University of Florida have learned, is to screen children for the presence of the damaging antibody. Type I diabetics have a genetic tendency to the disease, which usually must be triggered by something, possibly a virus.

Type II diabetes, *noninsulin-dependent,* usually occurs in persons over 30. Perhaps as many as nine to ten million persons have this form, although they have not necessarily been diagnosed. Many of them are obese at the time of diagnosis or have a history of obesity. Type II diabetics usually have a combination of insulin deficiency and inability to use insulin. Weight loss, controlled diet, and, if necessary, antidiabetic drugs can improve both aspects markedly. Type II becomes more common with increasing age.

Diabetes can also occur secondary to other conditions, such as pancreatic disease or Cushing's. A fourth type occurs during or after pregnancy and usually disappears spontaneously. These women do seem to have a tendency to develop the disease later, however.

Finally, impaired glucose tolerance is the name given subclinical diabetes. Excessive thirst, urination, and hunger with weight loss are classic symptoms of diabetes. Weakness, lethargy, itching, boils, fungus-type vaginal infections, blurred vision problems, retarded healing, and easy bruising are among the symptoms of manifest disease. Needless to say, complaints of tiredness and low energy and altered appetite, even blurred vision, will signal depression in the absence of gross physical signs. And, in true endocrinological style, diabetes causes its share of serious emotional symptoms. Patients who turned out to have diabetes have met all the criteria for major depression, schizophrenia, and personality disorders. One researcher has noted that undiagnosed diabetics may appear for psychiatric consultation because of impotence and marital problems.

Should testing for the autoimmune type of diabetes become widespread and prevention the rule, it will be interesting to see how many depressed people will "miraculously" be cured.

HYPOGLYCEMIA

A 55-year-old woman appeared in a hospital emergency room and started taking off her clothes in the waiting area. Clearly a "psych" case, concluded the nurses, who summoned a psychiatrist. In another emergency setting, a 45-year-old man was labeled drunk and crazy and the staff ignored him. A 39-year-old man was lying on a New York street babbling and looking wild-eyed. Inured to drunks and street people, pedestrians went around or stepped over him on their way to work. It made no difference that he was well dressed, wearing a suit and tie.

These "drunks" or "crazies" were all insulin-dependent diabetics who had taken too much insulin and were suffering hypoglycemic reactions; now they had too little glucose in their blood.

Hypoglycemia can produce bizarre behavior that in appearance is indistinguishable from schizophrenia, depression, dementia, or anxiety attacks. In less severe states, the person may appear drunk, with slurred speech, an unsteady walk, and some confusion. In chronic, undiagnosed conditions, personality changes, occasional attacks of paranoid psychosis, and progressive deterioration resulting in dementia may ultimately be irreversible.

Physically, depending on the cause, faintness, weakness, hunger, shakiness, nervousness, headache, and visual problems can progress to palsy, loss of consciousness, convulsions, and coma.

Many conditions can cause hypoglycemia, including insulin-secreting tumors of the pancreas or overdose of insulin in diabetics. Early mild diabetes may cause so-called reactive hypoglycemia, which strikes a few hours after a meal rich in carbohydrates. It can happen for no apparent reason, however, in which case it is termed "functional." Fasting hypoglycemia, usually quite mild, is probably familiar to many of you who have missed a meal. If severe, however, it may signify underlying illness and should be checked out. Eating carbohydrates will take away the immediate symptoms, but the control of the condition depends, of course, on the cause.

Just don't tell your psychiatrist that you think you have hypoglycemia—he'll think you really *are* crazy. Hypoglycemia used to be the diagnosis of the hour—*everybody,* especially women, had it. As a result, now *nobody* has it.

Nevertheless, the psychiatrist should not overlook mild or subacute forms of hypoglycemia in his or her patients. Standards for its diagnosis are far more strict than in the overdiagnosing-it days, and the diagnosis can now be made with confidence.

The Parathyroids

Four tiny parathyroid glands lie behind the thyroid. They secrete parathyroid hormone, which increases blood concentration of calcium. The body is extremely sensitive to changes in calcium concentration: too little (hypocalcemia) and muscles go into spasm and the mind into depression, dementia, psychosis; too much (hypercalcemia) leads to severe emotional disturbance and heart malfunction. Both conditions result primarily from the respective undersecretion or oversecretion of parathyroid hormone. The alert physician can fingerprint a person's mood on the basis of his or her calcium level. Details of the effects of hypercalcemia, the far more common condition, are discussed in Chapter 9.

Hyperparathyroidism is usually caused by benign tumors, sometimes by cancer. Surgery is the usual treatment; yet it can lead to hypoparathyroidism. Thyroid surgery is one of the most common causes of hypoparathyroidism; the surgeon often removes the parathyroids, too, sometimes inadvertently.

The Sex Glands

Last but no one would dare say least, are the male and female sex glands and their hormones. The female sex glands are the two ovaries, which contain two endocrine structures each. The ovarian follicles secrete estrogens, and the corpus luteum secretes progesterone as well as estrogens. The hypothalamus and pituitary control the timing of these hormones in menstrual and reproductive behavior.

Also under hypothalamic-pituitary control are the endocrine interstitial cells within the testes. The more ICSH from the pituitary, the more testosterone is secreted, which ultimately reaches a high blood concentration and stops pituitary secretions (negative feedback).

Unfortunately, little systematic research has been conducted on the possible psychiatric presentations of sexual endocrinology. To judge from how bizarrely we can behave under the influence of *normal* sexual hormonal secretions, surely abnormalities of the sex glands are bound to be trouble!

Estrogens and progesterone have been given to women to influence mood states encountered during menopause and during premenstrual syndrome (PMS). Estrogen makes some women less depressed and other women more depressed. We'll talk more about this when we tackle PMS and postpartum depression in Chapter 23.

One of the cases I am most proud of concerned a woman in her mid-thirties whom I'll call Susan. Susan, a PhD biochemist, was referred to me for severe depression. She felt completely overwhelmed and had isolated herself in her home. This was the second time she had had such a crisis. The first was in 1976, while she was in graduate school and could not tackle her dissertation. She saw a psychiatrist at the time who gave her a very small amount of antidepressant medication. It had no effect. Susan gave up and quit the therapy and eventually she came out of her depression. She had been in and out of therapy for milder depressions several times since.

Susan's father was a psychologist and her brother was a gynecologist with an endocrinological subspecialty. What's more, Susan was referred to me by a very close friend of mine in another city. The pressure was really on to do something.

Susan's father and brother were very concerned about her. Her dad believed that her present episode had to do with Susan's recent promotion at the drug company for which she worked. Her brother was worried that she was going to blow a great career.

I began to take her history. While we were talking about her two major bouts of depression, Susan mentioned, "You know, making matters even worse, both times I got very hairy. My legs got hairy— my thighs, and particularly, my face. Ugh!" Susan made a vivid expression of revulsion. "Back in '76 and again now, the only time I go out is to see the electrolysist."

Unusual growth of hair—hirsutism—is an endocrine problem. Immediately I had Susan doing temperature charts to find out if she was ovulating. She wasn't. At first I thought she might be overproducing adrenal androgens, male hormones which females also have. But her level was normal. When I checked her pituitary-stimulating hormones to the ovaries, I confirmed this finding.

The other common cause for female hirsutism is polycystic ovaries, which would also be consistent with lack of ovulation. But here Susan threw me a curve ball. She said she'd had an abortion. That didn't fit with polycystic ovaries, because if she hadn't ovulated, she could hardly have become pregnant. Susan confessed that she had been sexually inactive at the time and couldn't imagine how she could have become pregnant. But she had missed her period and had all the signs of apparent pregnancy; the hospital where she went for the abortion tested her hormones and her progesterone was high enough for pregnancy. Then she told us that they hadn't found a fetus.

We sent for the pathology report and sure enough, no fetus. The doctors believed that she had had what is called an "exuberant growth" of the uterus, overstimulated by hormones. This, too, is consistent with polycystic ovaries.

We completed the diagnostic procedure that confirmed the existence of polycystic ovary disease in our "psychiatric" patient. But when Susan filed a claim for insurance reimbursement, her insurance company wanted to send us for peer review (a hearing before other psychiatrists). I wrote back saying fine, but the only psychiatrists whose judgment I was willing to accept were those who knew something about medicine, because this patient did not have a psychiatric diagnosis.

Susan had been in therapy for twelve years with a depression that came and went but always came back again—a dozen years of psychotherapy at a cost to her insurance company of thousands and thousands of dollars. No one had even hinted at a peer review, because to so many of my peers in the profession, that's the way it goes.

No peer review proved necessary. We diagnosed in our patient a condition that was missed probably her whole adult life. The insurance company saw the light. The best news is: Susan's all right.

Part III

Depression Is . . .

11

Of Depression and Elephants

Now WE KNOW WHAT depression is not. It is time we found out what depression *is*.

Take this quiz:

Is depression—
a. a normal part of life?
b. a psychological problem?
c. a symptom of medical and/or psychiatric illness?
d. an illness in itself?
e. several possible illnesses?

The answer depends on who's talking. "Depression" is a term with many seemingly contradictory meanings. To the individual who is aware of being depressed (and not everyone is), it signifies a miserable, subjective personal experience. When one friend says to another, "I'm so depressed," they both understand that *ugh* feeling upon which the statement is based.

Such easy agreement eludes the professionals who study depression and work with patients who suffer from it. Depression is a psychological reaction to early life experience, says one. Depression is the unavoidable reaction to oppressive social conditions, says another. You're all wrong, says a third: Depression is a learned behavioral style. No way, says a fourth: Depression is a biochemical disorder, entirely physiological. A fifth professional will insist that depression is an expression of a genetic behavioral trait.

It reminds me of the story of the blind men and the elephant. Four blind men encounter an elephant. They seek to understand this impressive phenomenon. The first man feels the tusk and thoughtfully concludes that an elephant is a kind of spear. The second man explores the elephant's legs and decides it is a tree, while the third

man, at the tail, insists it's a rope. The fourth man tells his friends that
this thing is a snake; moving back from the trunk, he cautions the
three to take care.

Their answers obviously depend on which part of the elephant
each man has experienced. The blind men have each discovered valid
aspects of elephantness. Now they require not sight but *insight* into
what all their data mean.

Similarly, my professional colleagues, past and present, are each
correct in what they have discovered about depression. The answer
to the above quiz is:

f. all the above—and then some.

Depression is a condition of the mind. It is a physical affliction.
It is environmentally induced. It is a genetic tendency. It is learned.
It is a "biological clock" disorder. It is many separate biochemical
illnesses.

No one point of view represents a complete understanding of
this complex and curious condition. Perhaps because biopsychiatrists
are the new guys on the block, with no preexisting biases or vested
interests in any one theory, we have been able to discern a shape to
this complex, many-faceted, often confusing, certainly contradictory
condition.

In science we are all blind. Therefore the best way to comprehend depression is first to approach it as if it were an elephant—to
encounter its many features and dimensions. Facts and facets will
build upon each other as the chapters proceed; by the end of this
section, we will perhaps have conjured the very nature of this most
oppressive beast.

12

Depression Is
a Feeling

DEPRESSION IS LIKE love: It is a state of mind that overwhelms and distorts the senses; the whole world looks and feels different. But whereas love seems to imbue all the molecules of the earth with a heavenly, light energy, depression increases the weight of the world until finally it is too dense and dark to stand up in. Worse, the self loses its value in such an atmosphere. The depressed person is but one more grain of sand washed up on an endless, meaningless beach.

"Ay, There's the Rub"

Like the man or woman in love, the depressed person can think of or feel little beyond that experience—it is all-encompassing. It is a feeling that colors life and living; in other words, it is a mood. A mood can exist for as little as a moment, called forth perhaps by a memory, but for that speck in time, the mood represents your perception of past, present, and future. The experience seems *final*—you can't imagine ever feeling differently; the joy and meaning that depression takes from you will never return. Never.

Some people feel angry when they get depressed. Others feel an inner apathy and/or a host of physical discomforts. Some harbor a secret burden of guilt for the duration. Others loudly blame the very heavens for this agony. A few people are not aware of anything wrong, or anything right.

Although most people who are depressed feel a lack of energy, a blunting of all appetites, the actual experience of depression is utterly individual.

My son Steven once said that "depression is like you really like to go fishing and then all of a sudden you don't really care about going fishing anymore."

A 55-year-old clergyman I treated reported: "It was like getting run over by a steamroller. You lie there flat on the ground with your brain telling your arms to move—but it's all going on in slow motion."

And a 16-year-old cheerleader told me, "All I could do was sleep and eat. It seemed like I was sleeping eighteen hours a day. I would eat and sleep and then eat and sleep some more until my boyfriend —he was the wide receiver on the football team—gave me some cocaine. Believe it or not, it made me so depressed that all I could do was sleep, eat, and cry for one whole day."

A 64-year-old clothing executive: "I worked my way up. I assure you, no one ever accused me of being a soft or sentimental woman. But last year I suddenly became tearful. I felt like crying after doing just about anything—going to a movie, reading the newspaper. One day I burst into tears when a young woman at the office said hello to me. After that I stopped going out to lunch—I felt like staying in my office with the door closed instead of having to eat with people."

A 42-year-old investment banker: "I didn't feel especially depressed—I just didn't feel the optimism that had always been with me."

A 39-year-old real estate agent: "I felt like Dr. Jekyll and Mr. Hyde. I'd go along, even-tempered and easy to be with. Then suddenly, right before I'd get my period, I'd get extraordinarily hostile to everybody—my husband, my kids, myself, my clients. But a few days later I'd wake up and feel my old self again."

A 20-year-old bass guitarist: "Usually I'm a very up guy—I'm on top of the world when I'm performing—high as a kite on nothing but my music. But after Shari and I broke up I was empty inside. The emptiness was unspeakably heavy—like a black hole. All pleasure had disappeared into blackness. I couldn't taste, feel, love. There was no music. I didn't want to go back to her, and I couldn't perceive a future that was any different from how I was feeling."

A prince of Denmark:

> To be or not to be: That is the question.
> Whether 'tis nobler in the mind to suffer
> The slings and arrows of outrageous fortune,
> Or to take arms against a sea of troubles,
> And, by opposing, end them. To die; to sleep;
> No more; and by a sleep to say we end
> The heartache and the thousand natural shocks
> That flesh is heir to. 'Tis a consummation

Devoutly to be wish'd.
To die; to sleep;—
To sleep? Perchance to dream! Ay, there's the rub;
For in that sleep of death, what dreams may come. . . .

This last speaker is of course Hamlet, desperately depressed. He cannot accept his heartache and, typical of depressed people, cannot foresee a time when this pain will end. He feels helpless to alter his fate, ever. He is angry and wishes to strike out. But how? Where? Against life itself?

A Glass Historically Half Empty

Past or present, there is no end to the descriptions of depression's torments. Shakespeare could have been no stranger to the feeling of depression, to have put this extraordinary soliloquy in Hamlet's mouth. He had a lot to say about depression throughout his plays. The people of Shakespeare's time were as familiar with depression as we are. Melancholy, or melancholia (meaning unwarranted sadness and the loss of the ability to achieve pleasure), was known as "The Elizabethan malady" in sixteenth-century England. "If there be a hell upon earth, it is to be found in a melancholy man's heart," commented Englishman Robert Burton some 360 years ago in a book called *The Anatomy of Melancholy.* It became a bestseller of its day.

Miseries were foremost in everyone's mind in those days: "One [melancholic] complains of want, a second of servitude, another of a secret or incurable disease; of some deformity of body, of some loss, danger, death of friends, shipwreck, persecution, imprisonment, disgrace, repulse, contumely, calumny, abuse, injury, contempt, ingratitude, unkindness . . . unfortunate marriages, single life, too many children, no children . . . etc.," wrote Burton.

Sound familiar? While everyone's experience of depression differs whether in the sixteenth or the twentieth century, feelings of despair, of loss, of frustration pervade thoughts. In the absence of depression, we may see the glass as half full; when depressed, it is half empty, and never to be filled.

Depression feels like a kind of death in life, the (usually) temporary disappearance of faith and hope. It shares many of the features of grief and mourning. Frequently it follows on the heels of loss—loss of love, of employment, of opportunity, of possessions, of youth, of everything, of anything.

COMPLAINTS OF PEOPLE WITH
AND WITHOUT DEPRESSION

With Depression		Without Depression
90%	impaired concentration	30%
85%	weakness	10%
60%	rapid breathing	4%
50%	constipation	15%
50%	ringing in ears	10%
40%	speech problems	5%
35%	loss of sex drive	4%

none	all	none	all
0	100%	0	100%

Medication-free outpatient depressives	Matched controls

The Feeling Is a Normal Adaptation

Three and a half centuries ago, Robert Burton recognized that depression "is either a disposition or habit. In disposition, it is that transitory melancholy which goes and comes upon every small occasion of sorrow, need, sickness, trouble, fear, grief, passion or perturbation of the mind. . . . And from these melancholy dispositions, no man is free."

When depression corresponds to a recent or present experience, and the degree of reaction is appropriate to the cause, it can be a completely normal adaptation. The bank forecloses on you and you lose the farm that has been in your family for generations. You would be abnormal if you *didn't* get depressed. You "close down," lick your wounds, and eventually begin to cope with the reality of your new situation, however unpleasant. You begin to hope for a better future; the urge to survive has returned. You may not be cheerful, but you are no longer depressed. You never did lose your capacity to obtain pleasure; a visit from your grandchildren was a joy, no matter how dark a time. And throughout the experience, no matter how bad you felt, you did not hate yourself.

Depression as a normal reaction is equivalent to unhappiness or sadness and can affect great numbers of people at any one time. There seem to be times in history—as in Robert Burton's day—when the incidence of this rotten mood is extraordinary. Apparently we are enduring such a time now. One writer estimated that 80 percent of the entire population is suffering from some type of depression at this very moment!

Life in sixteenth- and seventeenth-century Europe was marked by fundamental changes in all aspects of life—social, religious, economic—as people adjusted to Renaissance upheavals in long-standing traditions. Our times, too, are marked by extreme, and exceedingly rapid, changes. Throughout the world, we are in an era of social, political, and technological revolution. The science we learn in school is invalid by the time we reach adulthood. The computer is second nature to our children, but to many parents and grandparents this fundamental new tool will remain a mystery. Children have a power and independence unheard of just a short time ago. Teenagers murder. Teenagers commit suicide.

Life expectancy is longer, but money runs out. Conquer heart disease and what do you get? Cancer. Horrible diseases like AIDS appear out of nowhere. One plane crashes and five hundred people die. Acid rain. Toxic waste. Drug addiction. Child abuse. Park your car in a city and the cassette deck is gone when you come back. Terrorists blow up airplanes, shoot cripples. Nuclear war spells doom.

The operative word of our times: stress. Constant stress. You can't win. Your hopes for the future cannot be fulfilled. Today the turbulence is too much for you. Depression.

Tomorrow maybe you'll see it another way.

The Survival of the Depressed

Depression is perfectly human—or shall we say *mammalian?* Mammals get depressed, too, in reaction to stresses of loss and frustration (as well as from alcohol and other drugs, experimentally speaking). Remove an infant monkey from its mother, for example, and it will demonstrate characteristically depressed behavior. After displaying obvious, loud distress, like a human infant whose mother does not come, a young monkey will "despair," withdrawing, slouching, and curling up, ceasing to play. Its face will have that same downcast expression and gaze and furrowed brow that gives our human moods away, no matter how we might insist to others that we're feeling okay. Charles Darwin noted that all mammals will display this expression.

This animal response suggests one evolutionary advantage conferred by depressed behavior. There must be something useful about depression for the trait to hang on through the evolutionary millennia from mammals to humans. Isolated in the wild, the baby monkey becomes easy prey. The withdrawn, silent nature of depression insures that the monkey will not reveal itself to potential enemies and that it will not wander off before its mother returns or until other monkeys appear to whom it can attach itself. In addition, with all its functions slowed, it cannot deplete its energy reserves. Thus, the natural depressed response to separation enables the monkey to survive.

Animal response to loss and/or abandonment demonstrates how mood serves to motivate. A depressed mood motivates us to *inaction* when the appropriate response to stress is, in effect, to "play dead." Loss of a loved one, through death or severing of the relationship, is a terrible blow for most people, an extremely common depression trigger. A normal, adaptive "downing" allows us to temporarily remove ourselves from the fray and bandage our psychological wounds. This healing step is important, for a major loss often precedes the onset of serious illness. (Depression of the *maladaptive* type, however, can prove even more stressful than the loss that triggered it. Then the depression becomes the illness risk factor.)

Psychiatrists Paul Wender and Donald Klein reason that moods have survived because, as with animals, they help us to cope with a changing environment and with danger. If we are continually defeated by a hostile environment, it makes no sense to continue to take risks. The safest course is to throw in the towel. A pessimistic attitude that accompanies a depressed mood—"There's no point in trying; I lose no matter what I do"—evolves from an animal's avoidance of a losing battle.

By the same token, mania has its evolutionary advantages. An optimistic attitude, no matter how apparently unrealistic, maximizes use of available or scarce resources. Manics can be amazingly productive. They race around getting things done, not sleeping, hatching creative, seemingly crazy schemes and plans. They proceed whether others agree with them or not. They can be very likable, even charismatic. They'll attract a mate and reproduce their genes for sure. Their energy is bottomless—unless they crash. At their most intense, moods are nearly always short-lived. In an evolutionary sense, they guide our survival temporarily.

Yet another theory of the survival of depression suggests that the genetic trait may confer an evolutionary advantage that has nothing to do with depression. This follows the model of diseases such as sickle-cell anemia, a fatal anemia common among blacks. Inheriting the affected gene from only one parent appears to confer a resistance to malaria, a killer in ancestral Africa; anemia does not develop. Persons who had acquired this protective trait would have tended to survive; thus the gene would have proliferated. Unfortunately, possession of two of these genes, one from each parent, leads to the development of sickle-cell anemia.

This last theory may explain why pathological, long-lasting forms of depression afflict our species to the extent that they do. The nature of the possible genetic advantage associated with this miserable trait has yet to be suggested, however, let alone imagined.

Depression Is a Bad Feeling That Won't Go Away

Normal depression is a drain on energy and psychic resources. But it does not truly interfere with your ability to go about the necessary business of living, although it may well reduce your motivation. It does not, to repeat, rob you of self-worth. You remain the person you always were. Gloomy though you may be, you can do your work and relate to other people. You feel lousy, period. Normal depression is ultimately, if unpleasantly, benign.

NORMAL GRIEF

Trauma ⟶ Rumination ⟶ Resolution

Trauma	Rumination	Resolution
Crying	Depression	
Numb	Insomnia	
Sense of unreality ⟶	Loss of appetite ⟶	Regain interest in
Denial	Fatigue	people,
Disbelief	Thoughts of death	appearance, and
	Social isolation	activities
	Loss of pleasure	

Regardless of resolution, parental loss before the age of 17 is associated with a very high risk of eventual adult depression.

For some people, though, the mood creeps into every corner of life. Tomorrow's view of the world will be just about as negative as it is today and was yesterday. These individuals see and feel the bad side of everything, especially themselves—the mirror reveals nothing but flaws. All experience, no matter how objectively gratifying, is ultimately disappointing. Although those close to them are always telling them to stop looking at the dark side, their behavior is based on a genuinely pained perception of the world and of themselves that they cannot easily relinquish. Nor do they feel there is anything they can do about it.

Overall, it is a chronic misery, even though there will be periods in which it lifts.

This persistent depression is a *maladaptive* state of mind, hindering a normal experience of life. Generally it affects thinking, feeling, and energy, and results in a level of withdrawal from others. But the afflicted person can still participate in essential life activities.

Psychiatrists and psychologists have many names for depression with these descriptive symptoms, including "depressive personality disorder," "characterological depression," "depressive neurosis," and "minor depression." DSM-III calls it "dysthymic disorder" (meaning ill-humored), a term that is rarely used in practice.

Whatever its name, this persistent bad mood is usually considered to be either a largely psychological problem in and of itself or symptomatic of a psychiatric condition such as alcoholism or obsessive-compulsive neurosis.

But watch out for a psychiatrist or other practitioner who jumps immediately to this conclusion.

"How long have you been depressed?" Dr. X will ask. "All my life," you sigh. Immediately you are hustled off for psychotherapy, because to many therapists, "chronic" equals "neurotic."

Any depressive difficulty that has crossed to the maladaptive side requires a complete differential diagnostic procedure. Even if it is not symptomatic of a mimicker or of another psychiatric illness, who is to say it isn't biological? The symptoms may not be typical of biological depression (which we discuss in the next chapter), but symptoms are not the best way to tell what is going on inside your brain; laboratory tests provide objective data.

Keep in mind, too, that your "minor" depression (which feels far from minor) may have become chronic because nobody treated it right in the first place. This type of depression can begin following a bout with biological depression. Or vice versa: 15 percent of all biological (also called clinical, major, or endogenous) depressions erupt out of minor depression. We call this phenomenon double depression. The minor form tends to persist after the major form clears up.

Still, the most probable diagnoses are psychological for a clinical picture that consists mostly of a persistently depressed mood. Which doesn't mean the depression is not serious. Being depressed all the time is an awful way to live. Besides, anyone who is depressed runs the risk of suicide.

What does "psychological" or "neurotic" mean? In their broadest sense these terms refer to patterns of thinking and behaving caused by mental or emotional conflicts rather than by physiological factors. These conflicts may have been generated in early life in response to internal or external stresses or learned throughout life because of psychosocial factors, such as socioeconomic status.

Why a Rat Will Sing the Blues

Apparent depression can be experimentally induced in rats. Yoke two rats together in a cage with a wheel on one wall. Give control of the wheel only to the rat on the left. Now give them both an identical electric shock. The shock will stop when the rat on the left turns the wheel. Although the shock begins and ends at the same time for both rats, it's the rat on the right who gets depressed. This rat has had no control over what has happened to it, and ends up just giving up in life—the *learned helplessness* effect. Now put it in a situation where it will be able to escape the shock and it will not be able to learn how. It will eat less, lose weight, develop stomach problems, and be less aggressive.

"Learned helplessness" has been proposed as one model for human depression as well. Disadvantaged and/or scapegoated segments of society are at risk. Family dynamics can produce this kind of depression, in the child who learns through the horrors of experience that she or he is helpless and unable to control abuse; or, more subtly, in the family member, adult or child, who is consistently deprived of respect and power.

13

Depression Is an Affliction of Mind and Body

WHEN DEPRESSION PERSISTENTLY interferes with pleasure, social functioning, thinking, eating, working, initiative, sex, memory, satisfaction, sleeping, self-esteem, self-care, peace of mind, assessment of reality, movement, health, and will to live, the bad mood is often the least of it. This depression is more than maladaptive—it's downright pathological. This collection of symptoms has an exhausting list of names, a few of which are: *biologic depression, major depression, clinical depression, vital depression, endogenous depression.* Assuming I had already ruled out mimickers and other psychiatric illnesses, and that I had not yet discovered the subtype, I would simply refer to it as *primary depression* (see Chapter 5 for my preferred "nosology" of depression).

Besides cognitive (describing abilities to reason, comprehend, concentrate) and emotional symptoms, depression of this nature includes what we call *vegetative* symptoms. These refer to essential functions of the organism: to sleep, to eat, to procreate, to remain alert, and so forth. Vegetative symptoms, also termed *hypothalamic symptoms,* suggest brain malfunction, particularly at the hypothalamic level; the hypothalamus (see Chapters 10, 18, and 19) regulates these body functions.

Patient Portraits

Primary depression syndromes have any number of symptoms and symptom combinations.

Judy Y's symptoms presented perhaps the most common picture. She came to us with a fierce bad mood and a load of guilt. "This is a terrible thing I'm doing to my family," cried the 42-year-old mother of three, as if she had asked for this affliction. Her self-esteem was down at about ground level. She'd lost, she said, twenty-five pounds. She was five foot seven and fairly large-boned, but weighed only 125 pounds. She just didn't care about eating. Or about how she looked, to judge from her appearance; her hair just hung, unstyled, perhaps unwashed. Normally sexually active ("every night," she said with that guilty glance, as if something were wrong with that), Judy had "given up," as she put it. She was far less interested in sex now, but the major problem turned out to be that she could no longer have an orgasm.

Judy walked heavily and spoke very slowly, a sign of psychomotor retardation. She had difficulty concentrating. She wasn't interested in much of anything anymore, even the afternoon TV soap operas which for years she had tuned into with delicious anticipation. She was constipated (this, too, she "confessed" as if it were some kind of crime). Her worst time of day was morning, which is typical of most biologically depressed people, whose mood exhibits a diurnal variation, or fluctuation throughout the day. Mornings, she said, were when she wished she were dead. She said that she thought her husband probably wished the same for her, too.

Judy was having a horrible time, but some people have it even worse. They have delusions or hallucinations on top of everything else. These delusions have the same miserable, guilty, down tone as the depressed mood itself—they're "mood-congruent," as we say. The nature of the delusions or hallucination distinguishes this psychotic depression from schizophrenia. I had a patient, Harvey L., for example, who was utterly convinced that he had murdered his wife and that his execution was imminent. In fact, his wife had recently died from cancer. Harvey's depressive syndrome was of the psychotic type.

John R, 54, came in so agitated he couldn't stay seated. He spoke quickly as he moved nervously around the room, pulling variously at his sleeve, his hair, his pant legs. He complained less of a depressed mood than of this awful anxiety and restlessness. The remainder of his symptoms fit the depressed picture.

Finally, Ellen P, a 19-year-old college student, was plagued by a weight gain of fifteen pounds and an appetite that wouldn't quit. When she wasn't eating, she said, she was sleeping—twelve, even fourteen hours a day. She felt okay once she got up, though. By nighttime she was ready to kill herself.

A Backache, a Stomachache, Constipation, an Eating Problem, High Blood Pressure . . .

For some people, depression is few of the mental/physical experiences we have discussed so far. Instead, their depression manifests itself as stomach pains, headaches, backaches, palpitations, weird tingly feelings in the extremities *(parethesias),* dizziness, and a host of other entirely physical complaints. They claim to have no agonized, helpless, depressed feelings, although sometimes they'll admit to being upset about their health.

These individuals are depressed, but theirs is called *masked depression.* Their physical pains are real, but instead of signifying an actual physical illness, they become a physical expression of a mental phenomenon that is too painful to experience directly. Other names for a physical condition that serves as a masked depression are *depressive equivalent* and, when the patient is all smiles, *smiling depression.*

Persons suffering from this depressive syndrome consult internists and family physicians, not psychiatrists. Why would a physician suspect that a patient's physical complaint is depression? To the alert and concerned physician, these patients offer a host of clues. For one, the symptoms often will result in difficulty concentrating, sleep and memory problems, lack of appetite, and other depression-associated vegetative symptoms. Their "health problems" may provide the explanation for the social withdrawal so frequently found in depression. Drug use is another possible clue. The patient may have started taking drugs or drinking excessively to distance him- or herself further from the depression.

In addition, these individuals often look depressed—that nearly universal downcast expression and slow, heavy demeanor or jumpiness are important clues. For another, the pain or complaint frequently does not follow a disease pattern. Moreover, a family history of depression is common, and the appearance of symptoms often coincides with major losses or frustrations, which are common depression triggers. The final diagnostic factor is that thorough physical examination reveals no physiological basis for the distress.

Clues notwithstanding, the diagnosis of masked depression requires considerable care on the part of the physician, and caution on the part of the patient. Misdiagnosis presents two serious risks: Is it really masked depression, or is it a mimicker? Although the patient may present a masked-depression appearance, the physical symptoms may indeed express a disease process. Watch out for the doctor who announces a masked-depression verdict without taking an extensive history and physical. On the opposite side of the coin is the doctor who would rather treat a patient for bodily complaints than deal with his or her emotions. The physician's avoidance can result in inordinate expense and permanent suffering for the patient with masked depression whose aches and pains are taken too seriously, perhaps even treated surgically (about which more in Chapter 21).

PANIC DISORDERS AND EATING DISORDERS AS DEPRESSIVE EQUIVALENTS

One of the after-the-fact criteria for establishing a diagnosis of masked depression is whether antidepressants eliminate the symptoms. This is hardly a systematic way to go about making a diagnosis. Neither is it particularly accurate, since not all depressed people respond to antidepressants. But before biopsychiatry and laboratory tests, psychiatrists had to work with what they had.

Masked depression does not have to be exclusively somatic (bodily). Antidepressants can be effective in treating panic disorders and apparent anxiety. Recent attempts to treat eating disorders with these types of medications are hopeful. The question arises: Are these illnesses also depressive equivalents, or are the antidepressants effective in treating a number of different conditions?

Recent biopsychiatric studies suggest that some forms of bulimia ("binge-purge" syndrome) and anorexia nervosa (self-induced starvation) are related to depression in terms of both brain chemistry and brain function. (Other forms may be related to drug addictions.) This finding would explain the medications' effectiveness in these disorders. In addition, genetic studies indicate a multigeneration family "pedigree" of depression in persons with eating disorders, the significance of which we shall discuss in Chapter 16.

MISERABLE MOOD, MISERABLE BODY

Depressed people with classic symptoms are not excused from bodily ills. Aches and pains of all kinds are common. Many depressed people feel a kind of pressure in the chest or in the head. "I feel like I've been socked in the stomach," said one patient. The discomforts of constipation are all too familiar to depressed people. In addition to these miscellaneous aches and pains, however, folks who are chronically or frequently depressed are prone to three particular medical conditions: irritable bowel syndrome (IBS), hypertension, and fibromyalgia.

UNDIAGNOSED DEPRESSION

**Common Single Complaints of 100 Patients
Seeing Their Internists or Family Practitioners**

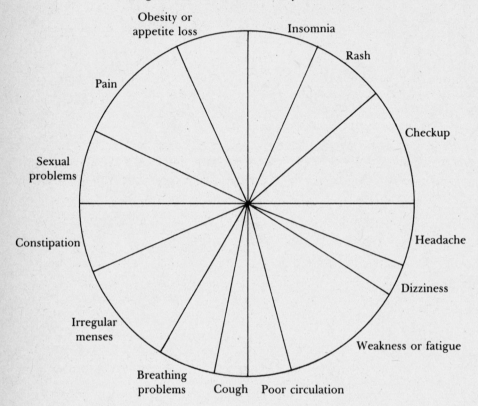

IRRITABLE BOWEL SYNDROME

IBS, in which the intestines are highly responsive to stress, is a chronic "functional" disturbance. In other words, the bowel does not work correctly, even though it is not diseased. It is not nearly as medically serious as it feels. The symptoms include constipation, diarrhea, nausea, cramps, and gas. It is often erroneously termed spastic colitis, which can be a very serious disease indeed.

IBS is an extremely common disorder, accounting for a high rate of worker absenteeism. Studies evaluating IBS sufferers find that as many as half have mood disorders. Nevertheless, comment psychiatrists Paul Wender and Michael Kalm in the *American Journal of Psychiatry,* "that psychiatrists are not familiar with [IBS] is illustrated by the fact that there is no discussion of it as a psychosomatic disorder in the current" premier psychiatric textbook.

HYPERTENSION

"Prevalence of depression in hypertensives is five times higher than the general population," declares Dr. Joseph Di Giacomo. Among psychiatric outpatients only, one study found diagnoses of major depression "three times as common among those with hypertensive disease as those without hypertension."

This relationship causes great difficulty in treating high blood pressure, because of the tendency for antihypertensive medication to cause or exacerbate depression (see Chapter 8).

FIBROMYALGIA (FIBROSITIS)

Chronic tenderness, pain, and stiffness of connective tissue in muscles, joints, tendons, and ligaments mark this common rheumatic condition. The pain can be severe and disabling. Fibromyalgia, also known as fibrositis, has a strong association with depression as well as with irritable bowel syndrome. Persons with the disorder, of which the cause is unknown, have a strong family history of depression. One study compared fibromyalgia patients and rheumatic arthritis patients. Seventy-one percent of fibromyalgia sufferers compared to 14 percent of rheumatic arthritis patients had a history of significant mood disorder.

14

Depression Is Half the Story

IF YOU HAVE EXPERIENCED a depressive episode, you are at risk for a manic episode as well. Mania is as up as depression is down, and equally unrealistic. During a depression you can't get moving. During a manic phase you can't stop moving.

Manics talk a mile a minute, but often cannot complete a thought before they go on to another one. They are impulsive, to say the least, and this, coupled with an overwhelming and unrealistic self-confidence, spells trouble.

Flying High with David, Crystal, and Ron

David S., 39, a stockbroker, had a manic "inspiration." He sank nearly a million dollars of his clients' funds into three worthless stocks, which he "knew" would rise to extraordinary heights. To no one's surprise but his, the stocks lost further ground. He lost his job and reputation and, by sheer good fortune, managed to avoid going to jail.

If David had been depressed, he might well have been unable to trust his experienced *good* sense of the market and therefore he would have had difficulty making an appropriate decision. Symptomatically depression and mania are polar opposites—hence the term *bipolar illness,* currently the preferred name for manic-depression (we will use them both interchangeably).

All the energy and appetite that is lacking in depression, mania has in spades. Manic individuals usually have little need for sleep. They often are overly social and inappropriate in their belief that the person they just met feels a special closeness to them. Hypersexuality is frequently a symptom, as it was with Crystal. A few years ago her mother phoned a colleague of mine in a panic. She had gone to visit her 25-year-old daughter. When she arrived, Crystal was standing naked by the elevator in her apartment house, issuing invitations for sex to any man who got off the elevator. Her mother could not convince her to stop and return to her apartment. When the police arrived, Crystal happily propositioned them, too.

The rotten mood of depression is matched by the euphoria of mania. The high, however, commonly turns to or is accompanied by irritability and a ferocious temper when a family member or associate prevents a manic person from undertaking ill-considered projects.

As discussed in earlier chapters, manics are commonly misdiagnosed as schizophrenic. This mistake is easy to make, for manics can become delusional on top of all their racing thoughts and peculiar speech. As it is in depression, the content of the delusions, or hallucination, is significant. The admitting psychiatrist must be alert to excessive self-esteem and grandiosity. Ron, 29, was directed by God to take a supersonic transport to London to be the bearer of holy tidings to Prince Charles and Princess Diana upon the birth of their first child. He was traveling without luggage because he expected to move in with the royal family, who would, of course, provide him with a new wardrobe.

That very night he was outfitted with pajamas and a robe, at the New York hospital where his before-takeoff ravings earned him a bed.

While the seemingly endless energy and reduced need for sleep may seem enviable, especially to those of us who have many projects to finish and little time, "before modern treatments for mania were available, it was a life-threatening illness: Approximately 15 percent of manic patients died from physical exhaustion," psychiatrist Nancy Andreasen reminds us, adding, "Even in the era of modern treatment, the excessive activity level continues to be a serious risk in patients with cardiac problems."

A fairly straitlaced Wall Street lawyer, Ron was later horrified at what he had attempted to do. It had been his first full-blown manic episode. While he claimed to be a "pretty even guy," after taking a history and speaking to Ron's parents and his wife, the psychiatrists were able to point out to Ron that he had had several, milder "ups" since his early twenties. These were interspersed with mild, infrequent downs. Ron had moved from bipolar II disorder to bipolar I.

Creative Highs and Woes

Psychologist Kay Jamison believes, as a weekly newsmagazine put it, "poetry is the most overrepresented occupation in the annals of manic-depression." She reached this conclusion after studying English and American poets, and after completing research on forty-seven successful living English writers and artists.

Byron, Shelley, Poe, Delmore Schwartz, Robert Lowell, Sylvia Plath, Anne Sexton, and Theodore Roethke are only a few of the bipolar poetic greats.

Among the present-day writers and artists Jamison studied, the rate of mood disorders was a whopping 38 percent, more than six times the rate found within the general population. All "bona fide" manic-depressives in Jamison's study were poets. Nearly 20 percent of them had been hospitalized for the disorder, and more than half had received medication for mania or depression. Well or ill, however, close to 90 percent of the writers and artists experienced powerful, productive creative highs for two weeks at a time—periods corresponding to the length of the usual manic high.

Jamison concludes that creativity and mood disturbance go hand in hand: no mood swings, no poetry. But one does not need such ups and downs to be a successful poet or creative artist, she adds. To which we might add that just because you're moody, you are not necessarily guaranteed a place in the pantheon of great ones.

Bipolar I

Bipolar I illness is classic manic-depression: major mania cycling with major depression. It is rarely a one-for-one cycle, though. One "pole" or the other usually predominates. Men tend to experience more manic episodes and fewer depressions. The reverse is true for women: more depression, less mania. Depressed phases generally last longer than manic periods.

Long periods can separate an episode of any kind, and during these times the person is fine, much better off, in fact, than persons who suffer from depression alone. Bipolars tend to experience more recurrences of the illness than do unipolars, however. The median lifetime episode frequency is ten. Those unfortunate persons who suffer four or more episodes per *year* are known as *rapid cyclers* and are problematic to treat. Generally bipolar I disorder is effectively controlled with lithium, a naturally occurring salt (see page 17 for a history of this drug).

While bipolar and unipolar depressions are symptomatically indistinguishable, diagnosis of the disorder from which each springs is all-important, even if a manic episode has not yet occurred. The focus of treatment in bipolar illness is to stabilize the cycling as well as to treat the particular mood. Treating the depression with tricyclic antidepressants (TCAs) alone, the most popular type of medication for depression, will send a bipolar patient flying into mania or increase the frequency of the cycles (from perhaps one up, one down episode per year to three of each). The reaction will help identify an undiagnosed bipolar disorder, but it is not the best way to go about helping a patient. Indeed, some persons suffer depression and mania at the same time, a truly miserable condition.

RANDY, THE RAPID CYCLER

He was a tall, thin, arrogant, aggressive CEO of a multinational corporation whose name was familiar to anyone who read the business pages or the gossip columns. Rumors of his sexual prowess spread round the world. Was it true that this 40-year-old self-made billionaire could have sex nonstop for six hours running?

Yes, during his once-a-month, week-long manic episodes. But then there was another week in which he could not get an erection.

Neither his associates, acquaintances, or lovers recognized Randy for the manic-depressive he was, although his wife knew something was wrong with him. He was a rapid cycler, riding the high waves two weeks a month, going under for one week, and floating in a calm sea for another week. In his high phase, one week would be truly manic, filled with work and sex and generally frenzied behavior accepted as allowably idiosyncratic by someone of his stature. His depressions, regular as clockwork, were severe only for two or three days, when he could not drag himself out of bed to go to work. The remaining down days were characterized by a general lack of energy or interest. He had to travel frequently and would try to arrange to fly during a down time, so he could sleep through it.

Randy came to me because his wife insisted; otherwise, she would have left him. Despite his numerous adulterous relationships, he could not bear to lose her, and during one of his depressed swings he nearly succumbed to suicidal despair.

Randy did not respond to lithium, but he is doing very well now on anticonvulsant medication (see page 189). He may appear less "brilliant" to columnists, but his wife, not to mention his board of directors, is far more pleased.

ADDICTION TO MANIA

Manic-depressive illness bears an intriguing resemblance to cocaine addiction. (Many of Randy's friends and colleagues believed his peculiar behavior was due to cocaine, which Randy had never used.) Sufferers become addicted to their own neurochemical manic explosions and prefer the sick state to any others. Like cocaine addicts, they do not come for help until their lives are in shambles, with job, finances, family, and health heading down the drain.

One of the greatest challenges in treating manic patients is keeping them on their medication. Once their lives are back in order, many manics prefer a recurrence of their illness to a normal experience of life. They stop taking the lithium and succumb to mania. Because this behavior is so common, programs such as ours at Fair Oaks incorporate lithium support groups into the treatment program—just as we do in our drug treatment programs. And, of course, we check blood levels of drugs—lithium for the manic-depressives, illicit drugs for the abusers.

The similarities between mania and a drugged state are widely recognized in research circles. Can drugs used to antagonize addictive states also combat mania? Experiments are ongoing.

Note that cocaine is not an antidote for depression. Cocaine makes severe depression worse, often triggering hallucinations. Manic-depressives often try cocaine or amphetamines to switch themselves from depression into mania. Some end up feeling a slight improvement before crashing to the depths within a couple of days.

Bipolar II

Until recently we believed the risk of bipolar disorder among depressed patients to be a relatively low 10 percent. That was before we discovered the existence of another, milder form of bipolar disorder, bipolar II. Now we believe that a high 25 to 35 percent of depressions actually represent the down side of all forms of bipolar disorder. About half the time the disease is bipolar I, half the time as yet undiagnosed bipolar II.

The manic phase of bipolar II disorder is what we call *hypomania*, meaning "low high." If you're hypomanic, your behavior does not appear bizarre, the way manic behavior often does. In fact you don't seem at all ill. You're in an extremely good mood, have a lot of energy, you feel sexy, you don't need a whole lot of sleep, your self-esteem is great, you're full of ideas and plans and enthusiasms. You're the ideal of the 1980s.

Is such a great state of mind really abnormal—or are psychiatrists a bunch of grouches?

The difference between normal and abnormal in all aspects of mood is often extremely subtle and may depend on the accumulation of consequences. Everyone has mood shifts. In bipolar II disorder, your judgment may be affected. Is your decision to change jobs based on a realistic appraisal of your abilities and opportunities, or on a sudden spurt of self-esteem? Do you really need all those new clothes or audio equipment or computer add-ons that you are about to buy? Even more to the point, can you really afford them?

Despite the consequences, however—and there may be few— who seeks psychiatric help for feeling good? Because it is the depression that brings a person with bipolar II to the psychiatrist's office, the illness is also called *pseudo-unipolar depression.* Yet another name is *atypical bipolar disorder.* It looks like a DSM-III form of depression, it acts like it, only it isn't. Even if the patient has never experienced hypomania, here too the psychiatrist has to be able to predict it in order to treat the depression. The pain that brought the patient in requires mood-stabilizing treatment in addition to antidepressants.

Obtaining an accurate history from a depressed patient is tricky, however. As psychiatrist Frederick Goodwin points out, "It is extremely difficult to get a past history of hypomania from individuals who are currently depressed and looking at the world through 'blue-colored glasses,' so to speak. Very commonly, however, one can pick this up from family members. In a study at the National Institute of Mental Health (NIMH)," says Goodwin, who is its Scientific Director, "physicians interviewed family members after having taken a history from the patient alone, and a substantial portion of the patients diagnosed as unipolar on the basis of the self-report were rediagnosed as bipolar II after obtaining histories from the family."

Is There a Mania in Your Future?

ASSESSING THE RISKS
For an average of about six and a half years, psychiatrist Hagop Akiskal and his colleagues followed 206 outpatients with a history of depression only. Mania eventually appeared in 20 percent of them.

This 20 percent differed in these six ways from the 80 percent who continued their depressed-only course:

1. They had had their first "clinically significant" depression before age 25.

2. and **3.** Not only did they have a history of bipolar illness in their families, they also had "loaded pedigrees," meaning at least three family members with the illness.

4. They suffered from depression following childbirth (postpartum depression).

5. When depressed, they tended to oversleep rather than to develop insomnia.

6. Antidepressant medication caused a hypomanic episode.

You could already be subject to mania but not know it, until you move to a particular geographic area. In some areas (west Texas, European spas and mineral springs, for example) high levels of lithium occur naturally in the drinking water and prevent the appearance of bipolar symptoms.

Bipolar II is of great interest to researchers. Bipolar I illness has the distinction of being probably the "truest" descriptive category among all the mood disorders in terms of consistency of symptom pictures, prognosis, and treatment indication. In other words, while psychiatrists like me question the DSM-III depression categories, we all agree that bipolar illness is a discrete illness in everything from symptoms to biochemistry.

Bipolar II is more cloudy. We know that patients have bipolar I in their families, and that their own illnesses began in the age range in which we generally begin to see manic-depressive illness.

Some of my colleagues have suggested that bipolar II is the category in which to place those depressed patients who have "reverse" symptom patterns: those who oversleep as opposed to those who can't sleep, and those who eat and eat instead of losing their appetites. Here, too, they place many patients with neurotic symptoms.

CYCLOTHYMIA

There is, however, a separate mood-shift category reserved for those whose ups and downs are believed to be caused by neurotic/character/personality difficulties. Cyclothymia is dysthymia with hypomanic phases as well.

Are all these descriptive categories legitimate? Are all these ups and downs truly separate illnesses? Recent evidence suggests, to the contrary, that cyclothymia is a low-level bipolar illness, and that cyclothymics come from bipolar families. They may not be any more or less neurotic than anyone else with a mood-cycling disorder.

We'll say it again: The actual categories of mental illness can never be described by symptoms alone. We must employ every diagnostic means available if we're ever going to provide treatment that makes sense.

Bipolar Disorder = Seizure Disorder?

Lithium is not the only medication used to control manic-depression. Anticonvulsant medications used in the treatment of epilepsy, such as carbamazepine (Tegretol) and sodium valproate, hold promise for treatment of bipolar disorder. Similarly, lithium acts also to control epileptic seizures. Antiseizure medications could be effective in both illnesses either because the two types of disorders are related, or because the drugs have many independent properties (like Valium, which relaxes muscles as well as relieves anxiety).

Two research psychiatrists from the National Institutes of Mental Health recently found that some bipolar patients (plus a relatively few unipolar depressives) and epileptics with complex partial seizures share a number of symptoms. These include: "illusions of significance, jumbled thoughts, altered sound intensity, altered odor intensity," hallucinations of hearing and smell, periods of amnesia, visual distortions of shape and distance, feelings of detachment from the environment, and others.

The scientists conclude that perhaps the electrical physiology of certain parts of the brain is similarly and subtly altered in both conditions, accounting for the common symptoms.

One small study does not prove the point, but there is no doubt that for many manic-depressives, anticonvulsants work. This is good news, as is the possible relationship to seizure disorders, for it is a line of research that can provide an understanding and eventual answers for those who suffer either disorder.

15

Depression Is a Fact

DEPRESSION IS THE MOST common adult psychiatric disorder. Ten to 25 percent of us all will experience an episode at some time in life—5 to 6 percent are in the throes of one right now. Depression is believed to be on the rise worldwide, perhaps even epidemic. In the United States alone, affective disorders (depression and bipolar illness) currently create havoc in the lives of nine to sixteen million people.

No one, rich or poor, white or yellow or brown or black, famous

---

U.S. President:

"I AM NOW THE MOST MISERABLE MAN LIVING"
He continued, "If what I feel were equally distributed to the whole human family, there would not be one cheerful face on earth. Whether I shall ever be better, I cannot tell; I awfully forebode I shall not. To remain as I am is impossible. I must die or be better, it appears to me."

These words belong to Abraham Lincoln, who was plagued with severe bouts of depression complete with headaches and profound fatigue.

"He was a sad-looking man; his melancholy dripped from him as he walked," wrote a former law partner, A. G. Herndon. So depressed was Lincoln the January day in 1841 on which he was supposed to marry Mary Todd that he did not appear at the ceremony. Alarmed, his friends went searching for him. They found him walking by himself, desperately depressed. Afraid he would kill himself, they instituted a suicide watch over him. Abe and Mary eventually married, presumably on a more cheerful day.

or unknown, infant to ancient, is immune to the mental and physical ravages of depression.

Depressive illness disrupts the lives of sufferers and their families. Whether or not they go for help—and more than two out of three will not—their illness will exact a heavy financial toll, in missed work and/or in medical expenses. Overall, the illness of depression costs this country $7 to $10 billion every year. According to a 1985 special report from the Institute of Medicine, "The affective disorders . . . are probably the most destructive group of mental illnesses in the United States in terms of prevalence, mortality, economic cost, and impact on families." As of 1979, affective illness was the third most commonly diagnosed condition in the United States, following cardiovascular disease and musculoskeletal disease.

Depressive illness is the most common cause of psychiatric hospitalization. It is the bread and butter of a psychiatrist's practice. Family and internal physicians see even more of it than do psychiatrists or psychologists, and they write most of the prescriptions for antidepressant medication.

Mood disorders are the most common psychological problems among college students. One out of three college students will have experienced a unipolar or bipolar episode by the time he or she has graduated. In the freshman year alone, one out of five experiences depression or manic-depression.

More Statistics

While depression is usually precipitated by a life event, its severity and course may be unrelated to the reality of that situation. In 80 to 85 percent of all cases, the episode will abate within six to nine months whether or not the illness is treated and no matter what triggered it.

It will also recur, treated or untreated. Seventy to 90 percent of persons who endure one episode of severe depression can expect to go through it again at least once. Four recurrences is the lifetime median. Months, years, or decades with or without related symptoms can pass between episodes. The risk of recurrence is said to be greatest within four to six months after initial symptoms pass. (Unfortunately, most studies use remission of symptoms as a measure of recovery. But symptoms provide no indication that the internal biological condition has abated.)

Episodes of bipolar disorder recur far more frequently; the median number is ten. However, lithium treatment for the majority of people will reduce the number of recurrences by half; for as many as 30 percent, it will put a halt to all future episodes.

Even though the symptoms of severe depression will most likely disappear in time, we treat it so that it will lift as quickly as possible. Severe depression is rarely a constructive experience. Indeed, evidence is building that the longer an episode of depression continues, the greater the risk of the illness becoming chronic.

In a chronic course, symptoms do not go away; they fluctuate between more or less intense. Inadequate treatment will assure this result as certainly as not seeking treatment. A panel convened by the National Institutes of Health (NIH) recently concluded that recurrent mood disorders are both underdiagnosed and undertreated. Other factors that appear to predict depression taking a chronic course are preexisting alcoholism, older age at onset, minor depression, other psychiatric disorders, and low income. ("The substantial association between lower family income and a more pernicious course seems all too familiar, and serves as a reminder that many powerful factors influencing the course of illness are not susceptible to the clinician's art and science," report the authors of one study.)

Epidemiology to the Rescue

All these statistics and those that follow come to us courtesy of psychiatric epidemiologists, who have contributed much to the overall understanding of depression.

Doctors treat disease in individual patients. No disease strikes but one person, of course, and any disease will be expressed differently in each individual. Epidemiologists are public health specialists who contribute to the understanding of disease by studying its expression within the population as a whole. Does it strike uniformly throughout the country, the world? Or are there geographical areas in which the disease is more prevalent? What are the factors that contribute to the isolated outbreaks? Does the disease strike equally among men and women and adults and children? Does it have similar manifestations among each age group? How is the disease transmitted? Does it appear in families? What factors or characteristics seem to favor the appearance of this disease? Other than the disease itself, do persons with the disease have anything in common? For example, can they trace their ancestry to one area of the world? Or do they also have any other illness? Are identical twins affected similarly?

In other words, epidemiologists unearth the incidence, distribution, and variations within the population of illness and health problems. In doing so they detect the factors that most influence its expression within the population or group, including social, economic, genetic, environmental, psychological, medical, and so forth. They also evaluate diagnostic criteria and treatment effectiveness.

Ultimately epidemiologists trace patterns of disease and identify vulnerability factors and risks. Without epidemiologists, what would we know about AIDS, for example? Long before the virus causing it was identified, someone had to discover the nature of the epidemic, pinpoint disease criteria, and identify key vulnerability factors and at-risk populations.

Knowing how the disease behaves within the larger population, the private physician can see the patient's reported symptoms and examination findings in a sufficiently broad context to begin to make a diagnosis. This holds true as well in mental illness. Epidemiology supplies many of the missing pieces that allow the puzzle to begin to reveal a clear picture.

Elicited during the history, or an interview with the family, an epidemiological finding can often clarify an otherwise "iffy" diagnosis. For instance, let's say that you do not know whether a patient's depression is symptomatic of bipolar II or unipolar illness. You find out that the first significant depression occurred in the patient's early twenties and that since then recurrences number at least three a year. Epidemiology has shown this to be a bipolar II pattern, so you begin to lean in this direction.

Biopsychiatrists and epidemiologists work hand in hand, often to correct flaws of an earlier era. Among these have been the notion that research among hospitalized populations can tell us all we need to know about the vastly larger number of persons "on the outside," most of whom have never even sought help for their depressions. Today ambitious "community studies" are shedding new light on old ideas, such as the ratio of depressed women to depressed men. For years everyone accepted that three women for every man were depressed. More recent work suggest the figure is closer to one and a half or two to one.

The Sex Difference

As just mentioned, more women than men are depressed. This is an overall figure, however, and the ratio does not hold true in all situations. For example, among married and divorced persons, women number among the more depressed. Men take the depressed cake among those who have never married or whose spouses have died. (You'll find more about women and depression in Chapter 23.)

Men experience more of the manic form of bipolar I, although men and women suffer the disease in equal numbers. Bipolar II claims more women on both sides.

Age at Onset

First appearances of bipolar illness patterns tend to cluster in the twenties, although about a third show up during adolescence.

The age of onset of unipolar depression is less easy to pinpoint, probably because the depressive syndrome represents many separate subtypes. Most cases appear from the late thirties to early forties, although depression can appear at any age from childhood to old age. In women the illness may occur somewhat earlier. The first episode of unipolar depression may in fact go undiagnosed, since it often appears as a masked condition or is dismissed as "just" a reaction to a life difficulty. Earlier-onset depressions are now believed to be bipolar II depressions.

Stand Up and Be Counted

Depression is so popular, so common, that there is no reason for anyone to avoid giving his or her suffering a name. The stigma attached to mental suffering that lingers in some communities, cultures, or families would crumble if all members who were concealing their pain, from themselves or others, stood up to be counted. Remember, there's safety in numbers.

16

Depression Is
in Your Genes

DEPRESSION RUNS IN families, often for generations. Scientists now believe that the neurochemical deficiencies that characterize depression are transmitted genetically from parents to offspring. Children who receive the affected gene or genes become vulnerable, or predisposed, to affective disorder. In other words, *depression is an inherited illness.*

Down Through the Generations

The family of Leslie Y. presents a typical depressed pedigree. Leslie is the oldest of four daughters; the second two are twins. Leslie has somehow managed to survive five suicide attempts. Her father had become severely depressed when he was in his forties. Leslie remembers that he developed a painfully sour outlook. Although he had been a successful lawyer, he began to believe that he was not good enough. He became convinced that he was about to have a heart attack and went from doctor to doctor seeking this diagnosis; some assured him he was fine; others suggested psychiatric help, which he angrily refused. Often he stayed home in bed rather than face the prospect of running his business, and he withdrew from friends and formerly enjoyable activities as well as from his family.

Leslie at first insisted that her mother was "more than okay mood-wise." Leslie's description, however, revealed a woman who arose daily at five A.M. because she couldn't sleep, and whom the children would not dare disturb before her morning coffee because her frame of mind was so awful. Once the morning mood passed, her mother sometimes became "speedy and superefficient," Leslie reported enviously, prone to apparently excessive socializing and occasional spending sprees. To us her mother's pattern strongly suggested a bipolar II pattern.

Although both sets of grandparents had died in Leslie's early childhood, she knew about them, and their moods, from her parents. Both grandmothers had also been depressed. Leslie's paternal grandmother, an Eastern European immigrant, could see no future for herself or her family, although her husband within a decade progressed from pushing a cart to owning buildings; her only son, Leslie's father, was far more educated and successful than his father had ever been. The woman was excessively fearful, a trait that Leslie's father exhibited as he grew older. Like his mother, too, Leslie's dad grew to believe that "everyone was out to get him."

Leslie's maternal grandmother suffered extreme mood swings, from fits of laughter to torrents of tears. Leslie's mother was the fourth of seven children; the older children cared for the younger, since their mother was often emotionally incapacitated.

Within Leslie's generation, both she and her youngest sister had a history of depression. Her sister's depressions, less severe, began in her mid-thirties, shortly after her second child was born. Her twin sisters were spared the family illness.

Leslie's own difficulties dated from high school; she attempted suicide the first time at age 17. Four attempts followed when her three-year marriage broke up in her late twenties. She was shocked to hear that we believed her to be bipolar, since her many previous psychiatrists had treated her only for depression. We had asked Leslie to describe the last time she remembered being happy—not an easy question for a depressed person whose dark state of mind dominates and distorts even memory. With pained nostalgia, Leslie described a period of euphoria, reduced need for sleep and food, and unusual productivity—hypomania, in a word.

Population Genetics

Family trees such as Leslie's first alerted scientists to the possible inheritability of depression. Evidence remains statistical. Biologically, it is highly suggestive but still not proved. Direct proof awaits further research, which itself depends on identification of the biochemical, neuroendocrinological, and neurophysiological components of depression. As you will soon see, this research is proceeding at a furious pace. Nonetheless, few doubt that there is a strong genetic component to affective illness. Genetic epidemiologists have been in the field for decades, gathering data. While early studies may be in doubt because of methodological problems, data from recent family, twin, and adoption studies are sufficiently convincing.

Family studies consist of interviews with as many members of the family of a depressed person as possible to determine diagnoses and ultimate family patterns of illness. Often family members will be asked to supply information about members of past generations.

THE AMISH STUDIES

Homogeneous populations, such as the Old Order Amish of Pennsylvania, are ideal for such studies because the number of complicating environmental and cultural influences are minimal. The Amish have maintained their own customs in rural communities separated from the non-Amish for two centuries. Their excellent record-keeping includes detailed family trees dating back to European times. Since they do not drink or take drugs, are all employed, and have strong family ties from birth to death, we can rule out many nongenetic influences in the development of mood disorders. Thus, when studies consistently show that mood disorders cluster along family trees within this population, too, genetic factors receive strong support.

The most recent studies among the Amish reveal a genetic link even to suicidal behavior. Suicide is uncommon in this group, because their religion forbids it. Nevertheless, the research team was able to find evidence of twenty-six suicides over the past century. Seventy-three percent of them occurred within only four families. One family claimed seven suicides in one hundred years. "The role of inheritance was suggested by the way in which suicides followed the distribution of affective disorders in these kinship lines," reported the researchers in the *Journal of the American Medical Association.* Lending further support for the inheritability of suicidal behavior is the team's finding that although the suicides occurred within families beset by mood disorders, other similarly loaded families claimed no suicides. Although the majority of suicides occur among depressed people, depression itself, then, may not be the sole deciding factor.

FAMILY RATES AND RISKS

Within the general population, if one family member has unipolar or bipolar illness, the risk of affective illness among first-degree relatives (parents, siblings, children) is two to three times higher than normal. According to some studies, if one parent and one child have a mood disorder, any other child in the family has a 25 percent risk of developing the disorder. The risk rises to 40 percent when both parents and one child are ill.

Depression à Deux

One in five married depressed patients has a depressed spouse. Geneticists especially want to know why. Is it "assortive mating"—our human tendency to pair off with someone who shares the same problems—that is responsible? Or is it that life with a severely depressed spouse can get you down? Obviously, the validity of many genetic epidemiological studies depends on a correct answer in each case. Unfortunately, the information may be impossible to obtain, especially for preceding generations.

Recent work by Yale University researchers showed that persons who suffered their first major depression before they reached age 20 had the most relatives with the same condition. On the other hand, those who first developed depression at 40 or older had a family rate of depression barely greater than normal.

Interestingly, inheritance patterns appear to differ among bipolar and unipolar groups. Bipolar individuals tend to have an equal number of first-degree relatives with bipolar as well as unipolar problems. Unipolar individuals, however, tend to have mostly unipolar relatives. This tantalizing finding suggests that there is a genetic relationship between the two manifestations of affective illness, with bipolar illness possibly the more severe form.

TWIN AND ADOPTION STUDIES

Twins are the darlings of epidemiological geneticists, for identical twins share an identical genetic makeup. If depression is inherited by one twin, the other should also develop the disorder. Studies do reveal a significant difference in "concordance" among identical twins and nonidentical (fraternal) twins. Depending on the criteria used to define depression, both identical twins become depressed in 40 to approximately 70 percent of the cases; rates for bipolar illness are even higher. Among nonidentical twins the corresponding rate is the same as it is for nontwin siblings, 0 to 13 percent.

To offset the notion that twins "copy" each other, or that one twin's depression would depress the other, epidemiological geneticists also study twins who have been raised apart from one another. The results are the same.

Studies of adopted children yield similarly valuable information. Scientists compare adopted children whose natural parents have mood disorders with adopted children whose natural parents are normal in this regard. They are trying to determine whether the adoptive parents or the natural parents have the most influence over the future moods of the children. It turns out that adopted children whose *natural* parents suffer from affective illnesses are most likely to develop similar difficulties.

Biological Genetics

Some geneticists believe that all affective disorders, from manic-depression to dysthymia, are controlled by one gene. Others claim that many genes must be involved. In either case, biological geneticists hunt for *trait markers* to reveal how the disorder is transmitted and who is vulnerable.

MAGIC MARKERS

A genetic trait marker, explain Brana Lobel and Dr. Robert Hirschfeld, chief of the NIMH Center for Studies of Affective Disorders, is "a biological characteristic that is clearly associated with a tendency toward clinical depression. If scientists had an ideal," they say, "it would be a trait marker that could be traced to a specific location on a particular chromosome; it would be inheritable; it would be observable in well but susceptible people and recovered ill people, not merely in those who were currently ill; and its presence would be associated with the illness—ill people would always have the marker, while their healthy relatives might or might not."

Linkage markers are one type of trait marker. These are characteristics unrelated to mood—color blindness, for example—which afflicted individuals and their relatives also inherit and whose genetic location is known.

We each inherit a pair of genes for every characteristic, one from our mothers and one from our fathers. Each pair is located on one of our forty-six chromosomes. Geneticists have discovered that genes that are close together on a chromosome tend to be inherited together—a group from mom, a group from dad. The linkage marker is one that presumably is inherited along with the gene that carries affective disorders.

The possible linkage markers that have been suggested apply primarily to bipolar illness, which is the form of affective illness geneticists tend to work with; bipolar illness is the most clearly defined of the affective disorders and, as population studies reveal, it has the strongest genetic pattern. Some of the inheritance mechanisms may prove to be the same as for unipolar depression.

The X (female) chromosome is "home" to many of the bipolar linkage markers, including red-green color blindness and a blood antigen. In other words, some geneticists have found that within certain families, the manic-depressives are also color-blind and have the blood factor. Not all families with bipolar pedigrees possess these traits, a fact that suggests that bipolar disorder can be transmitted in more than one way. And, to repeat, not all people who are color-blind are manic-depressive. There is no tie between these factors; color blindness and the blood antigen are no more than a convenient way of trying to locate the mood problem.

Other biologic geneticists search for biological trait markers specific to the physiology of the mood disorder itself. Genes control the activity of many enzymes, certain cell membrane processes, and immunological mechanisms, all of which are believed to be involved in the vulnerability to depressive disorders. The closer we come to identifying the biochemistry of depression, the easier their job will become. That day is dawning.

THE (SE)X FACTOR

If depression, at least in some families, is passed on via the X chromosome, it could explain why more females than males are depressed. The X and the Y chromosomes determine gender; females have two X chromosomes, males one X and one Y.

Some geneticists think that the depression trait is dominant. (Genes are either dominant or recessive. Of the pair of genes inherited, any dominant gene will determine the characteristic in the presence of a recessive gene.) The odds go against a female, who could be stuck with the vulnerability from either of her X chromosomes. The odds are better for a male, who has only one X of a chance to inherit the trait. If there is no depression lurking on the chromosome, presumably he's home free.

X-linkage is not reported in all studies, however. If it were valid, a depressed father could pass his vulnerability on only to a daughter. Every child automatically gets one of mom's X's. Should dad pass his X on to the next generation, the result has to be a depressed daughter. Various investigators have found father-son lines of inheritance.

Thus, either X-linkage is erroneous, or, more likely, it is true only in certain families.

Nature or Nurture?

Let us return to the family of Leslie Y. For at least three generations the Y's had suffered from depression. Statistical implications notwithstanding, their pattern does not prove that depression is genetically inherited. Might not Leslie's illness arise through the influence of her parents, who were unable to establish a healthy family experience because of their own mood problems and those of their parents? It is depressing to grow up with depressed parents. Did Leslie's dad learn his mother's attitudes? Was her mother mimicking her own mother? Did her mother's child-rearing practices contribute to Leslie's own problems?

Obviously, these are difficult questions to answer. "Assessing the relative contributions of genetic and environmental factors is . . . a complex problem," acknowledge the authors of a report issued by the National Institute of Mental Health. ". . . There may be more than one genetic predisposition capable of producing a clinical syndrome. Nongenetic factors that may be significant in the etiology of depression, such as poverty and child-rearing practices, tend to run in families from generation to generation just as genetic traits do."

Nature or nurture? Both. Nurture (environment) triggers nature (heredity). Or: Experience makes us vulnerable to our inherited predispositions. And experience makes it possible to *correct* many of them.

A tendency toward depression is but one of many predispositions we inherit. Perhaps you have a family history of Type II, or adult-onset, diabetes. Will you get it? Even if you inherit the vulnerability the answer at best is *maybe.* Predisposed does not mean predestined. Grow fat and you are more likely to awaken the tendency. But mend your nutritional ways after you receive the diagnosis, and in time you may not even know you have the disease.

In depression as in diabetes, geneticists calculate that many more persons possess the gene(s) than who actually develop the disorder. Environmental, biological, and/or social factors must trigger the predisposition; even then, other factors may offset it. In the words of another NIMH report: "Protective factors, genetic or environmental, interact with genetic predisposition or vulnerability and [can] prevent the expression of a disorder."

Leslie's twin sisters were at high risk to develop the family mood disorders, and yet they remain free of any sign of it. Perhaps their strong, positive attachment to one another acted as a kind of buffer against family and environmental stresses. In some families with a history of multigenerational depression, only one identical twin develops the illness. Genetically they are as close as any two people can be; clearly other factors intervene. Personality factors can influence a predisposition; for example, persons who are worriers and perfectionists are known to be vulnerable to depression. Extraordinarily dependent individuals as well as introverts are also at risk.

VULNERABILITY TRIGGERS

Other than personality factors, among the known or suspected genetic vulnerability triggers are early life experience, overall stress, illness, socioeconomic status (in itself or change in it), geographic mobility, nutrition, physical or mental illness, individual biochemistry, change in overall economic environment, and so on.

The contribution of these factors to the expression of an underlying predisposition probably depends both on the relative weight of both inheritance and experience at any given time. During any severe economic recession, the environment will likely awaken a depressive tendency in great numbers of people. (It is no coincidence that the disastrous economic times of the 1930s were called the Great Depression.) Similarly, among disadvantaged groups, rates of depression and mental illness in general are higher than among the remainder of the population. (Bipolar illness is a curious exception—it is a disorder of those who are well off.)

For strongly predisposed individuals, biochemistry alone may be sufficient to trigger the illness. And in families with many ill members, such as Leslie's, triggers may be almost impossible to avoid. Leslie was very close to her dad when she was young. For him to suddenly drop out when she was a teenager must have been a terrible blow.

THE BEST NEWS YET

Our genes are *not* our destiny; this is perhaps the great lesson of genetic research. Inborn errors can be corrected. Vulnerabilities can be avoided. We can change.

Biopsychiatric treatments for depression work because they counter or correct many of the genetic as well as experiential factors that trigger depression. The psychiatric lab is beginning to differentiate among several different biochemical subtypes of depression; we can then proceed to correct these genetically controlled processes. Similarly, specific psychotherapies have been developed to counter interpersonal, cognitive, and behavioral depression triggers; psychotherapy in general often helps to provide strength to cope with life-event and psychological stressors that can touch off a depression in a vulnerable individual.

As you will see in Chapter 21, you can do much yourself to strengthen your resistance to depression and at least soften the blow. Self-help measures in mild cases or self-help in conjunction with biopsychiatric treatment in more severe illness may even prevent the next depressive episode.

Prevention will be the greatest gift of genetic research. Once biological markers are found, children in high-risk families can be tested and treated before illness becomes a life pattern. This scenario is not necessarily far off, considering the progress we have made in the laboratory to detect the biologic underpinnings of depression. The future of genetic research, the development of accurate diagnostic procedures, specific treatments, and ultimately cures for this horrifyingly common source of human suffering depend on what we are doing in the psychiatric laboratory right now.

Let us not forget, as we depart this chapter, that inheritance is also a *good* thing. In Chapter 14 we mentioned Kay Jamison's study of writers and artists, which showed that they had more than six times the rate of mood disorders than one would expect within the general population. But even the healthy individuals in this group tended to experience creative, manic-like highs during which they were extremely productive. To geneticists these data suggest that a carrier of the manic-depressive gene or genes might receive a great gift instead of a disease. Genes confer the best as well as the worst possibilities.

17

Depression Is Mortal

"To TELL YOU THE truth, one of the reasons I chose psychiatry was because I couldn't deal with patients dying. The deaths that result most directly from psychiatric illness are suicides. Naive as I was, I believed I would be able to prevent or avoid them.

"Little did I realize the nightmare of sitting there session after session worrying about who was going to do it and who wasn't. The quiet ones—were they the risk? The ones who threatened time and time again? What if my attention wandered and I missed something that would be the 'giveaway'? Once I could afford to turn away patients, I began to accept only those whom I felt were not or would not become suicidal.

"Then one of my patients committed suicide—a 45-year-old woman whom I had seen three times. She had come to me because she felt stuck in life, she'd said. Her job was going nowhere, her marriage was boring. She seemed depressed, but not seriously. I asked her, as I asked all patients in the initial interview, whether she ever felt like killing herself. 'No,' she'd said matter-of-factly.

"She did not show up for her fourth session. I phoned her home and no one answered. I called her at work and they told me she had died. 'How?' I asked, shocked. Her secretary would not tell me. Finally I reached her husband, who told me she had shot herself in the head. His tone was icy cold—I felt he was aiming that gun at *me*. I wanted to throw the phone down and run. I don't remember what I said. The next thing I knew the phone was back on the receiver and I was crying. For her, for me. I had had no idea she was suicidal. What kind of psychiatrist was I?

"She shot herself!" repeated Dr. L., reliving the event as if it had happened last week, not twelve years before. Six months afterward, he abandoned the consulting room for the laboratory.

Many physicians fear death; some can translate this mortal fear into a powerful desire to save or extend their patients' lives. For the others, there are few corners in clinical medicine in which to hide. Psychiatry is not one of them.

"Psychiatric patients are known to have high death rates relative to the general population," comment Drs. Donald Black, Giles Warrack, and George Winokur, authors of a study of psychiatric mortality from 1972 through 1981. "During the last fifty years, in different samples, in different parts of the world, researchers have consistently shown this to be true. The excess of deaths has been found in all types of clinical settings and in patients with varied psychiatric diagnoses." Their own work, conducted among former hospital inpatients, revealed a high rate of unnatural deaths—i.e., suicide and accidents. Among depressed patients, these excessive deaths occurred particularly among women during the two years following their hospitalization. Often drugs and alcohol are contributing factors in the high death rate among all psychiatric patients.

Depression and Immunity

Depression affects the immune system, as we will be discussing in Chapter 19. Fatal diseases such as cancer have been linked to depression, although we do not have direct proof as yet.

The Awful Facts of Suicide

Accidental deaths, such as single-car automobile fatalities, are often a form of suicide. "Direct" suicide claims the lives of at least 15 percent of depressed patients. Many more persons try but fail. Among depressed nonpatients, no one really knows how many persons take their lives; suicides are grossly underreported to spare the family the stigma, and among those that are reported, we do not know who was or was not depressed. Psychiatrist-authors Wender and Klein suggest that "there may be ten thousand suicides for every million untreated episodes of the illness." The reported number of suicide deaths is thirty thousand per year. The NIMH estimates that the actual number is closer to seventy-five thousand.

The reported number alone makes suicide the tenth leading cause of death in this country. According to Dr. M. Harvey Brenner, a member of the National Commission on Mental Health and Unemployment, every time the U.S. unemployment rate goes up one point, suicides as well as homicides increase by 4 to 6 percent within the next six years.

MALE SUPERIORITY

Men have the tragic distinction of being "better" at suicide. While four times as many women as men attempt suicide, men tend to succeed; in other words, men outnumber women as suicides four to one. Explanations abound for this phenomenon. "For women, attempts often are a way to express their distress, something men may be less able to do until the pain has gotten too great," says NIMH psychiatrist Susan Blumenthal. It also may be that women take pills and men use more violent means, such as guns, which are more likely to succeed.

THE LINK WITH HOMICIDE

Men also commit more homicides, which we mention because of the deadly close relationship between suicide and homicide. Fact: Some 10 percent of homicides are associated with suicides, as when a mother kills herself and her children. Fact: Violent, murderous rage is one of many possible motives for suicide. (Among others: escape from pain and unconscious rebirth fantasies.) Fact: Depression may fuel homicidal as well as suicidal tendencies.

Here's another fact: Women are catching up both in homicides and violent suicides.

WHO'S AT RISK

By far the group at highest risk for suicide is the elderly. In persons over 65, the rate of suicide is fifteen times higher than among the population generally. Even so, the rate for persons over 44 is lower than it was in 1950. Not so for the under-44 set—especially the under-24s—among whom the rate of suicide has been on the rise.

For adolescents and young adults aged 15 to 24, the rate has more than doubled since 1950. Nobody seemed to notice this until the early 1980s. Now this alarming trend is taken seriously indeed. In a flurry of professional and public activity, we have developed a deeper understanding of adolescent depression and suicide and its warning signs. Turn to Chapter 23 for a discussion of depression's special populations, including children and older people.

Predicting Suicide

Speaking of warning signs, Dr. L. was not alone in his inability to foresee his patient's suicide. Prime risk factors include depression (a factor in 80 percent of all suicides), alcoholism, drug addiction, and schizophrenia, but none of these factors applied in this case. Dr. L's patient was depressed, but she had made no previous suicide attempts to his knowledge; she did not indicate her intention; she did not tell him she was writing a will or otherwise finalizing her affairs; she was not delusional; and she had not recently suffered a severe stress—all of which would have put him on a "suicide alert."

If Dr. L. knew that his patient was contemplating suicide, her degree of hopelessness could have proved an important predictor of eventual success. Chances are that her husband or a friend knew, though. Pity no one told her psychiatrist. Probably her husband did not want to face it either, or perhaps he was one of the many who expect a psychiatrist to be a mind-reader.

Dr. L. would have been overjoyed if someone had handed him a foolproof suicide-prevention checklist. Wouldn't we all! Many dedicated people have attempted to develop one. Unfortunately, while they are able to identify high-risk groups and characteristics of persons who have already committed suicide (such as family history of affective disorders and/or of suicide), they cannot predict that any individual will or will not do it. The greatest risk of suicide is when the patient is beginning to come out of a profound depression and has recovered sufficient energy to act on the deadly impulse. Apparent recovery brings the energy with which to act. Thus it remains up to the clinician to use his or her subjective judgment of the patient's behavior and attitude and shared thoughts to decide whether and when the patient is in danger. Possibly Dr. L's anxiety obscured his clinical skills; clearly he was not cut out to be a psychotherapist. Yet even the most competent, intuitive clinicians lose patients to suicide.

SUICIDE RISK FACTORS

1. A history of previous attempts.
2. A lethal suicide plan.
3. A family history of suicide is more common in suicidal patients than in the general population.
4. Marital status: Patients who have never married are at greatest risk, followed by those widowed, separated, and divorced, married with no children, and married with children.
5. Failure at or loss of occupation.

6. People with certain occupations (e.g., psychiatrists, police officers, musicians, lawyers) seem more prone to suicide.
7. Men are more likely to be successful at suicide, while women make more attempts.
8. Risk generally increases with age, although teenage suicides are increasing.
9. Health status: Certain patient populations are at high risk, including those recently having undergone major surgery, patients in great physical pain, and patients with a chronic or terminal illness.
10. Location: Rates are higher in urban areas than in rural ones.
11. Drug or alcohol use.
12. Paranoia: withdrawal from healthy human contact.
13. Hopelessness: sense of inevitable doom.
14. Being a recent surviving spouse.

Help! Suicidal Elephant Requires Hope!

Out of the biopsychiatric laboratory has come an extraordinary finding about the *biology* of suicide: Suicidal individuals have abnormally low levels of the brain chemical *serotonin*.

This finding, as well as others under study, promise the clinician objective, case-by-case, diagnostic data. For the patient, the same finding offers the hope of eliminating the violent urge to die.

Serotonin is one of the neurotransmitters strongly implicated in certain types of depression; it is also involved in the regulation of impulsive behavior and aggression, whether or not depression is present.

We determine serotonin brain levels indirectly, by measuring levels of its principal metabolic breakdown product, 5-HIAA (5-hydroxyindoleacetic acid), in the cerebrospinal fluid (CSF). A decade ago in Sweden, Dr. Marie Asberg began to notice the correlation between low CSF 5-HIAA levels and both suicide attempts and high levels of aggression. Her finding has been replicated again and again. In one study of suicide attempters who had had their CSF 5-HIAA measured, Asberg discovered that 20 percent of those with low levels succeeded in killing themselves during the subsequent year; of those with normal levels, only 2 percent killed themselves.

Asberg and numerous additional researchers have since found that persons prone to violent suicides (shooting, jumping, hanging) have especially low levels—as do violent criminals. In still another study, both unipolar and bipolar depressed patients with low CSF

5-HIAA levels scored particularly high on the anger-related items on a psychological questionnaire.

The serotonin discovery fits in nicely with genetic findings about suicide and depression. Identical twins tend to have similar levels of CSF 5-HIAA; nonidentical twins do not. Healthy persons with low values have significantly more affective illness in their families than do healthy persons with normal values. The serotonin factor thus marks an inherited trait (a trait marker) rather than a temporary state (a state marker). This is just the sort of information biopsychiatrists are searching for: biochemical markers linked to suicidal behavior. The markers are used to develop both reliable tests to identify persons at risk and medication to reverse the illness. Combine these objective "tools" with our additional clinical skills, and we will be able, as Dr. L. was not, to save our patients' lives.

Not that everyone who attempts suicide wants to be saved. True, many persons who attempt suicide have chosen this high-risk means of shrieking for help. Many die in the process. Others do indeed want out—they don't want anybody to interfere and, as they see it, perpetuate their pain. Discoveries such as the serotonin factor help us comprehend the biological nature of the disorder that produces the pain, so that we can treat it immediately and prevent it in the future.

Paula Was Saved

The desire to self-destruct is in itself a nightmare. Paula D., now 51, made four serious attempts on her life in a two-year period over ten years ago, after she discovered her husband's infidelities with two of her close friends. "At the time, I thought that the humiliation and betrayal I felt were the worst pain I had ever experienced. Looking back on it now, though," she muses, "the need to destroy myself was by far the most excruciating part of the whole horrible time."

That Paula survived seems proof that somebody up there wanted her to live. She lived through two gunshot wounds, one overdose of pills, and one attempt at gassing herself in a closed garage. She had been depressed much of her life, before and after the attempts. She was and is in treatment with a psychiatrist well known as a psychotherapist but who did not at the time believe in the use of medication. Paula herself urged him to prescribe antidepressants for her, which he did but at too low a dose to be effective, an all too common error. When Paula finally came to us for evaluation, tests revealed she was a good candidate for medication. Within one month her most recent depression had substantially lifted. At the end of the year, when we slowly tapered her off the pills, it was gone. She has not had a recurrence, or an urge to die, in four years.

"Now I know what most people mean when they say they're depressed," she says. "I get depressed. It's a down frame of mind, usually in response to something that's just happened or to something that has come up in my therapy—not a blackening of my entire existence. I deal with it and it goes away. Or I don't deal with it and it goes away!"

Paula's therapy is no longer a perpetual battle with her moods. "I've been able to understand and avoid the self-destructive relationships I was always getting myself into. I'm finally getting some work done there!" she says with a laugh and a grimace. Paula has been in therapy for almost twenty years.

The Beast Begins to Emerge

Thus far we have encountered numerous aspects of depression. Subsequent chapters will reveal still others, deeper and deeper inside the "elephant's" brain and body. Let us take a few steps back now, however, and see what we have so far.

WHAT IS DEPRESSION?

Depression is a psychobiological mood disorder—in other words, an interaction of psychological and biological variables. The ratio of psychological to biological factors in the expression of depression depends on the relative strength of environmental and genetic influences. Long-standing economic stress, chronic medical or psychiatric illness, destructive family patterns, or an overload of stressful situations can cause depression in the absence of predisposing genetic factors. Similarly, inherited body chemistry can assure the onset of depression in the presence of few or mild or, rarely, *no* apparent triggers. Factors and variables differ for everyone. Depression is utterly individual, utterly personal. The treatment of depression even as a brain disease depends on this understanding.

18
Depression Is a Brain Disease

IN MEDICINE WE OFTEN find the cure before we understand the illness. When we attempt to understand why the treatment works, we often end up understanding the illness. This knowledge leads us to more efficient treatment applications, to diagnostic tests, to new and better cures, and ultimately to preventive measures. So it has been with depression.

Depression *is* a brain disease. We know that because of two decades of extraordinary exploration of the brain as we have attempted to figure out why and how antidepressants achieve their results.

A Heady Time

The treatment of schizophrenia fell into our laps first. A French surgeon was searching for a drug to prevent the fall of blood pressure that leads to surgical shock. He tried an antihistamine on his patients; it did not achieve the desired results but it had interesting calming properties that left awareness intact. He added the drug to his presurgical repertoire. Other surgeons became interested; chemists set out to produce more effective compounds. Chlorpromazine (Thorazine) was far better. In the early 1950s this drug was elevated to Wonder Drug status when French psychiatrists discovered that it could do what no other treatment had ever accomplished: bring schizophrenic patients back into this world.

Then came the mad dash by pharmaceutical companies to come up with a drug that was even better and that had fewer side effects. A common strategy in doing this is to alter or add to the chemical formulation of the existing drug. By fiddling with chlorpromazine, Swiss chemists created imipramine (Tofranil). Unfortunately, it failed overall as an antipsychotic, except that it did seem to reduce depressive symptoms.

Thus was born the tricyclic class of antidepressant drugs. ("Tricyclic" refers to their chemical structure.) Meanwhile, physicians in tuberculosis hospitals happened upon the other major class of antidepressants, monoamine oxidase inhibitors (MAOIs). The MAOI iproniazid, an antibiotic developed specially for TB, seemed to lift the cloud off many of the depressed tubercular patients.

It was a truly heady time in the history of psychiatry. Freud himself had postulated a chemical imbalance in severe mental illness, but he lacked the technology to elucidate it. In our time, advanced technology was opening the portals to a golden age of neuroscience.

A major breakthrough came when research scientists were able to demonstrate that the nature of communication in the brain was electrical (which we knew) and chemical (which had been hypothesized but never confirmed). It became immediately clear that the chemical was the fundamental unit of communication between nerve cells. This finding gave biological psychiatrists and neuroscientists the go-ahead to search for the biochemical malfunctioning which they believed generated mental illness. Even so, physiological explorations of severe mental suffering continued to enjoy little support among the psychiatric establishment, which remained largely psychoanalytic and espoused psychological explanations for the entire spectrum of mental illness.

There could be little doubt, however, that antipsychotics and antidepressants worked by affecting the chemistry of the brain directly. Ready or not, it was time for psychiatry to widen its perspective. It was time for the brain to resume its proper place inside our heads, from which it had long before been banished in favor of the mind. The question remained: *How* do medications for the mind affect the chemistry of the brain?

The Communication Network of the Brain

Throughout much of the history of medicine, the brain has been off-limits. A brain at autopsy could reveal structural information but took to the grave most of its working secrets. Tinkering with a living brain would destroy it; the brain is the only organ in our bodies that does not generate new cells after birth. (It does, however, generate new connections between cells as we learn and experience.)

THE WHATS

The brain is essentially a mushy mass of nerve cells—ten billion to a trillion of them. These cells come in two types: glial cells and neurons. Glial cells outnumber neurons nine to one; besides keeping the brain supported, protected, and fed, their additional functions are poorly understood. As far as we know now, the neurons do all the actual brain work.

Nerve cells are organized into structures and specialized functional areas that often look identical but control quite different activities and systems.

The gross anatomical structures of the brain evolved over millions of years. The brain stem, rising from the spinal cord, is often called the "reptilian brain," because it is remarkably like a reptile's brain. Basic body functions necessary to survival—heart rate, breathing—are regulated here. All communication to and from the body passes through the brain stem. The cerebellum, one of the brain structures concerned with movement, is behind the brain stem.

The diencephalon is deep within the brain. It consists of groups of neurons sometimes called the "mammalian brain" because these structures are most highly evolved in mammals. Within this part of the brain is the limbic system, the "emotional brain," containing, among other structures, the hypothalamus and the pituitary gland. Body temperature, blood pressure, eating, sleeping, hormones, behavior, and emotions, including pleasure and displeasure—our mammalian selves—are kept in balance here. Or not, as the case may be. Those of us who study depression are most concerned with this area of the brain, particularly the hypothalamus. It is a limbic system regulator, integrating messages through this complex area. The hypothalamus appears also to be a major motivation center, highly influenced by rewarding stimuli.

Lying atop it all is the largest part of the brain, the cerebrum, site of our most evolved, cerebral selves. The cerebrum is covered with the eighth-inch of gray matter, the cortex, that contains our uniquely human capabilities: reason, planning, understanding, behavior control, speech, decisionmaking, imagination, writing, nuclear-bomb-making. . . .

The two hemispheres of the cerebrum are somewhat specialized. In most people, the left side is more logical, mathematical, and verbal. The right side is more "artsy-craftsy" and more concerned with patterns and spatial relationships. Each hemisphere controls opposite sides of the body—left hemisphere/right side, right hemisphere/left side.

The cortex is divided into four lobes, each with highly specialized areas corresponding to different body functions and systems, such as recognizing and processing visual stimuli, control of delicate movements, interpreting sounds, and so on.

The neuron is the basic functional unit of these structures and areas.

The neuron consists of a cell body, containing the nucleus. A web of tubular filaments called *dendrites* protrudes from the cell body. The dendrites receive information and deliver it to the cell body, which "gets the message" and communicates it to other neurons via the axon. The axon projects like a stem from the cell body. At the end of the axon are hundreds of branches, each with a terminal.

With each cell having a legion of dendrites and some as many as a thousand axon terminals, "in a single human brain the number of possible interconnections between these cells *is greater than the number of atoms in the universe!*" as Robert Ornstein and Richard F. Thompson appropriately exclaim in their book *The Amazing Brain*! That calculation should relieve the anxieties of those who worry that delineation of the anatomical structures and biologic processes of the mind robs them of individuality and free will.

THE HOWS

No two neurons are directly connected to one another. A space of a millionth of an inch—the synapse—always separates them. An electrical impulse zips down the axon from the cell body. Q: How does it get to the next neuron? A: It never does. Each axon terminal harbors vesicles containing chemicals; when the impulse reaches the end of the axon and triggers the vesicle to release its chemical contents, its job is done.

The chemicals at the terminals are called neurotransmitters. They diffuse across the synapse and attach to receptors on the adjacent neuron. A receptor will accept a chemical only with a particular molecular structure. The traditional analogy is that of a lock and a key. If the neurotransmitter fits precisely into the receptor molecule, changes will occur in the membrane of the next, or "postsynaptic," neuron; sodium ions will rush in and excite that next neuron into generating a new impulse, called an action potential. Thus the message continues from neuron to neuron.

Neurotransmitters deliver basically two messages: excite (fire); inhibit (don't fire). Translation: Gimme some more of that delicious neurotransmitter; I'm feeling really terrific today. Or: Turn the stuff off, will you? I'm in a crummy mood. When a neurotransmitter is delivering an inhibitory message, negatively charged chloride ions permeate the membrane and prevent the target neuron from firing. Actually it takes neurotransmitters from hundreds of terminals to get the message across to the neuron.

A neuron will use only one type of neurotransmitter at every connecting point, from dendrites to axon terminals. Probably the brain manufactures several hundred neurotransmitters. We have identified some thirty probable neurotransmitters so far. They are difficult to find because, for one, they are released in minute quantities. For another, unused or excess quantities are immediately withdrawn from the synapse, either by enzymes sent to break them down, or by the presynaptic terminal, which draws them back (a process we call "reuptake") to be broken down and recycled.

The Biochemistry of Depression

Once we had the technology to work at a cellular level in the brain, we could begin to understand how antidepressants worked.

THE CATECHOLAMINE HYPOTHESIS

Research with animals suggested that although the two types of antidepressant medication functioned differently, they both increased the concentration of the neurotransmitter norepinephrine in the synapses. The tricyclics prevented norepinephrine from being drawn back to the presynaptic neuron to be recycled. MAO is the enzyme that breaks down many neurotransmitters once they reach the next neuron; MAOIs prevent this process.

Scientists thus hypothesized that if symptoms of depression can be relieved by enhancing the availability of brain norepinephrine, the symptoms must then result from a deficiency of this chemical. Logically, mania must result from an excess of the chemical. It all seemed so simple.

Norepinephrine is one of the catecholamine type of biogenic amine neurotransmitters. These are manufactured, or synthesized, within the neurons from amino acids, protein constituents that often come from the food we eat.

We could not very well take tissue samples from the brains of depressed people. Verification of what was then called the "catecholamine hypothesis" among human subjects necessarily had to be indirect. Although now we have the technology for visualizing the brain in action (the PET scanner, explained shortly) we did not then and still cannot quite see the living brain at the neurotransmitter level. We can, however, infer that the levels of norepinephrine are low by measuring its principal breakdown metabolite, MHPG (3-methoxy-4-hydroxyphenylglycol), in urine.

The MHPG test was originally conceived as a test for depression. Results demonstrated that some unipolar and bipolar depressed persons were deficient in urinary MHPG. Although the test proved unreliable as a diagnostic tool, it remains in use today, to predict which patients are likely to improve on norepinephrine-increasing antidepressants.

THE BIOGENIC AMINE HYPOTHESIS

Soon scientists realized that the catecholamine hypothesis was at best a partial explanation. Laboratories throughout the world were providing other biogenic amine neurotransmitter "culprits." Depression seemed to be not one but several illnesses that shared a common symptom constellation. In other words, depression is a heterogeneous illness with several biochemical subtypes. DSM-III descriptive subtypes do not correspond to these biochemical subtypes. Many effective antidepressants do, however.

Imipramine was supplemented by other tricyclics, such as amitriptyline (Elavil). Amitriptyline influences serotonin rather than norepinephrine. Serotonin's metabolite, 5-HIAA, leaves the brain via the spinal fluid, where it can be measured. Some persons who respond to amitriptyline but not to imipramine do indeed have low levels of 5-HIAA. Very low levels of 5-HIAA often correspond to suicidal behavior or even homicidal behavior, as discussed in the previous chapter.

Further complicating the hypothesis were findings that some depressed people had high instead of low levels of norepinephrine and serotonin.

Although norepinephrine and serotonin remain the neurotransmitters most directly implicated in depression, other neurotransmitters have been added to the list, including dopamine, which was thought to be involved mostly in schizophrenia. Others undoubtedly play a role in mood alteration as well as in the production of antidepressant side effects. A common side effect, for example, is dry mouth—blame acetylcholine for that. And histamine is the apparent culprit when sedating side effects are noted.

NEUROPEPTIDES

Currently one of the most fascinating research areas involves a whole new class of chemical substances, the neuropeptides, also called polypeptides or just peptides. These are chemicals that have properties both of hormones and of neurotransmitters. They work in conjunction with neurotransmitters, making cells more or less receptive to the message.

The endorphins, a class of neuropeptides discovered a decade ago, have captured public and scientific imagination for their structural and functional similarity to opiate drugs such as morphine. Besides killing pain, opiates can bring on depression and elation (the "runner's high," for example). Our natural brain opioids (meaning they are opiate-like), the endorphins and related substances are clearly relevant to the biochemistry of depression. For example, my colleagues and I have found that persons with some types of minor depression have low beta-endorphin levels, particularly those patients who mutilate or cut themselves.

Somatostatin is a peptide at first thought to exist only in the gastrointestinal system. A recent discovery revealed it is manufactured in the brain as well. During a depressive episode, some depressed persons show a low level of this substance.

No doubt other of these many brain substances will prove to fluctuate along with moods—and will invite a new generation of drugs to alter their levels in the brain. It may turn out that some still-to-be-discovered neurotransmitter is the answer to everything. At present we can study only those substances that are both known and measurable.

The Biochemistry of the Placebo

Antidepressants, no matter which type, are guaranteed to work in at least one out of three patients. Aspirin would have the same effect if it were called an antidepressant, because these medications have a high placebo response rate. Medicine typically looks down its nose at placebo responders, as if their response to a pill with no active ingredients proves that they are not really ill.

The placebo, and the placebo responder, deserve more respect.

A research team appeared at a dental clinic in California. Dental pain is supposed to be the worst physical pain we feel, and they came bearing pain pills for the patients awaiting their dental work with the usual dread. Little did anyone in the waiting room know that half of them were about to receive placebos. Nonetheless, all subsequently reported a substantial reduction or elimination of pain.

Step Two. The team reappeared at the clinic. Again half the unsuspecting patients received genuine medication and half received placebos. Only this time half of the placebo group also received a drug called naloxone. The naloxone group was the only segment to report substantial pain.

Naloxone is an endorphin antagonist; it is designed to fit into endorphin receptors and block them so that our natural painkillers cannot work.

The results of this experiment, and many others before and since, tell us that the lowly placebo acts on our endorphin system. All it requires is belief that the medicine we're taking is the real thing.

We do not actually know whether endorphins are responsible for the placebo effect of antidepressants. We do know, though, that endorphin receptors are abundant in the limbic and hypothalamic areas linked to depression, and that endorphins regulate important catecholamine systems.

And now for the bad news: The placebo effect in depressive illness is usually short-lived. The good news: If it's an isolated bout, the placebo effect may be what cures you. Which is possibly why so many psychiatrists prescribe these extremely potent drugs with such abandon.

AMINO ACIDS

Certain amino acids, which are the building blocks of proteins and often occur naturally, have neurotransmitter properties. A few years ago the amino acid GABA (gamma-aminobutyric acid) was identified as our natural antianxiety neurotransmitter. Anxiety and depression are frequent companions, which may explain why low GABA levels have been found in some depressed people.

FOCUSING ON THE RECEPTOR

Evidence exists, however, that the functional defect in depression is not so much the transmitter itself but the receptor that receives it. In other words, the key is all right; it's the lock that is broken.

Focusing on the receptor could help answer a question that has continued to plague researchers: Why do antidepressants typically take two to three weeks to work when they increase the amount of available neurotransmitter immediately? Perhaps antidepressants end up changing the sensitivity of receptors, an adjustment that would take time.

This point of view has become the "new catecholamine hypothesis": that altered levels of neurotransmitters result from the brain's attempt to compensate for the reduced sensitivity of receptors. The synapses have feedback receptors that normally determine when the neurotransmitter levels are appropriate; they issue the order to cease fire. Depression has deafened them, however. The cell keeps pouring the stuff out and the synapse becomes flooded with neurotransmitter. The brain is always trying to keep itself in balance; thus receptors on the postsynaptic side refuse to respond. In time, the effect of the antidepressant would be to set those receptors straight once more.

SYSTEMS, ELECTROLYTES, ENZYMES

Another approach to the delayed effects of antidepressants is study of the relationships among adjacent neurotransmitter systems. When an antidepressant affects one neurotransmitter system, do neighboring systems adjust themselves accordingly to restore harmony?

Investigating electrolytes has also proved productive. Electrolytes such as sodium, calcium, potassium, and magnesium assist in electrical conductivity across cell membranes. Electrolyte imbalances appear in certain types of depression. Lithium, a salt that is similar to an electrolyte, appears to assist in transport of the sodium ion.

Then there's COMT (catechol-O-methyltransferase), an enzyme that breaks down neurotransmitters within the synapse (MAO performs that function within the cell body). High and low levels have been reported in differing types of depression.

MAO: The "Personality Enzyme"

When is a platelet not a little plate? When it is a component of blood cells. We can monitor levels of the neurotransmitter breakdown enzyme MAO in blood platelets, which resemble brain cells in numerous ways, including receptor and membrane function. Like the central nervous system, platelets contain MAO. Until recently, platelet MAO measurements have been used mostly to diagnose (MAO is low in bipolar depression), to determine MAOI medication responsiveness (the medication appears useful in persons with high MAO activity plus anxiety, agitation, and bodily complaints), and to improve MAOI response (reduction of platelet MAO by 50 to 80 percent).

Lately platelet MAO levels are also providing a quick and easy assessment of certain personality traits—easier than the paper-and-pencil psychological test approach. In study after study, decreased

MAO levels, associated with bipolar disorder, correlate with sensation or thrill-seeking and impulsivity. Low MAO is a possible "suicide marker," as is low serotonin, mentioned in the previous chapter.

Eventually, MAO levels may be able to predict future vulnerability to mood disorders. In one experiment, researchers measured MAO levels in college students then contacted them again two years later. Compared with the high-MAO and normal group, low-MAOers had more psychiatric and legal problems and had fallen an average half-year behind in school; those who had graduated or simply left school reported greater job instability. Some had experienced no serious problems, but they reported significantly more depression, alcoholism, suicide, and contact with the mental health system in their families. Platelet MAO levels may qualify therefore as a genetic trait marker, identification of which could potentially help prevent serious mental suffering.

Serotonin, by the way, also can be measured in blood platelets. It has additional personality correlates besides violence, impulsivity, and suicidality, which in some persons correspond to low levels of the neurotransmitter. A high level of serotonin is an apparent leadership quality. Dominant monkeys in one report had twice the amount of serotonin than the others—and in a college fraternity, the officers had higher serotonin values than the "brothers."

Mapping Depression in the Brain

To repeat: The neuron is the basic functional unit of the brain, the neurotransmitter the fundamental unit of communication. Our brain power comes from the "wiring" of neurons—the pathways—among the specialized structures and areas of the brain. Emotional reactions do not come blasting helter-skelter out of the limbic system. The circuitry connects the system to the cortex and many other areas of the brain, including memory centers, all of which may encourage or inhibit a response and determine how it is to be expressed. The response is different in every person because the interconnections among nerves are as individual as fingerprints. Interconnections are continually being formed by learning and experience.

Neurotransmitters carry the messages throughout the brain, but they do not determine it. The meaning of the message can be inferred from where in the brain it goes.

Following the pathways of norepinephrine (called the noradrenergic system), serotonin (the serotonergic system), and other biogenic amines reveals the brain areas we think are involved in depression.

The neurons in these systems have very long axons and plentiful terminals, so that their interconnections number in the many thousands. The cell bodies originate in the brain stem.

There are two noradrenergic brain pathways, one leading to the hypothalamus and limbic system, with terminals in the so-called "pleasure centers." The other is concentrated in a small brain stem area known as the locus coeruleus. This tiny brain area is associated with fear; monkeys who were electrically stimulated in the locus coeruleus became behaviorally and physiologically fearful. This area is also implicated in drug withdrawal states. From the locus coeruleus, this noradrenergic pathway terminates in the cortex and hippocampus, the latter involved in memory. It also projects down into the spinal cord and spreads throughout the cortex, as do the serotonin and dopamine systems.

The serotonergic system follows a pathway similar to that of norepinephrine, originating, however, in the raphe nuclei. In laboratory experiments, animals without these nuclei are agitated and insomniac.

One of the projections of the dopaminergic system connects the hypothalamus with the hypophyseal portal system, which proceeds to the pituitary gland. Other projections are found in an area of the cortex that is associated with emotional behavior.

These maps make it clear that depression affects us on many experiential and physiological levels. The neurotransmitters are particularly involved in the limbic system, paralleling depression's emotional and vegetative symptoms. The nerve patterns within the cortex demonstrate that depression affects the highest brain functions and controls.

HIGH-TECH MAPPING

Positron emission tomography (PET) offers an intriguing way to see where depression is located in the brain. It is a latter-day computer-assisted "X ray," which reveals body tissue in action. In research psychiatry, PET is used to picture rates of glucose metabolism in the brains of persons with various mental illnesses compared with those of a normal control group. Glucose—sugar—provides the energy for the brain. Subjects receive radioactively tagged glucose; forty minutes later their brains are scanned for about an hour. If certain areas of the depressed brain are more or less active during depression, they will show up using this procedure.

In a 1985 study, depressed persons revealed significant sluggishness in the part of the brain called the caudate nucleus. Connected to the limbic system but not actually part of it, the caudate nucleus helps to regulate movement and muscle tone, but it may be involved as well with attention and arousal. The caudate nucleus is one of the highest dopamine-containing areas of the brain.

One more difference showed up, but only in a segment of the subjects: The left side of the frontal lobe of the cortex was substantially slowed. For years there have been numerous reports of the brain's segregation of positive and negative emotions, with rotten moods being the right hemisphere's weight to bear. Stroke victims whose brains have been damaged in the left frontal areas show severe depression. So it seems that if your "cheerful side" is impaired, depression awaits you.

ELECTRIC "BEHAVIORAL" MAPS

How the brain responds to a brief stimulus, such as a flash of light, provides an inner look at a possible explanation for outward behavioral style. The method is called *evoked potential.*

The subject is attached to an electroencephalograph (EEG), which measures the brain's electrical response to changes in the stimulus (light, sound, etcetera). The response of depressed persons typically differs from that of nondepressed individuals. As the stimulus becomes more intense, their brain waves barely increase in amplitude; sometimes they may even show a reduction. In other words, brain activity in depression is inhibited, underaroused. Depressed persons cannot maintain appropriate sensory attention to the world around them—further indication that our responses to the environment depend on the electrical and chemical environment within the brain.

The hyperresponsiveness of mania is revealed in results of evoked potential tests: Brain waves intensify beyond the normal.

Evoked potential response parallels neurotransmitter defects. Give a depressed person L-dopa, which will increase dopamine, and brain-wave response will return to normal levels.

19

Depression Is
Too Many Hormones and a
Mistimed Bio-Clock

DEPRESSION LITERALLY FLOWS out of the brain and into the body. The endocrine system provides the channel.

So common are biochemical derangements of the endocrine system that we have come to regard them as state markers for biological depression. Unlike a trait marker, which is present in health and illness and signifies a vulnerability to disease, a state marker comes and goes with the illness. In other words, a state marker is a diagnostic "flag." In the biopsychiatric laboratory, your hormones are such a good indication of what is happening in your head that we call them:

A Window into the Brain

Some years ago, Dr. Edward J. Sachar began a study of the levels of the hormone cortisol among depressed persons undergoing psychotherapy. Cortisol is a stress hormone secreted by the cortex of the adrenal glands. Sachar wanted to see whether psychotherapy causes changes in stress levels. Instead he stumbled upon a major discovery about the biology of depression.

Sachar discovered that a large percentage of seriously depressed people have a level of cortisol in their bodies that is even higher than in persons suffering from severe anxiety or psychosis or other equally stressful conditions. It did not make any sense. For one, cortisol is an activating hormone, helping to stimulate body systems to respond to stress. But depressed persons with high cortisol levels were anything but stimulated. Secondly, while oversecretion of cortisol is a symptom of Cushing's disease (see page 154), Sachar's depressed subjects had normal adrenal glands.

NO FEEDBACK

Investigators began looking for other abnormal hormonal patterns in depressed persons. There soon came about yet another paradoxical finding. Many depressed persons with healthy thyroid glands showed evidence of excessive secretions of thyroid hormone. Persons with too little thyroid hormone (hypothyroidism) are often misdiagnosed as depressed (page 148), but as with cortisol, too much of the hormone generally produces opposite symptoms.

Indeed, evidence of "too many hormones" began to show up in many endocrine subsystems. But the glands themselves were normal.

The endocrine glands function to keep complex body systems in a well-balanced, well-regulated state, or homeostasis; they continuously and smoothly adapt to changes in our inner and outer environments. Clearly, depression disrupted this delicate balance. But neuroendocrinologists could find no evidence that the glands themselves were damaged.

The site of the malfunctioning had to be the brain. As we pointed out in Chapter 10, the endocrine system is a kind of extension of the nervous system into the remainder of the body. Indeed, the two are inseparable, since they are linked at the hypothalamus. We have seen that the hypothalamus and the limbic system of which it is a part are central to emotions in general, depression in particular. The hypothalamus also has charge of the endocrine system, via the same neurotransmitters implicated in depression. The imbalances in neurotransmitter-receptor systems that produce depression also influence the hypothalamus's ability to regulate the endocrine system.

Thus, via the hypothalamus, emotions influence the physiological functioning of the body, and the malfunctioning of body systems influence emotional experience.

We have seen as well that diseased endocrine glands are among the most common mimickers of depression. Disease causes a gland to oversecrete, undersecrete, or cease secreting hormones; the resulting hormonal imbalance produces emotional symptoms through neuroendocrine channels.

Depression, however, works from the brain downward. It affects the elaborate feedback mechanisms that establish and monitor the correct level of hormonal secretions throughout the endocrine networks. Some of these mechanisms function like thermostats, turning off secretions when hormone levels reach a certain set point. In biological depression, these sensors do not operate properly. The depressed person awakens at unusual hours and cannot return to sleep;

he loses his appetite; she does not get her menstrual period even though she is not pregnant.

ENDOCRINE TESTS FOR DEPRESSION

Thanks to the work of neuroendocrinologists and biopsychiatrists since Sachar's original discovery, we now have concrete physiological evidence of disruption in this essential homeostatic balance in depression. Since not all patients reveal the same endocrine abnormalities, we have developed a number of neuroendocrine measures. Most biopsychiatrists need to administer only two such tests to detect the vast majority of biologically depressed persons.

The dexamethasone suppression test (DST) and the TRH stimulation test are both "challenge," or "provocative," tests. We administer a dose of hormone and challenge the system to behave or misbehave.

Dexamethasone is a synthetic version of the adrenal hormone cortisol. We administer a level of dexamethasone that the hypothalamus should monitor as excessive cortisol. The normal, nondepressed hypothalamus responds by telling the pituitary gland to signal the adrenal cortex to stop its usual daily secretions of cortisol for at least twenty-four hours, until levels return to normal. But in about half of depressed people, no such response takes place. In the absence of functioning feedback mechanisms, the adrenal cortex continues to secrete cortisol.

The TRH stimulation test, also known as the TRH–TSH test, was described in Chapter 10.

Together the DST and the TRH stimulation tests can identify biological malfunction in approximately 85 percent of unipolar depressives. The DST alone will identify about half of them; the TRH stimulation test alone is abnormal in nearly 64 percent. Thirty percent of patients show abnormalities on both tests.

We know that these endocrine disinhibitions are depression-related, because treating the depression banishes them; they go away. Normal endocrine regulation resumes. Thus we use these tests not only to detect biological depression but also to determine as well when the episode truly has ended. Symptoms may disappear, but when the underlying imbalance remains, we now know that depression is bound to return. The tests are our feedback mechanisms. Once they are normal, we can cease aggressive treatment of the acute phases and move on to long-term prevention.

The Clock That Couldn't

Dr. Sachar's work led to another important discovery about hormonal functioning in depressed persons. Sometimes their overall levels of hormones are normal, but the timing of secretions is odd indeed. For example, take cortisol. In normal individuals, levels are lowest in the middle of the night and highest at about eight A.M. and four P.M. Depressed persons often reveal no day-night differences or even show a reversed pattern, with the high occurring in the wee hours.

Emotionally, depressed persons are out of sync with the rest of the world. Biologically, too, they march to a different drummer.

A SAD PATIENT

I remember the first time I heard her voice. It was during the World Series. Before I flipped on the TV to catch the game, I reached over to turn off the radio. She started to sing and the quality of that voice —you would know what I meant if I could reveal her name—transformed the next several hours of my life. Even when the song had ended, I remained mesmerized. The baseball game was exciting, but it takes second place in my memory of that long-ago day.

I bought a number of her recordings over the years, for hers was the kind of voice and personality that live forever. But then she stopped singing. I heard a vague rumor that she was ill. Cancer, somebody said. I shook my head in sadness.

Shock is too mild a word for my reaction when she was shown into my consulting room. My appointment book indicated a new patient, but the name was not hers. She had used her real name instead of the stage name the world knew her by.

She certainly did not look like she had cancer. Her shapeliness had disappeared under the thirty pounds she said she had gained in the last few months. "I get these cravings," she admitted. "Anything sugary or sweet. I could eat a box of donuts this minute—all of them, no joke."

Our tests ruled out cancer along with other mimickers. Nonetheless she was severely ill—desperately depressed. At that moment she was spiraling downward, she said, but sooner or later she would "snap upward like a released rubber band." While she had been going back and forth like this for at least ten years, it hadn't been a significant problem until three years ago. Diagnosed manic-depressive, she had been through the gamut of psychological and pharmaceutical therapies without noticeable change. She had had a brief flirtation with alcohol, marijuana, and cocaine in order to keep up with her demanding career. She ended up on such a "bummer," she said, that she gave them up along with her career.

During depressed phases she drifted away from everybody she knew. She had no energy. Mostly she slept. At first she would return to the world when her spirits lightened. Her disappearances lasted so long, however—half the year—that she lost contact with most of her circle. She traveled for a while but found it too difficult, ultimately, to keep up the interest or the pace. Even in a good phase she felt a little lonely and lost. She spent most of the time sleeping in her hotel rooms in some of the most fascinating places in the world.

Only one trip seemed to bring her out of it, she said. She'd spent part of one winter in the Caribbean at the estate of an old friend. She had had a wonderful time. She didn't do anything special; she just felt great, like her old self again. She went back to New York to see about resuming her career, and within the week she had plummeted.

The proverbial light bulb went off in my head. Close questioning revealed a pattern to her moods: down in fall and winter, up in spring and summer. "I've always been down in winter," she said, "since I was a kid. But it was nothing like what's happened to me during the last few years. I've spent a lot of time talking to shrinks about why I close up in winter." She added, "I'm really neurotic about it."

"Maybe, maybe not," I said. "Your mood swings may be physiological. We have recently discovered that some depressed people are highly responsive to light, or rather the absence of it. Their moods fluctuate seasonally in response to the length of day and the intensity of the light."

Her visit occurred about five years ago, when the discovery of seasonal affective disorder (SAD) was brand-new. Now we know a great deal more about it, including the hormone that seems to be responsible: melatonin. Melatonin is produced by the pineal gland, located in the brain. Not that the seasonal nature of moods had escaped notice. Even Hippocrates had known that mania and depression peak in spring and fall.

In our time we have seen these seasonal moods as psychologically motivated events, as they often are. But sometimes they have to do with the biological rhythm of melatonin.

Why we secrete melatonin has long been a mystery. We have known that in animals it controls seasonal reproductive rhythms; offspring are born as the hormonal secretions diminish in spring and summer. Melatonin secretions occur in the dark of night; nights grow longer into winter, when few animals give birth and many hibernate. Darkness stimulates melatonin; light suppresses it.

Human reproductive behavior does not follow such a pattern. Light and dark have far less of an overall influence on our behavior, or so we have long believed.

Nonetheless, our pineal glands secrete melatonin at night. Natural or bright light will suppress it. Those afflicted with SAD are sensitive to this hormone. Other than depression, their symptoms, which grow stronger as days grow shorter, suggest impending hibernation: lethargy, large appetite and overeating, weight gain, carbohydrate craving. And according to one report, women with SAD tend to conceive in late summer, giving birth at a low-melatonin point nine months later.

SHE SINGS IN SUNLIGHT

The treatment for SAD is simple: more light. Spend the winter closer to the equator or sit under intense light, five to ten times brighter than usual indoor light, for three hours each at the beginning or end of the day or for five hours at the end. My singer-patient chose the "Caribbean cure." Every year she winters with her friend or in Florida. She'll come north for brief concert dates or recording sessions, since it takes about three days for the depressive syndrome to return.

Light put her back in sync with the rest of the world. She sings again. All depressed people wish to sing again in their own way. Resynchronization may just be the key.

The World Through Rose-Colored Glasses or Blue-Green Ones

Put on a pair of specs with 50 percent rose-gradient plastic lenses and you'll be cured. Unless you are one of those persons who require blue-green lenses, says Dr. Peter Mueller. He refers to the novel treatment he has developed for the seasonal down-up phenomenon he calls light-sensitive Seasonal Energy Syndrome (SES).

Dr. Mueller studied a group of severely seasonally affected individuals for whom light therapy did not work. He discovered they had an unusual set of mental and physical symptoms for each of the fall/winter and spring/summer illness phases.

During the fall/winter period, for example, besides the symptoms ordinarily found in SAD, his patients commonly suffered from such vascular problems as chronic migraine, easy bruisability, and Raynaud's phenomenon (in which fingers and toes become extremely cold and painful). Women, he also found, were markedly more depressed as a group than were the men during this phase.

In the spring/summer phase, men now suffered the most extreme emotional symptoms. All patients were "up" in this period, but the men as a group tended to lose control, become violent, and move into psychosis. Migraine was common at this time, too, but tended to be acute instead of chronic.

Dr. Mueller performed extensive tests on these patients, including EEGs and CAT scans. Most of them, he discovered, suffered from attention deficit disorder (which in children used to be called hyperactivity) and about half had a form of epilepsy.

Light exposure did not work—and the worst of the symptoms, the violent behavior, occurred during periods of ample light.

He traced most of the symptoms to melatonin and its chemical precursors. He prescribed medications where necessary—and glasses.

For the fall/winter group, rose-colored glasses did the trick; for the spring/summer set, blue-green polarized lenses. On the basis of this initially fortuitous discovery, he suggests that visible light in the red spectrum inhibits the melatonin, while the blue-green increases it.

THE LOSS OF RHYTHM

We live in a world of cycles and rhythms, daily, monthly, yearly, lunar, seasonal. No matter how "civilized" we become, our existences are tied inextricably to them. When the weather grows colder we must dress more warmly, to cite but one simple but essential example.

The basic unit of our lives is the twenty-four-hour day; we must adapt all our activities—sleeping, working, eating, playing, maintaining a family—to this environmentally imposed cycle. Our bodies have corresponding rhythms, some attuned to the outward environment, some working only according to internal, repetitive rhythms, and all working in complex harmony with one another.

From the cycles of sleeping/waking and rest/activity to body temperature rhythms and hormonal secretions, smooth and ordered functioning of our biological clocks is essential to physical and mental well-being. Think of the havoc that jet lag can wreak on our lives. Adjusting our daily clocks a few hours ahead or back can throw off concentration, energy, digestion, behavior, sleep, hunger, immunity to illness, and mood.

Physiologically, jet lag is the result of our two daily oscillators, or pacemakers, losing their mutual synchronization. Researchers believe that our daily rhythms are driven by at least two such oscillators. One is strong and consistent; it controls body temperature ups and downs, some hormonal secretions, and REM (dream) sleep. The other oscillator controls sleep/waking, activity/rest, and sleep-dependent hormones. It is said to be weaker and more capable of fluctuating in time. For instance, unless you have insomnia, you can go to bed at eleven tonight and two A.M. the next night and midnight the night after that without too much difficulty getting to sleep and sleeping the night through. But your temperature will doggedly stick to its pattern; it will peak at the same time every afternoon and dip to its lowest in early morning.

Both of these systems are usually keyed to the day-night, light-dark cycle imposed from the outside, which also keeps them in sync with each other. Head for Bora Bora, however, and these cycles will have to adapt to a different day-night cycle. According to one calculation, after a five-hour flight west, the sleep/wake pacemaker will catch on in two days, while the more "stubborn" temperature system will continue on home time for three more days. Misery. Only when this cycle eventually adapts to the change and operates in harmony with the weak oscillator will you feel yourself again.

Evidence is mounting that depression represents a periodic de-synchronization with respect to internal and environmental stimuli, especially when hormonal secretions are out of sync. Experiments have been conducted in which normal volunteers spend time in environments with no clocks or windows or other time cues. Characteristically their days lengthen to an average twenty-five hours (called a "circadian" rhythm, meaning "about a day"), their two pacemakers separate, and they end up with biological rhythms much like those of depressed people. Some subjects also become seriously depressed.

Depression has its own pathologic rhythms. Bipolars have two distinct mood cycles. All mood disorders are episodic, sometimes better, sometimes worse. Recurrences often occur with precise regularity. Besides a seasonal worsening, for most depressed people the bad mood intensifies in the morning, letting up a little toward the end of the day. Some persons exhibit the reverse pattern. Twenty-eight-day lunar rhythms in depressed moods occur in women with premenstrual syndrome (PMS).

THE SLEEP OF DEPRESSION

Virtually all persons with mood problems experience irregularities in the sleep/wake cycle, which is the most fundamental rhythm in our lives. Some can't fall asleep, others can't stay asleep, most awaken too early in the morning. Still others require enormous amounts of sleep.

Sleep researchers have been peering into sleeping depressed

brains for some time. Using EEGs they have discovered that the sleep cycles of depressed people run backwards.

Sleep consists of four stages plus REM (rapid eye movement) sleep, in which dreaming occurs. All stages plus REM repeat themselves every ninety minutes throughout the night, although the different stages occupy more or less of the time relative to each other as the night progresses. The typical, normal pattern is for deepest sleep to take up most of the ninety minutes at the beginning of sleep and to grow shorter toward morning. REM sleep, however, which is close to a waking state, occupies perhaps as little as ten minutes per ninety-minute cycle early in sleep but can lengthen to as much as an hour as wakeup approaches.

The pattern is reversed in depression. REM sleep occurs far more quickly after the onset of sleep (we call this "shortened REM latency") and diminishes toward morning. The shortened REM latency is so characteristic that it has become the single most accurate diagnostic test for biological depression, with an 85 percent yield.

Depressed people also get less overall deep sleep, which is the most restorative and refreshing of all.

This peculiar pattern of depressed sleep is evidence of desynchronization, since REM sleep and sleep/wake are on separate timing "devices."

The REM finding also supports the view that the basic disturbance in depression is of the biological clock. Other distorted biorhythms are the previously mentioned cortisol, body temperature, and secretions of hypothalamic TSH and prolactin. MHPG, the metabolite of norepinephrine, also reveals an "off" rhythm. Explanation: The temperature/REM pacemaker is running too fast in relation to the sleep/activity cycle. The good news is that antidepressants slow the cycle and return the biological clock to its proper, complex timing system.

THE MASTER TIMEKEEPER

Our biological rhythm pacemakers are a central nervous system phenomenon, requiring contact with both the outside and inside world. When changes occur, the brain works hard to correct them and to resume the balanced, functioning state (homeostasis) that enables us to survive. Introduce cocaine into your brain, for example, and your brain will feel as if it's received a rush of norepinephrine, which cocaine resembles. Keep on flooding those receptors, though, and soon the brain will fight to regain its "composure," the receptors becoming insensitive to the drug. Balance is achieved anew—unless the dose of cocaine is increased, which will start the process over again. Keep on increasing and eventually you'll die from the effects of the drug on the cardiovascular system.

Depression can be seen as a similar phenomenon. You go out of sync and the brain eventually resets the clock. It goes out of sync again, though, because the illness remains. Thus the struggle continues. If, however, the depression is not treated, and if suicide does not intervene, the brain will begin to see depression as normal. It will no longer work to resume its previous balance. The depressed state will become chronic.

The puzzle is: Where in the brain does this timing control emanate? We don't actually have little machines spinning around in there, or ticking, for that matter. Chronobiologists (chrono = time) believe that they may have located such a center. Guess where they found it? Right, the hypothalamus. Which brings us back, like a well-functioning clock, to neurotransmitters and hormones.

The suprachiasmatic nuclei (SCN) are small cell clusters in the hypothalamus that are linked to the pineal gland and to the eyes. They are believed to be the brain area that integrates daily rhythms, if not all biological rhythms, according to the most prominent environmental stimulus, light. Via the nerve pathways excited by the neurotransmitter acetylcholine, light travels from eyes to SCN, then via a norepinephrine pathway to the pineal. Here norepinephrine acts as an inhibitor, to stop the manufacture of melatonin. In the absence of light, melatonin—called the "chemical tick tock"—is synthesized directly from serotonin. The pineal, in fact, possesses the highest concentration of serotonin in the body.

THE FINAL COMMON PATHWAY

"The major neurotransmitters which we relate to depression are all involved in the control of melatonin synthesis," noted pioneering researcher Daniel F. Kripke, MD.

"So what you're saying," an interviewer responded, "is that light may affect the metabolism of these key neurotransmitters, and that this can lead to an effect on melatonin secretion (which regulates the body's circadian rhythms—one of which may involve mood)."

"Correct," said Dr. Kripke. "We don't know the full details of where and how melatonin acts, but it appears that melatonin acts on the hypothalamus in a way that alters the secretion of hypothalamic polypeptides. Thus, melatonin secretion appears to influence the secretion of [certain] hypothalamic-releasing hormones."

We have seen that many types of depressive syndromes (psychological, drug-induced, biological) produce similar symptoms. Is the SCN-to-pineal pathway the "final common pathway" that produces this constellation? "Genetic, biological, environmental, and psychological effects could all trigger disorders of this system," says Dr. Kripke.

THE GOOD NEWS
The biological clock can be reset. Antidepressants and lithium are one way, light another, eyeglasses another. Careful use of melatonin itself, or of other drugs that affect these mechanisms, may prove to alleviate depression. Shifting "synchronizers" has been attempted with some success—such as treating chronic depression by timing bedtime and waking five or six hours earlier, then gradually returning to the usual time. If this doesn't lift mood, it may nonetheless increase the effectiveness of antidepressants. Waking a depressed person during REM phases has sometimes also been successful in the treatment of acute depression.

Or skip a synchronizer altogether. Stay up all night. The next day you'll feel fine. It's one of the best ways we know to snap somebody out of depression. Unfortunately, it does not necessarily work for long. By Day Two you'll probably be feeling lousy again. You'll be ripe for more long-lasting, perhaps permanent treatments.

You might try the "natural, organic" approach. Lead a regular life. Every day, even on weekends, get up at the same time, go to sleep at the same time, eat at the same time, and so on. All these activities are synchronizers that may ease you back on track. Also, stay away from drugs and alcohol, which are desynchronizers. This path is commonly recommended to persons suffering from insomnia, chronic headaches, and stress-triggered problems of all kinds.

Depression, Hormones, Clocks, and the Immune System

Our nervous, endocrine, and circadian systems all share mind/body links. The immune system may be the last missing link. It, too, is modulated by hypothalamic hormones as well as by adrenal, thyroid, sex, and growth hormones. Depression alters the secretions of all these hormones.

A brand-new field called psychoneuroimmunology is busy turning out evidence of these and other extraordinary interrelationships. Among them:

1. Depression indeed influences susceptibility to disease. Lymphocytes are the primary disease-fighting units of the immune system. Several studies now show weakened lymphocyte response among severely depressed patients, which would make them more vulnerable to disease. Intense grieving resembles depression in many ways, and landmark studies have demonstrated similar changes in lymphocytes following bereavement, particularly among men.

Depression increases vulnerability to certain infections, including those caused by the herpes simplex virus. Possibly it raises the risk of cancer.

2. Cortisol plays a powerful role in suppressing the immune response. At least half of all biologically depressed persons oversecrete this hormone.

Normally, cortisol may turn off the system in response to hormonal signals that the "invaders" are done for. However, in depressed persons, feedback mechanisms do not function normally, and cortisol continues to flow, damaging the body's ability to fend off illness.

3. States of learned helplessness (page 175) in animals parallel some types of human depression. Laboratory animals in which learned helplessness is induced show impaired immune systems.

When rats are subjected to stressful experiences early in life, including loss of a mother, their immune responses function poorly even in adulthood.

Loss among human beings has been associated with the onset of many diseases, including hypertension, rheumatoid arthritis, skin conditions, and ulcers.

4. Loss of circadian hormonal rhythms can adversely affect the efficiency of the immune system.

5. Just as a depressed mind can suppress the immune system, positive emotions can enhance it. A study of depressed persons undergoing psychotherapy showed a strong relationship between increased hopefulness and improved lymphocyte function.

6. Antidepressants and lithium help to regulate immune system reactivity and return it to normal.

Part IV

The State of the Art:
Treatment of Depression in Psychiatry's New Age

20

The New Technology

RESEARCH IS THE backbone of biopsychiatry. Treatment of men, women, and children is the flesh and blood—the life—of our new field.

In the following chapters we describe tests, procedures, and therapies that enable the practitioner to diagnose depression, to identify the precise treatment, to predict response, to monitor results, to foresee and even to prevent relapse. You will see how the science of psychiatry merges with the practitioner's art to produce a fast and lasting cure. You will see too how biopsychiatry improves upon or diverges from traditional practices.

LABORATORY TECHNOLOGIES THAT CAN HELP DIAGNOSE AND TREAT DEPRESSION

Test Technology	Aids in Treatment
Radio immunoassay (RIA)	Measures hormones that if out of balance can mimic depression
Flame photometric assay	Measures hormonal response to challenge tests (TRH, DST), to aid in diagnosis and treatment
High-performance liquid chromatographic assay (HPLC)	Measures the amount of antidepressants in blood, for the same reasons as measuring lithium
	Measures brain chemicals and byproducts (MHPG), to help select antidepressants
	Predicts optimum dosage range for medication

LABORATORY TECHNOLOGIES THAT CAN
HELP DIAGNOSE AND TREAT DEPRESSION *(Continued)*

Test Technology	Aids in Treatment
Gas chromatographic assay (GC)	Measures neuroleptics in blood, for the same reasons as measuring lithium
Atomic absorption spectroscopy plasma emissions	Measures lithium and other metals more accurately than GC
	Measures brain enzyme activity (MAO), to insure enough medication is taken; also used in diagnosis
Radio receptor assay	Measures actual biological activity of neuroleptic medications and all metabolites at a cellular (receptor) level
Enzyme immunoassays	Measures the amount of antiepileptic medications sometimes given in depression, for the same reasons as measuring lithium
	Measures various commonly abused substances (PCP, THC etc.) that can cause depression
Gas chromatography mass spectroscopy	Confirms with 100 percent certainty a substance is present that can cause depression
	Measures brain chemicals in blood and urine, to isolate imbalances

The Birth of the
Psychiatric Laboratory

Our vastly improved treatment results would not be possible without the clinical psychiatric laboratory, a biopsychiatrist's ever-present partner. A decade ago, such a thing did not exist. Psychiatric tests were performed only by researchers like me, then a fellow in neurobehavior at Yale University School of Medicine, fortunate to be working alongside some of the greats in biopsychiatric medicine. My Yale coworkers and other colleagues took the first big step in establishing the usefulness of biological markers (DST, TRH, MHPG) and antidepressant blood levels for the National Collaborative Study on Depression, a massive nationwide research project.

Access to new, ultra-advanced technology, such as the gas chromatograph/mass spectrometer and radioimmunoassay techniques made our work at Yale possible; we could actually detect the minute amounts of metabolites and hormones that spelled the difference between normal and abnormal functioning.

It was exhilarating to observe the improvement in depressed persons participating in research studies whose treatment was moderated by test results (even though our understanding was rudimentary when compared with what we know today). All had previously failed to respond to months or even years of the traditional "prescribe and pray" approach. Yet I soon began to wonder what was the point of all our work if results would not be applied to all persons who came for help. It made little sense that to receive the most modern and efficient treatment, patients had to first endure an unsuccessful effort.

Psychiatry has an unfortunate tradition of separating research from clinical practice. Researchers keep testing and retesting each other's findings, while clinicians continue their routine practices. In other medical specialties, when a respected journal announces a new test that may yield information that could alter the natural course of a disease, practitioners jump in to try it. They use the test in their work with patients to judge whether it helps them and their patients. In turn, they report their results to their colleagues. Thus the clinicians themselves field-test and continuously improve the tests or procedures that were developed for them in the first place. In psychiatry, to this day residents at some of the nation's finest teaching hospitals may routinely order laboratory tests only for patients on research units; they must relinquish the more up-to-date techniques when they treat the majority of patients in their care.

In 1976, I became determined to create reliable testing systems that could be used by all psychiatrists for all their patients. Before the year was out I had a plan. Psychiatric Diagnostic Laboratories of America (PDLA)—the first and largest full-service psychiatric laboratory delivery of state-of-the-art analyses to psychiatric clinicians across the United States—was born in 1978.

PDLA began as a one-room research lab at Fair Oaks Hospital, crammed with a high-pressure liquid chromatograph for the development of an antidepressant blood-level monitoring system; a gas chromatograph with nitrogen detector for the development of systems for monitoring medication and for the analysis of urinary

MHPG; and a radioimmunoassay system and counter for neuroendocrine measurements.

Within five years, PDLA grew from that one room at Fair Oaks to one floor of a building next to the hospital to a clinical laboratory occupying 20,000 square feet in suburban New Jersey. Once the clinical laboratory became self-funding, I had accomplished my mission; using the tools of the new psychiatry, practitioners could now assure the best possible test and treatment results to every patient. PDLA is now a full-fledged commercial operation, independent of us, with equipment several generations more advanced than what we began with.

Consulting the Oracle

Judging from the growth of PDLA and the establishment of other such commercial laboratories, psychiatrists are making use of the new treatment technology in increasing numbers.

Nonetheless, the majority of depressed persons who visit a psychiatrist today will not be tested for anything, much less be aware that such tests exist. It is no small undertaking to incorporate laboratory procedures into psychiatric practice. Because psychiatry is traditionally a nontechnological medical specialty, practitioners are unlikely to be well grounded in laboratory medicine. To start testing patients requires vast reeducation, without which psychiatrists are unlikely to understand or apply the results correctly. Laboratories are our modern-day oracles; the results they deliver are only as good as the person interpreting them. The psychiatrist must know how to take advantage of the information the tests yield and not be led astray by false implications. No test provides *the* answer. Every test has specific limitations and invalidating factors. With the DST, for example, a normal result does not rule out a biological depression, since depression can also result from other biological dysfunctions (which is why I recommend using two diagnostic tests). An abnormal result can also be caused by a mimicker, or by malnourishment, stress, many types of drugs, alcohol withdrawal, a laboratory error, and many other factors.

Pretend you are a psychiatrist. Should you give all your patients the DST to find out which ones are biologically depressed? Definitely not. Even if you eliminate those patients whose test results could be influenced by any of the above confounding factors, the DST is not a *screening* test. It will not tell you who does or does not have a biological depression. You must evaluate the results patient by patient in the context of a total differential diagnosis. In the words of Dr. Barney Carroll, who is responsible for developing this test for psychiatric use, you must "look at the lab test result in relation to the patient's clinical state."

Although some psychiatrists insist that a test with these limitations has little use, most medical tests are similarly imperfect. For example, the blood test for the presence of the AIDS virus when it was introduced was touted as a great step forward in the detection of this terrible scourge. Yet, like the DST, it cannot itself diagnose AIDS. It provides evidence only of exposure to the virus; a small percentage of those who have the resulting antibodies eventually develop the disease. In the presence of other signs and symptoms of illness, however, this information becomes crucial to an accurate diagnosis.

In his frequent lectures to psychiatrists, Dr. Carroll demonstrates that the DST is comparable to other state-of-the-art medical tests, such as the one used in coronary care units to diagnose a heart attack, or the test to detect cancer of the prostate. "I show you this," he says, "to dispel any magical thinking that you may still have that those other doctors have perfect and one-hundred-percent reliable laboratory tests whereas we don't. The tests that are emerging now . . . are fully comparable in their performance characteristics with those available in other areas of medicine."

A normal test result may be only somewhat informative. An abnormal DST is another story. Once you have ruled out confounding conditions and factors, you can be 90 percent certain that your patient is biologically depressed. Knowing this, you know what to do to relieve this patient's suffering.

It beats guessing.

21

Treatment That Works

DEPRESSED PEOPLE DESERVE and require help as quickly as possible. Biopsychiatric methods can usually achieve results that are faster and more lasting than traditional psychiatric treatments. We have no magic elixir or arcane cures. Like most psychiatrists, we use one or a combination of the same treatment modalities—medication, psychotherapy, sometimes ECT (shock therapy). The difference in effectiveness lies mostly in how we use them.

By introducing "high-tech" and other modern medical concepts into the practice of everyday psychiatry, we have managed to:

1. drastically reduce the often long wait for therapeutic effectiveness

2. increase the odds against first-time failure

3. prevent relapse for a vast number of patients

4. limit distressing side effects

5. contribute to the storehouse of knowledge that can be applied to all depressed patients

The result is a 90 percent success rate in the treatment of depression. Eight out of ten patients experience complete relief promptly; the remaining 20 percent will experience the same freedom with additional treatment.

Even for those patients who respond quickly and thoroughly, the treatment of depression is rife with inherent difficulties. Pharmacological therapy alone is far more complex than take-two-antidepressants-and-call-me-in-the-morning. A traditional psychiatrist (one who uses both organic and psychotherapeutic treatments) and a biopsychiatrist confront the treatment hurdles differently. Let us examine the manner in which traditional and new psychiatrists work with patients and make decisions concerning what is best for you.

The Traditional Treatment of Depression

In standard practice, psychiatrists effectively skip the diagnostic phase and begin to treat patients immediately. Many write prescriptions for medication during their patients' first visit, choosing the antidepressant with which they are most familiar. In general, within six weeks of dutiful pill taking, at least half of their depressed patients will begin to feel much, much better.

Forty to 50 percent will not be so fortunate. Eventually, some may respond to a different medication. For those who do not, yet a third medication trial, or shock therapy, will be the turning point. Each change of medication or modality extends the treatment time and requires a degree of hopefulness that is rare in a depressed person. The risk of suicide increases as the "cure" drags on.

THE SIX-WEEK-TO-SIX-MONTH WAIT

Many factors influence the amount of time a patient must wait before feeling better. Antidepressant drugs never take effect immediately. While symptoms such as insomnia may disappear within a week or two, the heart of the depression hangs on for another week or two. Before antidepressants can do their job, you must be taking the full therapeutic dosage.

Therapeutic dosage signifies the amount of medication you require daily in order to receive the maximum antidepressant benefit. This amount varies greatly from individual to individual. An effective dosage for you may leave another person as depressed as ever, and it may prove literally poisonous for a third person. Everyone metabolizes antidepressant drugs differently. How much ends up in the blood for delivery to the brain depends on factors such as genetics, other drugs, age, and the overall health of your liver.

Response to an antidepressant drug, if any, will be seen within ten days to three weeks at full therapeutic dosage. Since you must build up to your maximum dosage slowly, the wait to know whether this drug is right for you will be closer to six weeks.

How does the psychiatrist determine your therapeutic dosage? A traditional practitioner can only guess. Should he or she estimate correctly and you respond quickly, well and good. But if you remain depressed, the guesswork becomes complicated: Is it because you have received insufficient medication or are you perhaps nonresponsive to this particular pill? Possibly you are not a candidate for medication to begin with.

When the patient does not respond to the medication, many psychiatrists increase the dosage, then watch and wait. Still no response? Then the time has come to try a different drug.

Unfortunately, switching medications may waste precious time. In some cases, the patient may have to be off all medication for as long as two weeks before beginning the new drug. And the second medication trial may drag on as long as the first. Can the patient hang in there? Patients commonly blame themselves when the medicine does not work ("I'm a failure at everything, even getting better"). Or they blame the doctor for being unable to provide effective treatment.

THE INFLUENCE OF SIDE EFFECTS

Antidepressants are powerful chemicals that can adversely affect many body systems. Thus, you begin with a small amount and build up to the presumed therapeutic dosage as your body accustoms itself to the chemical. The faster you can achieve your necessary dosage, the faster you'll feel better. The side effects, however, may hold you back.

Depending on the specific antidepressant, side effects can include dry mouth, constipation, headaches, blurry vision, orthostatic hypotension (fall in blood pressure when you stand up or stand still, resulting in dizziness, falling, or fainting), sedation, agitation, memory loss, insomnia, excessive appetite, heart palpitations, and/or more serious effects on the heart. Usually most of these are transitory and mild, no more than a nuisance for many people. A number of persons prove extremely sensitive to them, however.

Almost a third of patients cannot tolerate the side effects of antidepressants and are forced to discontinue treatment. For those who muddle through despite a sensitivity, building up to the therapeutic dosage must proceed very slowly—further extending the time necessary to reach therapeutic dosage level. Months may pass before the psychiatrist can fairly evaluate the treatment and if necessary change it.

THE TREATMENT-REFRACTORY GROUP

It has become virtually axiomatic in traditional psychiatry that 20 to 35 percent of depressed patients will prove ultimately refractory to antidepressant treatment. Their suffering, compounded by the frustration of ineffective treatment, may be much worse than it was when they first came for help. Now the psychiatrist may choose to refer the patient for specialized evaluation or for therapy. The conclusion that the patient must be "characterological," i.e., neurotic, can be tempting at this point. (Some psychiatrists use failure to respond to medication as evidence that psychotherapy is the more appropriate treatment, even though they have not prescribed the medication appropriately or given it a fair try.) Other options include still other drugs or more innovative treatments, if the patient has not given up and stayed home, figuring depression is something you have to learn to live with. Or die from.

TREATMENT PITFALLS

Inadequate trials for drugs

Improper patient screening

Inadequate dosage

Short maintenance period

Sudden withdrawal

Inadequate patient counseling about side effects, drug and dietary interactions

Seeing the patient too frequently

Failure to individualize therapy

Inadequate "lines of communication"

Inadequate follow-up

Biopsychiatric Treatment Techniques

How an individual biopsychiatrist proceeds depends, of course, on the style of the practioner and the needs of the patient. I'll show you my variations on our common themes. Notice how I incorporate neuroscientific understandings and laboratory findings in all my decisions.

HISTORY AND DIAGNOSIS
1. Extensive history taking, including questionnaires for the patient, family history, and interviews with family members where possible.
   2. Drug-free interval, laboratory testing, and psychological testing to rule out the mimickers and/or identify other psychiatric illness. (A biopsychiatric axiom: Persons who are least likely to respond to treatment for depression are most likely to be suffering from an altogether different disease.) Where necessary, patients are referred to an appropriate specialist or drug-treatment program.
   3. Laboratory tests to identify neuroendocrine markers of bio-

logical depression. The DST plus one other neuroendocrine test is usually sufficient. I prefer the TRH–TSH test. A patient may be a normal "suppressor" and still reveal a hypothalamic-pituitary-thyroid abnormality. If results of both tests are negative but my clinical nose tells me that the picture suggests a biological condition, I may continue the search.

TREATMENT CHOICE

4. My clinical assessment combined with objective data from the history, family pattern of illness, and laboratory results all contribute to this critical decision.

The most common treatment alternatives include medication and psychotherapy. All recent evidence indicates that a combination of both modalities is better for major (biological) depression than either one alone. Positive neuroendocrine measures both verify an active organic underpinning to the disease and predict response to antidepressants. If I remain unsure that medication is appropriate, I might try another response prediction test. Mood improvement following a single dose of amphetamine, for example, suggests early antidepressant success.

Many psychiatrists hedge their bets and prescribe antidepressants to everyone, just in case they might work. Not me. Drugs are not the answer to everything, in medicine or in life. Diagnostic tests for depression are designed to help the psychiatric physician render a specific diagnosis that *pinpoints* a specific treatment.

The pharmacological treatment of the depressed patient can be one of the most rewarding aspects of psychiatric practice. When used properly *in the depressed patient likely to respond,* they can help patients to resume a normal, healthy state of mind within weeks, with a minimum of side effects. Otherwise the drugs can prove to be no more than highly toxic chemicals, potent weapons for suicidal patients.

On the other hand, certain types of psychotherapy can benefit all comers, about which more in the next chapter. Psychotherapy alone becomes the treatment of choice when neuroendocrine testing is consistently negative. (Note that negative testing does not imply that the depression has no biological basis. Tests tend to normalize just before symptoms disappear, or as a result of spontaneous remission or successful treatment.)

PRESCRIBING AN ANTIDEPRESSANT

5. I will try tricyclic antidepressants first. Additional testing can dispel the which-one-will-work-and-at-what-dosage? quandary. Here the

MHPG urine test comes in handy. We have found that patients who excrete the least amount of MHPG respond preferentially to noradrenergic antidepressants. These include nortriptyline (Aventyl, Pamelor), desipramine (Norpramin, Pertofrane), and imipramine (Tofranil). The highest MHPG excretors may respond to a broad spectrum of treatment if continued over a long term. The intermediate group is treated most successfully with serotonergic antidepressants, including amitriptyline (Elavil), or perhaps trazadone tryptophan.

The tricyclic dose prediction test ascertains how a patient metabolizes the selected medication. We give a test dose and twenty-four hours later measure how much of it remains in the blood plasma. From this measurement we can predict the therapeutic dosage and thus minimize dose changing and unnecessary side effects.

6. Side effects will also influence the choice of medication as well as the manner in which I prescribe it. Giving a working corporation executive a heavily sedating drug is asking for failure, especially if prescribed at intervals throughout the day. On top of the depression, any further inability to function may be the last straw; the patient may become even more depressed and possibly suicidal, or will quit treatment. The psychiatrist who is fully aware of all the drugs and their side effects can prevent the high dropout effect, safeguard patients' health, and even use side effects to advantage. Prescribe a sedating drug in a single large dose at bedtime, and the insomniac executive will finally begin to get some sleep, yet be alert during working hours. After the first week of real night-long sleep in months, the patient may even think there may be something to this treatment after all.

MONITORING ANTIDEPRESSANT BLOOD LEVELS
7. Tests to monitor the level of medication in the blood replace the guesswork that can drag treatment on for months. They are among the most valuable tests in the biopsychiatrist's bag of tricks.

All antidepressants are ineffective below a certain concentration in the blood plasma. We now know, too, that some of them are nothing but trouble above another level: Effectiveness decreases and side effects multiply, endangering patients with cardiovascular disease in particular. The psychiatrist must prescribe sufficient medication to "hit" only within this narrow range, which we call the "therapeutic window." Blood-level tests at last make this target visible. Performed one or more times during treatment, this simple procedure reassures us that we are prescribing correctly, with least risk and discomfort to all patients. If the medication fails to work, we can change treatment strategy without having to agonize over whether the dosage was right.

TRACKING COMPLIANCE
8. Monitoring antidepressant blood levels also reveals whether the patient is taking the medication as prescribed.

> A quiz: How many persons taking antidepressant medication neglect to follow the treatment regimen?
> **A.** More than half
> **B.** About half
> **C.** Less than half

You'll find the correct answer along with a discussion of noncompliance at the end of this chapter. Suffice to say here that not following the doctor's orders—increasing or decreasing dosage, altering the timing, even failing to take the medication altogether—can lead to treatment failure.

ALTERING TREATMENT
9. Eighty-five percent of my patients will respond within about three weeks of medication maintained at the target level. Including the diagnostic phase, about four weeks will have elapsed since the time they despondently set foot in my office.

For the nonresponding 15 percent, it is time to alter treatment. Supplementing the medication rather than changing it will quickly do the trick for many. Small amounts of thyroid hormone, tyrosine (a naturally occurring amino acid, especially effective with the low MHPG group), tryptophan (another natural amino acid, by itself a possible treatment for depression, pain, and/or insomnia) or even lithium often will trigger antidepressant action. For depressed patients who are already taking lithium, thyroid hormone can have profound results, largely because lithium slows down the thyroid gland. Treatment supplements generally work within a week or two. If not, I discontinue them and try something new.

10. What's next depends on my assessment of why treatment failed and/or the urgency of immediate response. Trouble with tricyclic side effects encourages some of my colleagues to put the patient on a "second generation" antidepressant, such as maprotiline (Ludiomil) or trazodone (Desyrel). These are the newest types of antidepressant medication. They seem to have fewer debilitating side effects. (Let me stress *seem:* All drugs have side effects; we'll know the full story when these medications have been in use as long as the older formulations.)

Otherwise I might try a second tricyclic or begin my patient on an MAO inhibitor.

SWITCHING TO AN MAO INHIBITOR

11. MAO inhibitors, as explained in Chapter 18, function somewhat differently from tricyclics, although they work just as well. Years ago MAO inhibitors developed a reputation for extreme dangerousness, so psychiatrists stopped prescribing them. The dangers of these medications—including phenelzine (Nardil), isocarboxazid (Marplan) and tranylcypromine (Parnate)—turn out to be exaggerated. There is one serious risk, resulting from the interaction of these drugs with certain foods, drinks, and other medications. Aged cheese, red wine, and cold medications are among the substances that can trigger a loss of blood pressure control and a corresponding, potentially fatal hypertensive crisis. Patients who follow certain dietary restrictions will avoid this uncommon consequence. MAO inhibitors can work when all else fails, but the psychiatrist has to be sure the patient will follow the rules.

CREATIVE PRESCRIBING

12. The rare person will remain depressed despite all efforts. A psychiatrist may recommend ECT (see below), but even if the patient refuses it, there is no reason for either the patient or the psychiatrist to throw in the towel. The psychiatric literature of innovative treatments grows fat as practitioners report novel treatments that work with individual patients. Innovative uses of drugs such as anticonvulsants or combinations of medications—stimulants with MAO inhibitors, MAO inhibitors with tricyclics—can pull the rug out from under a tenacious chronic depression.

Let me share with you a note from my colleague Jerrold G. Bernstein, MD, director of the Boston Psychopharmacologic Institute:

> Since many of my patients suffer from what has been called refractory depression—that is to say, depression which is difficult to treat—I have to be flexible. If necessary I will try a variety of medication regimens, combining two, three, even four medications simultaneously. Oftentimes, small doses of antipsychotic medications, even for patients who are not psychotic, will spell the difference between a satisfactory re-

sponse and utter incapacity. Some depressed women approaching menopause experience a considerable improvement in their mood when estrogenic hormones are added to the antidepressant regimen.

We must remember that each patient is an individual and that no particular treatment works for everyone. The difference between a favorable and unfavorable outcome may be directly proportional to the willingness of the physician and the patient to experiment with changing treatment regimens or with more complicated regimens involving the administration of multiple medications simultaneously.

The good news is that most depressed patients will be better if they and their physicians persist long enough, and if they are willing to be flexible and try different approaches to treatment.

SHALL I SHOCK YOU?

13. For the actively suicidal or homicidal depressed patient, or for the patient whose physical condition precludes medication, time may be running out. The psychiatrist may decide to forgo another medication trial and instead choose electroconvulsive therapy—ECT, also known as shock or electroshock therapy.

Shock therapy has had an awful reputation, mostly well deserved. Since its introduction in 1938, it has at times been used indiscriminately, punitively, and dangerously.

In this type of treatment, electricity passes through electrodes attached to the patient's head. The "shock" to the brain causes a convulsion, or seizure. The seizure is essential to the treatment, not a side effect (although some physicians bill patients for "nonconvulsive ECT"). Depression lifts after a series of treatments. In the past, psychiatrists zapped patients' brains with high-energy currents while they were fully awake. Patients had to be tied down because their whole bodies went into horrific convulsions; vertebrae snapped from the violence of the seizure. Sometimes their hearts stopped. They were forced to endure this treatment—no one bothered getting their consent—because they were neurotic or psychotic or had a behavior problem.

Today low-energy electrical currents are briefly aimed at either one or both sides of the brain (at issue is which method works better and with fewer side effects). The patient is relaxed and asleep, courtesy of muscle relaxants and short-acting anesthesia, and receiving oxygen. Monitors check vital signs. The major known side effects are confusion and memory loss, usually short-term but sometimes longlasting. Lasting damage to the brain may be possible, however, especially for the patient who is subjected to numerous treatments. And use of a general anesthesia carries its own risks.

Electroshock therapy is no longer the torture it once was, although the image persists. ("It may be hard for the average person to separate the image of the therapeutic electric-shock device from the torture of the electric chair," writes a popular journalist. "Correcting a malfunction of the brain with a jolt of electricity may sound too much like kicking a television set to adjust its fine-tuning.") The fact is, it works to relieve the symptoms of depression faster than any other treatment we have. A series of treatments—perhaps three a week for two to three weeks—will jolt the depression out of existence within a couple of weeks. But the effect may be temporary. For this and other reasons, I do not recommend it to many of my patients.

It worked for one man in his late fifties, a Washington politician who was convinced he was emanating an odor that was poisoning the nation's capital. He believed he had to kill himself in order to save the country. This man had received excellent care for the previous several months from qualified biopsychiatrists. He was one of the rare true nonresponders. ECT had not been tried; we had to work fast because he was actively suicidal. ECT worked. Within six weeks he had returned to the business of government, where he remains, free of relapses, to this day.

ECT is enjoying a new surge of popularity among psychiatrists, including some biopsychiatrists. Probably electroshock has its place, generally as a last resort for all but a limited number of patients. We have been shocking patients for a half-century, but we know too little still about why it works or how the treatment changes the brain for better and for worse.

In June 1985, the National Institutes of Health (NIH) sponsored a conference on ECT. The panelists ranged from psychiatrists and psychologists to lawyers and laypersons. In their consensus report they agreed: "The physician's decision to offer ECT to a patient and the patient's decision to accept it should be based on a complex consideration of advantages and disadvantages of ECT compared with alternative treatments. An ongoing consultative process, requiring time and energy on the part of both patient and physician, should occur." I agree.

MONITORING PROGRESS

14. The patient looks and acts great: smiling, sleeping, eating, feeling sexy, walking tall. The symptoms of depression have flown, but what about the biology? I must repeat the DST and other diagnostic tests. If the biological state markers of depression have vanished, I can be certain that treatment has worked. If the markers remain, I know that my patient is heading for a relapse.

PREVENTING RELAPSE AND/OR SUICIDE

15. Why take medication if you do not need it? Once a patient's biological status remains normal, he or she has no reason to expect a recurrence, certainly not immediately. Persons who have suffered frequently recurring episodes very often were never treated adequately, so the depression kept returning; their symptoms may have cleared, but the underlying condition remained. Generally, treatment should continue sixteen to twenty weeks after symptoms disappear.

No matter the outward signs, patients whose tests remain abnormal should be (1) continued in treatment, and/or (2) watched carefully for early signs of recurrence, so that treatment can be reinstituted before symptoms get out of hand. For potentially suicidal patients, a nonnormalizing DST means Suicide Alert, for virtually all patients who later kill themselves come from this group.

Bipolar patients taking lithium generally continue their medication in order to prevent manic episodes.

Sometimes the vegetative symptoms will clear and the tests return to normal, but attitude remains in the pits. Psychotherapy now becomes the treatment of choice. Now physiologically functional, the patient is in good shape to benefit from it. Even for those whose tests reveal still-active depressive disease, psychotherapy can help prevent recurrence by strengthening coping abilities and by helping to undo the learned style of life that accompanies chronic depression.

A What's What and Who's Who of Treatment Errors

In practice, biopsychiatric treatment of depression need not be as complicated as the foregoing description might suggest. Few patients require numerous tests and procedures; most patients respond quickly and thoroughly, and that's that. Even those who sought treatment repeatedly rarely prove so difficult to help. Biopsychiatrists get credit from patients and their families for "miracle cures" when all we've done is spot, then correct, someone else's treatment errors.

By far the most common treatment errors fall into the following categories:

UNDERTREATMENT

There is "an international undertreatment of depression," claimed a commentator in the *British Journal of Psychiatry*. Despite accumulating evidence that a combination of pharmacotherapy and psychotherapy is best for major depression, psychotherapy alone continues to be the most common treatment. In a representative report, only 34 percent of patients received antidepressant medication, and only 12 percent of these received doses that were high enough to work.

All too many practitioners prescribe the same dosage level for all adult patients, regardless of differing blood plasma levels. Clinicians continue to underdose many patients with medication after medication, until the patient is termed refractory or nonrespondent or treatment-resistant. Another study of this group of patients showed that almost two-thirds had not received an adequate antidepressant trial.

NONPSYCHIATRIC PHYSICIANS
Statistically the clinicians most guilty of undertreatment are not the psychiatrists whom we have been exhorting to act more like doctors. Neither are they the psychologists or other nonmedical mental health specialists who treat depressed persons but cannot act like doctors because they lack the credentials.

The fact is, those "regular" doctors—family physicians, GPs, pediatricians, internists, surgeons, neurologists, etcetera—see more cases of depression than do all mental health professionals, psychiatrists included. Depression is believed to be the most common illness in family practice. Nonpsychiatric physicians write 70 percent of the prescriptions for antidepressant drugs. And they are responsible for most of the treatment failures, undertreatment and incorrect treatment included.

A 1982 report stated that "60 percent of the estimated 32,000,000 sufferers from mental illness in the United States receive treatment within the primary care system exclusively." These physicians "manage most of these patients entirely within their practice and refer only 10 percent . . . to a psychiatrist. Unfortunately, despite extensive contact with psychosocial issues in the care of their patients, most physicians have had little formal training in the evaluation of these factors."

It is hard enough for psychiatrists to stay abreast of developments in their own specialty. For nonpsychiatric physicians, the task is nearly impossible. Consequently, they practice according to often long-abandoned notions acquired during medical school or hospital training.

We used to distinguish, for example, between *endogenous* depression, meaning occurring from within, and *reactive* depression, caused by a reaction to an outside event. We would provide medication only for the endogenous variety. Psychiatry now rejects this dichotomy in the face of evidence that the stress of life events can trigger all types of depression.

Nonetheless the distinction lingers in primary practice, with sometimes deadly consequences. Family practitioner Joseph H. Talley, MD, reports, "In a survey of a series of suicides in which the patients had seen their physicians within three weeks of their demise, it was found that the physicians had not in fact missed all of the depressions; they had simply elected not to treat because there appeared to [be] a 'reason' for their patients' depression."

Although they prescribe antidepressants frequently, nonpsychiatric physicians are similarly unfamiliar with principles of treatment. They prescribe any antidepressant rather than tailor the choice to the patient's particular depression. To avoid side effects, they generally prescribe a low dosage even though such a small amount of medication cannot work. Unlike psychiatrists, nonpsychiatric physicians usually do not attempt to adjust dosage or try other types of medication. Dr. Talley believes that most nonpsychiatric physicians find antidepressants ultimately unrewarding. They get nowhere with them so frequently that they are thus less inclined to make the treatment work. Instead they load the patient with multiple medications, including tranquilizers and sleeping pills for symptomatic relief, along with ineffective antidepressants. The patient is still depressed, and now at increased risk of serious consequences (drug dependency, suicide) from all these drugs. One antidepressant prescribed correctly would suffice to relieve the depression and associated symptoms.

Perhaps even more commonly, nonpsychiatric physicians do not recognize the symptoms of masked depression (Chapter 13). Most depressed persons who consult their family doctor are concerned more with exhaustion, digestive problems, insomnia, nervousness, and other somatic symptoms than with mood. Nonpsychiatric physicians may be uncomfortable with the patient's emotions and thus do not probe in the right places. The doctor who does not recognize masked depression can do as much harm as the doctor who fails to diagnose a mimicker. Indeed, the scope of this type of misdiagnosis and mistreatment is staggering: *one-third to two-thirds of all hospitalized medical and surgical patients over 40 are suffering from masked depression and not the disease for which they are receiving treatment.*

Esther R. was a chronically depressed woman who had had eighteen unnecessary operations on her spine in as many years—all performed by the same doctor, who preferred to ignore her head and concentrate rather too narrowly on her lower back.

In a 1985 article appearing in the journal *Psychosomatics,* titled "The High Cost of Treating a Psychiatric Disorder as a Medical Problem," the authors report the case of a woman with psychiatric illness whose bills for unnecessary medical treatment totaled $46,000 for one year alone.

Los Angeles psychiatrist Harvey Sternbach tells of a case in which both a man and his mother had long been treated for myasthenia gravis, a chronic disease characterized by muscle weakness. The 50-year-old son came to Dr. Sternbach complaining of weakness, apathy, and excessive sleep. Dr. Sternbach hospitalized him for testing as well as to detoxify him from the prescribed and nonprescribed drugs he'd been taking to self-medicate his symptoms.

The man had taken antidepressants from time to time, and his reaction was among the factors that made Dr. Sternbach doubt the medical diagnosis. Antidepressants worsen the symptoms of myasthenia gravis, and yet this patient always felt better, rather too much so; the drugs sometimes triggered hypomania. The man had had other spontaneous "up" episodes along with his slow, weak, sleepy phases. His mother revealed the same pattern. Complete evaluation easily ruled out myasthenia gravis and ruled in bipolar illness. For the first time, mother and son were treated for what really ailed them.

Two True

Although antidepressants have become routine in the treatment of depression, misunderstanding of their uses and abuses runs rampant among practitioners and patients. Some see them as a great evil foisted upon an ignorant public, while others tout them as a cure-all. Attitudes toward treatment of course will influence its outcome. A patient who fears their power will not take them correctly, just as a clinician who thinks them a waste of time will not prescribe them properly, if at all.

How much do you really know about antidepressants? Which two of the following statements are true? The correct answers are on page 258.

1. All antidepressants are equally effective.

2. The new or "second generation" antidepressants work better than their predecessors.

3. Antidepressant therapy will help virtually all seriously depressed persons.

4. Like all mood-elevating drugs, antidepressants have abuse potential.

5. Antidepressants can be addicting.

6. Antidepressants are overprescribed.

7. Antidepressants cover up the symptoms of depression; the underlying condition remains.

8. Because antidepressants are toxic drugs, a low dosage is always preferable to a high one.

9. Antidepressant response runs in the family.

10. Antidepressants treat depression. They do not cure it.

YOU

Patients are themselves responsible for treatment failure more often than one might imagine. The *majority* of persons do not take their medicine as prescribed, and not just psychiatric patients. Here we are scratching our heads over why treatment is not working, and it turns out the medication is not entering the mouth, let alone the brain.

The problem pervades all of medicine today and accounts for a substantial number of treatment failures. Twenty to 25 percent of *all* hospital admissions result from noncompliance. Among psychiatric patients who end up labeled treatment-refractory, 12 percent have not followed the treatment regimen.

Many people adjust their own dosage, even increasing it in the mistaken belief that they will achieve greater benefit. They may decide to supplement their medication with other drugs they have around the house, which may throw off antidepressant effectiveness and/or cause serious side effects. They may take their medicine only when the mood begins to worsen, even though the instructions clearly say to take one or two times a day, every day. Apparently people who stop taking their antidepressants because they are feeling a little better, only to take it again when they begin to feel worse, do not understand how antidepressant therapy works. Often the prescribing physician is at fault for not making this essential point.

Many persons stop or reduce the dosage of the drug because of side effects. Some of them do not wish to hurt their nice, caring doctor's feelings by admitting they cannot tolerate the drug the doctor assured them would be so wonderful. Others become angry at the doctor for their discomforts, so they just quit taking the pills. Always it's up to the practitioner to inquire about the side effects. A little reassurance can go a long way: Many of the side effects in time will pass, and isn't just a little discomfort worth the eventual payoff? Once informed, the doctor may wish to adjust dosage or switch the patient to another drug that he or she can better tolerate.

Brown University professor, psychiatrist Andrew Edmund Slaby, MD, PhD, provides an example of how sensitivity to the patient's individual experience can counter noncompliance:

"An eighty-year-old woman presented with a five-year history of depression," he tells us. "Her husband was an invalid, and her mother, in her late nineties and living in a nursing home, was demented. Six months before she came for treatment, one of her two sons, who was in his fifties, was killed in a car accident. She became extremely depressed. All attempts to treat her with antidepressants failed because of a lack of response or difficulty with side effects."

When Dr. Slaby prescribed Parnate, an MAO inhibitor, "she began sleeping and eating well. Her energy level increased markedly, as did her sexual interest. But because she felt 'very sexual,' she stopped the medication. She protested that her husband was not sexually interested in her and that she believed masturbation and extramarital affairs were wrong."

So Dr. Slaby cut the dosage in half. The patient agreed to give it another try. The lower dosage worked without the side effect that this particular patient could not tolerate.

Noncompliance can be sparked by the depression itself, which may foster a what's-the-use attitude: Why bother with this miserable stuff? Nothing's going to help me anyway, ever. Forgetfulness, the result of depression or of the medication, also contributes. Did I take my afternoon pills? Well, I'll take two more, just to be sure. Family members can help out immeasurably by encouraging compliance with the doctor's orders and by keeping track.

Finally, some persons resent being dependent on pills, especially those who believe that they should have psychological control over themselves. One of my patients went off on a two-week vacation to a tiny Caribbean island and "forgot" the medication that had brought him out of the pits and enabled him to go off to have a good time. He felt that his biological depression was the "fault" of his neurosis. He returned in pretty bad shape. He was lucky, though, that he did not suffer any adverse physiological reactions from going off the medication so abruptly (one discontinues antidepressant medication the same way one begins: a little at a time). This patient told me he had not taken his pills; most people do not bother to inform their doctors.

They join the ranks of the nonresponders when indeed they are responding quite appropriately to an inadequate dosage.

I never rely on patients to tell me. Blood-level testing gives me all the information I need to monitor—and correct—this curious, complicated, utterly human reaction. A couple of blood tests during treatment protects patients from nonresponse—and keeps psychiatrists from getting too depressed over their nonperformance.

A Case of "False Noncompliance"

I had a young woman patient who responded beautifully to treatment in the hospital. She continued on the same level of medication when she returned home and resumed treatment with her regular psychiatrist.

Crash—she's depressed again. Her family's yelling at me that I'm a lousy psychiatrist, her psychiatrist's accusing her of not taking her medicine, and she is back to not sleeping, not eating, not working, and not believing that there is hope.

I peered through the "therapeutic window": Her blood levels were way down. When she insisted that she was taking her pills, I believed her—especially when I saw her light up a cigarette. She had started smoking again, three packs a day. Any good biopsychiatrist knows that smoking is one of the many factors which will alter the way antidepressants are metabolized, in this case speeding it up and removing it from the body so that less is available. She would not stop smoking, so I increased the dosage. The depression departed. Case closed.

Two True, Continued

Here are the answers to the true/false quiz appearing on page 255:

1. *All antidepressants are equally effective.*

True. When we judge performance of different types of antidepressants within a large patient population, we note no differences in overall efficacy. Of, say, three thousand patients, about the same percentage will respond to imipramine as respond to phenelzine as respond to nomifensine, and so on.

Which is not to say that every individual will respond to the same antidepressant. Some persons respond to phenelzine but not to imipramine or nomifensine, etcetera. The psychiatrist must attempt to match the person to the drug.

2. *The new or "second generation" antidepressants work better than their predecessors.*

False. Despite promotional efforts of drug companies and fads in prescribing, new is not necessarily better. To receive FDA approval, an antidepressant must only be equal in efficacy to old-timers amitriptyline or imipramine. Drug companies try to develop antidepressant drugs that work about as well as the old ones but have fewer side effects. Thus the only difference between old and new antidepressants supposedly is reduced toxicity, not efficacy. However, the more experience we have with these drugs, the greater the number of side effects we find. Already at least one new antidepressant has had to be withdrawn because of fatal reactions. Others appear to induce seizures, even to cause tardive dyskinesia.

3. *Antidepressant therapy will help virtually all seriously depressed persons.*

False. Antidepressants work only in the presence of true biological illness. Since depression can be caused as well by a mimicker or by psychological conflicts, antidepressant therapy will not necessarily be helpful.

4. *Like all mood-elevating drugs, antidepressants have abuse potential.*

False. These medications are not mood-elevators; depressed persons who take them do not end up feeling wonderful. They simply feel normal again. (Some persons do experience a manic state, but this is generally a transitory side effect.) Moreover, antidepressants have no positive effects on persons who are not biologically depressed. The medication has been compared in this regard to aspirin, which will bring down a high fever but not significantly alter normal body temperature.

Antidepressants will not alleviate normal feelings of grief, loss, or painful frustration. They are not intoxicating. Thus, unlike many of the prescribed psychoactive drugs, including sleeping pills, tranquilizers, stimulants, and painkillers, antidepressants have no abuse potential.

5. *Antidepressants can be addicting.*

False. Again, this type of medication cannot be lumped into the same category with prescribed "head" drugs that can "hook" the patient.

6. *Antidepressants are overprescribed.*

False. They are *under*prescribed. Overall, biologically depressed patients remain deprived of essential pharmacological treatment. Psychotherapy remains the most common treatment for depression.

7. *Antidepressants cover up the symptoms of depression; the underlying condition remains.*

False. A painkiller will remove pain but not the condition which causes it; the pain will return when the medication wears off. Cough medication may tame the hacking, but you're in for it again later while your flu hangs on. Antidepressants operate at a more fundamental level, restoring the brain to normal functioning. Should your symptoms return when antidepressant therapy stops, probably the treatment did not last long enough. Or possibly the symptoms indicate a withdrawal reaction from stopping abruptly rather than tapering off.

In other words, antidepressants are not the easy out that this erroneous but common belief implies. They are not a crutch, they do not prevent you from working out your problem, and you are not "bad" if you take them.

8. *Because antidepressants are toxic drugs, a low dosage is always preferable to a high one.*

False. Although these drugs are rife with side effects, most of which abate over the long term, a high dosage frequently is required before the drug will work. Antidepressants either do the job or they don't; a low dosage will not produce mild improvement. Too much medication can be dangerous, however. Fortunately, the clinician can perform tests to predict and monitor the proper dosage, which is the amount necessary to provide adequate working blood levels.

9. *Antidepressant response runs in the family.*

True. First-degree relatives are apt to share the same type of biological depression. Thus if your mother or father, sister, or brother has ever responded to a particular type of antidepressant medication, be sure to tell your doctor. This information can save testing time.

10. *Antidepressants treat depression. They cannot cure it.*

False. They *can* cure it. After antidepressant therapy many persons lead a life free of this debilitating illness. The outlook is especially hopeful when we catch it early. For those with a chronic condition, however, a treatment "package" of medication and psychotherapy can substantially reduce the number of future episodes. We believe that medication may actually "teach" the brain's neurons to respond differently. Possibly, too, the medication returns the neurons to a level of functioning at which the brain's own restorative mechanisms can take over.

22

Psychotherapy for Depression

PSYCHOTHERAPY FOR DEPRESSION *can* help. While we are unable to show that psychotherapy in general effectively cures depression, we have proof now that at least two forms of psychotherapy work as well as medication (prescribed traditionally and without blood-level measurements) in some cases. We know too that in severe depression, one or another of these treatments—cognitive therapy or interpersonal therapy—combined with medication cures depression better than medication alone.

Cognitive therapy and interpersonal therapy are what we call disorder-specific; they were developed to treat certain depressions only. The two therapies are practical, directed attempts to deal with the mental and behavioral components of depression: the way you think and the way you act. They focus on present difficulties, paying little heed to past problems. And they are short-term approaches, rarely lasting more than half a year. Deeper, underlying difficulties may remain after the conclusion of therapy, at which time psychoanalysis or other extended types of psychotherapy may be appropriate. But you won't be depressed—and that's what you came for.

What Is Psychotherapy and Why Do We Need More Types?

As psychiatric epidemiologist Myrna M. Weissman has remarked, "Psychotherapy in the marketplace has been an ostentatious success." Ever since Sigmund Freud developed techniques to uncover the deepest layers of our mental processes and to use this knowledge to produce change, Americans especially have consumed psychotherapy with gusto. We believe that psychotherapy will eliminate mental illness and its symptoms, improve our functioning, free us from fear, enhance our relationships, help us to gain real pleasure from our lives, even reshape our personalities. The more goals we develop for psychotherapy, from relief of severe emotional suffering to self-improvement, the more types of treatment appear in the marketplace.

HOW IT WORKS

In psychoanalytic types of therapy, which have become the norm throughout most of this century, the individual talks and relates to a trained professional in conditions of utter privacy. The therapist listens and observes with empathy, slowly and appropriately aiding the patient to understand thoughts, feelings, ideas, and actions in terms of unconscious patterns extending far into the past. "Psychotherapy adds insight to injury," in the words of one psychiatrist.

The deepening intellectual and emotional awareness of self allows the individual to free him- or herself from the grip of the unconscious and to establish new, healthier, more adaptable patterns. In this way, the person undergoing therapy unlearns old ways of behaving and relearns new ones.

Behavioral psychotherapy (also called behavior modification) tackles this relearning more directly. Therapists manipulate reward and/or punishment to condition, or train, a new habit pattern. A behavior therapist will have little interest in the psychic origins of, say, a fear of dogs. Instead he or she may guide the phobic individual first to look at pictures of dogs, then to be in the same room with a caged dog, then to touch a leashed and muzzled dog, and so on. With each step mastered, the fear diminishes and the sense of accomplishment increases.

Hundreds of specific therapies have sprung from these two and the so-called "experiential" approaches, these based on the healing release of emotional and/or spiritual energy. Orthodox or unusual therapies continue to attract persons with symptoms of mental suffering or with a desire to improve themselves and their performance.

DOES IT WORK?

Unquestionably certain individuals benefit from certain therapies. Still, we do not know the percentage of patients in general who improve. We cannot predict which person will benefit from which type of psychotherapy. Despite the overwhelming commercial success of psychotherapy, we cannot even provide proof that most forms of treatment work.

Traditional forms of psychotherapy do not lend themselves to objective measurement. For example, the treatment is a highly personal, subjective experience whose continuation, if not success, depends on a good match between therapist and patient and on the privacy of their interaction; an observer cannot be present to assess the treatment. Because the diagnosis of the patient, the goals and strategy of the therapy, treatment length, and the determination of success vary from therapist to therapist, researchers cannot design studies to compare results.

Considering the vast numbers of depressed persons who enter the health-care system, we need more objective data about the efficacy of the psychotherapies as treatment techniques. Is psychotherapy overall an efficient use of our mental-health-care resources? Can it help acutely ill patients fast? Psychiatry has been hard-pressed to provide evidence that its favorite treatment modality is worth the time and the price.

Cognitive and interpersonal approaches can be studied, even observed in action, by researchers without compromising the outcome. Recent studies show that these forms of psychotherapy can indeed assist recovery from as serious a mental health problem as depression. Importantly, both types of treatment emphasize precise diagnosis, targeted treatment, and administration of the treatment by specially trained practitioners according to a preexisting protocol.

Cognitive Therapy

"If we see things as negative we are likely to feel negative and behave in a negative way," says psychiatrist Aaron Beck, MD, founder of cognitive therapy.

Depressed persons perceive themselves and the world darkly: "No matter how hard I try, I never do well enough." "It's no use; no one will ever understand me." "If only I had worked harder fifteen years ago, I would be a success today." "I do not have what it takes to be happy in life." When a depressed person measures life experiences, he or she sees only the failures, never the successes. No matter how vehemently one might insist, "Stop talking like that, it's not true!" the depressed person is convinced his/her convictions are correct.

Bad feelings accompany negative thoughts. What anguish to see yourself a failure after all the effort you have put in! A future without hope of change is a nightmare. And the behavior that results from such a dark, pained view of the universe can be nothing short of self-defeating. If you're such a rotten egg, why bother to try again?

If the future stretches on in unremitting agony, why go on? If you cannot see alternatives, of course you have no hope.

Thoughts, feelings, actions all feed upon one another and do indeed make life worse, confirming the depressed person's certainties. True to his or her perceptions, the depressed person goes nowhere but down.

But the depressed perception of the world is inaccurate. What the depressed person sees results from the faulty information processing that is symptomatic of depression.

ERIC FALLS IN LOVE AGAIN; TIM DOESN'T, YET

Tim, a screenwriter in his late thirties whose eight-year marriage had broken up some months before, was telling me about a conversation he had had with his friend Eric. Eric had been divorced a few years earlier and was about to be married a second time. Eric's happiness was hard on Tim, who was deeply depressed and "knew" that a happy marriage was not in the cards for him. Tim had loved and admired his wife, but once he found out about her long history of affairs, he could no longer tolerate her presence. Unspeakably wounded, and privately convinced that had he been the man he should have been she would not have cheated on him, Tim had moved out.

Tim had been out with a lot of women lately, so many he could hardly remember their names. Out of bed, everybody bored him; no one came close to having the qualities of Jeanne, his estranged wife.

Eric was a sensitive guy and tried to reassure his friend that in time everything would work out. "Eric told me that after he and his wife had split up he was a hundred percent certain he'd never find another woman," Tim told me. "He went to bars and picked up women and the next morning woke up next to a strange, naked, female body. She'd be warm and affectionate, he'd be hung over and cold. He hated the parting scenes, when she would be hanging around waiting for some sign that he wanted to see her again. Eric felt nothing but contempt for her suffering. When the door would close behind him, he would go back to bed in despair, knowing he would never be happy again."

Tim was astonished to learn that the friend he so admired and envied had even considered killing himself. One Sunday morning Eric woke up alone in such anguish that he felt he couldn't go on. He knew he had plenty of sleeping pills and pain pills left over from a knee operation. All he had to do was get up, get the pills from the medicine chest, and wash them down with the rest of the bottle of bourbon he had opened the night before.

"Eric said that when he realized what he was thinking—that he was actually planning to end his life—he was jolted back into reality. Just like that the fog in his head cleared," Tim said. "He understood suddenly that he'd been through painful endings of relationships before his marriage and had always gotten over them. He would recover this time, too. And he'd fall in love again, the way he always had before."

The logic was inescapable. Once Eric no longer believed that things would not work out, he could begin to take care of himself again. He started facing up to his drinking problem, and he treated women with renewed respect. Six months later, Eric met Tina, the woman he was now about to marry.

I thought Tim's story about his friend was a great example that what a person thinks ("I'll never fall in love again") influences what he does (refusing to be with a woman with his wits about him and then rejecting her) and his feelings ("This is so bad I must die"). It demonstrated too that once he realizes that his basic assumption is illogical ("Of course, I'll fall in love again, because I always have before), he can act differently ("No, thanks, I'm not drinking tonight—by the way, what's your number? May I call you again?) and feel terrific ("I love Tina and I know we will build a good life together").

Unfortunately, Tim processed his friend's story through his deeply depressed mind. "Well and good for Eric," he told me gloomily. "He may have had a good love life before he was married, but I didn't. All my relationships were terrible." Tim could remember only the painful endings, not the hopeful, happy beginnings that always followed, eventually.

Tim's a good candidate for cognitive therapy.

CHANGING YOUR MIND

Cognitive therapists set out to correct their depressed patients' thinking style. They aid them to identify their false assumptions and the feelings and behavior that result from them. Then they work with the patients to replace the mental distortions with a more balanced view that allows them to function, achieve, feel confident, and have faith.

Although research has not verified Dr. Beck's theory that the thoughts themselves cause the depression, certain types of depression may be a disease that is commonly associated with these thoughts. For many people the therapy can provide a swift return to reality. And learning to distance oneself from the symptoms of the illness proves useful in dealing with any recurrence of the darkness. Once you know that the hopelessness is a symptom of the illness and not the fate of your life, you can struggle against accepting such a deadly assumption. You can change your emotional response.

Patient and therapist work hard for sixteen to twenty weeks. Without vigorous effort and cooperation with the therapist, treatment cannot work. (Becoming physiologically normal and able to concentrate on the work is the job of medication, about which more below.)

Interpersonal Therapy

Depression distorts all aspects of a person's functioning, relationships with other people certainly included. The illness colors how a person thinks and feels about and reacts to others. Troubled relationships with spouses, lovers, friends, bosses, coworkers, parents, children are the rule for almost every depressed person during the illness, if not before. Indeed, depressed symptoms often appear in a context of other people, such as a shattered relationship. Psychiatrist Gerald Klerman and epidemiologist Myrna Weissman discovered that a short-term therapy to help patients identify and resolve their here-and-now problems with other people in their environment could assist in the recovery from the depression itself. They developed a set of techniques and in 1979 published a procedural manual for therapists to follow. Despite its brief history of practice, interpersonal therapy scores as favorably as cognitive therapy in efficacy studies.

Whether the disturbed relationship triggers the depression or the depression gives rise to the interpersonal problem is unimportant to the conduct of the treatment. The interpersonal therapist helps determine the nature of the relationship problem, then sets out to find solutions.

Most often interpersonal problems involve role transitions or role disputes. Transitions from married to single, single to married, married to widowed, with children at home to empty nest, having day-to-day relationships with coworkers to home alone retired—all coexist with depression.

Role disputes commonly involve differing expectations of the relationships among lovers, spouses, family members. The depressed person will be at a loss to change the nature of the relationship. She wants him to share the child care and housework so she can devote more time to her career; he says, "No way!" She's convinced she loves him more than he loves her. She's stuck; she doesn't want to leave him, but she can't go on this way. There's nothing she can do. Her future is bleak. The interpersonal therapist treats both persons involved in role disputes, helping them to communicate, negotiate, and see things as they really are. There are *always* alternatives; depression blinds us to them.

Interpersonal therapy also helps the isolated person who lacks the self-esteem and social skills necessary to establish a relationship with another human being. The dependent person who can't break away is a candidate for interpersonal therapy too.

Combination Cures

For the largest number of severely depressed persons, a combination of pharmacological and psychotherapeutic treatments produces the best results. The order of treatment is important. Every depressed person requires some supportive therapy, and this comes first. The psychiatrist immediately establishes a trusting, accepting, and encouraging relationship with the depressed person: *You're not alone in this. I'm here to help you. You are suffering from an illness—you have done nothing to deserve this. We will work together and everything will be okay.*

The patient can now begin active pharmacotherapy and/or psychotherapy in a comfortable, mutually honest partnership with the psychiatrist. Importantly, the biologically depressed person will now have a reliable person to turn to should side effects of medication threaten to sidetrack treatment.

Once the medication begins to work and confusion lessens, energy improves, and sleeping and eating patterns return to normal, the individual can move into an active problem-solving psychotherapy, be it cognitive or interpersonal. Psychotherapy before the patient can think straight is almost guaranteed to fail, and to contribute to the certainty that there's no way out.

Entering the right therapy at the right time increases the odds of success. "Nondirective" therapies in which the therapist mostly listens instead of actively working with and supporting the patient can be dangerous. Severely depressed persons misinterpret the therapist's attitude as profoundly rejecting. Self-esteem dips below zero, and helplessness overwhelms. In studies assessing benefits of psychotherapy and medication, patients who receive nondirective psychotherapy fare worse than the control group, who receive no treatment. When the therapist actively directs the patient's returning energy into accomplishing specific goals, the resulting self-mastery can feel wonderful. After being utterly at a loss for months or years, it's a godsend.

The new-found strength that can result from short-term psychotherapies complements medication therapy and, as studies are beginning to show, helps prevent relapse. Persons who are better able to control their emotions and better adjusted socially by the end of all treatment are significantly less vulnerable to a return of the depression. This result holds true for people of all ages, even if they have a long history of depression.

Patients on medication will probably continue it after short-term psychotherapy concludes. They will appear and feel normal; they will not be suffering, and they will have learned how to cope for the present. For those who wish to go on to a longer-term, deeper type of psychotherapy, now is the time.

The Chicken or the Egg?

Events or the environment can trigger brain changes which cause depression. Psychotherapy can correct the malfunctioning of these brain neurochemicals. Similarly, medication alone can completely reverse depression's psychological symptoms, including low self-esteem and negative thinking. Does the psychological cause the biological or the biological produce the psychological? Does our misery change our brain chemistry or our brain chemistry alter our happiness?

The only way to resolve this quandary is to recognize the interrelationships of psychological (mind) and biological (body) processes. The communication among billions of brain cells makes these processes and their interrelationships possible. Any intervention into depression in one way or another affects these brain cells.

Drugs work at the level of the individual brain cell and chemically challenge them to resume normal functioning, leading to changes in biological and psychological processes. Psychotherapy works from the highest brain level to the cells, possibly resulting in new connections and/or enhanced functioning among brain cells. We know now that our experiences from the moment we are born, possibly before, can and do alter the function and even the structure of brain cells. Psychotherapy is a set of experiences directed at accomplishing these changes. The mind/body connections through which techniques such as meditation and biofeedback alter blood pressure, heart rate, and body temperature also provide the pathways through which psychotherapy influences emotional and behavior response patterns.

Long-term Psychotherapy

Because the stresses that trigger depression are so complex and varied, for some individuals additional therapy may insure more lasting change. It is important to understand that just because we cannot design studies to demonstrate that long-term therapies work does not mean that they do not help many persons.

An article by an unnamed recovering patient that appeared in the *American Journal of Psychiatry* in January 1986 underscores the value of psychotherapy when used along with medication in the treatment of severe mental suffering. The article was written by a recent Harvard graduate who had spent "half my college life . . . at a private psychiatric hospital." For this valiant individual, the suffering took the form of schizophrenia. However, many of his or her words apply equally to anyone who has long battled with depression. We will substitute "depression" for "schizophrenia" as we quote a few paragraphs from this article that explain the reasons for and rewards of psychotherapy from this patient's point of view:

> Even if one adheres to the belief that psychotherapy lends itself more to emotionally oriented problems than to something which appears to be more biochemical, one must take into consideration the emotional aspects of [depression]. Besides the day-to-day stress of contending with what often seems to be a monster raging inside one's mind, there are emotional problems that have evolved and accumulated over the course of the patient's life. Assuming that a person is biochemically predisposed to the illness, there are certain problems which appear before its onset. I believe that several incidents during my lifetime occurred because of something "different" about me; perhaps I was physically and emotionally abused because my abusers sensed some vulnerability in my nature. I have learned that some of the basic elements of my illness may have been present since early childhood, in which case the way I related to my family and early acquaintances must have been affected and probably influenced the way other people related to me, even on an unconscious level.
>
> . . . Even if medication can free the [depressed] patient from some of his torment, the scars of emotional confusion remain, felt perhaps more deeply by a greater sensitivity and vulnerability.
>
> . . . I was once told that I had a very strong observing ego, and I was fascinated and encouraged to think of my mind having that power to step away from the [depression], to look at it and understand it. Perhaps that is why therapy has worked so well for me—this capacity and a strong motivation to develop it have driven me to uncover what

it is about my mind that makes me retreat into [depression] when the stresses of my life, real or imagined, become unbearable. I do not believe I had this observing ego when I began therapy. It took me time to develop and, more importantly, it took the skill and patience of a therapist who was willing . . . to work very hard. . . . I know I have a long road ahead of me, but I can honestly say that I am no longer without hope.

Who Is the Best Psychotherapist?

Only a biopsychiatrist has the training and experience necessary to provide a complete diagnostic evaluation and to determine the best type of treatment for a depressed person. While any MD can legally prescribe medication for depression, not every physician, indeed not every psychiatrist, has the expertise to provide the most up-to-date pharmacotherapy and laboratory testing. The biopsychiatrists listed in the Appendix are highly competent and well regarded in their field.

Which mental health specialists are best equipped to provide psychotherapy is a far more difficult question to answer. One does not need to be a biopsychiatrist, or even a psychiatrist, to practice psychotherapy. Psychologists (PhDs), social workers (MSWs), and nurses (MSNs) may be equally competent, sometimes even better trained in certain psychotherapeutic techniques. The training, competency, and ethics of each practitioner must be judged individually. Since psychotherapy is one piece of the total evaluation and treatment of the depressed person, the biopsychiatrist is probably the best source of information on qualified psychotherapists in the community, particularly those practitioners who offer depression-specific therapies. Remember not to "take the cure" before you know the actual nature of the depression. It bears repeating again and again that complete medical/psychiatric—i.e., biopsychiatric—evaluation and diagnosis must come first.

Curing Yourself of the Blues

You can treat a mild depression on your own, even help a severe depression heal faster by using some of the techniques of cognitive and interpersonal therapies as well as stress management. In particular:

1. Observe yourself when you are depressed. Listen to the self-critical language of your thoughts. Do you find yourself thinking: "I can't . . ." "I'll never . . ." "If only I had" done such and such . . . "I'm not" good enough or smart enough or attractive enough, or a good friend, parent, spouse, sibling. . . .

How do you talk to yourself? If you make a mistake, do you silently curse yourself or call yourself a "jerk," a "dope," a "fool," or some such?

Do you have a hard time thinking of alternatives? Do you think in black-and-white terms, such as "If my wife dies before I do, I won't survive" or "If I don't get this promotion, I will be a failure"?

The point of self-observation is to establish distance between you and your depressed thoughts. You will weaken the grip of depression once you are able to accept (even if you can't fully feel) that you are perceiving the world through depressed eyes. You are not a jerk or a failure or a worthless human being; you're depressed.

Techniques of meditation make self-observation easier.

2. Distract yourself. Depressed thoughts feed upon each other. If you retreat to your bed and stare into space thinking how awful things are, you will feel worse and worse. Trick your mind by occupying it with other things—especially with other people. Do not retreat from social activities no matter how much you may want to, and despite your feelings that you're a real drag.

3. Exercise. Most people find it impossible to be depressed while they are actively exercising. Aerobic exercise, which increases oxygen intake, counteracts depression even in severely depressed people. Jogging, aerobic exercises or dancing, distance swimming, weight lifting, brisk walking—any exercise that keeps you moving for at least twenty minutes practiced four times a week or more is sufficient to keep depression at bay temporarily. Probably aerobic exercise alters the release of brain neurotransmitters. Aerobically fit individuals respond better to stress overall, with less anxiety and depression.

4. Avoid drugs and alcohol. While they may help to lift your spirits briefly, they make matters much, much worse overall. Indeed, the depression you feel may have more to do with the drugs you take to relieve it than the blues you felt in the first place. Do without the drugs and see how you feel.

5. Seek help. The best way to help yourself may be to admit that you can't do it alone.

6. Join the National Depressive and Manic Depressive Association (NDMDA), a rapidly growing organization of self-help, education, and support groups throughout the United States and Canada. For a list of local chapters, write or call: NDMDA, Merchandise Mart, Box 3395, Chicago, Illinois 60654; (312) 446-9009.

Part V

The Chosen

23

Depression in Groups: Women, Children, and the Elderly

THUS FAR IN THESE many chapters we have focused on depression as a disease that strikes individuals, each with certain vulnerability factors. Depression also strikes groups. Women are depression's favorite sex, children its newest victims, older persons its chosen age group. It seems fitting to conclude this book by looking at the needs of these groups, for to make an inroad on this widespread disease we must successfully diagnose and treat people by the millions.

The special needs of women, children, and the elderly, groups into which all sufferers of depression do now or ultimately will fall, have in the past been largely overlooked or disregarded. The good news is that biopsychiatrists are beginning to identify the diagnostic and treatment issues particular to these groups to stem the tide of the epidemic of depression in our society.

Women

Women are twice as likely as men to be depressed. They go to doctors more often than men do, for many reasons. Physicians have long believed that women have "weak constitutions." As one doctor expressed it in 1827, the female "is far more sensitive and susceptible than the male and extremely liable to those distressing affections which for want of some better term have been determined nervous, and which consist chiefly in painful affections of the head, heart, side, and indeed of almost every part of the system."

In the late-twentieth century, actions speak more powerfully: Physicians write 75 percent of all prescriptions for mood-altering drugs to women, who represent only 60 percent of the patients they see daily in their offices. Many of these prescriptions are for addicting tranquilizers.

Medicine still clings to the notion that "the remorseless biological demands placed by nature on womanhood" explains the higher incidence of depression and other "nervous affections" among this group. We have not progressed far in the objective understanding of the psychobiological functioning of women. Even though medicine has lately recognized the medical validity of the set of symptoms known as premenstrual syndrome (PMS), its diagnosis and treatment has been fraught with partial understanding and downright error.

A joint panel of the American Psychological Association, the Women and Health Roundtable, and the Federation of Organizations for Professional Women concluded that women's mental health needs are not being met. The panel reported that research, training, diagnosis, and treatment are all oriented toward men.

Biopsychiatrists are beginning to devote serious attention to the study of women. What we have learned so far is how much we *don't* know.

PMS

We know that women's suicide attempts and threats, as well as their admissions to psychiatric hospitals, increase premenstrually.

We know that over two-thirds of women with a history of severe depression have significant premenstrual lows.

We know too that women with premenstrual mood problems are likely to have a family history of depression.

In other words, we know that there is a strong relationship between the menstrual cycle and depression. But we don't know—despite the increasing frequency of the PMS diagnosis (and self-diagnosis) for women who become depressed premenstrually—that just because a woman suffers from depression in the premenstrual phase of her cycle, she indeed has PMS.

A differential diagnosis, which few doctors perform, could reveal a thyroid deficiency; hypothyroidism, as we pointed out in Chapter 10, is by far more common among women, and some studies show that hypothyroid women almost always suffer from premenstrual depression. It might show a premenstrual exacerbation of a chronic depression problem, which is most noticeable at that time of the month. Or it might turn up dysmenorrhea (painful menstruation) or endometriosis (a disorder in which tissue from the lining of the uterus, the endometrium, becomes detached and grows elsewhere in the abdomen). Appropriate, safe treatment demands a correct answer.

WHAT IS PMS?

The answer to this question is as complicated as what is and isn't depression, to which we have devoted numerous chapters of this book. We know less about PMS, however. Probably PMS (or premenstrual changes, premenstrual tension, premenstrual stress) comprises a number of different subtypes that occur in the luteal phase of the menstrual cycle, a week to ten days before the onset of the menstrual flow. "Premenstrual syndrome has come to include any of a number of different symptoms, both physical and emotional, which occur in a cyclic fashion just prior to the menstrual flow. These symptoms should begin to abate with the menstrual flow. Individual patients may have some symptoms and not others. Many patients have predominantly affective symptoms with very mild somatic symptoms, while other patients, particularly in an outpatient general gynecological practice, may have physical symptoms with few affective symptoms. It is not known whether these different groups have similar etiologies," report Steven J. Sondheimer, MD, Ellen W. Freeman, PhD, Beth Scharlop, MD, and Karl Rickels, MD.

We should note that not all the reported symptoms are unpleasant or uncomfortable. Ten to 15 percent of women feel *better* premenstrually.

To merit a diagnosis of PMS, the symptoms must be markedly more severe in the twenty-first through the twenty-eighth day of the cycle (counting from the first day of menstrual flow) compared with the sixth through the twelfth days, when symptoms should be virtually absent. Also, the symptoms must recur for at least two consecutive cycles. PMS studies and specialists require that patients keep a daily mood diary to determine whether they meet these two criteria. Most women do not.

Meeting the criteria establishes the diagnosis of premenstrual syndrome, but it does not explain what it is or where it comes from. Most important as far as the woman herself is concerned, the diagnosis does not indicate treatment. While over three hundred possible treatments for PMS have been reported, *none has proved more effective than placebo.* Some work for some women, others work for other women. None is a cure-all, no matter what you may read.

And some are dangerous. Dr. Jean A. Hamilton and her colleagues caution that "many self-help booklets currently recommend doses of vitamin B6 that may be neurotoxic, and levels of progesterone that exceed those currently being explored by the FDA, much less tested in controlled trials. As with all treatments, possible side effects of progesterone (e.g., headache, exhaustion, lightheadedness, uterine bleeding) must be clearly weighed against possible benefits.''

A CALL FROM A FRIEND OF A FRIEND

Susan T., 34, read a popular book on PMS and recognized many of her own symptoms. She too became painfully bloated and irritable almost beyond measure. "I feel like Dr. Jekyll and Mrs. Hyde," she told her gynecologist. "I really worry that I'm going to kill somebody —like my kid. Then I get my period and the next day I'm normal and nice." She was extremely relieved to discover that she was suffering an extremely common, physiological disorder that could be treated. The book spoke well of treatment with the hormone progesterone. Susan asked her gynecologist to prescribe it for her.

Her doctor refused. He said, "I do not know that you have PMS. That is a difficult diagnosis to make, far more complicated than your book suggests—and I don't want to start prescribing hormones for you unless I am absolutely certain you need them. In fact, Susan," he told her, "we don't really know what PMS is. The symptoms you have could be caused by a number of different disorders. I understand you want to get to the bottom of these mood changes. They're awful for you and for your family. Here's the best way I can help you." The doctor advised Susan to undergo a thorough examination at a PMS evaluation clinic at a nearby university hospital. He said he would be glad to call and set up an appointment for her, but Susan was miffed that he would not give her the medication she was certain would cure her. Without another word she put on her coat and left his office.

Susan is a friend of a friend, and when she got home she called me. She believed that her gynecologist had mistreated her by refusing to prescribe progesterone. Although it sounded to me that he had behaved responsibly, I said I'd call and talk to him. We ended up having an interesting conversation about diagnostic issues related to PMS. He told me about the work being done at the clinic he had recommended to Susan. I called her back and explained, too, that progesterone could have serious side effects, including uterine bleeding. I told her that the PMS clinic sounded like a good idea. Or, I said, she might want to come here to Fair Oaks and be evaluated for depression.

"Well, I'll think about it," she said, now disappointed with me, too. I heard several weeks later that she had found a gynecologist who "took her seriously" and prescribed progesterone to her. As far as I know she still suffers bouts of depression premenstrually, the cause and the treatment of which have never been determined.

OR IS IT DEPRESSION?

Given the stigma that continues to be associated with mental suffering, "it may be more socially acceptable for women to think of their mood problems as a premenstrual phenomenon rather than a more generalized disorder, and consequently they present their difficulties in this context," observe Wilma M. Harrison, MD, Judith G. Rabkin, PhD, and Jean Endicott, PhD.

As mentioned previously, most women who suffer from severe depression have a worsening of symptoms in the days just prior to their periods. Women with milder mood problems also tend to have premenstrual mood changes. At other times of the month the depression may not be so intrusive. A woman may "become more aware of the unpleasant symptoms only when these symptoms worsen" in the premenstrual phase, say Harrison and colleagues. Before being evaluated for PMS, she may be unaware that she has a chronic mood problem.

Drs. Harrison, Rabkin, and Endicott discovered that the large majority of women who volunteered to participate in a PMS treatment study did not in fact have the disorder. Even many of those who passed the initial screening were later excluded when closer evaluation revealed that their distress could just as well be caused by another psychiatric or medical illness (58 percent) or by use of a drug or medication (31 percent).

"The most frequently reported premenstrual mood symptoms are irritability, tension, anxiety, depression, and mood swings, which not only are not specific to premenstrual syndrome but may characterize any number of . . . disorders," note Harrison, Rabkin, and Endicott.

Medication and the Menstrual Cycle

The way a woman's body metabolizes medication, including antidepressants and lithium, may vary throughout the menstrual cycle. Lithium levels may decrease premenstrually. Depressed women whose moods have returned to normal with antidepressants often experience a temporary premenstrual return of symptoms. All the more reason for the psychiatrist to monitor antidepressant blood levels frequently and to adjust dosage or supplement accordingly. And as Drs. Harrison, Rabkin, and Endicott suggest, researchers especially should note a woman's menstrual phase when evaluating her response to antidepressant treatment. "It is still rare even in well-controlled studies to find that the menstrual phase has been recorded or considered in evaluation of placebo response, relapse, or treatment outcome," they note.

POSTPARTUM DEPRESSION

We may know little about PMS; we know less about postpartum depression, which in its mildest form affects an estimated 70 to 80 percent of all women following the birth of a child. From 10 to 20 percent of new mothers experience a full-blown clinical depression. A far smaller number, approximately one in one thousand, develop a postpartum depressive psychosis. Despite the high incidence of depression following childbirth, the often desperate new mother may receive inappropriate or inadequate treatment—or, most likely, no treatment at all. Psychiatrists, notes a commentator in the *Journal of the American Medical Association,* are not taught to differentiate these mood disorders from those not related to childbirth; "psychiatry training programs and texts refuse to separate them from non-postpartum conditions, or recognize them as distinct disorders.

"And even if psychiatrists are aware of" this type of illness, she adds, "the people most likely to encounter it firsthand—obstetricians, general physicians, nurses, and husbands—are even less likely to know anything about it. Because 'postpartum psychiatric problems lie midway between obstetrics and psychiatry,' in the words of James Alexander Hamilton, MD, '. . . these problems fail to receive the attention of specialists in either field.' "

It is vital that we understand this set of disorders, for the sake of the mother and for the infant as well. Recent research has revealed that a mother's depression in the baby's first years may affect the child's subsequent emotional and cognitive development (more about this later in this chapter). "This doesn't mean a child's future is profoundly determined," says British psychiatrist Harold L. Caplan, MD, "but there now seems sufficient evidence in terms of the development of the child . . . to justify strenuous efforts to detect and treat maternal depression."

DIFFERENTIAL DIAGNOSIS

The research effort has begun to strengthen. Throughout the world scientists at over one hundred laboratories are attempting to determine the connections that must exist between the many hormonal, metabolic, and psychological changes that take place at childbirth and the high incidence of depression. Differential diagnosis is of course essential. What may result from a thyroid insufficiency in one woman may be caused by a combination of sensitivity to hormonal shifts and the stress of giving birth and adjusting to a new role in another. As always, appropriate, effective treatment depends on pinpointing a diagnosis.

Identification of vulnerability factors will help identify and ultimately prevent this type of suffering. As with premenstrual depressions, a history of depression increases the risk of postpartum depression. Since the postpartum depression for some women is the first in a long series of depressive episodes, discovery of biological markers and other risk factors would be a boon. Hypothyroidism commonly develops in women following childbirth; autoimmune thyroid disease can be detected by the existence of antibodies early in pregnancy in time to treat it and prevent its severe emotional consequences.

THE SUBTYPES

For most women, postpartum depression is temporary. Treatment, if any, consists of relief of symptoms, which themselves depend on the type of postpartum depression the woman has. Whether a woman receives medication may depend on whether or not she is breastfeeding her infant.

The vast majority of women endure "maternity blues." Frequently on the third day following delivery, the new mother becomes tearful, sleepless, tense, and angry. Episodes come and go for twenty-four hours to a week, then they lift. Understanding the biologic underpinnings of this essentially normal state would shed light on the more pathological postpartum conditions.

Ten to 20 percent of new mothers will move from the blues to a full clinical depression. The depression may last two to eight weeks, but sometimes it may continue for as long as a year. Some psychiatrists and obstetricians refer to this type of depression as "postpartum neurotic depression" because stress factors, including changing family roles and insufficient preparation for motherhood, often are prominent. Since the biological mechanisms of postpartum mood disorders have not been identified, we should be wary of jumping to conclusions.

A small number of women have to be hospitalized with a full-blown postpartum depressive psychosis. Although most recover, the separation of mother and infant threatens that most important bond.

A BETTER START

A postpartum clinical depression is not "natural" or "normal," no matter what anyone might tell a suffering new mother. "Most obstetricians don't have great insight into the emotional problems of childbirth," admits David N. Danforth, MD, PhD, professor emeritus of obstetrics and gynecology at Northwestern University School of Medicine in Chicago. The mother deserves help as soon as possible, so that she and her new baby get off to a good start, and so that she can be sure to prevent future episodes. To be on the safe side, seek a biopsychiatric evaluation, which includes a medical and psychological workup and the most advanced types of treatment. If the depression begins during pregnancy, get help right away.

THE FUTURE OF PMS
AND OTHER MOOD DISORDERS AMONG WOMEN

We do not yet fully understand a woman's normal hormonal cycling, much less the abnormal. The more we discover about the neuroendocrine mind/brain/body links in depression, no doubt the more we will understand how sex hormones specifically influence depression and behavior. Researchers are finding evidence of the influence of sex hormones on neurotransmitter functioning, but this is true equally of male sex hormones. Men, however, do not experience a similar periodic hormonal cycling; nor do they experience the sudden reduction of hormones which women undergo at menopause (and which may be responsible in part for the depression some women must deal with at that time). The desynchronization of monthly and other periodic hormonal cycles in relation to other biologic-clock variables may be the key to understanding cyclic depressions in women.

We can expect most progress to be made in the diagnosis and treatment of PMS, if only because lately it's a hot topic. As with depression itself, research is likely to reveal specific, identifiable PMS biologic subtypes and biologic markers. The next step will be treatments that are actually effective, which cannot be said for present-day approaches. Remember, PMS has only recently become a legitimate area of medical investigation; much work remains to be done. Progress with menopausal depressions, which are even foggier than premenstrual and postpartum syndromes, will follow.

THAT SEX DIFFERENCE

Overall the greatest progress for women may stem from the design of better research studies, which determine more accurately the causes for the sex differences in depression. That a woman's biological differences determine her vulnerability to this disease advances the old anatomy-is-destiny argument.

In an attempt to explain sex differences in the incidences of depression, British physicians Rachel Jenkins and Anthony W. Clare in 1985 took a hard look at epidemiological studies. They determined that most epidemiologists have not studied a homogeneous sample. The men and women included in the studies that have revealed a preponderance of depressed women have differed in terms of social variables such as occupation and status. The few studies Jenkins and Clare found in which men and women were equivalent on all variables revealed no sex difference in the incidence of depression. We need more homogeneous studies to confirm these findings. For now, conclude Jenkins and Clare, "All claims that the excess of depression in women is explained by their reproductive biology—or indeed by their constitution in general—should be treated with grave caution."

Children

Twenty years ago psychiatrists believed that depression in children did not and could not exist. Now experts in child health are sounding an alarm. Declare psychiatrists Donald H. McKnew, Leon Cytryn, and Herbert Yahraes: "From three to more than six million American children suffer from depression—much of it unrecognized and untreated." The terrible truth has caught psychiatrists and pediatricians by surprise. Often it takes a child's attempt at suicide for the parents to get the message. For the families of the 5,000 to 10,000 children who succeed in killing themselves each year, that message comes too late.

Depression in children can result in learning problems, school failure, drug abuse/addiction, disturbed relationships with other people, tendency to illness and or psychosomatic disorders, suicide, even homicide. If depression in a child is not detected and treated, the child may be in for a lifetime of suffering. If a suicide attempt fails now, another may succeed later.

Depressed kids must get help. But most kids can't do that on their own. An adult first has to recognize the problem, or recognize it for what it really is and take it seriously. That's the hard part.

DIAGNOSIS AND MISDIAGNOSIS
Depression in adults and children is remarkably alike, from incidence to biological subtypes. While the symptoms too are similar—sleep

and appetite disturbance, bodily complaints, hopelessness, guilt, lack of self-esteem, loss of ability to experience pleasure, confusion, fatigue, and so on—kids do not express them the same as grown-ups. The child's facial expression, posture, and tone of voice may present an eloquent picture. But ask what's wrong, and the little one may only shrug and pout. The older child may not wish to share his or her feelings. Especially if parents have other things on their minds, they may not find that anything is particularly out of the ordinary. The extremely well-behaved child who always tries to please is being good, right? As for that sulky and sloppy and irritable one who's not eating or doing his homework—he's just a normal rebellious teenager. He'll grow out of it. . . .

The sudden flurry to comprehend the increase in adolescent suicide, which has tripled since 1950, has led to a discovery about adolescence: Private anguish and unpredictable, downright obnoxious behavior are not necessarily a normal part of growing up. They are symptoms, often, of depression.

MASKS

As in adults, masked depression in children is common. Depression in adults is often cloaked in physical complaints. Children, too, may be treated for headaches or stomach problems when depression is the real problem. Other, perhaps more, kids tend to mask their symptoms in behavior problems, including disruptiveness, fighting, delinquency, school difficulties, bed-wetting, alcohol and drug abuse, and so on. Many kids end up being treated for hyperactivity and learning disabilities, punished for laziness, or even placed in detention for aggressive, destructive behavior, when depression is the primary problem.

Learning Disabilities = Depression
Depression = Learning Disabilities

Psychologist David Goldstein conducted a five-year study of 159 learning-disabled children in Philadelphia and found that nearly all of them were depressed. The school problems caused the depression in most of them; but for about one-third, depression produced the school problems. When the depression was treated, school performance improved.

MIMICKERS

By the same token, kids may seem depressed and get hauled off to therapists or school counselors when they are in fact physically ill. "When a nine-year-old suddenly can't function in his environment, refuses to go to school, or becomes very aggressive, you also have to look at whether something is going on organically," says child psychiatrist Nancy Roeske, MD. "Every child with a problem needs a thorough physical examination. For example, at nine and ten the child is entering an age where diabetes or epilepsy may begin to show up. . . . And, unfortunately, you also need to think about whether the child has become involved with drugs or alcohol."

Drug and alcohol abuse is by far the major mimicker among apparently depressed children. Thyroid deficiency is also common, particularly among adolescents. Not long ago, we evaluated twenty-eight consecutive adolescents who were being admitted to Fair Oaks with symptoms of depression and lack of energy. After a comprehensive thyroid evaluation of them all, we discovered that 11 percent were suffering from subclinical hypothyroidism.

A host of other diseases that appear with emotional symptoms can also strike children, from lead poisoning to cancer. A New Mexico child psychiatrist tells us of an 8-year-old boy whose mother brought him in for treatment of depression. The mother, a young widow, had moved to the Southwest from Pennsylvania after her husband's sudden death the previous year. Paul, her little boy, had been deeply depressed the whole year, and the move appeared to worsen his symptoms, which included pains in his leg. In Pennsylvania, Paul's mother had taken him to a pediatrician who had found no signs of physical illness. He recommended a child psychiatrist, who treated Paul with no apparent success. Paul had had another physical before entering his new school in New Mexico. His mother had told the pediatrician that Paul had been having leg pains off and on since his father had died. Again the pediatrician noted nothing unusual and recommended a local child psychiatrist.

Paul's new psychiatrist was concerned about the boy's physical symptoms. They did not seem to conform to the usual pattern of psychosomatic aches and pains. And, after working with the boy for a few weeks, he did not think that a psychiatric condition was at the root of Paul's problem. He urged Paul's mother to seek a particular pediatric specialist for a thorough medical workup. Paul's mother refused; she'd been to two pediatricians already.

The Christmas holidays came, and the psychiatrist left town on a week-long ski trip with his family. When he returned, Paul's mother called to cancel her son's next appointments. Paul had fallen and badly twisted his leg. It was his right leg, the one that had been giving him so much trouble. At the emergency room where she took him, the doctors X-rayed the leg and discovered bone cancer.

Paul was operated on three days later. He lost the leg, but he survived. Four years have passed and the psychiatrist still wonders whether there wasn't some way he could have convinced Paul's mother to take her boy for evaluation earlier. Who knows, he might have been able to help save the boy's leg.

DEPRESSION IN THE FAMILY

Depression is a family affair in more ways than one. The predisposition to develop depression can be inherited, as we discussed in Chapter 16. Many investigators now believe that children who begin a depressed course before puberty are probably genetically driven into such an early expression of the illness.

Relationships within the family, which is the world for younger children in particular, also trigger depression. Children whose parents abuse them are at great risk for depression. So are kids whose parents are overly critical and who focus on their child's inadequacies. Depression is common in kids whose parents don't pay them genuine, thoughtful attention. A parent may dismiss as trivial an anxious, striving teenager's crisis over a failure to get a grade he wanted, then claim that the suicide attempt "came out of nowhere."

Not that parents necessarily understand what they are doing, or intend to do it. The struggle to get by financially, to endure a separation or divorce, to deal with kids in a drug-sex-crime-infested world, may overwhelm or distract a parent. Sometimes, when parents have too much to deal with in their own lives, although they may be hard-pressed to admit it, they just don't want to know about their kids' problems. When the parents are themselves depressed, they can hardly take care of their own needs, much less their kids'. They may not recognize that depression in kids is not normal, since they were themselves depressed as children. Conflicts and difficulties mark the families of most depressed people.

Kids take it personally when a depressed parent withdraws, or becomes suddenly angry, irritable, critical, and punishing. They think: "I'm bad" or "There's something wrong with me." Mommy gets depressed and turns from warm and nurturing to icy and impatient. The child may try desperately to please, not understanding that Mommy can't be pleased until she feels better.

Even infant children of depressed mothers become depressed, we now know. The effects can be devastating. Some withdraw and slow down, often failing to make eye contact or to smile. They develop digestive problems, such as colic. They may grow and develop much slower than normal. The future is cloudy for these kids unless someone intervenes. In the past, when extended families were the rule, the baby would be able to make a good attachment with a grandmother or an aunt. Today infant psychiatrists, as they are called, and other specialized health-care workers, step in to correct the mother-child interaction—if the mother comes for help.

Mostly, however, children in depressed families continue to fall through the cracks in the health-care system. Studies reveal a 40 to 45 percent rate of psychiatric disorders, mostly depression, among children of parents with mood disorders. "Early infancy and adolescence seem to be the stages in which children are particularly vulnerable," report psychiatrists William R. Beardslee, MD, Jules Bemporad, MD, Martin B. Keller, MD, and Gerald L. Klerman, MD. Nonetheless, even when the parents are in treatment, the physicians and therapists rarely stop to think that the patient's children are probably affected. "The seriousness of the impairment and the finding that few of these children received any treatment at all strongly suggest the need for heightened awareness among clinicians about the seriousness of depression in children whose parents have affective disorders," state Beardslee and colleagues. Likewise, parents of depressed kids should be evaluated and treated for depression.

Good Treatment for Depressed Kids

Provided that they receive a thorough biopsychiatric evaluation, many types of treatment are available to children, too. Antidepressants are often prescribed for teenagers; increasingly they are being given to seriously depressed younger children, "despite the lack of FDA approval for the use of these medications in doses usually required in the treatment of depression," notes child psychiatrist Elva Poznanski, MD. Medical management of kids taking antidepressants is essential, since they metabolize these drugs differently from adults and are much more at risk of side effects. Drs. Cytryn and McKnew recommend that tricyclic antidepressants be used judiciously "in children in whom a depressive illness has been reliably diagnosed and who failed to respond to psychotherapy and environmental manipulation." Careful monitoring of side effects and increments in dosage as indicated by medication blood levels are definitely indicated. Blood pressure, blood levels, pulse, and EKG should be screened regularly.

As in adults, biological tests can be used to diagnose and monitor depression in youngsters. Hypersecretion of cortisol tends to increase with age; the dexamethasone can detect this biologic marker of depression beginning in adolescence. Younger biologically depressed children often oversecrete growth hormone during sleep.

Psychotherapy is the traditional treatment approach. Child psychiatrists and psychotherapists speak "childese"; they are trained to talk to kids and understand the meaning of their behavior and feelings. They can find out what is really disturbing the younger or older child in a supportive, trusting environment free of the parent-child conflicts. Then they can help find solutions. Sometimes that means the parents must recognize their own problems and their effects on their children. Child psychotherapy, especially with younger children, must involve the parents, who are the only persons in a position to make the changes that the child requires. A child may benefit from a different type of school, for example. Perhaps the child is suffering from the loss of a grandparent; the parents may need to talk more openly about the death with the whole family. Or the parents may need to learn that they are putting too much pressure on the child to achieve. When the whole family is in crisis, family therapy can be extremely effective in helping all members understand their effects on each other.

Cognitive therapy has been adapted for kids, and group therapy can be very helpful, since depressed children almost always have trouble relating comfortably to their peers.

Drug rehabilitation is essential for depressed kids who abuse alcohol and/or drugs. Kids may take to drugs to try to escape their pain. Or they may become depressed as a result of the drugs. In either case the depression will recur if drug use remains or resumes. And in all cases, treatment for depressed kids' drug or alcohol problems begins immediately.

Take It Seriously

- More than eight out of ten children who threaten suicide attempt it.
- Suicide has overtaken homicide as the second leading cause of death among youths aged 15 to 24. Accidents are first; among these, many single-car automobile accidents may in fact be unreported suicides.

- The only age group in the United States with a constantly rising mortality rate is 15- to 24-year-olds. Suicide is the fastest-growing cause.
- Forty percent of teenagers who attempt suicide are drug and/or alcohol abusers.
- Two thirds of suicidal kids report poor relationships with their parents. Ninety percent say their parents don't understand them.

The child is at the end of his or her rope. Pay attention. Listen. Watch for:

—Increased sadness, tearfulness, moodiness, or irritability.

—Withdrawal from favorite activities and relationships with favorite people.

—Evidence of drug or alcohol use (these can both weaken the inhibitions against suicide and provide the means to do it).

—Changes in sleeping and eating habits, and lack of attention to clothes and appearance.

—Sudden failures or difficulties in school.

—Preoccupation with death and dying ("I hope I can come here again before I die," said a 7-year-old boy to his favorite aunt three weeks before he tried to hang himself with his sister's jump-rope. A 15-year-old girl was reading *Death Be Not Proud,* John Gunther's account of his teenage son's death from brain cancer, the night she overdosed on pills.)

—Distribution of "worldly goods," such as favorite records and tapes, toys, or clothing.

—A recent personal loss (such as a boyfriend or girlfriend) or rejection (not invited to join a club or go to a dance) or failure (got a B in math instead of an A).

Teachers often prove more able to detect depression in kids than do their parents. If the child's teacher calls to say something's up, believe it. If you are worried about your child and want more information, call the teacher.

If an attempt appears imminent, don't waste time feeling guilty, angry, or upset. Act. Call a suicide or crisis intervention hot line, the psychiatric unit at a local hospital, or a trusted pediatrician or psychiatrist (but if you can't get through, don't wait for him or her to return your call).

Don't wait to see if the child feels better in the morning. Most attempts by kids take place at home in the late afternoon or evening with family members present.

By all means, talk to your child. The notion that talking about suicide encourages it is false and dangerous. Kids are human. We all feel better when someone hears us out. Express understanding of the child's anguish and reassure him or her that there is a solution to the problem and that you will do everything you can to help find it. As someone once said, suicide is a permanent solution to a temporary problem.

For further information regarding the prevention of adolescent suicide contact:

National Committee on Youth Suicide Prevention
67 Irving Place South
New York, N.Y. 10003
Linda Laventhall, Executive Director

The Elderly

Twentieth-century medicine continues to indulge Americans in their wish to live longer. The improvement in diagnosis, treatment, and prevention of formerly deadly diseases has resulted in a huge increase in the numbers of older persons in this country. Today the fastest-growing segment of the population is over 85. Evidence suggests no halt to this trend. At present about 12 percent of Americans are over 65. Within fifty years that percentage will approach 20 percent. By the middle of the next century, life expectancy will be in the nineties.

But, in the words of T. S. Eliot, "as we grow older/The world becomes stranger, the pattern more complicated."

Living into old age means contending with loss. Loss of health, vigor, opportunities, strength, physical and mental prowess, friends, spouses, siblings, work, earnings, independence, residences, and support networks. Loneliness, boredom, and helplessness threaten. Esteem diminishes in a society which does not respect its elderly. The longer we live, the more pain we have to contend with. To live long requires a continuous expenditure of energy simply to survive. Canadian psychiatrist H. E. Lehmann, MD, perceives that "the elderly are in double jeopardy as the aging process invariably reduces a person's ability to adapt and to cope at a time when this is most needed, as life stresses increase."

The risk of depression increases as ability to tolerate biologic and psychosocial stressors decreases. Thus the incidence of depressive illness is highest in old age. Depression is four times more prevalent among the elderly as among the general population. The rate of suicide is fifteen times higher. While persons over 65 account for 12 percent of the population, they commit 25 percent of all suicides. Ninety percent of all suicide attempts succeed.

The view prevails that the loneliness, isolation, difficulties in sleeping and eating; the loss of energy, sexual interest and ability, mental function, and peace of mind; the constipation and other physical discomforts that accompany depression are normal to this phase of life.

They are not.

When living to an advanced age was not a realistic expectation, no one paid much attention to the quality of life in the late decades. Now persons at the height of their powers are beginning to foresee that these humiliations are bound to be their fates. Suddenly we are witnessing a massive medical effort to deal with the aging of America. Biopsychiatry has played a major role in this turnaround. We have contributed to research in physiology and psychology of the aging mind and body. We have determined that the quality of mental life can be restored to a depressed person. With treatment, even a person of advanced years can recover sufficient energy and coping ability to lead a dignified life.

DIAGNOSIS AND MISDIAGNOSIS

Most elderly depressed persons do not now receive treatment, because they either (1) deny their symptoms; or (2) accept them as normal and do not come for treatment; or because they (3) receive an incorrect diagnosis when they do seek help. Differential diagnosis of depression in this age group is tricky for even the most skilled clinicians.

THE MASKS OF DEPRESSION IN OLDER AGE

Dr. Lehmann teaches physicians: "Frequently, clinical depression is missed in a person over sixty because the affective disorder is masked by a host of physical symptoms and somatic complaints. The physician may find in his depressed patient hypertension, emphysema, diabetes, or a chronic urinary infection, and may then miss the associated depression which, in its own right, may have become the most important and most urgent pathological condition." Sometimes, too, the physician will diagnose a disease such as Alzheimer's and ignore the patient's depression, thinking that it is inseparable from the illness and in itself untreatable.

Or, says Dr. Lehmann, the depression may be cloaked entirely in "complaints about bowel functions, urinary frequency, dizziness, peculiar taste, burning on urination, or various aches and pains without organic basis, but the underlying depression may not be recognized." The individual receives treatment which he or she does not require, increasing the likelihood of drug interactions that worsen both the psychiatric symptoms and the risk to the patient.

THE MIMICKERS

In part because physicians too accept, even promote, the usual stereotypes of old people, they often leap to psychiatric diagnoses when a patient is grouchy, complaining, apathetic, confused, and annoying. In the absence of obvious signs of physical illness, or when a patient is unable to provide a complete and lucid history, the doctor may not investigate thoroughly. He or she will proceed to overlook the medical diagnosis to which the psychiatric symptoms should have provided clues. Because susceptibility to disease increases with age, the elderly are the most vulnerable to most of the mimicking illnesses that we discussed in detail in Part II. Brain tumors, pancreatic cancer, thyroid disease, rheumatoid arthritis, and cardiovascular disorders, for example, are much more common in this age group. A combination of gastrointestinal illness and poor diet may produce malnutrition, which physicians will frequently encounter in their geriatric patients, if they look for it.

RX + RX + RX

The elderly take 25 percent of all prescribed drugs. Not surprisingly, a much overlooked medical condition that mimics depression in older persons is adverse reactions to prescribed drugs. The wide majority of persons 65 and over take an average of over seven medications regularly. Many of these drugs separately or in combination can cause symptoms of depression, among other, often dangerous reactions.

Some physicians multiply the suffering and the dangers either by neglecting to ask about other medications, forgetting to discontinue unnecessary drugs, failing to substitute more tolerable formulations, and/or prescribing still more drugs to counteract the symptoms.

A Florida physician asked psychiatrist David A. Gross to look in on his father. The 73-year-old man had retired the previous year and was looking forward to the good life in a new home in another state. No sooner had he arrived than he had to be hospitalized with an acute ulcer. The man did not recover his health. He became so depressed and confused that he was unable to take care of himself. His son brought him back to Florida and placed him in a nursing home where he would be able to receive the constant care and attention he now needed.

Antidepressants provided no improvement and were discontinued. The man's condition grew worse. He developed tremors and other neurological symptoms which led to a diagnosis of Parkinson's disease in addition to depression. When Dr. Gross first saw him, the man could not maintain a train of thought or even stay awake for long periods. He barely moved or spoke spontaneously. His face was devoid of expression.

Dr. Gross recognized the problem. He suggested a change in the man's blood pressure medication and the elimination of one of his ulcer prescriptions. Gradually but steadily the physician's father recovered his spirits, his mind, and his happy interactions with other human beings. He left the nursing home to return once more to the pursuit of the good life.

ALCOHOL, ETC.

Abuse of drugs and alcohol is not confined to youth. Years of use can produce a pattern of symptoms that will seduce an unsuspecting physician into the wrong diagnosis.

"I was recently consulted by an internist to see a ninety-four-year-old woman who had been diagnosed as having mild to moderate Alzheimer's disease," Colorado psychiatrist Troy Thompson, MD, recently told us. The woman had insisted on living on her own and had managed it despite her confusion, memory loss, and other symptoms of dementia. She had been thoroughly evaluated, including a CAT scan of the head, which revealed brain changes which Dr. Thompson considered unrevealing in a patient of this age. Her internist and neurologist had found no specific cause for dementia, "so as a diagnosis of exclusion she was thought to have Alzheimer's.

"But she didn't seem so demented to me," he says. "She had a devilish gleam in her eye, unlike anything I have ever seen in a truly demented patient. So I asked about her drug and alcohol use. She freely admitted to 'nipping a little Scotch to take off the chill.'

"I asked her how often she felt the chill.

"She smiled and said, 'All day every day.' She'd been drinking over half a fifth a day since her second husband died just before World War II. To help get to sleep she also took two to three over-the-counter antihistamine-based sleeping pills nightly. 'If one is good, two to three should be better,' she added."

Dr. Thompson disagreed. He suggested that she cut back to two to three jiggers of Scotch a day, and he prescribed a sedative-hypnotic for sleep which would be more effective and which would clear her system faster.

She followed the doctor's regimen, and "her 'Alzheimer's' improved markedly over the next month."

PSEUDODEMENTIA

The worst misdiagnosis for a depressed person to be stuck with is Alzheimer's disease or senile dementia.

GERIATRIC DEPRESSION

Common Physician Errors

Underdiagnosis, including overdiagnosis of dementia or assumption that depressive complaints are a normal part of aging

Failure to prevent overdose or other suicide

Failure to evaluate concurrent medical or neurological illnesses (e.g., hypothyroidism, cardiovascular disease, Parkinson's disease)

Failure to add vitamin and nutritional supplements to regimen

Failure to reduce or to discontinue unnecessary medications (e.g., central nervous system depressants, such as hypnotics, or excessive doses of antihypertensives or hypoglycemic agents)

Failure to utilize blood levels: undertreatment with antidepressant medication (e.g., use of homeopathic doses)

Failure to monitor important side effects of antidepressant medication (e.g., orthostatic hypotension, constipation)

Use of dosages more suitable for younger depressed patients, resulting in signs of toxicity (e.g., confusional states)

Failure to define trial with blood levels operationally

Failure to maintain medication for a sufficient length of time, leading to recurrence of symptoms

Failure to educate patients and families about depression, especially about the high risk of recurrence

Factors Contributing to the Vulnerability of the Elderly to Depression

Heredity

Poor diet (e.g., essential amino acids)

Central nervous system changes associated with aging (e.g., catecholamine decreases)

Concurrent medical/neurological disorders (e.g., diabetes, hypertension, cancer, thyroid disease, and Parkinson's disease) and drugs used to treat these disorders

Significant psychosocial changes (bereavement, retirement, financial changes)

Diminishing psychological, psychosocial, and physiological reserves

GERIATRIC DEPRESSION *(Continued)*

Symptoms of Depression in the Elderly

Various dysphoric states (the patient may deny feeling sad but admits to pervasive feelings of uselessness, pessimism, or helplessness)

Neurovegetative changes, such as trouble staying asleep at night, loss of appetite and loss of weight, agitation or retardation, loss of interest or pleasure in usual activities (including sex), worsening of symptoms in the morning or evening

Feelings of self-reproach (guilt)

Feelings that life is not worth living (suicidal ideation)

Prominent somatic concerns out of proportionto any demonstrable abnormality

Prominent concerns about memory or cognitive problems out of proportion to any demonstrable deficits

Reversible cognitive impairment (e.g., inattentiveness with difficulty learning new material)

The diagnosis of Alzheimer's disease or senile dementia (see Chapter 7) can have horrifying consequences to a depressed person. Dr. Thompson's patient fortunately had sufficient wits about her to insist on taking care of herself. Most Alzheimer's patients, whether correctly or incorrectly diagnosed, are considered incurable; they end up in nursing homes for sometimes long years until finally they die. Confusion, loss of memory and intellectual functions, inability to recognize familiar persons—the mental deterioration people and doctors associate with senility—characterize depression as well as Alzheimer's. Everybody used to think that "old" and "senile" were synonymous. Nowadays, as Alzheimer's becomes more recognized, "senile" means "Alzheimer's"; sometimes it is diagnosed with reckless abandon. More older persons with these mental symptoms are depressed than have Alzheimer's—so many that the syndrome merits it own name: *depressive pseudodementia.*

In 1982, a total of 213 patients were treated and discharged from the geriatric service of New York Hospital–Cornell Medical Center at White Plains. Sixty percent of them had pseudodementia. Correctly diagnosed and treated for depression, they recovered.

They were lucky. When Alzheimer's is diagnosed instead and the depression not treated, the condition becomes chronic and can lead to true, irreversible dementia.

Because depression and dementia can coexist, and because the depressed symptoms may mask a true dementia (see the case of Mr. R in Chapter 7), the physician must perform a most thorough diagnostic workup. The depression that frequently accompanies Alzheimer's can often be treated with antidepressants, by the way, making the illness somewhat less intolerable to the sufferer, who is aware of what's happening in the early stages.

BIOLOGICAL DEPRESSION

We are discovering some reasons why older persons are so much more prone to biological depression. It seems that the supply of crucial brain neurotransmitters decreases and monoamine oxidase enzymes, which metabolize these neurotransmitters, increase. The maintenance of mood and balance depends in part on the steady supply of these brain chemicals. Also, aging brain cells become less able to maintain necessary homeostatic balance in the face of stresses and deterioration of body systems. The body's timekeepers tend also to slow down and possibly to go out of sync with one another. In the face of these biological stresses, depression may develop for the first time. In persons with previously existing illness, episodes of depression increase and worsen.

Biological tests for depression can be used in this age group, in which biological signs become most evident. Oversecretion of cortisol, for example, is highest in this age group.

THE TREATMENTS

The aim is to save time. Older patients benefit least from traditional trial-and-error approaches to treatment. They haven't time to wait to see if they are going to feel better and get a little enjoyment out of life. Therefore the biopsychiatrist will use all available technology to determine which is the most appropriate, safest, and by all means fastest way to effect a cure. Because it can work so quickly, some clinicians more readily consider electroshock (ECT) for patients in this age group, particularly those for whom medication may prove too dangerous. However, the clinician must exercise caution in its use and know how to minimize the resulting, temporary confusion and memory loss. (See the discussion of ECT in Chapter 21.)

ANTIDEPRESSANT DRUGS

Antidepressants can work wonders. They can also inflict suffering, permanent damage, and death. The difference between cure and disaster balances on the knowledge and skill of the prescribing physician. Be sure you can count on it.

The aging body absorbs, metabolizes, distributes, and excretes drugs much differently from that of the average youthful individual. Generally, older persons end up with much more of the drug in their systems. They overdose on amounts that a younger person wouldn't even notice. This age group is more vulnerable and sensitive to drug effects and side effects overall. Persons "over age 70 have approximately twice as many adverse drug reactions as do people under age 50," reports Boston psychiatrist Jerrold G. Bernstein, MD.

Many antidepressants can be deadly to a weakened heart, but that is only one of the potential dangers. The physician has to know the positive and negative effects of each and every antidepressant drug as well as their potentially dangerous interactions. Which drug is likely to cause such a drop in Mrs. Blum's blood pressure so that she'll faint, fall, and break her hip? Which ones will be so sedating as to throw Mr. Jones into utter confusion? Can I trust Miss Brown to follow the dietary restrictions if I prescribe monoamine oxidase inhibitors? Is Ms. Cruz really going to remember how many of these pills she's already taken? Do I dare prescribe these pills to Mr. Eklund following his heart attack? Which drug will block the effect of Mr. Yamamoto's blood pressure medication and throw him into a hypertensive crisis? If I prescribe these pills to Mrs. O'Malley, will she use them to kill herself?

Too many physicians, psychiatrists included, who prescribe antidepressants to their aging patients would fail this test. And too few monitor medication blood levels to be sure they are prescribing a safe and effective dosage.

PSYCHOTHERAPY

For older persons, too, medication and psychotherapy combined provide best results. The short-term therapies are just the thing, with their emphasis on immediate problem solving and coping skills. Sex therapy, even, can do a world of good. (When depression lifts, the recovered patient is probably going to feel sexy again, perhaps for the first time in years. The therapist can help the man or woman overcome inhibitions against behaving sexually "at my age.") Interpersonal therapy can help the older person out of his or her isolation. Marital therapy helps couples meet the needs of this stage of life.

When they can, some geriatric psychotherapists involve the families of their older patients, who may be having difficulty themselves dealing with the individual's symptoms. Sometimes patient and family can work with the therapist to help each other. Most people feel better about themselves when they can have something useful to do. Dr. Lehmann: "Examples of activities I have found useful for this purpose are Xeroxing papers, polishing silverware, feeding and walking pets and watering, repotting, and otherwise caring for plants, not only for the patient's family, but also for others who would appreciate help with such chores." The activities of course depend on the health and vigor of the older person. Once energy and interest return, a recovering person may reap great rewards from volunteer work.

Increasingly psychotherapists treating older persons recommend exercise, from walking to supervised aerobic programs.

Because of the interrelated medical and psychosocial considerations involved in treating older individuals, a biopsychiatrist who also practices psychotherapy may be your best bet. Nonmedical therapists must be medically aware and willing to work closely with physicians. In every case, the practitioner must be particularly sensitive to people at this stage of life. Not everyone can work with the older patient. Sometimes a clinician's own fears of getting old, difficulties dealing with his or her own aging parents, or attitudes about investing time in patients who have little life remaining can get in the way. Make sure you find someone who shows warmth, caring, and understanding.

Dr. Troy Thompson: "A refined elderly gentleman consulted me regarding memory problems. He detailed exactly when and how his memory had failed him over a period of months, so much so that there was little question in my mind that his memory was excellent. He somewhat sheepishly explained that he did well with 'numbers, presidents, and the news items'—the types of memory gaps we check for in mental status exams—but that he continually forgot things around his apartment.

"I sensed there was a hidden agenda, so I asked what he thought would help him most. He related that he had read about a tablet that improves memory and which must be taken three or four times daily. But, he added, since his memory was so erratic, he would have to have someone remind him several times a day to take it.

"I asked who he had in mind. He mentioned a widow who lived in his building, and he asked if I might call her to see whether she would be willing to assist him. This shy gentleman had seen the lovely widow numerous times in the building elevator and had chatted with her once or twice about the weather. But he was embarrassed to proceed further 'without a proper introduction.'

"I called the woman and asked if she would oversee twice daily what I was certain was a harmless dosage of a widely advertised memory enhancer. She eagerly agreed 'to do anything to help a needy neighbor.' I was invited to their wedding four months later, where my former patient informed me with a wink that he no longer needed the memory pill."

A Good Ending

When medicine and psychiatry take up arms together we can work miracles. The accomplishments of biopsychiatry in the treatment of older individuals ranks among the best news of which we have spoken throughout these many pages. After a long, hardworking life, one has the right to hope for peace of mind. Eighty percent of depressed, confused, hopeless elderly persons can immediately be treated and returned to dignified existence.

All they need to do is come for treatment. For this to happen, word of the advances in diagnosis and care must spread to the suffering individuals and their families, to their physicians, to medical students, to insurance companies, and to helping agencies throughout the community. Persons who become aware that much of the mental and physical agony of later life is reversible will demand better care for themselves or for members of their family.

The same can be said for mental health care at every age. Demand better for yourselves. The skill and technology is there and you will get it if you insist on it.

We have good reason to expect that at the present rate of advance in biopsychiatric research and understanding and the rapid development of psychiatric laboratory technology, we can halt the epidemic of depression that is sweeping our country in this century. Right now biopsychiatrists can identify and treat acute depression in most cases from infancy onward. Steadily we will improve our ability to diagnose state and trait markers and develop pharmacological agents that will target precise receptors without adversely affecting others. Identification of genetic markers will follow; manipulation of affected genes possibly awaits us in the next century. Psychiatrists will become highly skilled physicians, and physicians will become skilled in the recognition of mental and physical disease in their patients. Increasingly we will understand how the mind and brain and body are linked. We will elucidate the biological mechanisms of depression. We will know better how to harness the mind to better its own existence. Depression will lose its stigma.

By the time the baby boomers have reached the venerable years, depression, the illness, will cease to be a problem. When sadness comes, it will go away.

Appendix:
A Biopsychiatric Referral List

The following is a partial listing of biopsychiatrists throughout the United States. For each of these practitioners we include address and phone number, as well as university/hospital affiliations. Numerous additional psychiatrists practice biopsychiatric medicine. Any of the men and women mentioned on this list may in turn refer you to other practitioners in your area.

ALABAMA

Michael J. Kehoe, MD
University of Southern Alabama
2451 Fillingim Street
Mobile, AL 36617
(205) 479-3072

John R. Smythies, MD
University of Alabama at
  Birmingham
University Station
Birmingham, AL 35294
(205) 934-2011

ARIZONA

Michael E. Brennan, MD
3352 East Camelback Road
Suite H
Phoenix, AZ 85018
(602) 957-7996

Dennis C. Westin, MD
Palo Verde Hospital
P.O. Box 40090
Tucson, AZ 85717-0090
(602) 795-4850

ARKANSAS

Frederick Guggenheim, MD
University of Arkansas for Medical
  Sciences
4301 W. Markham - Slot 589
Little Rock, AR 72205
(501) 661-5483

CALIFORNIA

Victor I. Reus, MD
University of California, San
  Francisco
Medical Director
Langley-Porter Institute
401 Parnassus Avenue
San Francisco, CA 94143
(415) 476-7478

Geoffrey J. Newstadt, MD
Cedars-Sinai Medical Center
Rm. 4525
8700 Beverly Blvd.
Los Angeles, CA 90048
(213) 855-3465

Robert H. Gerner, MD
The Center for Mood Disorders
UCLA Neuropsychiatric Institute
12301 Wilshire Blvd
Suite 210
Los Angeles, CA 90025

Monte Buchsbaum, MD
University of California, Irvine
California College of Medicine
Room D402
Irvine, CA 92717
(714) 856-4244

John Deri, MD
2154 Broderick St.
San Francisco, CA 94115
(415) 921-3311

Michael J. Gitlin, MD
UCLA Neuropsychiatric Institute
Center For Mood Disorders
12301 Wilshire Blvd
Suite 210
Los Angeles, CA 90025
(213) 471-1876

Forest S. Tennant, Jr., MD, PhD
University of Southern California
Community Health Projects, Inc.
336 ½ South Glendora Avenue
West Covina, CA 91790
(818) 919-1879

John Feighner, MD
University of California, San Diego
San Luis Rey Hospital
1011 Devonshire Drive, Suite E
Encinitas, CA 92024
(619) 753-2301

Harvey A. Sternbach, MD
UCLA Neuropsychiatric Institute
11645 Wilshire Blvd-Suite 901
Los Angeles, CA 90025
(213) 820-6126

Ferris N. Pitts, Jr., MD, FAPA
University of Southern California
  School of Medicine
7500 East Hellman Avenue
Rosemead, CA 91770
(818) 571-4866

Robert Fusco, MD
French Hospital Medical Center
4131 Greary Boulevard
San Francisco, CA 94118
(415) 944-1733 or 666-8877

COLORADO

Troy Thompson, MD
University of Colorado School of
  Medicine
4200 East 9th Avenue
Denver, CO 80262
(303) 394-8370

CONNECTICUT

Laurence Rossi, MD
Institute of Living
400 Washington Street
Hartford, CT 06106
(203) 241-8000

L. Michael Sheehy, MD
Columbia College of Physicians and
  Surgeons
Silver Hill Foundation
P. O. Box 1177
New Canaan, CT 06840
(203) 966-3561

Selby C. Jacobs, MD
Yale University School of Medicine
Yale New Haven Hospital/2039CB
333 Cedar Street
New Haven, CT 06510
(203) 785-2619

J. Craig Nelson, MD
Yale University School of Medicine
Yale New Haven Hospital
20 York Street
New Haven, CT 06504
(203) 785-2157

Dennis Charney, MD
Yale University School of Medicine
333 Cedar Street
New Haven, CT 06510
(203) 789-7329

DC AREA

David Pickar, MD
National Institute of Health
Clinical Center, NIH,
Bldg. 10, 4N214
Bethesda, MD 20205
(301) 496-4303

Robert M. Post, MD
National Institute of Mental Health
NIMH, Bldg. 10, 3N212
9000 Rockville Pike
Bethesda, MD 20205
(301) 496-4805

William Z. Potter, MD, PhD
National Institute of Mental Health
NIMH, Bldg. 10, 2D46
9000 Rockville Pike
Bethesda, MD 20205
(301) 496-5082

S. Charles Schulz, MD
Georgetown University
National Institute of Mental Health
5600 Fishers Lane
Rockville, MD 20857
(301) 443-4707

Robert L. DuPont, MD
Georgetown University
6191 Executive Boulevard
Rockville, MD 20852
(301) 468-8980

FLORIDA

Abraham Flemenbaum, MD
2500 E. Hallandale Beach Blvd.
Suite 508
Hallandale, FL 33009
(305) 454-5544

Steve Targum, MD
University of South Florida
Sarasota Palms Hospital
1650 South Osprey Avenue
Sarasota, FL 33579
(813) 366-6070

Brian Weiss, MD
University of Miami
4300 Alton Road
Miami, FL 33140
(305) 674-2194

Otsenre Matos, MD
150 Sunset Blvd, Suite 12
New Port Richey
Tampa, FL 33552
(813) 849-2005

Arnold L. Lieber, MD
University of Miami
St. Francis Hospital
Neuroscience Unit, 11th Floor
250 West 63rd Street
Miami Beach, FL 33141
(305) 868-2747

David A. Gross, MD
Fair Oaks Hospital at Boca/Delray
5440 Linton Blvd
Delray Beach, FL 33445
(305) 495-1000

John Adams, MD
University of Florida Medical School
Department of Psychiatry
Box J-256, JHMHC
Gainesville, FL 32610
(904) 392-3681

William Rea, MD
Lake Hospital of the Palm Beaches
1710 Fourth Avenue North
Lake Worth, FL 33460
(305) 588-7341

Irl Extein, MD
Medical Director
Fair Oaks Hospital at Boca/Delray
5440 Linton Blvd
Delray Beach, FL 33445
(305) 495-1000

Richard C. W. Hall, MD
University of Florida College of
   Medicine
Florida Hospital
601 East Rollins Street
Orlando, FL 32803
(305) 897-1801

James Adams, MD
2329 Sunset Point Road, Suite 203
Clearwater, FL 33575
(813) 796-0038

Luis A. Herro, MD
Morton F. Plant Hospital
Clearwater, FL

GEORGIA

G. Douglas Talbott, MD
Emory University School of
  Medicine
Georgia Alcohol & Drug Associates
4015 South Cobb Drive
Smyrna, GA 30080
(404) 435-2570

Ronald C. Bloodworth, MD
Medical Director
Psychiatric Institute of Atlanta
811 Juniper Street, NE
Atlanta, GA 30308
(404) 881-5800

Melvin Udel, MD
Emory University School of
  Medicine
3985 South Cobb Drive, Suite 110
Smyrna, GA 30080
(404) 436-6667

Bob Robinson Maughon, MD
1953 Seventh Avenue
Columbus, GA 31904
(404) 324-5447

John Curtis, MD
650 Oglethorpe Avenue
Suite #6
Athens, GA 30606
(404) 354-4045

Arnold Tillinger, MD
515 East 63rd Street
Savannah, GA 31405
(912) 352-2921

HAWAII

John McDermott, MD
Chairman, Department of
  Psychiatry
John A. Burns School of Medicine
1960 East West Road
Honolulu, HI 96822
(808) 948-8287

ILLINOIS

John M. Davis, MD
University of Illinois
Illinois State Psychiatric Institute
1601 West Taylor
Chicago, IL 60612
(312) 996-1065

Jan Fawcett, MD
Rush Presbyterian/St. Lukes
  Medical Center
1720 West Polk Street
Chicago, IL 60612
(312) 942-5372

Dale Giolas, MD
University of Illinois
520 North Ridgeway
Chicago, IL 60624
(312) 722-3113

INDIANA

John Nurnberger, Jr., MD
Indiana University Medical Center
791 Union Drive
Indianapolis, IN 46223
(317) 274-8382

Iver Small, MD
Indiana University School of
  Medicine
Larue D. Carter Memorial Hospital
1315 W. Tenth Street
Indianapolis, IN 46202
(317) 634-8401

Joyce Small, MD
Indiana University School of
  Medicine
Larue D. Carter Memorial Hospital
1315 W. Tenth Street
Indianapolis, IN 46202
(317) 634-8401

IOWA

Nancy C. Andreasen, MD, PhD
Department of Psychiatry
University of Iowa
500 Newton Road
Iowa City, IA 52242

George Winokur, MD
University of Iowa College of
  Medicine
500 Newton Road
Iowa City, IA 52242
(319) 353-3719

William Coryell, MD
University of Iowa College of
  Medicine
500 Newton Road
Iowa City, IA 52242
(319) 353-3898

KANSAS

Thad H. Billingsley, MD
The Benessere Ctr.
7000 Squibb Rd.
Mission, KS 66202
(913) 432-9900

Donald Goodwin, MD
University of Kansas
Department of Psychiatry
39th and Rainbow
Kansas City, KS 66103
(913) 588-6402

Sheldon H. Preskorn, MD
University of Kansas Medical School
Chief of Psychiatry
VA Hospital #116
5500 East Kellogg
Wichita, KS 67218
(316) 685-2221 X 3386

KENTUCKY

John J. Schwab, MD
University of Louisville School of
  Medicine
Department of Psychiatry, RM 503
Louisville, KY 40292
(502) 588-5387

Karley Y. Little, MD
University of Kentucky Medical
  Center
Annex 2
Lexington, KY 40536
(606) 233-5552

Daniel Nahum, MD
University of Kentucky
Department of Psychiatry
John Chambers Bldg
820 South Limestone
Lexington, KY 40536
(606) 233-5444

LOUISIANA

Wayne Julian, MD
Tulane
5610 Read Blvd
New Orleans East, LA 70127
(504) 244-5661

Michael R. Madow, MD
Methodist Psychiatric Pavillion
5610 Read Blvd
New Orleans, LA 70127
(504) 244-5661

Rudolph Ehrensing, MD
Ochsner Clinic
1514 Jefferson Hwy
New Orleans, LA 70121
(504) 838-3000

Gene L. Usdin, MD
Louisiana State University
Ochsner Clinic
1514 Jefferson Hwy
New Orleans, LA 70121
(504) 838-3965

Gregory C. Khoury, MD
Medical Director
JoEllen Smith Psychiatric Hospital
4601 Patterson Road
New Orleans, LA 70131
(504) 367-0707

Stanley Roskind, MD
Tulane University
Medical Director
JoEllen Smith Psychiatric Hospital
4601 Patterson Road
New Orleans, LA 70114
(504) 367-0707

MARYLAND

Frank J. Ayd, Jr., MD
1130 East Cold Spring Lane
Baltimore, MD 21239
(301) 433-9220

Solomon Snyder, MD
Johns Hopkins University School of
   Medicine
Wood's Basic Science Bldg. Rm 813
725 North Wolfe Street
Baltimore, MD 21205
(301) 955-3024

Paul R. McHugh, MD
Johns Hopkins University School of
   Medicine
Johns Hopkins Hospital
600 North Wolfe Street
Baltimore, MD 21205
(301) 955-3130

Bruce T. Taylor, MD
Taylor Manor Hospital
College Avenue P.O. Box 396
Ellicott City, MD 21043
(301) 465-3322

MASSACHUSETTS

Johnathan O. Cole, MD
Harvard Medical School
McLean Hospital
115 Mill Street
Belmont, MA 02178
(617) 855-3205

Harrison G. Pope, Jr., MD
Harvard Medical School
McLean Hospital
115 Mill Street
Belmont, MA 02178
(617) 855-2255

Jerrold G. Bernstein, MD
Harvard Medical School
Massachusetts Institute of
   Technology
830 Boylston Street-Suite 200
Chestnut Hills, MA 02167
(617) 738-8650

Lloyd I. Sederer, MD
Department of Psychiatry
Mount Auburn Hospital
330 Mount Auburn Street
Cambridge, MA 02138
(617) 499-5054

Alan F. Schatzberg, MD
Harvard Medical School
McLean Hospital
115 Mill Street
Belmont, MA 02178
(617) 855-2201

Paul Barreira, MD
Department of Psychiatry
University of Massachusetts Medical
   Center
55 Lake Avenue North
Worcester, MA 01605
(617) 856-4087

MICHIGAN

Samuel Gershon, MD
Wayne State University School of
   Medicine
Lafayette Clinic
951 E. Lafayette
Detroit, MI 48207
(313) 745-3553

John Francis Greden, MD
University of Michigan School of
   Medicine
1405 E. Ann, Box 11
Ann Arbor, MI 48109
(313) 763-9629

MINNESOTA

Paula J. Clayton, MD
University of Minnesota
Dept. of Psychiatry
Box 77 Mayo Memorial Build.
420 Delaware St. S.E.
Minneapolis, MN 55455
(612) 626-3532

James Halikas, MD
University of Minnesota
Department of Psychiatry
Box 393 Mayo Memorial Hospital
420 Delaware Street, SE
Minneapolis, MN 55455

Mood Disorders Clinic
Dept. of Psychiatry
Box 393 Mayo Memorial Bld.
420 Delaware St. S.E.
Minneapolis, MN 55455
(612) 626-3698

MISSISSIPPI

Howard Freeman, Jr., MD
Charter Hospital of Jackson
East Lakeland Drive
Jackson, MS 39216
(601) 939-9030

MISSOURI

Samuel Guze, MD
Washington University School of
  Medicine
4940 Audubon Avenue
St. Louis, MO 63110
(314) 362-7005

Stuart Ozar, MD
St. Louis University School of
  Medicine
1221 South Grand
St. Louis, MO 63104
(314) 577-8000

NEW HAMPSHIRE

John Docherty, MD
Nashua Brookside Hospital
11 Northwest Blvd.
Nashua, NH 03063
(603) 886-5000

NEW JERSEY

Michael Orlosky, MD
Rutgers University Medical School
133 Franklin Corner Road
Lawrenceville, NJ 08648
(609) 896-1211

Charles A. Dackis, MD
Columbia University College of Phy-
  sicians and Surgeons
Hampton Hospital
Rancocas Road
CN-7000
Mt. Holly, NJ 08060
(609) 267-0288

Patricia L. McGuire, MD
Fair Oaks Hospital
19 Prospect Street
Summit, NJ 07901
(201) 522-7095

Peter S. Mueller, MD
601 Ewing Street
Princeton, NJ 08540
(609) 924-4061

Donald R. Sweeney, MD, PhD
Yale University School of Medicine
Fair Oaks Hospital
19 Prospect Street
Summit, NJ 07901
(201) 522-7000

Jeffrey R. Berlant, MD
Summit Medical Group
120 Summit Avenue
Summit, NJ 07901
(201) 273-4300

NEW YORK

Donald F. Klein, MD
Columbia University School of
Medicine
722 West 168th Street
New York, NY 10032
(212) 305-2500

James W. Flax, MD
242-D North Main Street
New City, NY 10956
(914) 638-3358

Richard Altesman, MD
Harvard School of Medicine
Stony Lodge Hospital
P. O. Box 1250
Briarcliff Manor, NY 10510
(914) 941-7400

Robert Cancro, MD
NYU School of Medicine
550 First Avenue
New York, NY 10016
(212) 340-6214

David E. Sternberg, MD
Yale University School of Medicine
Falkirk Hospital
Estrada Road
Central Valley, NY 10917
(914) 928-2256

NORTH CAROLINA

Arthur Prange, MD
University of North Carolina
School of Medicine
BSRC-220H
Chapel Hill, NC 27514
(919) 966-1480

Bernard J. Carroll, MD, PhD
Duke University
P. O. Box 3950
Durham, NC 27710
(919) 684-5616

Charles B. Nemeroff, MD, PhD
Duke University
P. O. Box 3950
Durham, NC 27710
(919) 684-6562

OHIO

Herbert Y. Meltzer, MD
Case Western Reserve University
2074 Abington Road
Cleveland, OH 44106
(216) 844-8750

David Garver, MD
University of Cincinnati Medical
School
7303 Medical Science Bldg.
231 Bethesda Avenue
Cincinnati, OH 45267
(513) 872-5400

A. James Giannini, MD
Ohio State University
Northeast Ohio Medical College
3040 Belmont Avenue
Youngstown, OH 44504
(216) 759-8685

Gregory B. Collins, MD
The Cleveland Clinic Foundation
9500 Euclid Avenue, Desk P68
Cleveland, OH 44106
(216) 444-2970

OKLAHOMA

Gordon H. Deckert, MD
University of Oklahoma College of
Medicine
P. O. Box 26901
Oklahoma City, OK 73190
(405) 271-5251

OREGON

Alfred Lewy, MD
Oregon Health Sciences University
L-469, Department of Psychiatry
Portland, OR 97201
(503) 225-7746

PENNSYLVANIA

Stuart Yudofsky, MD
Columbia University College of Physicians and Surgeons
Allegheny General Hospital
320 East North Avenue
Pittsburgh, PA 15212
(412) 359–3131

Joseph Mendels, MD
University of Pennsylvania
1015 Chestnut Street-Suite 1303
Philadelphia, PA 19107
(215) 923-2583

Peter Whybrow, MD
University of Pennsylvania
305 Blockly Hall
Philadelphia, PA 19104
(215) 662-2818

Joaquim Puig-Antich, MD
University of Pittsburgh School of Medicine
3811 O'Hara Street, Rm E720
Pittsburgh, PA 15213
(412) 624-1436

Daniel Van Kammen, MD
University of Pittsburgh School of Medicine
VA Medical Center/Psychiatry Services
Highland Drive
Pittsburgh, PA 15206
(412) 363-4900 Ext. 483

David Kupfer, MD
University of Pittsburgh School of Medicine
3811 O'Hara Street
Pittsburgh, PA 15213
(412) 624-2353

Kenneth R. Sandler, MD
University of Pittsburgh School of Medicine
Fairmount Institute
561 Fairthorne Street
Philadelphia, PA 19128
(215) 487-4000

RHODE ISLAND

Richard Goldberg, MD
Brown University
Rhode Island Hospital APC-9
593 Eddy Street
Providence, RI 02902
(401) 277-5488

Andrew Edmund Slaby, MD, PhD, MPH
Brown University
Rhode Island Hospital APC-9
593 Eddy Street
Providence, RI 02902
(401) 277-5488

SOUTH CAROLINA

Raymond F. Anton, Jr., MD
Medical University of South Carolina
Assoc. Prof. of Psychiatry
171 Ashley Ave.
Charleston, SC 29425
(803) 792-4037

James Ballenger, MD
Medical University of South Carolina
171 Ashley Avenue
Charleston, SC 29403
(803) 792-2010

TENNESSEE

Hagop Souren Akiskal, MD
University of Tennessee School of Medicine
66 North Pauline Street
Suite 633
Memphis, TN 38163
(901) 528-6449

TEXAS

James Buckingham, MD
4800-A Northeast Stalling Drive
Nacogdoches, TX 75961
(409) 564-9785

Lee Emory, MD
1103 Rosenberg
Galveston, TX 77550
(409) 763-0016

A. John Rush, MD
Department of Psychiatry
University of Texas Health Science
  Center
5323 Harry Hines Boulevard
Dallas, TX 75235

Edward Gripon, MD
University of Texas Medical Branch
3560 Delaware, Suite 502
Beaumont, TX 77706
(409) 899-4472

Annette Marie Shelton, MD
Psychiatric Institute of Fort Worth
815 Eighth Avenue
Ft. Worth, TX 76104
(817) 335-4040

R. Michael Allen, MD
University of Texas, Dallas
1788 Highway 157 North-Suite 102
Mansfield, TX 76063
(817) 473-0662

Frederick Goggans, MD
University of Texas, Dallas
Health Science Center
1814-B Eighth Avenue
Ft. Worth, TX 76110
(817) 924-1036

Alan C. Swann, MD
University of Texas Medical School
6431 Fannin Street
Suite 5218
Houston, TX 77030
(713) 792-5541

James Maas, MD
University of Texas
Health Science Center
7703 Floyd Curl Drive
San Antonio, TX 78284
(512) 691-7315

UTAH

Bernard Grosser, MD
University of Utah Medical Center
50 North Medical Drive
Salt Lake City, UT 84132
(801) 581-4888

VIRGINIA

Robert O. Friedel, MD
Medical College of Virginia
University of Virginia
Charter Westbrook Hospital
1500 Westbrook Avenue
Richmond, VA 23227
(804) 261-7124

C. Gibson Dunn, MD
Springwood Psychiatric Institute
Route 4, Box 50
Leesburg, VA 22075
(703) 777-0810

WASHINGTON

Gary Tucker, MD
University of Washington
R.P. #10
Seattle, WA 98195
(206) 543-3750

David Dunner, MD
University of Washington
Harborview Medical Center
325 Ninth Avenue, ZA#15
Seattle, WA 98104
(206) 223-3404

WEST VIRGINIA

James M. Stevenson, MD
West Virginia University School of
  Medicine
Morgantown, WV 26506
(304) 293-2411

WISCONSIN

James Jefferson, MD
University of Wisconsin Medical
  School
600 Highland Avenue
Madison, WI 53792
(608) 263-6078

Barry Blackwell, MD
Mount Sinai Medical Center
950 North 12th Street
P.O. Box 342
Milwaukee, WI 53201
(414) 289-8620

Burr Eichelman, MD
University of Wisconsin Medical
  School
VA Hospital
2500 Overlook Terrace
Madison, WI 53705
(608) 262-7015

In addition, you can contact the National Depressive and Manic
Depressive Association (NDMDA) at (312) 993-0066

Bibliography

Adler, Stephen N., Mildred Lam, and Alfred F. Connors, Jr. *A Pocket Manual of Differential Diagnosis.* Boston and Toronto: Little, Brown and Co., 1982.

"AIDS." *Newsweek* (August 12, 1985):20–27.

Akiskal, Hagop Souren. "Dysthymic Disorder: Psychopathology of Proposed Chronic Subtypes." *American Journal of Psychiatry* 140 (January 1983):11–20.

Alper, Joseph. "Biology and Mental Illness." *The Atlantic Monthly* (December 1983):70–76.

American Psychiatric Association. *Diagnostic and Statistical Manual of Mental Disorders.* 3rd edition. Washington, D.C.: American Psychiatric Association Press, 1980.

Andreasen, Nancy C. *The Broken Brain: The Biological Revolution in Psychiatry.* New York: Harper and Row, 1984.

Anthony, Catherine Parker, and Gary A. Thibodeau. *Structure and Function of the Body.* 7th edition St. Louis: Times Mirror/Mosby College Publishing, 1984.

Aschoff, Juergen. "The Circadian System in Man." Chapter 8 in *Neuroendocrinology,* edited by Dorothy T. Krieger and Joan C. Huges. Sunderland, Massachusetts. A Hospital Practice Book, Sinauer Associates, Inc., 1980.

Ayd, Frank, Jr., ed. *Clinical Depressions: Diagnostic and Therapeutic Challenges.* Baltimore: Ayd Medical Communications, 1980.

Baldessarini, Ross J. *Biomedical Aspects of Depression and Its Treatment.* Washington, D.C.: American Psychiatric Association Press, Inc., 1983.

Barikolate, Gina. "Clinical Trial of Psychotherapies Under Way." *Science* 212 (April 24, 1981):432–433.

Baxter, Lewis R., Jr., Michael E. Phelps, John C. Mazziotta, et al. "Cerebral Metabolic Rates for Glucose in Mood Disorders." *Archives of General Psychiatry* 42 (May 1985):441–447.

Beardslee, William R., Gerald L. Klerman, Martin B. Keller, Philip W. Lavori, and Donna L. Podorefsky. "But Are They Cases? Validity of *DSM-III* Major Depression in Children Identified in a Family Study." *American Journal of Psychiatry* 142:6 (June 1985):687–691.

———, Jules Bemporad, Martin B. Keller, and Gerald L. Klerman. "Children of Parents With Major Affective Disorder: A Review." *American Journal of Psychiatry* 140:7 (July 1983):825–832.

Beck, Aaron T., Robert A. Steer, Maria Kovacs, and Betsy Garrison. "Hopelessness and Eventual Suicide: A 10-Year Prospective Study of Patients Hospitalized With Suicidal Ideation." *American Journal of Psychiatry* 142:5 (May 1985):559–563.

Belson, Abby Avin. "New Focus on Chemistry of Joylessness." *New York Times* (March 15, 1983):C1, C8.

Benevenga, N. J., and R. D. Steele. "Adverse Effects of Excessive Consumption of Amino Acids." *Annual Review of Nutrition* 4 (1984):157–181.

Bernstein, Jerrold G., ed., *Clinical Psychopharmacology.* 2nd edition. Boston, Bristol, and London: John Wright PSG, Inc., 1984.

———. "Neurotransmitters and Receptors in Pharmacopsychiatry." Chapter 4 in *Clinical Psychopharmacology,* edited by Jerrold G. Bernstein. 2nd edition. Boston, Bristol, and London: John Wright PSG, Inc., 1984.

———. "Pharmacological Management of The Elderly Patient." Chapter 12 in *Clinical Psychopharmacology,* edited by Jerrold G. Bernstein. 2nd edition. Boston, Bristol, and London: John Wright PSG, Inc., 1984.

Bird, Stephanie J. "Presymptomatic Testing for Huntington's Disease." *Journal of the American Medical Association* 253:22 (June 14, 1985):3286–3291.

Black, Donald W., Giles Warrack, and George Winokur. "Excess Mortality Among Psychiatric Patients." *Journal of the American Medical Association* 253:1 (January 4, 1985):58–61.

Bloodworth, Ronald C. Personal communication to Mark Gold, spring 1985.

Boffey, Phillip M. "Rare Disease Proposed as Cause for 'Vampires.' " *New York Times* (May 31, 1985):A15.

Boxill, Diana. "Teenage Suicide: Prevalent Problem." *Dispatch* (February 14, 1982).

Brayshaw, N., and M. S. Gold. "Thyroid Dysfunction in Premenstrual Syndrome." *APA Abstract* 102 (1985):191.

Brody, Jane E. "Personal Health: Detecting Signs and Preventing Teen-Age Suicide." *New York Times* (March 7, 1984):C7.

Brown, Marvin R., and Laurel A. Fisher. "Brain Peptides as Intercellular Messengers: Implications for Medicine." *Journal of the American Medical Association* 251:10 (March 9, 1984):1310–1315.

Buchsbaum, Monte S., and Richard J. Haier. "Psychopathology: Biological Approaches." *Annual Review of Psychology* 34 (1983):401–430.

Burch, E. A., and T. J. Goldschmidt. "Depression in the Elderly: A Beta-Adrenergic Receptor Function." *International Journal of Psychiatry in Medicine* 13:3 (1983–84):207–213.

Cohen, Martin R., David Picker, Irl Extein, et al. "Plasma Cortisol and B-Endorphin Immuroreactivity in Nonmajor and Major Depression." *American Journal of Psychiatry* 141:5 (May 1984):628–632.

Cohn, Victor. "Gene Defect Linked to Manic-Depression." *Miami Herald* (August 1, 1984):Section F.

"Commission Releases Findings on Unemployment and MH." *Psychiatric News* 20:18 (September 20, 1985):1.

Consensus Development Panel of the NIMH/NIH Consensus Development Conference. "Mood Disorders: Pharmacologic Prevention of Recurrences." *American Journal of Psychiatry* 142:4 (April 1985):469–476.

Corfman, Eunice. *National Institute of Mental Health: Science Reports: Depression, Manic-Depression and Biological Rhythms.* U.S. Government Printing Office, Washington, D.C.: National Institute of Mental Health, 1982. 0-377-011.

Coryell, William. "The Organic-Dynamic Continuum in Psychiatry: Trends in Attitudes Among Third-Year Residents." *American Journal of Psychiatry* 139:1 (January 1982):89–91.

Crayton, John W. "Adverse Reactions to Foods: Relevance to Psychiatric Disorders." *Journal of Clinical Immunology,* in press, 1985.

" 'Creativity and Madness Are Linked,' Study Says." *New York Times* (September 23, 1984):63.

Cytryn, Leon, and Donald H. McKnew. "Treatment Issues in Childhood Depression." *Psychiatric Annals* 15:6 (June 1985):401–403.

Dackis, Charles A., and M. S. Gold. "Bromocriptine as Treatment of Cocaine Abuse." *Lancet* 1:8438 (1985):1151–1152.

———, M. S. Gold, A. L. C. Pottash, and D. R. Sweeney. "Evaluating Depression in Alcoholics." *Psychiatry Research* 17 (1986):105–109.

———, and Mark S. Gold. "Opiate Addiction and Depression: Cause or Effect." *Drug and Alcohol Dependence* 2 (1983):105–109.

———, Joyce Bailey, A. L. C. Pottash, et al. "Specificity of the DST and the TRH Test for Major Depression in Alcoholics." *American Journal of Psychiatry* 141:5 (March 1984):680–683.

Davidson, Jonathan, Craig Turnbull, Rosemary Strickland, and Michael Belyes. "Comparative Diagnostic Criteria for Melancholia and Endogenous Depression." *Archives of General Psychiatry* 41 (May 1984):506–511.

DelBello, Alfred B. "Needed: A U.S. Commission on Teen-Age Suicide." *New York Times* (September 12, 1984):A31.

deMilio, Lawrence T., and Lynne Weisberg. "Subclinical Hypothyroidism Presenting as Adolescent Depression." Unpublished manuscript, 1985.

"Depression: A Problem for Learning-Disabled Young." *American Medical News* (March 8, 1985):35.

"Depression, Violent Suicides Tied to Low Metabolite Level." *Journal of the American Medical Association* 250:23 (December 16, 1983):3141.

Deptula, Dennis J., Alan Manevitz, and Allen Yozawitz. "Lateralization of Memory Deficits in Depression." Paper presented at American Psychiatric Association, May 1984.

"Diagnostic Tests." *Healthfacts* 9:62 (July 1984):1–6.

Di Giacomo, Joseph. "Treating the Depressed Hypertensive Patient." *Medicine and Psychiatry* 1:1 (Summer 1983):3.

"Don't Overlook Homicidal Tendencies in Depressed Patients, Report Warns." *Psychiatric News* (July 5, 1985):10

Dorland's Illustrated Medical Dictionary. 26th edition. Philadelphia: W. B. Saunders Company, 1981.

Edwards, Neil. "Mental Disturbances Related to Metals." Chapter 17 in *Psychiatric Presentations in Medical Illness: Somatopsychic Disorders,* edited by Richard C. W. Hall. New York, London: SP Medical and Scientific Books, 1980.

Elsenga, S., and R. VanDenHoofdakker. "Clinical Effects of Sleep Deprivation and Clomipramine in Endogenous Depression." *Journal of Psychiatric Research* 17:4 (1982–83):361–374.

"Enhanced Sensitivity to Light: A Risk Factor for Depression?" *Currents* 4:8 (August 1985):14.

Evans, Dwight L., Gail A. Edelsohn, and Robert N. Golden. "Organic Psychosis Without Anemia or Spinal Cord Symptoms in Patients With B12 Deficiency." *American Journal of Psychiatry* 140:2 (February 1983):218–221.

Extein, Irl, A. L. C. Pottash, M. S. Gold, and R. W. Cowdry. "Changes in TSH Response to TRH in Affective Disorders." In *Neurobiology of Mood Disorders* by Robert M. Post, M.D. and James C. Ballenger, M.D. Volume 1 of *Frontiers of Clinical Neuroscience.* Baltimore, London: Williams and Wilkins, 1984.

———, G. Rosenberg, A. L. C. Pottash, and M. S. Gold. "The DST in Depressed Adolescents." *American Journal of Psychiatry* 139:12 (1982):1617–1619.

———, and M. S. Gold, eds. *Medical Mimics of Psychiatric Disorders.* Washington, D.C.: American Psychiatric Association Press, 1986.

———, and M. S. Gold. "Psychiatric Applications of Thyroid Tests." *Journal of Clinical Psychiatry* 47:1 (1986):13–16.

———, M. S. Gold, and A. L. C. Pottash. "Psychopharmacological Treatment of Depression." *Psychiatric Clinics of North America* 7:3 (1984):503–517.

———, A. L. C. Pottash, and M. S. Gold. "Thyroid Tests as Predictors of Treatment Response and Prognosis in Psychiatry." *Psychiatric Hospital* 16:3 (1985):127–160.

———, A. L. C. Pottash, and M. S. Gold. "The TRH Test in Affective Disorders: Experience in a Private Clinical Setting." *Psychosomatics* 25:5 (1984):-379–389.

———. Memo to Mark Gold, March 29, 1985.

"Family Medical and Health Guide." *Consumer Guide Magazine Health/Exercise Bimonthly* 383 (March 1985):59.

Ferrell, Tom. "Some Sad People, It Seems, Are Unhappy as a Matter of Habit." *New York Times* (November 15, 1983):C2.

Fieve, Ronald R. *Moodswing.* New York: William Morrow and Co., 1975.

Fishbein, Morris. "Is Affective Illness on the Increase?" *Journal of the American Medical Association* 241:6 (February 9, 1979):545.

Freud, Sigmund. "Analysis Terminable and Interminable." Volume 23, 1937. In standard edition of *The Complete Psychological Works.* London: Hogarth Press, 1953–74.

Fulcha, Robert, Joy Stapp, and Marlene Wicherski. *Detailed Statistical Tables: 1979 and 1980 Doctorate Employment Surveys.* American Psychological Association report, November 1982.

Gada, M. T. "A Cross Cultural Study of Symptomatology of Depression: Eastern Versus Western Patients." *International Journal of Social Psychiatry* 28:3 (Autumn 1982):195–202.

Garelik, Glenn, and Gina Maranto. "Multiple Murderers." *Discover* (July 1984):26–29.

Garvey, M. J., and G. D. Toliefson. "Post-Partum Depression." *Journal of Reproductive Medicine* 29:2 (1984):113–116.

Geertsma, Robert H., and Donald R. Ginols. "Specialty Choice in Medicine." *Journal of Medical Education* 47 (July 1972):509–517.

"Genetic Link in Suicide Supported by Study of Amish." *Psychiatric News* (September 6, 1985):20–21.

Gershon, Elliot S., Judith Schreiber, Joel Hamovit, Eleanor Dibble, et al. "Clinical Findings in Patients With Anorexia Nervosa and Affective Illness in Their Relatives." *American Journal of Psychiatry* 141:11 (November 1984):-1419.

Giannini, A. James, William A. Price, and Robert H. Loiselle. "Prevalence of Mitral Valve Prolapse in Bipolar Affective Disorder." *American Journal of Psychiatry* 141:8 (August 1984):991–992.

—————. Personal communication to Mark S. Gold, May 1985

Gittleman, Rachel, and Andres Kanner. "Overview of Clinical Psychopharmacology in Childhood Disorders." Chapter 10 in *Clinical Psychopharmacology,* edited by Jerrold G. Bernstein. 2nd edition. Boston, Bristol, and London: John Wright PSG, Inc., 1984.

Goggans, Frederick C. "Nutritional Deficiency Syndromes in Clinical Psychiatry." Chapter 9 in *Diagnostic and Laboratory Testing in Psychiatry,* edited by M. S. Gold and A. L. C. Pottash. New York and London: Plenum Publishing Corp., 1986.

—————. "Thyroid Disorder in Psychiatric Practice." In *Medical Mimics of Psychiatric Disorders,* edited by Irl Extein and Mark S. Gold. Washington D.C.: American Psychiatric Association Press, 1986.

Gold, Mark S., R. B. Lydiard, and J. S. Carman, eds. *Advances in Psychopharmacology: Predicting and Improving Treatment Response.* Boca Raton, Florida: CRC Press, Inc., 1984.

—————, A. Carter Pottash, Donald Sweeney, et al. "Antimanic Antidepressant, and Antipanic Effects of Opiates: Clinical Neuroanatomical, and Biochemical Evidence." *Annals of The New York Academy of Sciences* (1982):-140–150.

—————. "The Challenge of Misdiagnosis." In *Biopsychiatric Insights on Depression: PDLA Depression Monograph,* (1985):14–21.

—————, and M. Kronig. "Comprehensive Thyroid Evaluation in Psychiatric Patients." Chapter 1 in *Handbook of Psychiatric Diagnostic Procedures,* edited by R. C. W. Hall and T. P. Beresford. New York: Spectrum Publications, 1984.

—————, B. Lydiard, A. L. C. Pottash, and D. M. Martin. "The Contribution of Blood Levels to the Treatment of 'Resistant' Depression." In *Special Treatments of Resistant Depression,* edited by J. Zohar and R. H. Belmaker. Jamaica, N.Y.: Spectrum Publications, 1986 (in press).

—————, and H. R. Pearsall. "Depression and Hypothyroidism." *Journal of the American Medical Association* 250:18 (1983):2470–2471.

—————, A. Carter Pottash, Donald Sweeney, et al. "Diagnosis of Depression in the 1980s." *Journal of the American Medical Association* 245:15 (April 17, 1981):1562–1564.

—————. *800-COCAINE.* New York: Bantam Books, 1984.

—————, and H. R. Pearsall. "Hypothyroidism—Or Is It Depression?" *Psychosomatics* 24:7 (1983):646–657.

—————, A. L. C. Pottash, T. W. Estroff, and I Extein. "Laboratory Evaluation in Treatment Planning." In *The Somatic Therapies,* edited by T. B. Karasu, 31–50. Part I of *The Psychiatric Therapies.* APA Commission on Psychiatric Therapies. Washington, D.C.: American Psychiatric Association Press, 1984.

————, A. L. C. Pottash, A. Stoll, D. M. Martin, L. B. Finn, and I. Extein. "Nortriptyline Plasma Levels and Clinical Response in Patients with Familial Pure Unipolar Depression and Blunted TRH Tests." *International Journal of Psychiatry in Medicine* 13:3 (1983):215–220.

————, and H. Rowland Pearsall. "Platelet and Trait Markers." Chapter 8 in *Diagnostic and Laboratory Testing in Psychiatry*, edited by M. S. Gold and A. L. C. Pottash. New York and London: Plenum Publishing Corp., 1986.

————, A. L. C. Pottash, and I. Extein. "The Psychiatric Laboratory." In *Clinical Psychopharmacology*, edited by Jerrold G. Berstein, 29–58. Boston, Bristol and London: John Wright PSG, Inc., 1984.

————. "The Risk of Misdiagnosing Physical Illness as Depression." *Directions in Psychiatry* 4:27 (1984):1–7.

————. "The Role of the Laboratory." In *Biopsychiatric Insights on Depression: PDLA Depression Monograph*, (1985):34–38.

————, A. L. C. Pottash, J. S. Carman, and R. B. Lydiard. "The Role of the Laboratory in Psychiatry." Chapter 12 in *Advances in Psychopharmacology: Predicting and Improving Treatment Response*, edited by M. S. Gold, R. B. Lydiard, and J. S. Carman. Boca Raton, Florida: CRC Press, Inc., 1984.

————. "The Serotonin Subtype." Chapter 5 in *Advances in Psychopharmacology: Predicting and Improving Treatment Response*, edited by M. S. Gold, R. Bruce Lydiard, and John S. Carman. Boca Raton, Florida: CRC Press, Inc., 1984.

————, T. W. Estroff, and A. L. C. Pottash. "Substance Induced Organic Mental Disorders." Chapter 12 in *American Psychiatric Association Annual Review, Vol. 4*, edited by Robert E. Hales and Allen J. Frances. Washington, D.C.: American Psychiatric Association Press, 1985.

————, A. L. C. Pottash, and I. Extein. "The TRH Test in the Diagnosis of Affective Disorders and Schizophrenia." In *Psychoneuroendocrine Dysfunction*, edited by N. S. Shah and A. G. Donald. New York and London: Plenum Publishing Corporation, 1984.

————, and H. Rowland Pearsall. "What's New in Laboratory Testing Procedures For Psychiatrists?" *The Psychiatric Hospital* 15:1 (Winter 1984): 3–9.

Gold, Phillip W., George Chrousos, Charles Kellner, et al. "Psychiatric Implications of Basic and Clinical Studies With Corticotropin-Releasing Factor." *American Journal of Psychiatry* 141:5 (May 1984):619–627.

Goldsmith, Marsha F. "Psychiatrists Analyze Their Present Problems, Project a Bright Future." *Journal of the American Medical Association* 252:6 (August 10, 1984):737–740.

————. "Research on Aging Burgeons As More Americans Grow Older." *Journal of the American Medical Association* 253:10 (March 8, 1985):1369–1370.

————. "Steps Toward Staging, Therapy of Dementia." *Journal of the American Medical Association* 251:14 (April 13, 1984):1812.

Golemann, Daniel. "Clues to Suicide: A Brain Chemical Is Implicated." *New York Times* (October 8, 1985):C1.

Goodwin, Donald W. "What is Mental Illness?" *American Journal of Psychiatry* 141:8 (August 1984):1001.

Goodwin, Frederick K. "Epidemiology and Clinical Description of Depression." In *Biopsychiatric Insights on Depression.* Symposium report, Psychiatric Diagnostic Laboratories of America, 1985.

Gore, Mary Jane. "The Psychological Input." *Psychology Today* (August 1984):17.

Gray, Gregory E., David Baron, and Joseph Herman. "The Importance of Medical Anthropology in Clinical Psychiatry." *American Journal of Psychiatry* 142:2 (February 1985):275.

Greist, John, and James W. Jefferson. *Depression and Its Treatment.* Washington, D.C.: American Psychiatric Association Press, 1984.

Gross, David A., Fair Oaks Hospital at Delray Beach, Florida. Personal communication to Mark S. Gold.

Gurpegui, M., I. Extein, M. S. Gold, and D. R. Sweeney. "The Study of the Hypothalamic-Pituitary-Thyroid Axis in the Psychiatric Disorders: A Review." *Archive de Neurobiologie* 46:2 (1983):79–108.

Haalenar, John·F. "Maybe Doctors Aren't Doing Enough Testing." *Medical Economics* (July 7, 1980):63–65.

Hall, Richard C. W., Thomas P. Beresford, Earl R. Gardner, and Michael K. Popkin. "The Medical Care of Psychiatric Patients." *Hospital and Community Psychiatry* 33:1 (January 1, 1982):25–33.

———. "Psychiatric Effects of Thyroid Hormone Disturbance." *Psychosomatics* 24:1 (January 1983):7–18.

———, Thomas P. Beresford, Earl R. Gardner, Michael K. Popkin. "Unrecognized Physical Illness Prompting Psychiatric Admission: A Prospective Study." *American Journal of Psychiatry* 138:5 (May 1981):629ff.

Hamilton, Jean A., Barbara L. Parry, Sheryle Alagna, Susan Blumenthal, and Elizabeth Herz. "Premenstrual Mood Changes: A Guide to Evaluation and Treatment." *Psychiatric Annals* 14:6 (June 1984):426–435.

Hamilton, Max. "The Effect of Treatment on The Melancholias (Depression)." *British Journal of Psychiatry* 140 (1982):223–230.

Hammer, Signe. "The Mind as Healer." *Science Digest* (April 1984):47–50, 100.

Harden, Blaine. "Why Psychiatrists are Blue." *The Washingtonian* (July 1984):-95–97, 136–137.

Harrison, Wilma M., Judith G. Rabkin, and Jean Endicott. "Psychiatric Evaluation of Premenstrual Changes." *Psychosomatics* 26:10 (October 1985):-789–799.

———, Thomas B. Cooper, Jonathan W. Stewart, et al. "The Tyramine Challenge Test as a Marker for Melancholia." *Archives of General Psychiatry* 41 (July 1984):681–685.

Hatsukami, Dorothy, and Roy W. Pickens. "Post-Treatment Depression in an Alcohol and Drug Abuse Population." *American Journal of Psychiatry* 139:12 (December 1982):1563–66.

Hopkins, Joyce, Marsha Marcus, and Susan B. Campbell. "Postpartum Depression: A Critical Review." *Psychological Bulletin* 95:3 (1984):498–515.

Hudson, James I., Margo S. Hudson, Lillian F. Pliner, et al. "Fibromyalgia and Major Affective Disorder: A Controlled Phenomenology and Family History Study." *American Journal of Psychiatry* 142:4 (April 1985):441–446.

Hurst, Daniel L., and Mary Jane Hurst. "Bromide Psychosis: A Literary Case." *Clinical Neuropharmacology* 7:3 (1984):259–264.

Jenkins, Rachel, and Anthony W. Clare. "Women and Mental Illness." *British Medical Journal* 291 (November 30, 1985):1521–1522.

Kandel, Eric R. "From Metapsychology to Molecular Biology: Explorations Into the Nature of Anxiety." *American Journal of Psychiatry* 140:10 (October 1983):1277–1293.

Karasu, Toksoz B., ed. *The Psychiatric Therapies.* Washington D.C.: American Psychiatric Association Press, 1984.

Kashani, Javad H., and Marybeth Priesmeyer. "Differences in Depressive Symptoms and Depression Among College Students." *American Journal of Psychiatry* 140:8 (August 1983):1081–1082.

Katz, Jack L., Avi Kuperberg, Charles P. Pollack, et al. "Is There a Relationship Between Eating Disorder and Affective Disorder? New Evidence From Sleep Recordings." *American Journal of Psychiatry* 141:6 (June 1984):753–759.

Keller, Martin B., Phillip W. Lavori, Jean Endicott, William Coryell, and Gerald L. Klerman. " 'Double Depression': Two-Year Follow-Up." *American Journal of Psychiatry* 140:6 (June 1983):689–694.

Kinzie, J. David, Spero M. Manson, Do The Vinh, et al. "Development and Validation of a Vietnamese-Language Depression Rating Scale." *American Journal of Psychiatry* 139:10 (October 1982):1276–1281.

Klerman, Gerald L., George E. Vaillant, Robert Spitzer, and Robert Michaels. "A Debate on DSM-III." *American Journal of Psychiatry* 141:4 (April 1984):539ff.

———. "History and Development of Modern Concepts of Affective Illness." Chapter 1 in *Neurobiology of Mood Disorders* by Robert M. Post, M.D. and James C. Ballenger, M.D. Volume 1 of *Frontiers of Clinical Neuroscience.* Baltimore and London: Williams and Wilkins, 1984.

———. "Psychotherapy and Pharmacotherapy." Chapter 1 in *Clinical Psychopharmacology,* edited by Jerrold G. Bernstein. 2nd edition. Boston, Bristol, and London: John Wright PSG, Inc., 1984.

Kline, Nathan S. *From Sad to Glad.* New York: Ballantine, 1974.

Kolivakis, Thomas, and Jambur Ananth. "Think Depression! The Signs and Symptoms of Primary and Secondary Depression." In *Clinical Depressions: Diagnostic and Therapeutic Challenges,* edited by Frank Ayd, Jr. Washington, D.C.: American Psychiatric Association Press, Inc., 1983.

Konner, Melvin. *The Tangled Wing: Biological Constraints on the Human Spirit.* New York: Holt, Rinehart and Winston, 1982.

Kreiger, Dorothy T. "The Hypothalamus and Neuroendocrinology." In *Neuroendocrinology,* edited by Dorothy T. Kreiger and Joan C. Hughes. Sunderland, Massachusetts: A Hospital Practice Book, Sinauer Associates, Inc., 1980.

Kreiger, Richard B., Elinor M. Levy, Edgar S. Cathcart, et al. "Lymphocyte Subsets in Patients With Major Depression: Preliminary Findings." *Advances* 1:1 (Winter 1984):5–9.

Langsley, Donald G., and Marc H. Hollender. "The Definition of A Psychiatrist." *American Journal of Psychiatry* 139:1 (January 1982):81–85.

Lehmann, H. E. "Recognition and Treatment of Depression in Geriatric Patients." Chapter 5 in *Clinical Depressions: Diagnostic and Therapeutic Chal-*

lenges, edited by Frank Ayd, Jr. Washington, D.C.: American Psychiatric Association Press, Inc., 1983.

Leiber, Arnold L., and Nancy Newburg. "Use of Biological Markers in a General Hospital Affective Disorders Program." Unpublished paper, 1984.

Liebmann-Smith, Joan. "PMS, Insomnia . . . or Thyroid?" *American Health* (September 1985):76–81.

Leibowitz, Michael R. *The Chemistry of Love.* Boston and Toronto: Little, Brown and Company, 1983.

Leigh, Hoyle. "Comment: The Role of Psychiatry in Medicine." *American Journal of Psychiatry* 139:12 (December 1982):1581–1586.

Leitner, G. I. "Misdiagnosis of Affective Disorders in Adolescents." *American Journal of Psychiatry* 139:11 (November 1982):1527.

Leo, John. "The Ups and Downs of Creativity." *Time* (October 8, 1984): 76.

Lesse, Stanley. "Unmasking the Masks of Depression." Chapter 4 in *Clinical Depressions: Diagnostic and Therapeutic Challenges,* edited by Frank Ayd, Jr. Washington, D.C.: American Psychiatric Association Press, Inc., 1983.

Lipton, Morris A., and Robert N. Golden. "Nutritional Therapies." Chapter 3 in *The Psychiatric Therapies,* edited by Toksoz B. Karasu. Washington, D.C.: American Psychiatric Association Press, 1984.

Lobel, Brana, and Robert M. A. Hirschfeld. *Depression: What We Know.* Department of Health and Human Services Publication # (ADM)84–1318. Washington, D.C.: U.S. Government Printing Office, 1984.

MacDonald, Ewen, David Rubinow, and Markku Linnoila. "Sensitivity of RBC Membrane Ca2+: Adenosine Triphosphatase to Calmodulin Stimulation." *Archives of General Psychiatry* 41:5 (May 1984):487–493.

Malcom, Janet. "The Patient is Always Right." *New York Review of Books* 21:20 (December 20, 1984):13–14, 16, 18.

Maler, Steven F. "Animal Models of Depression: New Findings." *Psychopharmacology Bulletin* 19:3 (1983):531–536.

Malesky, Gale. "Troubleshooting Your Thyroid." *Prevention* (June 1985):-112–121.

Maranto, Gina. "The Mind Within the Brain." *Discover* (May 1984):34–43.

Martin, David M., and Frederick Van Lente. "On the Diagnostic Frontier: The Laboratory in Mental Illness." *Diagnostic Medicine* (May/June 1980):87.

Marx, Jean L. "Diabetes: A Possible Autoimmune Disease." *Science* (September 21, 1984):1381–1383.

McCormick, Richard A., Angel M. Russo, Luis F. Ramirez, et al. "Affective Disorders Among Pathological Gamblers Seeking Treatment." *American Journal of Psychiatry* 141:2 (February 1984):215–218.

McKnew, Donald H., Jr. Leon Cytryn, and Herbert Yahraes. *Why Isn't Johnny Crying?: Coping With Depression in Children.* New York: W. W. Norton, 1985.

"Melancholic Patients: A New Test to Identify Depression." *Lab World* (September 1981):25–29.

Melnechuk, Theodore. "Neuroimmunomodulation." *Advances* (1983):1.

Melvin, Tessa. "Depression in Aged Termed Reversible." *New York Times,* Section 22 (February 20, 1983):1–5.

Mick, Stephen S., and Jacqueline Lowe Worobey. "Foreign Medical Graduates in the 1980s: Trends in Specialization." *American Journal of Public Health* 74:7 (July 1984):698–703.

Miller, Sigmund S., ed. *Symptoms: The Complete Home Medical Encyclopedia.* New York: Avon Books, 1978.

"Mind-Body Confusion." *Science News* 118 (October 11, 1980):238.

Montandon, Cleopatra, and Timothy Harding. "The Reliability of Dangerousness Assessments: A Decision-Making Exercise." *British Journal of Psychiatry* 144 (1984):149–155.

"Mood Disorder Victims are Undertreated." *American Medical News* 27:18 (May 11, 1984):24.

Morris, Lois B. "Infants' Emotional Health." *Sunday Woman* (July 4, 1982).

———, et al. *The Little Black Pill Book.* Toronto, New York, London, Sydney: Bantam Books, 1983.

Motto, Jerome A., David C. Heilbron, and Richard P. Juster. "Development of a Clinical Instrument to Estimate Suicide Risk." *American Journal of Psychiatry* 142:6 (June 1985):684.

Mueller, Peter S., and N. Grace Allen. "Diagnosis and Treatment of Severe Light-Sensitive Seasonal Energy Syndrome (SES) and its Relationship to Melatonin Anabolism." *Fair Oaks Hospital Psychiatry Letter* 2:9 (September 1984).

Nelson, Bryce. "Despite a Blur of Change, Clear Trends Emerging in Psychotherapy." *New York Times,* (March 1, 1983):C1, C6.

Newson, Gary, and Neville Murray. "Reversal of Dexamethasone Suppression Test Nonsuppression in Alcohol Abusers." *American Journal of Psychiatry* 140:3 (March 1983):353–354.

Nurnberger, John I., Jr., and Elliot S. Gershon. "Genetics of Affective Disorders." Chapter 5 in *Neurobiology of Mood Disorders* by Robert M. Post and James C. Ballenger. Volume 1 of *Frontiers of Clinical Neuroscience.* Baltimore and London: Williams and Wilkins, 1984.

Ornstein, Robert, and Richard F. Thompson. *The Amazing Brain.* Boston: Houghton Mifflin Company, 1984.

Pardes, Herbert. "Medical Education and Recruitment in Psychiatry." *American Journal of Psychiatry* 139:8 (August 1982):1033–1035.

Pearsall, H. R., M. S. Gold, and A. L. C. Pottash. "Hypothyroidism and Depression: The Casual Connection." *Diagnosis* (1983):77–80.

Perry, Barbara. "Depression and Psychobiology in Women's Life Cycles." Tape of symposium at American Psychiatric Association Annual Meeting, Los Angeles, May 1984.

Perry, Paul. "The Ironic Epidemic." *American Health* (October 1984):41–43.

Peterson, Linda Gay, and Mark Perl. "Psychiatric Presentations of Cancer." *Psychosomatics* 23:6 (June 1982):601–604.

Pollner, Fran, Judy Alsofrom, Rochelle Green, and Liz Gonzalez. "Phenylalanine: A Psychoactive Nutrient for Some Depressives?" *Medical World News* 24:20 (October 24, 1983):21–22.

Pomara, N., and S. Gershon. "Treatment-Resistant Depression in an Elderly Patient with Pancreatic Carcinoma: Case Report." *Journal of Clinical Psychiatry* 45:10 (1984):439–440.

Post, Robert M., and James C. Ballenger. *Neurobiology of Mood Disorders.* Volume 1 of *Frontiers of Clinical Neuroscience.* Baltimore and London: Williams and Wilkins, 1984.

Pottash, A. L. C., M. S. Gold, and I. Extein. "The Use of the Clinical Laboratory." In *Inpatient Psychiatry: Diagnosis and Treatment,* edited by Lloyd I. Sederer. Baltimore and London: Williams and Wilkins, 1983.

Poznanski, Elva. "Depression in Children and Adolescents: An Overview." *Psychiatric Annals* 15:6 (June 1985):365–367.

Prange, Arthur J., Jr. "Depression and Thyroid Function: A Brief Review." *Fair Oaks Hospital Psychiatry Letter* 1:3 (March 1983).

Prasad, Ananda S. "Clinical, Biochemical and Nutritional Spectrum of Zinc Deficiency in Human Subjects: An Update." *Nutrition Reviews* 41:7 (July 1983):197–208.

"Preventing Affective Recurrence: An Interview with Robert F. Prien, Ph.D." *Currents* (1985):5–9.

Prose, Mel, David C. Clark, Martin Harrow, and Jen Fawcett. "Guilt and Conscience in Major Depressive Disorders." *American Journal of Psychiatry* 140 (July 1983):839–884.

"Psychiatric Diagnosis: Off The Mark." *Science News* 122 (September 11, 1982):168.

Puig-Antich, Joaquim. "Affective Disorders in Childhood: A Review and Perspective." *Psychiatric Clinics of North America* 3:3 (December 1980):417.

Rabkin, Judith G., Edward Charles, and Frederick Kass. "Hypertension and DSM-III Depression in Psychiatric Outpatients." *American Journal of Psychiatry* 140:8 (August 1983):1072–1074.

Rabkin, J. "Therapeutic Attitudes Towards Mental Illness and Health." In *Effective Psychotherapy: A Handbook of Research,* edited by A. S. Gurman and A. M. Razin. Oxford: Pergamon, 1977.

Rafuls, W. A., I. Extein, M. S. Gold, and F. C. Goggans. "Neuropsychiatric Manifestations of Endocrine Disorders." In *Textbook of Neuropsychiatry,* edited by R. E. Hales and S. C. Yudofsky. Washington, D.C.: American Psychiatric Association Press, 1986 (in press).

Ray, Richard A., and Peter Howanitz. "RIA in Thyroid Function Testing." *Diagnostic Medicine* (May 1984):55–70.

"A Recovering Patient: 'Can We Talk?' The Schizophrenic Patient in Psychotherapy." *American Journal of Psychiatry* 143:1 (January 1986):68–70.

Reus, Victor I., and Jeffrey R. Berlant. "Pituitary-Adrenal Dysfunction in Psychiatric Illness." In *Medical Mimics of Psychiatric Disorders,* edited by Irl Extein and Mark S. Gold. Washington, D.C.: American Psychiatric Association Press, 1986.

Rickels, Karl. "Premenstrual Syndrome, Introduction." *Psychosomatics* 26:10 (October 1985):785.

Rivinus, Timothy M., Joseph Biederman, David B. Herzog, et al. "Anorexia Nervosa and Affective Disorders: A Controlled Family History Study." *American Journal of Psychiatry* 141:11 (November 1984):1414.

Rogers, June. "Psychiatry Puts Itself on the Couch." *MacLeans* 95 (November 27, 1982):57–58.

Rogoff, Jerome. "Individual Psychotherapy." Chapter 12 in *Inpatient Diagnosis and Treatment,* edited by Lloyd I. Sederer, M.D. Baltimore and London: Williams and Wilkins, 1983.

Ross, C. A. "Biological Tests for Mental Illness: Their Use and Misuse." *Biological Psychiatry* 21 (1986):431–435.

Rouner, Sandy. "Healthtalk: Shedding Light on Moods." *Washington Post* (June 24, 1983):C-5.

Rubinow, David, Robert Post, Robert Savard, and Philip W. Gold. "Cortisol Hypersecretion and Cognitive Impairment in Depression." *Archives of General Psychiatry* 41 (March 1984):279–283.

Rush, A. John, Michael A. Schlesser, Carl Fulton, and Michael A. Allen. "Biological Basis of Psychiatric Disorders." Chapter in *Clinical Neurosciences*, Vol. 1, edited by R. Rosenberg. London: Churchill-Livingston, 1983:1679–720.

Sabelli, H., J. Fawcett, P. Epstein, et al. "PAA, MHPG, DST and Methylphenidate Test in Depression." Unpublished paper.

Schatzberg, Alan F., Paul J. Orsulak, Alan H. Rosenbaum, et al. "Catecholamine Measures for Diagnosis and Treatment of Patients with Depressive Disorders." *Journal of Clinical Psychiatry* 4:12 (December 1980):Section 2, 35–38.

———. "Clinical Diagnosis and Classification of Affective Disorders." In *The Brain, Biochemistry, and Behavior: Proceedings of the Sixth Arnold O. Beckman Conference in Clinical Chemistry*, edited by Robert L. Habig. Washington, D.C.: The American Association for Clinical Chemistry, 1984:29–46.

———. "Evaluation and Treatment of the Refractory Depressed Patient." Chapter 5 in *Clinical Psychopharmacology*, edited by Jerrold G. Bernstein. 2nd edition. Boston, Bristol, and London: John Wright PSG, Inc., 1984.

———, Paul J. Orsulak, Anthony J. Rothschild, et al. "Platelet MAO Activity and The Dexamethasone Suppression Test in Depressed Patients." *American Journal of Psychiatry* 140:9 (September 1983):1231–33.

Schleifer, Steven J., Steven E. Keller, Arthur T. Meyerson, et al. "Lymphocyte Function in Major Depressive Disorder." *Archives of General Psychiatry* 41 (May 1984):484–486.

Schmeck, Harold M., Jr. "Addict's Brain: Chemistry Holds Hope for Answers." *New York Times* (January 25, 1983):C1, C4.

———. "Domination is Linked to Chemical in The Brain." *New York Times* (September 27, 1983):C3.

———. "Grim New Ravage of AIDS: Brain Damage." *New York Times* (October 15, 1985):C1.

Schottenfeld, Richard, and Mark Cullen. "Organic Affective Illness Associated with Lead Intoxication." *American Journal of Psychiatry*, 141:11 (1984):1423–1426.

Schuckit, Marc A. "Prevalence of Affective Disorder in a Sample of Young Men." *American Journal of Psychiatry* 139:11 (November 1982):1431–1436.

Schuster, Joseph. "At Last, A Proven, Drug-Free Treatment for Depression." *Washington University Magazine* 54(2):27–29.

Schwartz, Richard H. "Suicide: A Pediatrician's View." *Epidemic . . .* Number 6. Straight, Inc., St. Petersburg, Florida.

Sederer, Lloyd I., ed. *Inpatient Psychiatry: Diagnosis and Treatment.* Baltimore and London: Williams and Wilkins, 1983.

Shamberger, Raymond J. "The Subtle Signs of Chronic Vitamin Undernutrition." *Diagnostic Medicine* (April 1984):61–70.

Shapiro, Robert W., Martin R. Keller. "Initial Six-Month Follow-Up of Patient with Major Depressive Disorder." *Journal of Affective Disorders* 3 (1981):206–220.

Shemo, John, et al. "A Conjoint Psychiatry-Internal Medicine Program: Development of a Teaching and Clinical Model." *American Journal of Psychiatry* 139:11 (November 1982):1437–1442.

Sherman, A. D., and F. Petty. "Learned Helplessness Decreases (3H) Imipramine Binding in Rat Cortex." *Journal of Affective Disorders* 6:1 (February 1984):25–32.

Siever, Larry J., Thomas W. Uhde, David C. Jimerson, et al. "Differential Inhibitory Noradrenergic Responses to Clonidine in 25 Depressed Patients and 25 Normal Control Subjects." *American Journal of Psychiatry* 141:6 (June 1984):733–741.

Silverman, Harold M., and Gilbert I. Simon. *The Pill Book.* 2nd edition. New York: Bantam Books, 1982.

Silverman, Joseph Shepsel, Julia Ann Silverman, and David A. Eardley. "Do Maladaptive Attitudes Cause Depression?" *Archives of General Psychiatry* 41 (January 1984):28–30.

Sim, Myre. "What it Means to be Depressed: Its Primary and Secondary Effects." Chapter 7 in *Clinical Depressions: Diagnostic and Therapeutic Challenges,* edited by Frank Ayd, Jr. Baltimore: Ayd Medical Communications, 1980.

Simons, Anne D., et al. "Cognitive and/or Pharmacotherapy: One Year Later." Paper delivered at American Psychiatric Association annual meeting May 9, 1984, Los Angeles.

Sinyor, D., S. G. Schwartz, F. Peonnet, et al. "Aerobic Fitness Level and Reactivity to Psychosocial Stress: Physiological, Biochemical, and Subjective Measures." *Psychosomatic Medicine* 45:3 (June 1983):205–216.

Slaby, Andrew E., and Barry S. Fogel. "Identifying Occult Neurological Illness on a Psychiatric Service." *Fair Oaks Hospital Psychiatry Letter* 2:8 (August 1984).

Slawson, Paul Fredric. "Psychiatric Malpractice: The California Experience." *American Journal of Psychiatry* 136:5 (May 1979):650–654.

———, and Frederick G. Guggenheim. "Psychiatric Malpractice: A Review of the National Loss Experience." *American Journal of Psychiatry* 141:8 (August 1984):979–981.

"Somatic Disease Rate Found High in Psychiatric Patients." *Psychiatric News* (March 1, 1985):17–20.

Sondheimer, Steven J., Ellen W. Freeman, Beth Scharlop, and Karl Rickels. "Hormonal Changes in Premenstrual Syndrome." *Psychosomatics* 26:10 (October 1985):803–809.

Stern, Theodore A., Albert Mulley, and George E. Thibault. "Life-Threatening Drug Overdose: Precipitants and Prognosis." *Journal of the American Medical Association* 251:15 (April 20, 1984):1983–1985.

Sternbach, H. A., I. Extein, D. R. Sweeney, M. S. Gold, and A. L. C. Pottash. "Cortisol Secretion and Urinary MHPG in Unipolar Depression." *International Journal of Psychiatric Medicine* 13:4 (1984):261–266.

———, L. Kirstein, A. L. C. Pottash, M. S. Gold, I. Extein, and D. R. Sweeney. "The TRH Test and Urinary MHPG in Unipolar Depression." *Journal of Affective Disorders* 5:3 (1983):233–237.

Stone, Alan A. "The New Paradox of Psychiatric Malpractice." *New England Journal of Medicine* 311:21 (November 22, 1984):1384–1387.

Strauss, Gordon D., et al. "The Cutting Edge in Psychiatry." *American Journal of Psychiatry* 141:1 (January 1984):38–43.

Sturgeon, Wina. *Depression: How to Recognize It, How to Treat It, and How to Grow From It.* Englewood Cliffs, New Jersey: Prentice-Hall, Inc., 1979.

Talbott, John A. "Psychiatry's Agenda for the '80s." *Journal of the American Medical Association* 251:17 (May 4, 1984):2250.

———. "Psychiatry's Unfinished Business in the 20th Century." Address presented by new president of the American Psychiatric Association at annual meeting, May 1984.

Talley, Joseph H. "When Antidepressants Don't Work." Chapter 13 in *Clinical Depressions: Diagnostic and Therapeutic Challenges,* edited by Frank Ayd, Jr. Baltimore: Ayd Medical Communications, 1980.

"Treating Depression with Light: An Interview with Daniel F. Kripke, M.D." *Currents* 4:5 (May 1985):5–8.

Thompson, James W., et al. "The Decline of State Mental Hospitals as Training Sites for Psychiatric Residents." *American Journal of Psychiatry* 140:6 (June 1983):704–707.

Topping, Robin. "Handicapped by a Misdiagnosis." *Newsday* (January 13, 1985):6, 23–24.

Torrey, E. Fuller. "The Death of Psychiatry: A Progress Report." Paper presented at annual meeting of American Psychiatric Association, May 1984.

———. "Hollywood's Pique at Psychiatry." *Psychology Today* 5 (July 1981):74–79.

"Treatment of the Winter Blues?" *Medical World News for Psychiatrists* (January 1985):7.

Tueting, Patricia. *National Institute of Mental Health Sciences Report: Special Report on Depression Research.* Washington D.C.: U.S. Government Printing Office, 1983. 0-418-733.

"Two-Year Follow-Up of Subjects and Their Families Defined as at Risk for Psychopathology on the Basis of Platelet MAO Activities." *Neuropsychobiology* 8 (1982):51–56.

Udelman, Donna. "Hope and the Immune System." Paper delivered at annual meeting of American Psychiatric Association, May 1984.

van Praag, H. M. "A Transatlantic View of the Diagnosis of Depressions According to DSM-III: Did the DSM-III Solve the Problem of Depression Diagnosis?" *Comprehensive Psychiatry* 23:4 (July/August 1982):315–329.

Vaughn, Lewis. "The 'Secret Threat' of Marginal Deficiencies." *Prevention* (August 1984):122.

von Zerssen, Detlev, Mathias Berger, Peter Doerr. "Neuroendocrine Dysfunction in Subtypes of Depression." Chapter 19 in *Psychoneuroendocrine Dysfunction,* edited by Nandkumer S. Shah and Alexander G. Donald. New York and London: Plenum Medical Book Company, 1984.

Wanbolt, Marianne Z., Ned H. Kalin, and Stephen J. Weiler. "Consistent Reversal of Abnormal DSTs After Different Antidepressant Therapies in a Patient With Dementia." *American Journal of Psychiatry* 142:1 (January 1985):100–103.

Ward, N. G., H. O. Doerr, and M. C. Storrie. "Skin Conductance: A Potentially Sensitive Test for Depression." *Psychiatry Research* 10:4 (December 1983):295–302.

Weissman, Myrna M., et al. "The Efficacy of Drugs and Psychotherapy in the Treatment of Acute Depressive Episodes." *American Journal of Psychiatry* 136:4B (April 1979):555–558.

————, and Jeffrey H. Boyd. "The Epidemiology of Affective Disorders." Chapter 4 in *Neurobiology of Mood Disorders,* by Robert M. Post and James C. Ballenger. Volume 1 of *Frontiers of Clinical Neuroscience.* Baltimore and London: Williams and Wilkins, 1984.

————, Priya Wickramaratne, Kathleen R. Merikangas, et al. "Onset of Major Depression in Early Adulthood: Increased Familial Loading and Specificity." *Archives of General Psychiatry* 41 (December 1984):1136–1143.

————, Elliot S. Gershon, Kenneth K. Kidd, et al. "Psychiatric Disorders in the Relatives of Probands with Affective Disorders." *Archives of General Psychiatry* 41 (January 1984):13–21.

————. "Psychotherapy in Comparison and in Combination with Pharmacotherapy for the Depressed Outpatient." Chapter 31 in *The Affective Disorders,* edited by John M. Davis and James W. Maas. Washington, D.C.: American Psychiatric Association Press, 1983.

Wender, Paul H., and Donald F. Klein. *Mind, Mood, and Medicine: A Guide to the New Biopsychiatry.* New York: New American Library (A Meridian Book), 1981.

————, et al. "Prevalence of Attention Deficit Disorder, Residual Type, and Other Psychiatric Disorders in Patients with Irritable Colon Syndrome." *American Journal of Psychiatry* 140:12 (December 1983):1579–1582.

Wilford, Bonnie Baird. *Drug Abuse, A Guide for the Primary Care Physician.* Chicago: American Medical Association, 1981.

Winokur, George, Mong T. Tsuang, and Raymond R. Crowe. "The Iowa 500: Affective Disorder in Relatives of Manic and Depressed Patients." *American Journal of Psychiatry* 139:2 (February 1982):209–212.

"Women's Mental Health Needs Are Not Met: Panel Report." *International Medical Tribune News* (April 1985):8.

Woo, Olga F. "Toxic Time Bombs: Understanding the Actions of Slow Poisons." *Diagnostic Medicine* (June 1984):57–62.

Yager, Joel, Katherine LaMotte, and Lynn Fairbanks. "Medical Student Attitudes Toward Psychiatry in Relation to Psychiatric Career Choice." *Journal of Medical Education* 57 (December 1982):949–951.

————, et al. "Medical Students' Evaluation of Psychiatry: A Cross-Country Comparison." *American Journal of Psychiatry* 139:8 (August 1982):1003–1009.

Yahraes, Herbert. *National Institute of Mental Health Science Reports: "Genes and Mental Health: The Mechanisms of Heredity in Major Mental Illnesses."* Washington, D.C.: U.S. Government Printing Office, 1978. 0-274-688 (ADM) 78-640.

Zarrow, Susan. "Out of Your Mind . . . Or Out of B12?" *Prevention* (September 1984):22–26.

Ziporyn, Terra. "Rare Hyper-, Hypothyroid States Require Unconventional

Therapies." *Journal of the American Medical Association* 253:6 (February 8, 1985):737–739, 743.

————. " 'Rip van Winkle Period' Ends for Puerperal Psychiatric Problems." *Journal of the American Medical Association* 251:16 (April 27, 1984):2061–2064, 2067.

Index

Acquired immune deficiency syndrome (AIDS), 88, 90, 241

Acromegaly, 157

ACTH. *See* Adrenocorticotropic hormone

Addison's disease, 49, 153–154

Adoption studies, 199

Adrenal glands, 141, 152–155

Adrenocorticotropic hormone (ACTH), 154, 156

Age, depression onset, 194
  see also Children; Elderly

AIDS. *See* Acquired immune deficiency syndrome

Akiskal, Hagop, 187

Alcohol
  dementia, cause of, 90
  depression, mimicker of, 104–111, 271, 285, 293–294
  and pancreatic disease, 82
  and vitamin deficiency, 123, 124

Alcoholics Anonymous, 106

Alpha methyldopa, 114

Aluminum. *See* Metals, aluminum

Alzheimer's disease, 92–93, 294–296

AMA. *See* American Medical Association

Amazing Brain!, The, 214

American Health, 129

American Journal of Psychiatry, 44, 97, 180, 269–270

American Medical Association (AMA), 110

American Psychological Association, 276

Amino acids, 125–126, 218

Aminophylline, 119

Amish, 197

Amitriptyline (Elavil), 7–8, 216, 247

Amphetamines, 118, 186

Anatomy of Melancholy, The, 169

Andreasen, Nancy, 183

Anemia, 106, 122–123, 129

Anesthesia, 117

Animals, depression in, 171–172, 175

Annual Review of Nutrition, 132

Anorexia nervosa, 179

Antabuse, 113

Antiarrhythmics, 114

Anticonvulsants, 115, 123, 189

Antidepressants
  blood levels, 239, 247–248, 258
  for children, 287
  for elderly, 296–297
  for masked depression, 179
  monoaminoxidase inhibitors (MAOIs), 64, 124, 212, 215, 219–220, 249
  placebo effect, 217–218
  quiz, 255–256, 258–260
  "second generation," 248

About the Author

Mark S. Gold, MD, is Director of Research at Fair Oaks Hospital in Summit, New Jersey and Delray Beach, Florida. He is the founder of both the National Cocaine Hotline and Psychiatric Diagnostic Laboratories of America.

Dr. Gold has received numerous awards for his research, involving the use of laboratory tests in psychiatric diagnosis and treatment, the identification and treatment of drug abuse, and the use of medicines in the treatment of patients with depression. He has written extensively for professional audiences. In addition Dr. Gold is the author of two books for general audiences: *The 800-COCAINE Book* and *Wonder Drugs*.